Deutsche Erzählungen   German Stories

DEUTSCHE ERZÄHLUNGEN

GERMAN STORIES

A Bilingual Anthology

Goethe
Hebel
Kleist
Hoffmann
Stifter
Keller
Fontane
Schnitzler
Mann
Kafka

Translated and Edited by

Böll

HARRY STEINHAUER

UNIVERSITY OF CALIFORNIA PRESS
Berkeley   Los Angeles   London

University of California Press
Berkeley and Los Angeles, California

University of California Press, Ltd.
London, England

Copyright © 1984 by The Regents of the University of California

Library of Congress Cataloging in Publication Data

Main entry under title:

Deutsche Erzählungen = German stories.

1. Short stories, German—Translations into English. 2. Short stories, English—Translations from German. 3. Short stories, German. I. Steinhauer, Harry, 1905–   . II. Title: German stories.
PT1160.E7D4   1984   833'.01'08   83–24306
ISBN 0–520–05049–5
ISBN 0–520–05054–1 (pbk.)

Printed in the United States of America

5 6 7 8 9

Inhalt Contents

Preface

This book is designed primarily to alleviate the agony that language learning in its early stages entails, when the foreign words in the sentence simply will not combine to make sense. Legions of beginners give up when they could have made it with the aid of a book like this. But for centuries schoolmasters have frowned on this device, calling it dirty names like crib, crutch, pony. But the truth is that highly educated and motivated people have learned to read a foreign language this way. The great German archaeologist Heinrich Schliemann, who knew many ancient and modern languages, acquired them by using Bernardin de Saint-Pierre's *Paul et Virginie* as a pony. There are many bilingual series, such as the Loeb Classics or the Bollingen series, which have gained high prestige.

Of course, real mastery of a language requires intensive study, with careful analysis of syntax, memorization of vocabulary, and composition in the foreign idiom. But extensive reading—yes, even skimming—is also useful, and for this purpose the dual language text is a legitimate tool, indeed a great boon. And the reader who feels tempted to skim the English text first may do so in good conscience; the old epics and early novels often used to give summaries of the content before each canto or chapter.

Ever since I began teaching I have believed that language learning should be done through the medium of the best literature and thought created by the culture whose language is being studied. I do not belong to *la plume de ma tante* school, which still dominates language teaching in this country. Television has shown us disadvantaged children in a Chicago school being taught Shakespeare and liking it. So I believe that high school, and certainly college, students would prefer to learn German by reading the works of the best German authors.

[VII]

This book originally appeared in the Bantam dual language series and was used in German and comparative literature courses because it offers a survey of the development of German shorter fiction from the late eighteenth century to the present. This new edition is more than a reprint of the Bantam book. Several of the Bantam stories have been removed and replaced by more suitable ones and some new texts have been added. The editorial apparatus has been completely rewritten and the notes greatly expanded.

I wish to express my thanks to Professor Steven Martinson of the University of California at Los Angeles for his critical evaluation of the manuscript, to Stanley Holwitz, assistant director of the University of California Press, for his encouragement all along the way, and to Amanda Clark Frost for her excellent job of editing the manuscript for the press.

Harry Steinhauer

University of California, Santa Barbara
September 1983

Note: A bilingual text creates a special typographical problem in aligning the two texts on the page. Since the English text is usually shorter than the German, the right hand page shows blank gaps. In a few instances where the German text is shorter, the blank spaces occur on the left hand page. These blanks should be disregarded or at least endured.

Introduction

Story telling, in verse and prose, is probably as old as cave painting and music making. Short stories have come down to us
from ancient Egypt, from India, from the Greeks and the Arabs.
The Bible contains some excellent short stories in both the Old
and New Testament and the Apocrypha; examples are the
books of Jonah, Ruth, and Esther, the parables attributed to
Jesus, the books of Tobit, Judith, and Susanna and the Elders.
Most likely these biblical writers did not think of themselves as
men of letters at all but as priests or laymen writing to glorify
God and the nation. But just as they were sensitive to good grammar, syntax, and precise statement, so they knew "by instinct"
how to compose a fine narrative and how to embellish a sentence
with literary ambiguities and to clothe their thought in striking
imagery.

It is a different story with the Greeks and Romans. They had
their schools of rhetoric and manuals of good writing. The
anecdotes that Herodotus wove into his *History*, the Aphrodite-
Ares episode from the eighth book of the *Odyssey*, the fables of
Aesop, the beautiful allegory of "Amor and Psyche" from *The
Golden Ass* by Apuleius, the tender idyll *Daphnis and Chloë*, and
Lucian's *Dialogues* are examples of classical short fiction. We
know that there was in ancient Greece a collection of stories
titled *The Milesian Tales*. There must have been others, but they
have not survived.

The Middle Ages produced a considerable body of short fiction: *nova* and *exempla, lais, fabliaux, tenzone,* collections of anecdotes like the *Deeds of the Romans* (*Gesta Romanorum*) and the
Arabian Nights. Much of this literature was didactic; little of it

can pretend to be high art, which at that time had to be clothed in verse. For just as high literature concerned itself with extraordinary happenings, so it scorned the lowly vehicle of prose; for don't we all, even M. Jourdain, speak and write prose? A true bard sings in numbers. Of course there are short stories in verse too: the medieval French *fabliaux*, Chaucer's *Canterbury Tales*, La Fontaine's *Contes*, Gessner's *Idylls*, Longfellow's *Tales of a Wayside Inn*, to mention only a few. But the great mass of short fiction is in prose. To keep their congregations awake, the preachers interlarded their sermons with parables and stories to illustrate the moral lesson of the day. These were the *exempla*. The literature of entertainment, the *fabliaux*, consisted of piquant tales depicting exciting events or intriguing situations (often bawdy), the conflict of wits, witty sallies, and the broad spectrum of sexual adventure.

Scholars are agreed that the short story as an art form came into being in the Renaissance and that its progenitor was Giovanni Boccaccio (c. 1313–75), whose *Decameron* (1348–53) has been of immense influence on the development of the genre. The *Decameron* contains a hundred stories, most of which are no more than three or four pages long. Boccaccio created the fiction that the stories were told orally by ten Italian ladies and gentlemen over a period of ten days in a country house to which they had retired in order to escape the ravages of the Black Death then raging in Florence. In the preamble to the book he calls these stories *novelle*, which indicated to his contemporaries that they were true stories taken from real life, as opposed to the traditional tales derived from classical mythology and medieval chivalry and romance, which were tediously familiar to cultivated people. Scholars have maintained that Boccaccio created a new literary genre, *the* novella, and from an analysis of the *Decameron* they have developed the rules that govern this literary form. But in the preface to his book Boccaccio states explicitly: "I shall narrate a hundred stories or fables or parables or histories or whatever you choose to call them," thus clearly underscoring the diverse character of the collection. The work is in fact a cornucopia of fables, parables, legends, anecdotes, serious love stories, tales of married life, philosophical debates,

satires, practical jokes, and witty sallies. Moreover, these stories are not taken from life; nine-tenths of them are derived from medieval and older sources. Nor is there any unity of theme, mood, or tone in the *Decameron;* the stories cover the whole emotional spectrum from tragedy to farce. What unity there is in the book derives from the personality of its author, who was a great artist.

Boccaccio's book made history. Chaucer's *Canterbury Tales* shows its influence. There were many imitations in various European literatures; the most important names are Masuccio, Bandello, Marguerite de Navarre, and La Fontaine.

One feature that the *Decameron* lacks is character study. Boccaccio describes actions that issue from a goal or line of thought without going into the psychological factors that motivate the actors. This feature was supplied by Miguel de Cervantes (1547–1616) in his *Exemplary Novellas* (1613). Cervantes added a sociological element; he set the action of his stories against the social background out of which they arose. To do this he needed more space than Boccaccio had allowed himself. So we get the long novella written with a serious purpose, not for mere entertainment. It is a moral (Cervantes says: exemplary) tale, but it is a moral tale told with realism, presenting real people and events rather than the abstractions that Boccaccio produces to illustrate the philosophical or ethical thesis that is the point of his story. The spirit and tone of the *Exemplary Novellas* is very different from that which pervades the *Decameron.* These Spanish tales not only tell an exciting story; their greater length and the attention they pay to the study of character and milieu make them short novels. Perhaps Cervantes thought of them as such, for the Spanish word *novela* covers both *novel* and *short story.* The influence of Cervantes on European literature was second only to that of Boccaccio, though the Spaniard's influence did not make itself felt until later in the eighteenth century.

We now have two models that short fiction was to follow. It could be a moral-philosophical tale, a descendant of the biblical parable and the medieval *exemplum,* whose essence was a message dressed up as a story. This type of fiction enjoyed great popularity in the Enlightenment, which favored the didactic in

literature. The subject is analyzed more fully below in the introduction to Goethe's story of the virtuous attorney.

The short story developed in another direction too, following
the model created by Cervantes and influenced by the development of the novel in the eighteenth century. It could aim at
painting a realistic picture of life, depicting real people who
face the problems which life provides for us all. There were a
few such realistic tales in Boccaccio; there is some realism even
in his didactic stories. But for genuinely realistic stories that
mirror the complexilty and depth of real life we must wait for
Cervantes and after him till the romantic movement discovered
"the people" and incidentally the art of Cervantes.

There is a third tradition in fiction which affects the development of the short story. Art, even serious art, is essentially play,
make-believe, a glorious game created by the imagination of
homo ludens. Architecture and music appeal almost wholly to
our aesthetic sense, to our instinct for form, harmony, and
intellectual play. Painting has at all times used abstract forms
to arouse pleasurable emotions, and so has literature. Side by
side with the artistic ideal that a work of fiction should mirror
real life, there has always existed a school of writers who create
purely imaginative literary structures that are autonomous, not
answerable to the laws that govern everyday reality. Just as
children ask us to make up a story for them, so these writers
make up stories for grown-ups. In *The Monk's Wedding (Die
Hochzeit des Mönchs)* by Conrad Ferdinand Meyer, the poet
Dante, who is the narrator of the story, makes up a story as he
tells it to his audience, incorporating their suggestions and even
weaving their personalities into the fabric of his tale. The French
poet La Fontaine brushed off the objections raised by critics of
his verse tales by pointing out that they were, after all, only
stories. The German writer Wieland conceived his cycle of
stories *The Hexameron of Rosenhain (Das Hexameron von Rosenhain)*
as a composite story-telling game in which the listeners were
to participate. The narrator would stop at a certain point and
ask someone else to continue. At the close of one story the
group of listeners considers an alternative ending to the one
given by the narrator. Gottfried Keller's *The Epigram (Das*

Sinngedicht) also exploits the play impulse to construct a masterly cycle of novellas that deal with various aspects of love. The writers of historical fiction and drama have always reserved the right to introduce fictitious elements into their work and even to alter the facts of history for aesthetic ends. We must never forget the factor of play in art. It is significant that in both English and German the popular word for drama is *play*. Some writers place a high value on purely aesthetic elements like symmetrical structure, imagery, metaphor, symbol, leitmotif, patterns of sound, rhyme, assonance, and meter. In the eighteenth century the first two types of short story existed side by side: the old medieval *exemplum*, appearing in a marvelously refined form as the *conte philosophique* and *conte moral,* and the realistic model of Cervantes, reinforced by the new emergent novel, which is by definition "a fictitious prose narrative of considerable length, in which characters and actions representative of real life are portrayed in a plot of more or less complexity."[1] This definition could serve for the Cervantean novella too.

Paradoxical though it may sound, it was the romantic movement that gave a strong impetus to realism in literature through its interest in local color, in resurrecting the past and describing it with authenticity, through its concern with rural life, and through its cult of what Victor Hugo called "the grotesque," that is, the ugly. Short fiction benefited from this development; for now the story became integrated into the mainstream of literature; its evolution henceforth runs parallel to that of the other genres: through realism, naturalism, neoromanticism or symbolism, expressionism, and back to realism.

●

It was noted above that the highly literate culture of the Greeks and Romans has left almost no prose fiction, long or short. A possible explanation for this lacuna is that this genre remained outside the canon of high letters; therefore it was not considered worth preserving for posterity. In fact, almost throughout the history of literature prose fiction has been disparaged as *mere* popular entertainment, probably because it

---

[1]*Oxford English Dictionary* (London, 1955), p. 1341.

was declaimed or written in prose. At the end of the eighteenth century Schiller could still write that prose fiction produced a nonpoetic effect on the reader, and later still Grillparzer belittled the novella as an inferior art form because it was written in prose. As late as 1967 Anthony Burgess wrote: "There are people who, despite the high example set by Cervantes and Flaubert and Henry James, insist on regarding the novelist as the lowest kind of literary practitioner: the novelist is more concerned with entertainment than with poetic or epic uplift; he doesn't ennoble the world but presents it as it is, with all its meanness, dirt, and sexuality."[2] Even after the novel had been accepted as a legitimate descendant of the old verse epic, the short story was treated as a stepchild, right into our own day. Somerset Maugham, a master of the genre, wrote: "The short story is a minor art and it must content itself with moving, exciting, and amusing the reader. . . . It is wise to read short stories for the entertainment they produce."

It is a paradox in the history of short fiction that although the genre was disparaged as mere flippant entertainment and often condemned as immoral, the didactic flavor clung to it for a long time. Its brevity made it an apt vehicle for conveying a moral or philosophical message. This does not imply that the fables, apologues, and *exempla* from which the modern short story evolved were necessarily dull. The age of the Enlightenment prized the moral tale highly and some of these tales (such as those by Voltaire and Diderot) and Lessing's fables have become classics in the sense of belonging to all time. Voltaire's *Candide* is as delightful to us as it was to readers in the eighteenth century, but one can smell the didactic intent, the primacy of the message. There is something artificial about the people and the situations they portray. Candide and Pangloss and Cunégonde are not real personages of fiction, like those we meet in Fielding, Balzac, Tolstoy, or Maupassant. And yet, long after the taste in fiction had changed, moving away from the didactic, stories emphasizing the moral kept reappearing in literature. Kleist, one of the first great realists of modern times,

[2]Anthony Burgess, *The Novel Now* (New York, 1967), p. 13.

still wrote moral tales; so did Goethe, Gotthelf, Dostoevski, Tolstoy, and Shaw. The latter was once asked by a critic whether one of his plays carried a message. "Sir," he replied sternly, "of course it does. Do you think I write to *amuse* the public?" Oscar Wilde wrote some beautiful parables; Bertolt Brecht's *Stories of Herr Keuner* (*Geschichten von Herrn Keuner*) are parables; George Orwell called his *Animal Farm* a fairy story, but it is really a parable; so are his *1984* and Aldous Huxley's *Brave New World.* James Thurber wrote witty modern parables that he called fables, and Kafka's work is almost wholly parabolic. But the great mass of nineteenth- and twentieth-century fiction aims at creating an illusion of real life.

●

Although there is a steady tradition of story telling in Germany from the Middle Ages, German literature lacks the equivalent of a Boccaccio, Chaucer, Cervantes, or Marguerite de Navarre. Not till the late eighteenth century did short fiction in Germany begin to rise to the status of high literature. Because the didactic strain in literature was stronger in Germany than elsewhere, the moral tale flourished there. The romantic period may be regarded as a watershed. The work of Kleist, Arnim, Brentano, Hoffmann, Chamisso, and Tieck depicts real life even when it introduces supernatural elements into the narrative. The greatness of the novel in the nineteenth century is based on this ever-growing closeness to life. In Germany this phenomenon manifested itself largely in the short story because German writers produced novellas rather than novels. Most of the outstanding writers were lured by this new art form. It is not possible here to pursue the various turns and twists that literary practice took in the last century and a half. It is enough to say that the short story was there, jogging along beside its longer-winded rival, the novel.

The German novella had scarcely begun to be legitimized when German literary science (Literaturwissenschaft) proceeded to erect a mountain of speculation as to its nature and characteristics. An academic industry has grown up around the novella; repeated efforts have been made to define it and to establish its relationship to other forms of narrative. French

scholars too have racked their brains to find a tenable distinction between a *conte* and a *nouvelle,* but they have very sensibly given up. Anglo-American scholars have shown little interest in these scholastic exercises. But German literary science has made up for the inertia of foreign scholarship in this field.

So much intellectual activity by men of great erudition cannot be ignored. But space permits only a few comments on the vast material that has been written on the novella. Anglo-American literary history does not seem to recognize the short story as a separate genre but treats it as a branch of fiction, governed by the same principles as the novel, making allowance for those practical adjustments imposed on the short story by its brevity. This seems a reasonable approach because the fortunes of the short story in modern times have paralleled those of the novel. Wellek and Warren, in their authoritative *Theory of Literature,* do not mention the short story or novella as a separate genre. In Anglo-American usage a "short story" is a *short* story, while the term *novella,* a recent import into the vocabulary of literary criticism, denotes "a work of fiction intermediate in length and complexity between the short story and the novel."[3]

Of course, size in art does affect composition. The miniature painter or sculptor works differently from the artist who paints on a large canvas or sculpts on a large block of stone. But it is wrong to argue, as many scholars have done, that because a novella or short story is relatively short it must confine itself to one episode in a sequence of events. It would be more scientific to say that the limitations of space compel the short-story writer to choose between two alternatives: he may either treat a large material in outline or develop a single event or situation in greater detail. There is no justification for dictating to an artist how he shall use his material. Flaubert made a great novel, *Madame Bovary,* out of a short-story plot; Goethe conceived his novel *The Elective Affinities* (*Die Wahlverwandtschaften*) as a novella; so did Thomas Mann with regard to *The Magic Mountain* and the *Joseph* tetralogy; and Joyce's *Ulysses,* too, grew out of

---

[3]*Webster's Third International Dictionary* (Springfield, Mass., 1966), p. 1546; the *Oxford English Dictionary* does not list the word.

what was to be a short story. The same principle applies to the portrayal of character: the author may fill the space at his disposal with detailed character study if he is willing to sacrifice other elements, such as plot or historical background. Or he may squeeze a goodly number of people into a novella by treating them more sketchily. James Joyce's masterly story *The Dead* is three-quarters preparation or atmosphere, with the real action compressed into the last few pages. From the point of view of orthodox composition it is a failure—but it is a masterpiece all the same.

Writers refuse—rightly—to be restricted by past conventions; they are an innovative and rebellious race. "All the genres are good," wrote Voltaire, "except the boring genre." Lessing made a similar statement regarding the drama. All the restrictions that *Literaturwissenschaft* has tried to impose on the short-story writer as to plot, character, atmosphere, tone, and style have been violated by the best practitioners of the art.

●

A final word about German terminology in this field. The terms in common use are *Geschichte, Erzählung, Novelle,* and *Kurzgeschichte. Geschichte* is the precise equivalent of the English word *story.* "Es ist eine alte Geschichte," wrote Heine, "doch bleibt sie immer neu." Paul Ernst, one of the masters of the short story in our century, named two of his collections *Stories in the German Manner (Geschichten von deutscher Art)* and *Stories of Actors and Rogues (Komödianten- und Spitzbubengeschichten). Erzählung* is the generic name for narrative fiction. It translates our words "narrative," "tale," or "story." It should also include stories of novel length, but it doesn't. Prose narrative, as applied to a novel, is *Epik* or *Prosaepos. Novelle* is a term that first appeared in the late eighteenth century to denote any work midway between the lengthy novel and the brief anecdote. In the nineteenth century it became popular in literary circles and displaced *Erzählung* as a generic term. In the Biedermeier period (1815–50) there were narrative works from two hundred to three hundred pages in length that were called *Novellen,* possibly in imitation of British usage, which at that time applied the term *novel* to denote all fiction, long or short. As long as

the term *Novelle* remained fashionable, it was used to include both short and long stories. It just happened that the long novella became popular among German writers as a substitute for the novel, which flourished in Western Europe.

In the twentieth century the term *Novelle* lost ground, as the long novella was replaced by the short story, which was now named *Kurzgeschichte*, no doubt under Anglo-American influence. The term *Novelle* still surfaced occasionally, as in Arnold Zweig's *Novellas Concerning Claudia* (*Novellen um Claudia*, 1930). Günter Grass called his long story *Cat and Mouse* (*Katz und Maus*) a *Novelle*. Were these authors aware of all the ink that had been spilled by scholars to define, delimit, and regulate the criteria that make a story a *Novelle* rather than an *Erzählung*? It is hard to say; but this much is certain: authors are often not bothered by the distinctions that worry scholars. There is even an occasional German scholar who takes a latitudinarian position on this matter of terminology. Thus Erich Trunz, the eminent Goethe scholar, shuttles back and forth between the terms *Geschichte, Erzählung,* and *Novelle* thirteen times on two pages, using the terms as synonyms.

I have called the stories that make up this book *Erzählungen*, using the generic term. Anyone following Anglo-American usage would call all of them, except the two by Stifter and Schnitzler, short stories.

In his *Journey through the Harz Mountains* (*Die Harzreise*) Heinrich Heine reports that in a restaurant in Klaustal he was served a smoked herring called "Bücking," and he gives an erudite gloss on the origin of the name. He then adds: "How delicious such a dish tastes when you know the historical data connected with it and eat it yourself." An apt observation: the proof of the pudding is in the eating. So whether this anthology contains *Geschichten, Erzählungen,* or *Novellen*, the important thing is to enjoy them and, incidentally, to learn some German in the process.

Johann Wolfgang von Goethe

1749–1832

Goethe[1] is usually regarded as the founder of the modern German novella, although it might be argued that this honor belongs to his contemporary Wieland. In 1793 Goethe reshaped a story he found in the fifteenth-century anonymous French collection *One Hundred New Novellas* (*Cent Nouvelles nouvelles*) and offered it to his colleague Friedrich Schiller[2] for the journal *Die Horen,* which Schiller edited; it appeared there in 1795.

[1]To condense Goethe's biography into a couple of pages is a feat that even Houdini could not perform. Whole books record his daily activities and his multifarious writings. Goethe is one of the world's greatest intellectual giants; his achievements encompass the spheres of literature in its many genres: lyric and epic poetry (his *Faust* alone runs to over 12,000 lines), drama, fiction, biography and autobiography, literary and art criticism. He was a translator and wrote thousands of letters. He was also a painter, a statesman and an experimental scientist. He has left treatises on physics, botany, geology, mineralogy, comparative anatomy and meteorology. The Weimar edition of Goethe's works comprises 143 volumes, of which 50 contain his letters and another 15 his diaries. This introductory note limits itself to a discussion of Goethe's role in the development of the German novella.

This is the tale of the virtuous attorney which opens our collection of stories. Goethe adapted other tales from earlier writers and created some from his own imagination. Taking his cue from Boccaccio, he framed these stories in a social setting that reflected the turbulent time in which they were composed. The frame gave them an outer unity and allowed him to interject a running commentary on the theme of each story and on the characteristics of the novella as a literary genre. The whole collection appeared in 1795 under the title *Conversations of German Emigrés (Unterhaltungen deutscher Ausgewanderten)*[3]

No two of Goethe's novellas are alike, and some of them anticipate later developments in German fiction. The story of the virtuous attorney may be described as belonging to an early form of fiction: the "moral tale" (*moralische Erzählung*) or apologue, which we find in the literatures of antiquity, in the parables of the Bible, and in the medieval *exempla*. These are didactic tales presenting an ethical or philosophical teaching in fictional garb. Examples are Addison's "Vision of Mirzah" (from the *Spectator*), Samuel Johnson's *Rasselas, Prince of Abyssinia*, Voltaire's *contes philosophiques* (especially *Zadig* and *Candide*), and, toward the end of the century, Diderot's philosophical tracts in fictional form, one of which, *Rameau's Nephew (Le Neveu de Rameau)*, was discovered by Goethe and made public in his German translation. In 1761 Marmontel published his *Moral Tales (Contes moraux)*, pleasant stories dealing with social and domestic problems, celebrating the triumph of virtue and the defeat of vice. They were widely read both in and outside of France. Wieland[4] and Goethe, the two principal German writers

---

[2]Schiller is the hero of Thomas Mann's novella *Schwere Stunde* (pp. 364–382). A short biographical note on him will be found on p. 380. The *Horae* are the seasons in Greek mythology.

[3]*Ausgewanderte* refers to aristocratic refugees who fled before the armies of the French Revolution.

[4]Christoph Martin Wieland (1733–1813), Goethe's older contemporary and friend, wrote short stories and novels in verse and prose. His romance in verse, *Oberon* (1780), was translated into English verse by John Quincy Adams. His novella *Love and Friendship Tested* is the opening story of *Twelve German Novellas* published by the University of California Press in 1977.

of fiction in the late eighteenth century, produced moral tales, although both were rather critical of the genre, and Heinrich von Kleist originally intended to name his collection of novellas *Moralische Erzählungen.*

Goethe's tale of the virtuous attorney is an adaptation of a rather farcical story in Boccaccio's manner. Prior to the romantic movement, with its cult of "original genius," writers borrowed freely from one another. Boccaccio, Chaucer, Shakespeare, the French tragedians—they all took from their predecessors, from classical literature, from the Bible, from medieval literature, and even from their contemporaries, reshaping the content in their own artistic mold. According to the older classical aesthetic canon, artistry lies not in the *what* but in the *how.* This attitude is encountered even in our own day. When Jean Giraudoux decided to write a play on the classical theme of Amphitryon, he found thirty-seven plays on the subject; so he named his work *Amphitryon 38.* That the reader already knew the story or even all thirty-seven extant versions did not matter; the artistic challenge lay in the new life that author No. 38 could breathe into the dry bones. The genius impresses his own stamp on the raw or borrowed material; therein lies his originality. James Joyce's *Ulysses* is no less an achievement because the modern author follows the outer structure of Homer's *Odyssey;* on the contrary. Pope put it brilliantly:

> True wit is nature to advantage dressed,
> What oft was thought, but ne'er so well expressed.[5]

In the same collection Goethe includes psychological and sociological stories and a romantic fairy tale, which he called

---

[5]*Essay on Criticism,* 1:297. In this context *wit* is "the quality of speech or writing which consists in the apt association of thought and expression calculated to surprise and delight by its unexpectedness" (Oxford English Dictionary). Nature is the raw material with which art works; this may be taken from life or from the work of other artists. The achievement of the artist lies in his "dressing of nature to advantage."

Das Märchen but which is really an allegory. His later novellas, incorporated in the novels *Wilhelm Meister* and *The Elective Affinities* (*Die Wahlverwandtschaften*), are also varied in type, with the moral tale perhaps predominating.

As the reader works through this anthology, he or she will become aware of a steady growth in complexity, subtlety, and sophistication in the evolution of Western fiction. The depiction and development of character, the description of political and social conditions and social problems, the conflicts between ideologies, the impact of science on the individual and on society—these and other themes form the backbone of the short story as it develops in the nineteenth century and beyond. Judged by these standards, Goethe's story, and Hebel's which follows it, are unmodern and unsophisticated. The characters are so little individualized that they are not even given names. There is no concern for milieu or for the social factors that govern the behavior of the principals in the action, features that the modern reader expects. So intently is Goethe's gaze fixed on the main business at hand, which is the moral lesson or wisdom that the young woman is to learn, that he makes no use of the difference in age between husband and wife as a motive for explaining her behavior. The structure of the story is equally simple. There is no playing with artistry, no subtle imagery, no hidden symbolism, such as the literature of the novella was to develop later and which Goethe himself uses in other stories. The tone is serious but not solemn. The reader's attention is held as the moral to be drawn from the events is built up.

But literary greatness does not depend on artistry or erudition. The story of Ruth in the Old Testament is told without artistry; yet it is one of the great masterpieces of narrative fiction. The power of Goethe's and Hebel's moral tales derives from a hidden source that transcends artistic gimmickry. It is the same power that draws us to the music of Vivaldi and Clementi, though it is naive compared to the ultrasophistication of Hindemith, Schönberg, and Krenek.

Drawing by Goethe for *Faust*

Der Prokurator

In einer italienischen Seestadt lebte vorzeiten ein Handelsmann, der sich von Jugend auf durch Tätigkeit und Klugheit
auszeichnete. Er war dabei ein guter Seemann und hatte große
Reichtümer erworben, indem[1] er selbst nach Alexandria[2] zu
schiffen, kostbare Waren zu erkaufen oder einzutauschen
pflegte, die er alsdann zu Hause wieder abzusetzen oder in die
nördlichen Gegenden Europas zu versenden wußte. Sein Vermögen wuchs von Jahr zu Jahr um so mehr,[3] als er in seiner
Geschäftigkeit selbst das größte Vergnügen fand und ihm keine
Zeit zu kostspieligen Zerstreuungen übrigblieb.

Bis in sein fünfzigstes Jahr hatte er sich auf diese Weise emsig
fortbeschäftigt und ihm war von den geselligen Vergnügungen
wenig bekannt worden, mit welchen ruhige Bürger ihr Leben
zu würzen verstehen; ebensowenig hatte das schöne Geschlecht, bei allen Vorzügen seiner Landsmänninnen, seine
Aufmerksamkeit weiter erregt, als insofern er ihre Begierde
nach Schmuck und Kostbarkeiten sehr wohl kannte und sie
gelegentlich zu nutzen wußte.

Wie wenig versah er sich daher auf die Veränderung, die in
seinem Gemüte vorgehen sollte, als eines Tages sein reich beladen[4] Schiff in den Hafen seiner Vaterstadt einlief, eben an
einem jährlichen Feste, das besonders der Kinder wegen[5]
gefeiert wurde. Knaben und Mädchen pflegten nach dem Got-
tesdienste in allerlei Verkleidungen sich zu zeigen, bald in Pro-
zessionen, bald[6] in Scharen durch die Stadt zu scherzen und
sodann im Felde auf einem großen freien Platz allerhand Spiele
zu treiben, Kunststücke und Geschicklichkeiten zu zeigen und
in artigem Wettstreit ausgesetzte kleine Preise zu gewinnen.

The Attorney

A long time ago, in an Italian seacoast town, there lived a merchant who had distinguished himself since his youth by industry and prudence. He was at the same time a good seaman and had acquired great wealth by taking trips to Alexandria to buy or exchange precious wares that he was then able to sell at home or to send on to the northern regions of Europe. His fortune increased from year to year, all the more since he found his greatest pleasure in his business and had no time left for costly amusements.

In this way he had busily occupied himself till his fiftieth year and had come to know little of the social pleasures with which sedate citizens manage to spice their lives. Nor had the fair sex, despite all the advantages enjoyed by his countrywomen, aroused his attention, except insofar as he knew very well their desire for jewelry and precious things and on occasion was able to make use of this knowledge.

How little, then, did he foresee the change that was to occur in his heart when one day his richly laden ship landed in the harbor of his native city—on the very day of an annual festival that was celebrated especially for children. Boys and girls in all sorts of costumes showed themselves after the church service, sporting through the city now in processions, now in bands, then playing all kinds of games in the field on a large, open square, performing stunts and feats of skill and winning small prizes offered in a friendly competition.

Anfangs wohnte unser Seemann dieser Feier mit Vergnügen bei; als er aber die Lebenslust der Kinder und die Freude der Eltern daran lange betrachtet und so viele Menschen im Genuß einer gegenwärtigen Freude und der angenehmsten aller Hoffnungen gefunden hatte, mußte ihm bei einer Rückkehr auf sich selbst sein einsamer Zustand äußerst auffallen. Sein leeres Haus fing zum erstenmal an, ihm ängstlich zu werden, und er klagte sich selbst in seinen Gedanken an:

„O ich Unglückseliger! warum gehn mir so spät die Augen auf? Warum erkenne ich erst im Alter jene Güter, die allein den Menschen glücklich machen? Soviel Mühe! soviel Gefahren! Was haben sie mir verschafft? Sind gleich[7] meine Gewölbe voll Waren, meine Kisten voll edler Metalle und meine Schränke voll Schmuck und Kleinodien, so können doch diese Güter mein Gemüt weder erheitern noch befriedigen. Je mehr ich sie aufhäufe, desto mehr Gesellen scheinen sie zu verlangen; ein Kleinod fordert das andere, ein Goldstück das andere. Sie erkennen mich nicht für den Hausherrn; sie rufen mir ungestüm zu: ‚Geh und eile, schaffe noch mehr unsersgleichen herbei! Gold erfreut sich nur des Goldes, das Kleinod des Kleinodes.' So gebieten sie mir schon die ganze Zeit meines Lebens, und erst spät fühle ich, daß mir in allem diesem kein Genuß bereitet ist. Leider jetzt, da die Jahre kommen, fange ich an zu denken und sage zu mir: ‚Du genießest diese Schätze nicht, und niemand wird sie nach dir genießen! Hast du jemals eine geliebte Frau damit geschmückt? Hast du eine Tochter damit ausgestattet? Hast du einen Sohn in den Stand gesetzt, sich die Neigung eines guten Mädchens zu gewinnen und zu befestigen? Niemals! Von allen deinen Besitztümern hast du, hat niemand der Deinigen[8] etwas besessen, und was du mühsam zusammengebracht hast, wird nach deinem Tode ein Fremder leichtfertig verprassen.'

„O wie anders werden heute abend jene glücklichen Eltern ihre Kinder um den Tisch versammeln, ihre Geschicklichkeit preisen und sie zu guten Taten aufmuntern! Welche Lust glänzte aus ihren Augen, und welche Hoffnung schien aus dem Gegenwärtigen zu entspringen! Solltest du denn aber selbst gar keine Hoffnung fassen können? Bist du denn schon ein Greis?

At first our seaman watched this celebration with pleasure. But when he had observed the high spirits of the children and the joy of the parents for a long time and had found so many people savoring an immediate happiness and the most pleasant of all hopes, he was bound to be struck by his lonely state when he returned to himself. His empty house began for the first time to become a source of anxiety to him and he accused himself in his thoughts:

"Oh, unhappy man that I am! Why are my eyes opened so late? Why do I recognize only in my old age those good things that alone make man happy? So much effort! So much danger! What have they brought me? Though my storehouses are full of goods, my chests full of precious metals, and my cabinets full of trinkets and jewels, these possessions can neither cheer nor satisfy my spirit. The more I amass them, the more companions they seem to demand; one jewel demands another, one gold coin another. They do not recognize me as master of the house; they call to me impetuously: 'Go and hurry, procure more like us! Gold is only happy with gold, and a jewel with another jewel.' So they have been commanding me all my life, and only of late do I feel that in all this there is no enjoyment for me. Unfortunately only now, when age is approaching, am I beginning to think and say to myself: 'You are not enjoying these treasures and no one will enjoy them after you! Have you ever adorned a beloved woman with them? Have you used them as a trousseau for a daughter? Did you put a son into the position of winning and holding the affection of a good girl? Never! Neither you nor anyone belonging to you has ever possessed any of your possessions, and what you have laboriously brought together a stranger will frivolously squander.'

"Oh, how differently will those happy parents gather their children about the table tonight, praise their achievement and encourage them to do good deeds! What pleasure shone from their eyes, and what hope seemed to spring from the present! But can you yourself not grasp at any hope? Are you an old man yet? Is it not enough to realize your neglect, now when

Ist es nicht genug, die Versäumnis einzusehen, jetzt, da noch
nicht aller Tage Abend[9] gekommen ist? Nein, in deinem Alter
ist es noch nicht töricht, ans Freien zu denken, mit deinen
Gütern wirst du ein braves Weib[10] erwerben und glücklich
machen, und siehst du noch Kinder in deinem Hause, so werden dir diese spätern Früchte den größten Genuß geben, anstatt
daß sie oft denen, die sie zu früh vom Himmel erhalten, zur
Last werden und zur Verwirrung gereichen."

Als er durch dieses Selbstgespräch seinen Vorsatz bei sich
befestigt hatte, rief er zwei Schiffsgesellen zu sich und eröffnete
ihnen seine Gedanken. Sie, die gewohnt waren, in allen Fällen
willig und bereit zu sein, fehlten auch diesmal nicht und eilten,
sich in der Stadt nach den jüngsten und schönsten Mädchen
zu erkundigen; denn ihr Patron, da er einmal nach dieser Ware
lüstern ward,[11] sollte auch die beste finden und besitzen.

Er selbst feierte[12] so wenig als seine Abgesandten. Er ging,
fragte, sah und hörte und fand bald, was er suchte, in einem
Frauenzimmer,[13] das in diesem Augenblick das schönste der
ganzen Stadt genannt zu werden verdiente, ungefähr sechzehn
Jahre alt, wohlgebildet und gut erzogen, deren Gestalt und
Wesen das Angenehmste zeigte und das Beste versprach.

Nach einer kurzen Unterhandlung, durch welche der vor-
teilhafteste Zustand sowohl bei Lebzeiten als nach dem Tode
des Mannes der Schönen versichert ward, vollzog man die
Heirat mit großer Pracht und Lust, und von diesem Tage an
fühlte sich unser Handelsmann zum erstenmal im wirklichen
Besitz und Genuß seiner Reichtümer. Nun verwandte er mit
Freuden die schönsten und reichsten Stoffe zur Bekleidung
des schönen Körpers, die Juwelen glänzten ganz anders an der
Brust und in den Haaren seiner Geliebten als ehemals im
Schmuckkästchen, und die Ringe erhielten einen unendlichen
Wert von der Hand, die sie trug.

So fühlte er sich nicht allein so reich, sondern reicher als
bisher, indem seine Güter sich durch Teilnehmung und An-
wendung zu vermehren schienen. Auf diese Weise lebte das
Paar fast ein Jahr lang in der größten Zufriedenheit, und er
schien seine Liebe zu einem tätigen und herumstreifenden
Leben gegen das Gefühl häuslicher Glückseligkeit gänzlich ver-
tauscht zu haben. Aber eine alte Gewohnheit legt sich so leicht

the evening of your life has not come yet? No, at your age it is not yet foolish to think of courting; with your property you will acquire a good wife and make her happy; and if you live to see children in your home, these late fruits will afford you the greatest enjoyment instead of becoming a burden and a source of confusion, as they often do to those who receive them too early from heaven."

When he had confirmed this plan in his own mind through this conversation with himself, he summoned two shipmates and revealed his thoughts to them. They, who were accustomed to be willing and ready in all situations, did not fail this time either but hastened into the city to inquire after the youngest and most beautiful girls; for their employer, having now become covetous of this type of goods, was to find and possess the best.

He himself was no more idle than his emissaries. He went, asked, saw, and heard and soon found what he was looking for in a woman who at this time deserved to be called the most beautiful in the whole city—about sixteen years old, of fine culture and good upbringing, whose form and whole being revealed the most pleasant prospects and promised the best.

After brief negotiations, by which the most advantageous conditions were secured for the beauty both during the life of her husband and after his death, the marriage was celebrated with great splendor and joy; and from this day on, our merchant for the first time felt that he was really possessing and enjoying his wealth. Now he joyfully employed the most beautiful and richest materials for clothing the beautiful body of his beloved; the jewels glittered very differently on her breast and in her hair than they had formerly done in the jewel box, and the rings received an infinite value from the hand that wore them.

So he felt not only as rich as, but richer than before, inasmuch as his property seemed to increase through sharing and use. In this way the couple lived for almost a year in the greatest contentment, and he seemed to have wholly exchanged his love of an active and roaming life for the feeling of domestic bliss. But an old habit is not so easily discarded, and a direction we have assumed early in life can be diverted for a time, no doubt, but never wholly interrupted.

nicht ab, und eine Richtung, die wir früh genommen, kann
wohl einige Zeit abgelenkt, aber nie ganz unterbrochen werden.
So hatte auch unser Handelsmann oft, wenn er andere sich
einschiffen oder glücklich in den Hafen zurückkehren sah,
wieder die Regungen seiner alten Leidenschaft gefühlt, ja er
hatte selbst in seinem Hause an der Seite seiner Gattin manchmal Unruhe und Unzufriedenheit empfunden. Dieses Verlangen vermehrte sich mit der Zeit und verwandelte sich zuletzt
in eine solche Sehnsucht, daß er sich äußerst unglücklich fühlen
mußte und zuletzt wirklich krank ward.

„Was soll nun aus dir werden?" sagte er zu sich selbst. „Du
erfährst nun, wie töricht es ist, in späten Jahren eine alte
Lebensweise gegen eine neue zu vertauschen. Wie sollen wir
das, was wir immer getrieben und gesucht haben, aus unsern
Gedanken, ja aus unsern Gliedern wieder herausbringen? Und
wie geht es mir nun, der ich bisher wie ein Fisch das Wasser,
wie ein Vogel die freie Luft geliebt, da ich mich in einem
Gebäude bei allen Schätzen und bei der Blume aller Reichtümer, bei einer schönen jungen Frau eingesperrt habe? Anstatt
daß ich dadurch hoffte, Zufriedenheit zu gewinnen und meiner
Güter zu genießen, so scheint es mir, daß ich alles verliere,
indem ich nichts weiter erwerbe. Mit Unrecht hält man die
Menschen für Toren, welche in rastloser Tätigkeit Güter auf
Güter zu häufen suchen; denn die Tätigkeit ist das Glück, und
für den, der die Freuden eines ununterbrochenen Bestrebens
empfinden kann, ist der erworbene Reichtum ohne Bedeutung.
Aus Mangel an Beschäftigung werde ich elend, aus Mangel an
Bewegung krank, und wenn ich keinen andern Entschluß
fasse,[14] so bin ich in kurzer Zeit dem Tode nahe.

„Freilich ist es ein gewagtes Unternehmen, sich von einer
jungen, liebenswürdigen Frau zu entfernen. Ist es billig, um
ein reizendes und reizbares Mädchen zu freien und sie nach
einer kurzen Zeit sich selbst, der Langenweile,[15] ihren Empfindungen und Begierden zu überlassen? Spazieren diese
jungen, seidnen Herrn nicht schon jetzt vor meinen Fenstern
auf und ab? Suchen sie nicht schon jetzt in der Kirche und in
Gärten die Aufmerksamkeit meines Weibchens an sich zu
ziehen? Und was wird erst[16] geschehen, wenn ich weg bin? Soll
ich glauben, daß mein Weib durch ein Wunder gerettet werden

And so our merchant, too, when he saw others boarding ship
or returning safely to harbor, had once more felt the stirrings
of his old passion; indeed he had even sometimes felt uneasiness
and dissatisfaction in his own home at the side of his wife. This
desire increased with time and was finally transformed into
such longing that he was bound to feel extremely unhappy and
at last became really ill.

"What is to become of you now?" he said to himself. "Now
you learn how foolish it is to exchange an old way of life for a
new one in later years. How can we banish from our thoughts,
indeed from our limbs, what we have always done and sought?
And what is my condition now—I who have until now loved
the water like a fish and the free air like a bird—when I've
locked myself up in a building with all my treasures and the
flower of all wealth, a beautiful young wife? Instead of what I
had hoped for—to gain contentment from it and to enjoy my
estates—it seems to me that I'm losing everything, since I'm
acquiring nothing more. It is wrong to regard those people
who seek to pile up property on property in restless activity as
fools; for activity is happiness; and for the man who can feel
the joy of an uninterrupted effort, the wealth that he has acquired is without meaning. I'm becoming wretched from a lack
of activity, sick from a lack of movement, and unless I alter my
course I shall be near death in a short time.

"Of course, it is a risky undertaking to separate oneself from
a young, attractive wife. Is it right to court a charming and
susceptible girl and after a short time abandon her to herself,
to boredom, to her emotions and desires? Aren't these young
gentlemen in silk even now parading up and down in front of
my windows? Aren't they already seeking to attract my wife's
attention in church and in the gardens? And what will happen
once I'm away? Am I to believe that my wife could be saved
by a miracle? No; at her age, with her constitution, it would be
foolish to hope that she could abstain from the joys of love. If

könnte? Nein, in ihrem Alter, bei ihrer Konstitution wäre es
töricht zu hoffen, daß sie sich der Freuden der Liebe enthalten
könnte. Entfernst du dich, so wirst du bei deiner Rückkunft
die Neigung deines Weibes und ihre Treue zugleich mit der
Ehre deines Hauses verloren haben."

Diese Betrachtungen und Zweifel, mit denen er sich eine
Zeitlang quälte, verschlimmerten den Zustand, in dem er sich
befand, aufs äußerste. Seine Frau, seine Verwandten und
Freunde betrübten sich um ihn, ohne daß sie die Ursache seiner
Krankheit hätten entdecken können. Endlich ging er nochmals
bei sich zu Rate[17] und rief nach einiger Überlegung aus: „Tö-
richter Mensch! du lässest es dir so sauer werden,[18] ein Weib
zu bewahren, das du doch bald, wenn dein Übel fortdauert,
sterbend hinter dir und einem andern lassen mußt. Ist es nicht
wenigstens klüger und besser, du suchst das Leben zu erhalten,
wenn du gleich in Gefahr kommst, an ihr dasjenige zu verlieren, was als das höchste Gut der Frauen geschätzt wird? Wie
mancher Mann kann durch seine Gegenwart den Verlust dieses
Schatzes nicht hindern und vermißt geduldig, was er nicht
erhalten kann! Warum solltest du nicht Mut haben, dich eines
solchen Gutes zu entschlagen, da von diesem Entschlusse dein
Leben abhängt?"

Mit diesen Worten ermannte er sich und ließ seine Schiffsgesellen rufen. Er trug ihnen auf, nach gewohnter Weise ein
Fahrzeug zu befrachten und alles bereit zu halten, daß sie bei
dem ersten günstigen Winde auslaufen könnten. Darauf erklärte er sich gegen seine Frau folgendermaßen:

„Laß dich nicht befremden, wenn du in dem Hause eine
Bewegung siehst, woraus du schließen kannst, daß ich mich zu
einer Abreise anschicke! Betrübe dich nicht, wenn ich dir gestehe, daß ich abermals eine Seefahrt zu unternehmen gedenke!
Meine Liebe zu dir ist noch immer dieselbe, und sie wird es
gewiß in meinem ganzen Leben bleiben. Ich erkenne den Wert
des Glücks, das ich bisher an deiner Seite genoß, und würde
ihn noch reiner fühlen, wenn ich mir nicht oft Vorwürfe der
Untätigkeit und Nachlässigkeit im stillen machen müßte. Meine
alte Neigung wacht wieder auf, und meine alte Gewohnheit
zieht mich wieder an. Erlaube mir, daß ich den Markt von
Alexandrien wiedersehe, den ich jetzt mit größerem Eifer be-

you go away, you will, upon returning, have lost your wife's affection and her fidelity together with the honor of your house."

These reflections and doubts with which he tormented himself for a while aggravated the condition in which he found himself to an extreme. His wife, his relatives, and friends were concerned about him without being able to discover the cause of his illness. Finally he consulted his inner mind once more and after some deliberation cried out: "Foolish man! You are taking so many pains to preserve a wife whom, if your sickness continues and you die, you will soon have to leave behind for another man. Isn't it wiser and better that you should at least seek to preserve your life even though you run the risk of losing in her what is treasured as woman's highest good? How many a man is there who cannot prevent the loss of this treasure even by his presence and who patiently surrenders what he cannot preserve. Why shouldn't you have the courage to give up such a treasure when your very life depends on this decision?"

With these words he took heart and sent for his shipmates. He charged them to load a vessel with cargo in the usual way and to be ready to sail at the first favorable wind. Then he explained the situation to his wife in the following words:

"Don't be alarmed if you see activity in the house from which you may conclude that I'm preparing for a journey. And don't feel sad if I confess to you that I'm thinking of undertaking a sea voyage again. My love for you is still the same as ever and will certainly remain so all my life. I recognize the value of the happiness that I've enjoyed at your side till now; these feelings would be even purer if I did not often have to reproach myself privately for my inactivity and negligence. My old inclination is awakening again and my old habit is attracting me once more. Permit me to see the market of Alexandria again; I shall now visit it with greater eagerness because I expect to gain there the most precious materials and the noblest treasures for you.

suchen werde, weil ich dort die köstlichsten Stoffe und die
edelsten Kostbarkeiten für dich zu gewinnen denke. Ich lasse
dich im Besitz aller meiner Güter und meines ganzen Vermögens; bediene dich dessen und vergnüge dich mit deinen Eltern
und Verwandten! Die Zeit der Abwesenheit geht auch vorüber,
und mit vielfacher Freude werden wir uns wiedersehen."

Nicht ohne Tränen machte ihm die liebenswürdige Frau die
zärtlichsten Vorwürfe, versicherte, daß sie ohne ihn keine
fröhliche Stunde hinbringen werde, und bat ihn nur, da sie
ihn weder halten könne noch einschränken wolle, daß er ihrer
auch in der Abwesenheit zum besten gedenken möge.

Nachdem er darauf verschiedenes mit ihr über einige Geschäfte und häusliche Angelegenheiten gesprochen, sagte er
nach einer kleinen Pause: „Ich habe nun noch etwas auf dem
Herzen, davon[19] du mir frei zu reden erlauben mußt; nur
bitte ich dich aufs herzlichste, nicht zu mißdeuten, was ich
sage, sondern auch selbst in dieser Besorgnis meine Liebe zu
erkennen."

„Ich kann es erraten", versetzte die Schöne darauf; „du bist
meinetwegen besorgt, indem du nach Art der Männer unser
Geschlecht ein für allemal[20] für schwach hältst. Du hast mich
bisher jung und froh gekannt, und nun glaubst du, daß ich in
deiner Abwesenheit leichtsinnig und verführbar sein werde.
Ich schelte diese Sinnesart nicht, denn sie ist bei euch Männern
gewöhnlich; aber wie ich mein Herz kenne, darf ich dir versichern, daß nichts so leicht Eindruck auf mich machen und
kein möglicher Eindruck so tief wirken soll, um mich von dem
Wege abzuleiten, auf dem ich bisher an der Hand der Liebe
und Pflicht hinwandelte. Sei ohne Sorgen; du sollst deine Frau
so zärtlich und treu bei deiner Rückkunft wiederfinden, als du
sie abends fandest, wenn du nach einer kleinen Abwesenheit
in meine Arme zurückkehrtest."

„Diese Gesinnungen traue ich dir zu", versetzte der Gemahl,
„und bitte dich, darin zu verharren. Laß uns aber an die äußersten Fälle denken; warum soll man sich nicht auch darauf
vorsehen? Du weißt, wie sehr deine schöne und reizende Gestalt
die Augen unserer jungen Mitbürger auf sich zieht; sie werden
sich in meiner Abwesenheit noch mehr als bisher um dich bemühen, sie werden sich dir auf alle Weise zu nähern, ja zu

I leave you in possession of all my goods and of my entire fortune; make use of it and enjoy yourself with your parents and relatives. The time of my absence will also pass, and we will see each other again with much joy."

Not without tears did his charming wife cast the most tender reproaches at him, assuring him that without him she would not spend one single happy hour. Since she could not hold him back and did not want to curb him, she merely begged him to think the best of her during his absence.

After he had discussed various matters concerning certain business and domestic affairs with her, he said after a brief pause: "I still have something on my mind about which you must permit me to talk freely; but I beg you most sincerely not to misinterpret what I am saying but to recognize my love even in this anxiety of mine."

"I can guess it," the beautiful woman replied, "you are concerned about me since, like all men, you consider our sex to be basically weak. Until now you have known me as young and gay; now you believe that in your absence I'll be frivolous and easily seduced. I don't condemn this line of thought, for it is usual with you men. But as I know my heart, I may assure you that nothing can make such an easy impression on me and that no possible impression can affect me so deeply as to lead me astray from the road on which I have walked hitherto, guided by the hand of love and duty. Don't worry; when you return you shall find your wife as tender and faithful as you found her each evening when you returned to my arms after a brief absence."

"I believe you are capable of this conviction," her husband replied, "and beg you to persevere in it. But let us think of an extreme situation; why shouldn't we be prepared for that too? You know how much your beautiful and charming person attracts the eyes of our young fellow citizens. In my absence they will pay you even more attention than till now; they will seek to approach you in every possible way and indeed to please

gefallen suchen. Nicht immer wird das Bild deines Gemahls, wie jetzt seine Gegenwart, sie von deiner Türe und deinem Herzen verscheuchen. Du bist ein edles und gutes Kind, aber die Forderungen der Natur sind rechtmäßig und gewaltsam; sie stehen mit unserer Vernunft beständig im Streite und tragen gewöhnlich den Sieg davon. Unterbrich mich nicht! Du wirst gewiß in meiner Abwesenheit, selbst bei dem pflichtmäßigen Andenken an mich, das Verlangen empfinden, wodurch das Weib den Mann anzieht und von ihm angezogen wird. Ich werde eine Zeitlang der Gegenstand deiner Wünsche sein; aber wer weiß, was für Umstände zusammentreffen, was für Gelegenheiten sich finden, und ein anderer wird in der Wirklichkeit ernten, was die Einbildungskraft mir zugedacht hatte. Werde nicht ungeduldig, ich bitte dich, höre mich aus!

„Sollte der Fall kommen, dessen Möglichkeit du leugnest und den ich auch nicht zu beschleunigen wünsche, daß du ohne die Gesellschaft eines Mannes nicht länger bleiben, die Freuden der Liebe nicht wohl entbehren könntest, so versprich mir nur, an meine Stelle keinen von den leichtsinnigen Knaben zu wählen, die, so artig sie auch aussehen mögen, der Ehre noch mehr als der Tugend einer Frau gefährlich sind. Mehr durch Eitelkeit als durch Begierde beherrscht, bemühen sie sich um eine jede und finden nichts natürlicher, als eine der andern aufzuopfern. Fühlst du dich geneigt, dich nach einem Freunde umzusehen, so forsche nach einem, der diesen Namen verdient, der bescheiden und verschwiegen die Freuden der Liebe noch durch die Wohltat des Geheimnisses zu erheben weiß.“

Hier verbarg die schöne Frau ihren Schmerz nicht länger, und die Tränen, die sie bisher zurückgehalten hatte, stürzten reichlich aus ihren Augen. „Was du auch von mir denken magst“, rief sie nach einer leidenschaftlichen Umarmung aus, „so ist doch nichts entfernter von mir als das Verbrechen, das du gewissermaßen für unvermeidlich hältst. Möge, wenn jemals auch nur ein solcher Gedanke in mir entsteht, die Erde sich auftun und mich verschlingen, und möge alle Hoffnung der Seligkeit mir entrissen werden, die uns eine so reizende Fortdauer unsers Daseins verspricht. Entferne das Mißtrauen aus deiner Brust[21] und laß mir die ganze reine Hoffnung, dich bald wieder in meinen Armen zu sehen!“

you. The image of your husband will not always banish them from your door and heart as his presence does now. You are a noble and good child, but the demands of nature are legitimate and powerful; they are in constant conflict with our reason and usually gain the victory. Don't interrupt me! During my absence, even while you are dutifully thinking of me, you will certainly feel the desire by which a woman attracts a man and is attracted by him. For a time I shall be the object of your wishes; but who knows what sort of conditions will occur, what opportunities will arise, and another man will reap in reality what your imagination had intended for me. Don't become impatient, I beg you, listen till I'm through.

"Should the case arise—although you deny this possibility and I don't wish to precipitate it—that you could no longer live without the company of a man nor easily forgo the pleasures of love, promise me only this: not to choose in my place any of those frivolous boys who, however polite they may look, are even more dangerous to a woman's honor than to her virtue. Dominated more by vanity than by desire, they go after every woman and find nothing more natural than to sacrifice one for another. If you feel inclined to look about for a friend, then look for one who deserves this name, who by his modesty and discretion can enhance the joys of love with the virtue of secrecy."

At this point the beautiful woman no longer concealed her pain, and the tears which she had until now repressed fell plentifully from her eyes. "Whatever you may think of me," she exclaimed after a passionate embrace, "nothing is further from my mind than the crime that you in a sense consider to be inevitable. If ever such a thought is born in my mind may the earth open and swallow me, and may I be deprived of all hope of that happiness that promises us such a charming continuation of our life. Remove the distrust from your heart and leave with me the whole, pure hope of soon seeing you in my arms again!"

Nachdem er auf alle Weise seine Gattin zu beruhigen gesucht, schiffte er sich den andern[22] Morgen ein; seine Fahrt war glücklich, und er gelangte bald nach Alexandrien.

Indessen lebte seine Gattin in dem ruhigen Besitz eines großen Vermögens nach aller Lust und Bequemlichkeit, jedoch eingezogen, und pflegte außer ihren Eltern und Verwandten niemand zu sehen, und indem die Geschäfte ihres Mannes durch getreue Diener fortgeführt wurden, bewohnte sie ein großes Haus, in dessen prächtigen Zimmern sie mit Vergnügen täglich das Andenken ihres Gemahls erneuerte.

So sehr sie aber auch sich stille hielt und eingezogen lebte, waren doch die jungen Leute der Stadt nicht untätig geblieben. Sie versäumten nicht, häufig vor ihrem Fenster vorbeizugehen, und suchten des Abends durch Musik und Gesänge ihre Aufmerksamkeit auf sich zu ziehen. Die schöne Einsame fand anfangs diese Bemühungen unbequem und lästig, doch gewöhnte sie sich bald daran und ließ an den langen Abenden, ohne sich zu bekümmern, woher sie kämen, die Serenaden als eine angenehme Unterhaltung sich gefallen[23] und konnte dabei manchen Seufzer, der ihrem Abwesenden galt, nicht zurückhalten.

Anstatt daß ihre unbekannten Verehrer, wie sie hoffte, nach und nach müde geworden wären, schienen sich ihre Bemühungen noch zu vermehren und zu einer beständigen Dauer anzulassen. Sie konnte nun die wiederkehrenden Instrumente und Stimmen, die wiederholten Melodien schon unterscheiden und bald sich die Neugierde nicht mehr versagen zu wissen, wer die Unbekannten und besonders wer die Beharrlichen sein möchten. Sie durfte sich zum Zeitvertreib eine solche Teilnahme wohl erlauben.

Sie fing daher an, von Zeit zu Zeit durch ihre Vorhänge und Halbläden[24] nach der Straße zu sehen, auf die Vorbeigehenden zu merken und besonders die Männer zu unterscheiden, die ihre Fenster am längsten im Auge behielten. Es waren meist schöne, wohlgekleidete junge Leute, die aber freilich in Gebärden sowohl als in ihrem ganzen Äußern ebensoviel Leichtsinn als Eitelkeit sehen ließen. Sie schienen mehr durch ihre Aufmerksamkeit auf das Haus der Schönen sich merkwürdig machen als jener eine Art von Verehrung beweisen zu wollen.

After trying to calm his wife in every possible way, he took ship the following morning. His voyage was successful and he soon reached Alexandria.

Meanwhile, his wife lived in the full enjoyment and comfort the serene possession of a great fortune afforded her, but in retirement; apart from her parents and relatives she was in the habit of seeing no one. While her husband's affairs were carried on by loyal servants, she lived in a large house, in the splendid rooms of which she joyfully renewed every day the memory of her husband.

Yet, however quiet and withdrawn a life she led, the young men of the town had not been idle. They did not fail to pass frequently under her window and in the evenings sought to attract her attention with music and songs. The beautiful recluse at first found these endeavors inconvenient and annoying but soon became used to them, and during the long evenings she accepted the serenades as a pleasant entertainment, without caring where they came from. At such times she could not repress many a sigh that was meant for her absent husband.

She had hoped that her unknown admirers would gradually grow tired; instead, their efforts merely increased and took on a quality of permanence. She was already able to distinguish between the recurring instruments and voices and the repeated melodies and could soon no longer deny her curiosity to know who the unknown and especially the persistent men might be. She might well permit herself such an interest as a mere pastime.

She therefore began to look down into the street through her drapes and half-shutters from time to time to observe the passersby and especially to distinguish the men who kept their eyes on her windows the longest. They were mostly handsome, well-dressed young men who revealed, however, frivolity and vanity both in their gestures and in their whole physical appearance. They seemed to be more intent on calling attention to themselves by the attentions they paid to the beautiful woman's house than on demonstrating a kind of admiration to the beautiful woman herself.

„Wahrlich", sagte die Dame manchmal scherzend zu sich
selbst, „mein Mann hat einen klugen Einfall gehabt! Durch die
Bedingung, unter der er mir einen Liebhaber zugesteht,
schließt er alle diejenigen aus, die sich um mich bemühen und
die mir allenfalls gefallen könnten. Er weiß wohl, daß Klugheit,
Bescheidenheit und Verschwiegenheit Eigenschaften eines ruhigen Alters sind, die zwar unser Verstand schätzt, die aber
unsre Einbildungskraft keinesweges aufzuregen noch unsre
Neigung anzureizen imstande sind. Vor diesen, die mein Haus
mit ihren Artigkeiten belagern, bin ich sicher, daß sie kein
Vertrauen erwecken, und die, denen ich mein Vertrauen schenken könnte, finde ich nicht im mindesten liebenswürdig."

In der Sicherheit dieser Gedanken erlaubte sie sich immer
mehr, dem Vergnügen an der Musik und an der Gestalt der
vorbeigehenden Jünglinge nachzuhängen, und ohne daß sie es
merkte, wuchs nach und nach ein unruhiges Verlangen in
ihrem Busen, dem sie nur zu spät zu widerstreben gedachte.
Die Einsamkeit und der Müßiggang, das bequeme, gute und
reichliche Leben waren ein Element, in welchem sich eine un-
regelmäßige Begierde früher, als das gute Kind dachte, entwickeln mußte.

Sie fing nun an, jedoch mit stillen Seufzern, unter den Vorzügen ihres Gemahls auch seine Welt- und Menschenkenntnis,
besonders die Kenntnis des weiblichen Herzens zu bewundern.
„So war es also doch möglich, was ich ihm so lebhaft abstritt",
sagte sie zu sich selbst, „und so war es also doch nötig, in einem
solchen Falle mir Vorsicht und Klugheit anzuraten! Doch was
können Vorsicht und Klugheit da, wo der unbarmherzige Zufall nur mit einem unbestimmten Verlangen zu spielen scheint!
Wie soll ich den wählen, den ich nicht kenne? Und bleibt bei
näherer Bekanntschaft noch eine Wahl übrig?"

Mit solchen und hundert andern Gedanken vermehrte die
schöne Frau das Übel, das bei ihr schon weit genug um sich
gegriffen hatte.[25] Vergebens suchte sie sich zu zerstreuen; jeder
angenehme Gegenstand machte ihre Empfindung rege, und
ihre Empfindung brachte, auch in der tiefsten Einsamkeit,
angenehme Bilder in ihrer Einbildungskraft hervor.

In solchem Zustande befand sie sich, als sie unter andern
Stadtneuigkeiten von ihren Verwandten vernahm, es sei ein

"Really," the lady said jokingly to herself at times, "my husband had a clever idea. Through the condition under which he grants me a lover, he excludes all those who are paying me attention and who could possibly please me. He knows well that prudence, modesty, and discretion are the characteristics of mature age which our reason certainly values but which are unable to stir our imagination in any way or to stimulate our affection. I am certain that these men who are besieging my house with their attentions cannot awaken my confidence and those to whom I could give my confidence I don't find in the least attractive."

In the security of these thoughts she permitted herself more and more to linger over the pleasures offered her by the music and the figures of the passing youths. Without her noticing it there gradually grew in her breast a restless desire that she thought of resisting only too late. The loneliness and the idleness, the comfortable, good, and plentiful life were elements in which an illicit desire was bound to develop earlier than the good child thought.

She now began, though with quiet sighs, to admire among her husband's good points also his knowledge of the world and of people, particularly of the female heart. "So it was really possible—what I so vigorously contested," she said to herself, "and it was really necessary to advise caution and prudence in such an eventuality! But what power have caution and prudence where merciless chance seems to be merely playing with a vague desire? How am I to choose the man whom I don't know? And will there still be a choice on closer acquaintance?"

With these and a hundred other thoughts the beautiful woman increased the evil that had already affected her enough. In vain she sought to distract herself; every pleasant object stirred her emotion into life and her emotion provoked pleasant images in her imagination, even in her deepest solitude.

This is the state she was in when she heard from her relatives, among other items of city news, that a young lawyer had just

junger Rechtsgelehrter, der zu Bologna[26] studiert habe, soeben
in seine Vaterstadt zurückgekommen. Man wußte nicht genug
zu seinem Lobe zu sagen. Bei außerordentlichen Kenntnissen
zeigte er eine Klugheit und Gewandtheit, die sonst Jünglingen
nicht eigen ist, und bei einer sehr reizenden Gestalt die größte
Bescheidenheit. Als Prokurator hatte er bald das Zutrauen der
Bürger und die Achtung der Richter gewonnen. Täglich fand
er sich auf dem Rathause ein, um daselbst seine Geschäfte zu
besorgen und zu betreiben.

Die Schöne hörte die Schilderung eines so vollkommenen
Mannes nicht ohne Verlangen, ihn näher kennenzulernen, und
nicht ohne stillen Wunsch, in ihm denjenigen zu finden, dem
sie ihr Herz, selbst nach der Vorschrift ihres Mannes, überge-
ben könnte. Wie aufmerksam ward sie daher, als sie vernahm,
daß er täglich vor ihrem Hause vorbeigehe; wie sorgfältig
beobachtete sie die Stunde, in der man auf dem Rathause sich
zu versammeln pflegte! Nicht ohne Bewegung sah sie ihn endlich vorbeigehen, und wenn seine schöne Gestalt und seine
Jugend für sie notwendig reizend sein mußten, so war seine
Bescheidenheit von der andern Seite dasjenige, was sie in
Sorgen versetzte.

Einige Tage hatte sie ihn heimlich beobachtet und konnte
nun dem Wunsche nicht länger widerstehen, seine Aufmerksamkeit auf sich zu ziehen. Sie kleidete sich mit Sorgfalt, trat
auf den Balkon, und das Herz schlug ihr, als sie ihn die Straße
herkommen sah. Allein wie betrübt, ja beschämt war sie, als er
wie gewöhnlich mit bedächtigen Schritten, in sich gekehrt[27] und
mit niedergeschlagenen Augen, ohne sie auch nur zu bemerken, auf das zierlichste seines Weges vorbeiging.

Vergebens versuchte sie mehrere Tage hintereinander auf
ebendiese Weise, von ihm bemerkt zu werden. Immer ging er
seinen gewöhnlichen Schritt, ohne die Augen aufzuschlagen
oder da- und dorthin zu wenden. Je mehr sie ihn aber ansah,
desto mehr schien er ihr derjenige zu sein, dessen sie so sehr
bedurfte. Ihre Neigung ward täglich lebhafter und, da sie ihr
nicht widerstand, endlich ganz und gar gewaltsam. „Wie!" sagte
sie zu sich selbst, „nachdem dein edler, verständiger Mann den
Zustand vorausgesehen, in dem du dich in seiner Abwesenheit
befindest würdest, da seine Weissagung eintrifft, daß du ohne

returned to his native town from his studies in Bologna. They could not say enough in his praise. Along with an extraordinary knowledge, he demonstrated a cleverness and adroitness that were not common to youth and he possessed the greatest modesty together with a handsome appearance. He had soon gained the confidence of the citizenry and the respect of the judges as a lawyer. He went daily to the town hall to look after and transact his affairs.

The beautiful lady did not hear the description of such a perfect man without desiring to get to know him better and not without the secret wish that she might find in him the man to whom she could give her heart, even in conformity with her husband's prescription. How attentive did she therefore become when she heard that he went past her house daily; how carefully did she observe the hour when meetings in the city hall took place. Not without emotion, she finally saw him pass by, and if his handsome figure and his youth were bound to charm her, his modesty was, on the other hand, what caused her anxiety.

She had secretly observed him for some days and could no longer resist the wish to attract his attention. She dressed carefully, stepped on the balcony, and her heart beat fast as she saw him coming down the street. But how sad, indeed how ashamed was she, when he walked by, most gracefully, as usual with measured steps, absorbed in thought, his eyes downcast, without even noticing her.

In vain she sought for several days in succession to be noticed by him by the same method. He always walked with his usual step, without raising his eyes or turning them in this or that direction. But the more she looked at him, the more he seemed to her to be the man whom she needed so badly. Her interest grew more lively with every day and, since she did not resist it, it finally became very powerful indeed. "What!" she said to herself, "since your noble, understanding husband has foreseen the condition in which you would find yourself in his absence, when his prophecy that you can't live without a friend and

Freund und Günstling nicht leben kannst, sollst du dich nun
verzehren und abhärmen zu der Zeit, da dir das Glück einen
Jüngling zeigt, völlig nach deinem Sinne, nach dem Sinne
deines Gatten, einen Jüngling, mit dem du die Freuden
der Liebe in einem undurchdringlichen Geheimnis genießen
kannst? Töricht, wer die Gelegenheit versäumt, töricht, wer
der gewaltsamen Liebe widerstehen will!" Mit solchen und vielen andern Gedanken suchte sich die schöne Frau in ihrem
Vorsatze zu stärken, und nur kurze Zeit ward sie noch von
Ungewißheit hin und her getrieben. Endlich aber, wie es begeg-
net, daß eine Leidenschaft, welcher wir lange widerstehen, uns
zuletzt auf einmal dahinreißt und unser Gemüt dergestalt
erhöht, daß wir auf Besorgnis und Furcht, Zurückhaltung und
Scham, Verhältnisse[28] und Pflichten mit Verachtung als auf
kleinliche Hindernisse zurücksehen, so faßte sie auf einmal den
raschen Entschluß, ein junges Mädchen, das ihr diente, zu dem
geliebten Manne zu schicken und, es koste nun, was es wolle,
zu seinem Besitze zu gelangen.

Das Mädchen eilte und fand ihn, als er eben mit vielen Freunden zu Tische saß, und richtete ihren Gruß, den ihre Frau sie
gelehrt hatte, pünktlich aus. Der junge Prokurator wunderte
sich nicht über diese Botschaft; er hatte den Handelsmann in
seiner Jugend gekannt, er wußte, daß er gegenwärtig abwesend
war, und ob er gleich von seiner Heirat nur von weitem gehört
hatte, vermutete er doch, daß die zurückgelasssene Frau in der
Abwesenheit ihres Mannes wahrscheinlich in einer wichtigen
Sache seines rechtlichen Beistandes bedürfe. Er antwortete deswegen dem Mädchen auf das verbindlichste und versicherte,
daß er, sobald man von der Tafel aufgestanden, nicht säumen
würde, ihrer Gebieterin aufzuwarten. Mit unaussprechlicher
Freude vernahm die schöne Frau, daß sie den Geliebten nun
bald sehen und sprechen sollte. Sie eilte, sich aufs beste an-
zuziehen, und ließ geschwind ihr Haus und ihre Zimmer auf
das reinlichste ausputzen. Orangenblätter und Blumen wurden
gestreut, der[29] Sofa mit den köstlichsten Teppichen bedeckt.
So ging[30] die kurze Zeit, die er ausblieb, beschäftigt hin, die ihr
sonst unerträglich lang geworden wäre.

Mit welcher Bewegung ging sie ihm entgegen, als er endlich
ankam, mit welcher Verwirrung hieß sie ihn, indem sie sich

favorite has come true, are you to waste and pine away at a time when fortune shows you a youth wholly after your own heart and your husband's, a youth with whom you may enjoy the pleasures of love in impenetrable secrecy? Anyone who misses the opportunity is foolish, as is he who wants to resist the power of love!" With these and many other thoughts the beautiful woman sought to strengthen herself in her resolution and for only a short time longer was she driven hither and thither by uncertainty. But finally, as it happens that a passion that we resist for a long time at last carries us away suddenly and elevates our soul in such a way that we look back with contempt on anxiety and fear, self-restraint and shame, realities and duties as trivial hindrances, she suddenly formed the swift resolve to send a young girl in her service to the beloved man and to possess him at whatever cost.

The girl hurried and found him sitting at dinner with many friends; she conveyed to him her mistress's greeting precisely as it had been given her. The young advocate was not astonished at this message. He had known the merchant in his youth, he knew that he was away now; and although he had heard of his marriage only in a vague way, he surmised that the wife he had left behind probably needed legal help on some important matter during her husband's absence. He therefore gave the girl a most courteous answer and assured her that he would not fail to call on her mistress as soon as the dinner was over. With inexpressible joy the beautiful woman heard that she was soon to see and speak to the man she loved. She hurried to put on her best dress and quickly gave her house and her rooms a thorough cleaning. Orange leaves and flowers were strewn about, the sofa was covered with the most precious carpets. Thus the short span of time till he came, which would otherwise have become insufferably long for her, passed busily.

When he finally came, with what emotion did she go to meet him; when she sat down on the couch, with what confusion did

auf das Ruhebett niederließ, auf ein Taburett sitzen, das zunächst dabeistand! Sie verstummte in seiner so erwünschten Nähe, sie hatte nicht bedacht, was sie ihm sagen wollte; auch er war still und saß bescheiden vor ihr. Endlich ermannte sie sich und sagte nicht ohne Sorge und Beklommenheit:

„Sie sind noch nicht lange in Ihrer Vaterstadt wiederangekommen, mein Herr, und schon sind Sie allenthalben für einen talentreichen und zuverlässigen Mann bekannt. Auch ich setze mein Vertrauen auf Sie in einer wichtigen und sonderbaren Angelegenheit, die, wenn ich es recht bedenke, eher für den Beichtvater als für den Sachwalter gehört. Seit einem Jahre bin ich an einen würdigen und reichen Mann verheiratet, der, solange wir zusammenlebten, die größte Aufmerksamkeit für mich hatte und über den ich mich nicht beklagen würde, wenn nicht ein unruhiges Verlangen zu reisen und zu handeln ihn seit einiger Zeit aus meinen Armen gerissen hätte.

„Als ein verständiger und gerechter Mann fühlte er wohl das Unrecht, das er mir durch seine Entfernung antat. Er begriff, daß ein junges Weib nicht wie Juwelen und Perlen verwahrt werden könne; er wußte, daß sie vielmehr einem Garten voll schöner Früchte gleicht, die für jedermann so wie für den Herrn verloren wären, wenn er eigensinnig die Türe auf einige Jahre verschließen wollte. Er sprach mir daher vor seiner Abreise sehr ernstlich zu, er versicherte mir, daß ich ohne Freund nicht würde leben können, er gab mir dazu nicht allein die Erlaubnis, sondern er drang in mich und nötigte mir gleichsam das Versprechen ab, daß ich der Neigung, die sich in meinem Herzen finden würde, frei und ohne Anstand folgen wollte."

Sie hielt einen Augenblick inne, aber bald gab ihr ein vielversprechender Blick des jungen Mannes Mut genug, in ihrem Bekenntnis fortzufahren:

„Eine einzige Bedingung fügte mein Gemahl zu seiner übrigens so nachsichtigen Erlaubnis. Er empfahl mir die äußerste Vorsicht und verlangte ausdrücklich, daß ich mir einen gesetzten, zuverlässigen, klugen und verschwiegenen Freund wählen sollte. Ersparen Sie mir, das übrige zu sagen, mein Herr, ersparen Sie mir die Verwirrung, mit der ich Ihnen bekennen würde, wie sehr ich für Sie eingenommen bin, und erraten Sie aus diesem Zutrauen meine Hoffnungen und meine Wünsche."

she bid him sit on the stool close by! She fell silent in his presence, which was so desirable to her; she had not reflected on
what she wanted to say to him; he too was silent and sat modestly
before her. Finally she summoned her courage and, not without
anxiety and embarrassment, said:

"You haven't been back in your native city for any length of
time yet, sir, but you are already known everywhere as a richly
talented and trustworthy man. I too am putting my confidence
in you in an important and strange matter that, when I think
about it, is more suitable for a father confessor than for an
attorney. For one year I have been married to a worthy and
rich man who was most attentive to me as long as we lived
together and about whom I would not complain if a restless
desire to travel and to trade had not torn him from my arms
some time ago.

"As an intelligent and just man he probably felt the injustice
he was doing me through his absence. He realized that a young
wife could not be stored like jewels and pearls; he knew that
she rather resembles a garden full of beautiful fruits that would
be lost for everyone as well as for the owner if he were to lock
the gate stubbornly for some years. He therefore spoke very
earnestly to me before his departure, he assured me that I
would not be able to live without a friend, he not only gave me
his permission to find one but urged me and, so to speak, made
me promise that I would freely and without hesitation follow
the inclination that would arise in my heart."

She stopped for a moment, but soon a very promising look
from the young man gave her enough courage to continue with
her confession:

"My husband added one single condition to his otherwise so
tolerant permission. He recommended the greatest caution to
me and requested expressly that I should choose a sedate, re-
liable, clever, and discreet friend. Spare me the need to say the
rest, sir, spare me the confusion with which I would confess to
you how very much I am taken by you and surmise from this
confidence my hopes and my wishes."

Nach einer kurzen Pause versetzte der junge, liebenswürdige
Mann mit gutem Bedachte: „Wie sehr bin ich Ihnen für das
Vertrauen verbunden, durch welches Sie mich in einem so
hohen Grade ehren und glücklich machen! Ich wünsche nur
lebhaft, Sie zu überzeugen, daß Sie sich an keinen Unwürdigen
gewendet haben. Lassen Sie mich Ihnen zuerst als Rechtsgelehrter antworten; und als ein solcher gesteh ich Ihnen, daß ich
Ihren Gemahl bewundere, der sein Unrecht so deutlich gefühlt
und eingesehen hat, denn es ist gewiß, daß einer, der ein junges
Weib zurückläßt, um ferne Weltgegenden zu besuchen, als ein
solcher anzusehen ist, der irgendein anderes Besitztum völlig
derelinquiert und durch die deutlichste Handlung auf alles
Recht daran Verzicht tut. Wie es nun dem ersten besten[31] erlaubt ist, eine solche völlig ins Freie[32] gefallene Sache wieder
zu ergreifen, so muß ich es um so mehr für natürlich und billig
halten, daß eine junge Frau, die sich in diesem Zustande
befindet, ihre Neigung abermals verschenke und sich einem
Freunde, der ihr angenehm und zuverlässig scheint, ohne Be-
denken überlasse.

„Tritt nun aber gar wie hier der Fall ein, daß der Ehemann
selbst, seines Unrechts sich bewußt, mit ausdrücklichen Worten
seiner hinterlassenen Frau dasjenige erlaubt, was er ihr nicht
verbieten kann, so bleibt gar kein Zweifel übrig, um so mehr,
da demjenigen kein Unrecht geschieht, der es willig zu ertragen
erklärt hat.

„Wenn Sie mich nun", fuhr der junge Mann mit ganz andern
Blicken und dem lebhaftesten Ausdrucke fort, indem er die
schöne Freundin bei der Hand nahm, „wenn Sie mich zu Ihrem
Diener erwählen, so machen Sie mich mit einer Glückseligkeit
bekannt, von der ich bisher keinen Begriff hatte. Seien Sie
versichert", rief er aus, indem er die Hand küßte, „daß Sie
keinen ergebnern, zärtlichern, treuern und verschwiegenern
Diener hätten finden können!"

Wie beruhigt fühlte sich nach dieser Erklärung die schöne
Frau. Sie scheute sich nicht, ihm ihre Zärtlichkeit aufs lebhaf-
teste zu zeigen; sie drückte seine Hände, drängte sich näher
an ihn und legte ihr Haupt auf seine Schulter. Nicht lange
blieben sie in dieser Lage, als er sich auf eine sanfte Weise von
ihr zu entfernen suchte und nicht ohne Betrübnis zu reden

After a brief pause the young, charming man replied with mature reflection: "How deeply obliged I am to you for the confidence by which you honor me and make me happy to so high a degree! I wish so much to convince you that you have not turned to an unworthy man. Let me reply to you first as a lawyer; as such I confess to you that I admire your husband for having felt and realized his injustice so clearly; for it is certain that anyone who leaves a young wife behind to visit distant parts of the world is to be regarded exactly like the man who abandons any other possession and by this most unequivocal action gives up all rights to it. Now, just as it is permitted to any man who comes along to take possession of such a fully liberated object, I must consider it all the more natural and proper that a young wife who finds herself in this situation should once again bestow her affection and give herself without hesitation to a friend who appears to her to be pleasant and trustworthy.

"But when, as is the case here, the husband himself, conscious of his injustice, in explicit words permits the wife he left behind him what he cannot forbid her, there is no doubt left in the matter, all the more as no injustice is done to the man who has declared himself willing to bear it.

"If you now choose me as your servant," the young man continued with a totally different look in his eyes and the most animated expression, taking his beautiful friend by the hand, "you introduce me to a happiness of which until now I had no conception. Be assured," he exclaimed, kissing her hand, "that you could not have found a more devoted, more tender, more loyal and discreet servant."

How soothed the beautiful woman felt after this declaration. She did not hesitate to show him her tenderness in the most ardent fashion. She pressed his hands, moved up closer to him, and laid her head on his shoulder. They had not been long in this position when he sought to move away from her gently and began talking, not without sadness: "Can a man possibly

begann: „Kann sich wohl ein Mensch in einem seltsamern Verhältnisse befinden? Ich bin gezwungen, mich von Ihnen zu
entfernen und mir die größte Gewalt anzutun in einem Augenblicke, da ich mich den süßesten Gefühlen überlassen sollte.
Ich darf mir das Glück, das mich in Ihren Armen erwartet,
gegenwärtig nicht zueignen. Ach! wenn nur der Aufschub mich
nicht um meine schönsten Hoffnungen betrügt!"

Die Schöne fragte ängstlich nach der Ursache dieser sonderbaren Äußerung.

„Eben als ich in Bologna", versetzte er, „am Ende meiner
Studien war und mich aufs äußerste angriff, mich zu meiner
künftigen Bestimmung geschickt zu machen, verfiel ich in eine
schwere Krankheit, die, wo nicht mein Leben zu zerstören,
doch meine körperlichen und Geisteskräfte zu zerrütten
drohte. In der größten Not und unter den heftigsten Schmerzen tat ich der Mutter Gottes ein Gelübde, daß ich, wenn sie
mich genesen ließe, ein Jahr lang in strengem Fasten zubringen
und mich alles Genusses, von welcher Art er auch sei, enthalten
wolle. Schon zehn Monate habe ich mein Gelübde auf das
treulichste erfüllt, und sie sind mir in Betrachtung der großen
Wohltat, die ich erhalten, keineswges lang[33] geworden, da es
mir nicht beschwerlich ward, manches gewohnte und bekannte
Gute zu entbehren. Aber zu welcher Ewigkeit werden mir nun
zwei Monate, die noch übrig sind, da mir erst nach Verlauf
derselben ein Glück zuteil werden kann, welches alle Begriffe
übersteigt! Lassen Sie sich die Zeit nicht lang werden und ent-
ziehen Sie mir Ihre Gunst nicht, die Sie mir so freiwillig
zugedacht haben!"

Die Schöne, mit dieser Erklärung nicht sonderlich zufrieden,
faßte doch wieder bessern Mut, als der Freund nach einigem
Nachdenken zu reden fortfuhr: „Ich wagte[34] kaum, Ihnen einen
Vorschlag zu tun und das Mittel anzuzeigen, wodurch ich
früher von meinem Gelübde entbunden werden kann. Wenn
ich jemand fände, der so streng und sicher wie ich das Gelübde
zu halten übernähme und die Hälfte der noch übrigen Zeit mit
mir teilte, so würde ich umso geschwinder frei sein, und nichts
würde sich unsern Wünschen entgegenstellen. Sollten Sie nicht,
meine süße Freundin, um unser Glück zu beschleunigen, willig
sein, einen Teil des Hindernisses, das uns entgegensteht, hin-

be in a stranger situation? I am compelled to leave you and to impose the greatest violence on myself at a moment when I ought to abandon myself to the sweetest feelings. I must not at this moment take possession of the happiness that awaits me in your arms. Ah, if only the postponement does not cheat me of my fairest hopes!"

The beautiful lady inquired anxiously for the cause of this strange utterance.

"Just as I was finishing my studies in Bologna," he replied, "and was making the utmost efforts to prepare myself for my future career, I became seriously ill with an ailment that threatened to shatter my physical and mental powers, if not to destroy my life. In my extreme distress and in the most violent pain, I made a vow to the Mother of God that if she allowed me to recover, I would spend a year in strict fasting and abstain from all enjoyment, of whatever nature it might be. For ten months now I have kept my vow most faithfully and, in view of the great benefit I received, these months have in no way appeared long, since it was not difficult for me to do without many an accustomed and familiar pleasure. But what an eternity the two months that still remain will become for me, since only after they have run their course may I partake of a bliss that transcends all understanding. Don't let the time hang heavy and don't withdraw from me the favor you were so willing to bestow on me."

The beautiful woman, who was not particularly satisfied with this explanation, took courage again when her friend continued after some reflection: "I scarcely dare to make a proposal to you and to indicate the means by which I can be released from my vow sooner. If I were to find someone who would undertake to keep the vow as strictly and unfailingly as I do, and who would share with me half of the remaining period, I would be free all the sooner and nothing would stand in the way of our wishes. Would you not be willing, my sweet friend, in order to hasten our bliss, to remove a part of the hindrance that stands in our way? I can transfer a share in my vow only to the most trustworthy person. It is stringent, for I may only eat bread and water twice a day, may spend only a few hours of every

wegzuräumen? Nur der zuverlässigsten Person kann ich einen
Anteil an meinem Gelübde übertragen; es ist streng, denn ich
darf des Tages nur zweimal Brot und Wasser genießen, darf
des Nachts nur wenige Stunden auf einem harten Lager zubringen und muß ungeachtet meiner vielen Geschäfte eine
große Anzahl Gebete verrichten. Kann ich, wie es mir heute
geschehen ist, nicht vermeiden, bei einem Gastmahl zu
erscheinen, so darf ich deswegen doch nicht neine Pflicht hint-
ansetzen, vielmehr muß ich den Reizungen aller Leckerbissen,
die an mir vorübergehen, zu widerstehen suchen. Können Sie
sich entschließen, einen Monat lang gleichfalls alle diese Gesetze
zu befolgen, so werden Sie alsdann sich selbst in dem Besitz
eines Freundes desto mehr erfreuen, als Sie ihn durch ein so
lobenswürdiges Unternehmen gewissermaßen selbst erworben
haben."

Die schöne Dame vernahm ungern die Hindernisse, die sich
ihrer Neigung entgegensetzten; doch war ihre Liebe zu dem
jungen Manne durch seine Gegenwart dergestalt vermehrt worden, daß ihr keine Prüfung zu streng schien, wenn ihr nur
dadurch der Besitz eines so werten Gutes versichert werden
konnte. Sie sagte ihm daher mit den gefälligsten Ausdrücken:
„Mein süßer Freund! das Wunder, wodurch Sie Ihre Gesund-
heit wiedererlangt haben, ist mir selbst so wert und verehrungs-
würdig, daß ich es mir zur Freude und Pflicht mache, an dem
Gelübde teilzunehmen, das Sie dagegen[35] zu erfüllen schuldig
sind. Ich freue mich, Ihnen einen so sichern Beweis meiner
Neigung zu geben; ich will mich auf das genaueste nach Ihrer
Vorschrift richten, und ehe Sie mich lossprechen, soll mich
nichts von dem Wege entfernen, auf den Sie mich einleiten."

Nachdem der junge Mann mit ihr aufs genaueste diejenigen
Bedingungen abgeredet, unter welchen sie ihm die Hälfte
seines Gelübdes ersparen konnte, entfernte er sich mit der
Versicherung, daß er sie bald wieder besuchen und nach der
glücklichen[36] Beharrlichkeit in ihrem Vorsatze fragen würde,
und so mußte sie ihn gehen lassen, als er ohne Händedruck,
ohne Kuß, mit einem kaum bedeutenden Blicke von ihr schied.
Ein Glück für sie war die Beschäftigung, die ihr der seltsame
Vorsatz gab, denn sie hatte manches zu tun, um ihre Lebensart
völlig zu verändern. Zuerst wurden die schönen Blätter und

night on a hard bed and must say a large number of prayers, regardless of my many professional duties. If, as happened to me today, I cannot avoid appearing at a banquet, I must not on that account neglect my duty, but must rather seek to resist the attractions of all the delicacies that pass by me. If you, too, can resolve to follow all these laws for a month, you will then rejoice all the more in possessing a friend, since you will in a sense have won him yourself through such a meritorious undertaking."

The beautiful lady heard with displeasure of the hindrances that blocked her inclination. However, her love for the young man had been so much increased by his presence that no test seemed too hard to her if it could only assure her the possession of such a worthy prize. She therefore said to him in the most gracious terms: "My sweet friend! The miracle through which you have regained your health is so precious and venerable to me, too, that I will make it my joy and duty to share in the vow that you are bound to fulfill. I am glad to give you such certain proof of my affection. I will follow your instructions most precisely, and until you release me nothing shall take me off the road into which you are leading me "

After the young man had discussed with her in the minutest detail the conditions under which she could spare him half of his vow, he left with the assurance that he would visit her again soon, to inquire how she had succeeded in persevering in her resolve. And so she had to let him go, when he took his leave without pressing her hand, without a kiss, with only a barely meaningful glance. It was lucky for her that the strange resolve kept her busy, for she had much to do to change her way of life completely. First the beautiful flowers and leaves that she had had scattered for his reception were swept out; then, in

Blumen hinausgekehrt, die sie zu seinem Empfang hatte
streuen lassen; dann kam an die Stelle des wohlgepolsterten
Ruhebettes ein hartes Lager, auf das sie sich, zum erstenmal
in ihrem Leben nur von Wasser und Brot kaum gesättigt, des
Abends niederlegte. Des andern Tages war sie beschäftigt,
Hemden zuzuschneiden und zu nähen, deren sie eine be-
stimmte Zahl für ein Armen- und Krankenhaus fertig zu
machen versprochen hatte. Bei dieser neuen und unbequemen
Beschäftigung unterhielt sie ihre Einbildungskraft immer mit
dem Bilde ihres süßen Freundes und mit der Hoffnung
künftiger Glückseligkeit, und bei ebendiesen Vorstellungen
schien ihre schmale Kost ihr eine herzstärkende Nahrung zu
gewähren.

So verging eine Woche, und schon am Ende derselben fingen
die Rosen ihrer Wangen an, einigermaßen zu verbleichen.
Kleider, die ihr sonst wohl paßten, waren zu weit und ihre sonst
so raschen und muntern Glieder matt und schwach geworden,
als der Freund wieder erschien und ihr durch seinen Besuch
neue Stärke und Leben gab. Er ermahnte sie, in ihrem Vorsatze
zu beharren, munterte sie durch sein Beispiel auf und ließ von
weitem die Hoffnung eines ungestörten Genusses durchblik-
ken. Nur kurze Zeit hielt er sich auf und versprach, bald wieder-
zukommen.

Die wohltätige Arbeit ging aufs neue muntrer fort, und von
der strengen Diät ließ man keinesweges nach. Aber auch, leider!
hätte sie durch eine große Krankheit nicht mehr erschöpft
werden können. Ihr Freund, der sie am Ende der Woche abermals besuchte, sah sie mit dem größten Mitleiden an und stärkte
sie durch den Gedanken, daß die Hälfte der Prüfung schon
vorüber sei.

Nun ward ihr das ungewohnte Fasten, Beten und Arbeiten
mit jedem Tage lästiger, und die übertriebene Enthaltsamkeit
schien den gesunden Zustand eines an Ruhe und reichliche
Nahrung gewöhnten Körpers gänzlich zu zerrütten. Die Schöne
konnte sich zuletzt nicht mehr auf den Füßen halten und war
genötigt, ungeachtet der warmen Jahreszeit sich in doppelte
und dreifache Kleider zu hüllen, um die beinah völlig ver-
schwindende innerliche Wärme einigermaßen zusammen-

place of the upholstered couch a hard bed was brought in, on which she lay down at night for the first time in her life, after barely satisfying her hunger on bread and water. The following day she was busy cutting out and sewing shirts, of which she had promised to supply a definite number for a poorhouse and hospital. During this new and uncomfortable occupation she entertained her imagination with the image of her sweet friend and with the hope of future bliss; and with these very images her frugal fare seemed to afford her a nourishment that strengthened her heart.

Thus a week passed and at the end of it the roses in her cheeks had already begun to pale somewhat. Clothes that normally fitted her well had become too large for her, and her usually swift and vigorous limbs had become weary and weak when her friend appeared again and through his visit gave her new strength and life. He exhorted her to persevere in her resolution, encouraged her by his example and faintly hinted at the hope of an undisturbed enjoyment in the far distance. He stayed only a short time and promised to come again soon.

The work of benevolence was resumed more briskly, and there was no letup in her strict diet. But, alas; she could not have been more exhausted by a severe illness. Her friend, who visited her again at the end of the week, looked at her with the greatest sympathy and strengthened her with the thought that half the test was already over.

The unaccustomed fasting, praying, and working now became more burdensome to her with every day and the exaggerated abstinence seemed to ruin completely the healthy condition of a body used to rest and plentiful nurture. The beautiful lady was finally unable to stand on her feet and was compelled, in spite of the warm season, to cover herself with double and triple layers of clothing to conserve somehow the inner warmth that had almost completely vanished. Indeed she

zuhalten. Ja sie war nicht länger imstande, aufrecht zu bleiben, und sogar gezwungen, in der letzten Zeit das Bett zu hüten.

Welche Betrachtungen mußte sie da über ihren Zustand machen! Wie oft ging diese seltsame Begebenheit vor ihrer Seele[37] vorbei, und wie schmerzlich fiel[38] es ihr, als zehn Tage vergingen, ohne daß der Freund erschienen wäre, der sie diese äußersten Aufopferungen kostete! Dagegen aber bereitete sich in diesen trüben Stunden ihre völlige Genesung vor, ja sie ward entschieden. Denn als bald darauf ihr Freund erschien und sich an ihr Bett auf eben dasselbe Taburett setzte, auf dem er ihre erste Erklärung vernommen hatte, und ihr freundlich, ja gewissermaßen zärtlich zusprach, die kurze Zeit noch standhaft auszudauern, unterbrach sie ihn mit Lächeln und sagte: „Es bedarf weiter keines Zuredens, mein werter Freund, und ich werde mein Gelübde diese wenigen Tage mit Geduld und mit der Überzeugung ausdauern, daß Sie es mir zu meinem Besten auferlegt haben. Ich bin jetzt zu schwach, als daß ich Ihnen meinen Dank ausdrücken könnte, wie ich ihn empfinde. Sie haben mich mir selbst erhalten; Sie haben mich mir selbst gegeben, und ich erkenne, daß ich mein ganzes Dasein von nun an Ihnen schuldig bin.

„Wahrlich! mein Mann war verständig und klug und kannte das Herz einer Frau; er war billig genug, sie über eine Neigung nicht zu schelten, die durch seine Schuld in ihrem Busen entstehen konnte, ja er war großmütig genug, seine Rechte der Forderung der Natur hintanzusetzen. Aber Sie, mein Herr, Sie sind vernünftig und gut; Sie haben mich fühlen lassen, daß außer der Neigung noch etwas in uns ist, das ihr das Gleichgewicht halten kann, daß wir fähig sind, jedem gewohnten Gut zu entsagen und selbst unsere heißesten Wünsche von uns zu entfernen. Sie haben mich in diese Schule durch Irrtum und Hoffnung geführt; aber beide sind nicht mehr nötig, wenn wir uns erst mit dem guten und mächtigen Ich bekannt gemacht haben, das so still und ruhig in uns wohnt und so lange, bis es die Herrschaft im Hause gewinnt, wenigstens durch zarte Erinnerungen seine Gegenwart unaufhörlich merken läßt. Leben Sie wohl! Ihre Freundin wird Sie künftig mit Vergnügen sehen; wirken Sie auf Ihre Mitbürger wie auf mich; entwickeln Sie

was no longer able to remain upright and in the end was even
compelled to keep to her bed.

What reflections she was compelled to make concerning her
condition! How often did this strange event pass before her
mind, and how painful it was to her when ten days passed
without her friend appearing, he who cost her these extreme
sacrifices! During these gloomy hours, however, her complete
recovery was being prepared, indeed it was decided. For when
her friend appeared soon after that and sat down beside her
bed on that same stool on which he had heard her first declaration and admonished her in friendly, indeed in tender tones
to hold out steadfastly for the short period still remaining, she
interrupted him with a smile and said: "I need no further
urging, my dear friend, and I will endure my vow during these
few days with patience and in the conviction that you have
imposed it on me for my own good. I am too weak now to be
able to express my gratitude to you as I feel it. You have saved
me for myself; you have given me to myself, and I recognize
that from now on I owe you my whole existence.

"Truly, my husband was understanding and clever and knew
a woman's heart. He was fair enough not to scold her for an
inclination that might arise in her heart through his fault; indeed he was generous enough to place his rights behind the
demands of nature. But you, sir, are reasonable and good. You
have made me feel that there is something in us other than
desire which can balance it so that we are capable of renouncing
everything of value to which we are accustomed and to give up
even our most cherished wishes. You have led me into this
school through error and hope; but both are no longer necessary, once we have become acquainted with the good and mighty
'I' that dwells within us so silently and so serenely and so long
that it gains mastery in the house or at least makes its presence
known through delicate reminders. Farewell! Your friend will
see you in future with pleasure; influence your fellow citizens
as you have influenced me; do not merely unravel the confu-
sions that arise only too easily over property but show them

nicht allein die Verwirrungen, die nur zu leicht über Besitz-
tümer entstehen, sondern zeigen Sie ihnen auch durch sanfte
Anleitung und durch Beispiel, daß in jedem Menschen die
Kraft der Tugend im Verborgenen keimt; die allgemeine Achtung wird Ihr Lohn sein, und Sie werden mehr als der erste
Staatsmann und der größte Held den Namen Vater des Vaterlandes verdienen."

Notes: Goethe, *Der Prokurator*

1. *indem . . . pflegte,* equivalent to the gerund: *by being accustomed to.*
2. *Alexandria* (more commonly Alexandrien): in Egypt.
3. *um so mehr,* all the more.
4. *beladen.* Grammar requires *beladenes.*(The omission of the adjective ending is older usage.)
5. *der Kinder wegen,* because of the children.
6. *bald . . . bald,* now . . . again.
7. *gleich = obgleich.*
8. *der Deinigen,* of your kin.
9. *aller Tage Abend,* i.e., the end of your life.
10. *Weib,* older word for *wife, woman.*
11. *ward* = older form of *wurde.*
12. *feiern,* to stop work, be idle.
13. *Frauenzimmer,* the older word for *woman,* now used only in a comical or derogatory sense.
14. *keinen . . .* literally: form no other resolve.
15. *Langenweile,* usual form: *Langweile.*
16. The force of *erst* is: more than ever, even more.
17. *ging . . . Rate:* literally: he went inside himself for counsel.
18. *du . . . werden,* you take such great pains.
19. *davon = wovon.*
20. *ein für allemal,* once and for all.
21. German often uses *Brust* where we would say *heart.*
22. *andern,* following.
23. *ließ . . . gefallen,* allowed [it] to please her; i.e., accepted.
24. *Halbläden,* shutters covering only the lower half of the windows.
25. *um sich gegriffen hatte,* literally: had reached all about her.

also through gentle guidance and by example that in every human being the power of virtue secretly germinates. Your reward will be general esteem, and you will deserve the name of Father of our native land more than the foremost statesman and the greatest hero."

26. *Bologna,* city in Italy; seat of a famous university.
27. *in sich gekehrt,* literally: turned in on himself.
28. *Verhältnisse,* literally: relationships, conditions; i.e., reality as opposed to wish.
29. *der Sofa,* usually *das.*
30. *ging . . . hin,* passed.
31. *dem ersten besten,* i.e., the first is as good as any other.
32. *ins Freie,* into the open.
33. *lang,* i.e., tedious.
34. *wagte,* imperfect subjunctive expressing deference: would venture.
35. *dagegen,* i.e., in return for the miracle.
36. *glücklich,* i.e., successful.
37. *Seele,* soul, psyche, often used in German for *mind, heart.*
38. *fiel,* was.

Johann Peter Hebel

1760–1826

Hebel was born in Basel, Switzerland, of humble parents, both of whom were in the service of a patrician family of that city. He lost his father, who was a mercenary soldier and a self-taught scholar of some attainments, at the age of two; his mother died when he was thirteen. Through the generosity of family friends and the Basel patrician employer of his parents, the boy was given a good education. He took up the study of theology and was ordained a Lutheran clergyman but had difficulty in finding a living. After suffering many frustrations he was offered a post as teacher and preacher at the *Gymnasium*[1] in Karlsruhe in the duchy of Baden. His fortunes began to mend; in a few years he became headmaster of the *Gymnasium* and later was appointed prelate, the highest ecclesiastical office in the duchy. He was an ex officio member of the Baden diet. In his youth he loved and was loved by Gustave Fecht, a girl of his own age, but they had been too poor to set up a household. They were

---

[1] *Gymnasium.* The type of German secondary school in which the humanities are stressed.

never united in marriage but remained close friends and corres-
pondents for life.

Hebel's literary career began with the publication of a slim
volume of verse in the Alemannic dialect: *Alemannische Gedichte*
(1803). The book enjoyed considerable popularity and won
high praise from Goethe and Jean Paul Richter.[2] In the same
year Hebel began to contribute to the calendar issued by the
church for the edification of the rural population. He took over
its editorship in 1808 and changed its name to *The Rhenish
Family Friend* (*Der Rheinländische Hausfreund*). In 1811 the pres-
tigious firm Cotta published a selection of the stories Hebel
had contributed to the church calendar; the collection appeared
under the title *The Little Treasure Chest of the Rhenish Family
Friend* (*Das Schatzkästlein des Rheinischen Hausfreundes*). The book
achieved immediate popularity in all parts of Germany and
won the acclaim of prominent men of letters. Throughout the
nineteenth century stories from it were reprinted in school
textbooks. But it was not until our own century that Hebel was
recognized for what he is: a writer of classical stature and a
stylist of the highest order.

The *Schatzkästlein* is a collection of anecdotes, short stories,
moral reflections, and practical suggestions. It is a little *Decameron*, minus the bawdy element, plus the delightful verbal
wit that Hebel had in abundance but Boccaccio lacked. Hebel
had a universal curiosity about mankind, "an open heart for
all life and all being" as Jean Paul put it. His subjects range
from the emperor Napoleon to a begging artisan and a Parisian
water carrier. The "family friend," as the narrator calls himself,
emerges as an enlightened Christian, a true son of the *Auf-
klärung*, standing above creed, large-minded, wise. He endorses
the tried, old-time virtues of honesty, integrity, fidelity,
brotherly love, and belief in a benevolent Deity. But he is no
simple-minded "pure fool"; on the contrary, he is a sharp customer in his knowledge of human nature and its addiction to
selfishness, greed, rapacity, cunning, and violence. But though

[2]Johann Paul Friedrich Richter (1763–1825), who wrote under the pen name
of Jean Paul, is the author of novels that enjoyed widespread popularity among
educated readers during his lifetime. He is still counted among the classic
writers of German literature.

he knows every trick and wile in the arsenal of villainy, he is not soured in his ultimate belief in a just world order; for he is a sincere and devout Christian.

There is deep wisdom in these seemingly simple stories, wisdom for the sophisticated and the subtle too, as our century has come to realize. True, the family friend backs the traditional virtues, but his mind is alert enough to recognize that the conventional wisdom can be wrong in the eyes of God. Thus the moral of *The Water Carrier* (*Der Wasserträger*) would make a bishop and a banker shake their heads in dismay—until they thought it over. Hebel stirs them to thought by his sly comment at the end of the story: "The family friend has some ideas about this but he won't say what they are."

Hebel was not a "literary" type. He was primarily a theologian and a teacher, and at one time he thought of studying medicine. But he had a delightful sense of humor and mischief. He saw his calendar as a fine vehicle for teaching and entertaining, for teaching through entertainment. He was a consummate artist but he knew the art of concealing art. Many of his stories are frankly didactic, some even pointing a moral at the beginning or end. But that does not detract a whit from their artistic effect on the reader. Hebel knew the rustic public for whom he was writing and he never talked above their heads; but he never prostituted himself to attain popularity. Consequently, his stories, as the philosopher Ernst Bloch noted, are written for children and for the most sophisticated adults.

The quality of Hebel's literary achievement has been adequately realized by the finest minds of our century, by men of the most diverse outlook and taste: Hermann Hesse, Bertolt Brecht, Walter Benjamin, Franz Kafka, Ernst Bloch, Heinrich Böll. According to Kafka's friend Max Brod, Kafka held the *Schatzkästlein* in highest esteem and prized our story *An Unexpected Reunion* (*Unverhofftes Wiedersehen*) especially for its *Ganzheit* (wholeness or integrity), its directness and rugged honesty, a quality that characterizes all of Hebel's wonderful tales. But "rugged honesty" should not be taken to indicate a lack of polish; Walter Benjamin aptly called the *Schatzkästlein* "one of the purest works of goldsmith-crafted German prose." Hebel was a storyteller by the grace of God; he had an unerring sense

for the piquant, stirring event and for the telling detail. He takes time to mention that the working man went to an eating place to order a meal of Limburger cheese. And when he mentions "mouse droppings" (in *Kannitverstan*), he prefixes a polite "salvemini," that is, begging your pardon. Some of his stories have been subjected to careful literary analysis and found to be replete with effective structural devices, symbols, and leitmotifs. Our story, for instance, is rich in suggestions and overtones of death and resurrection, time and eternity, the grave and the marriage bed, the kerchief in black and red, the dark night of mortality, and the bright day of eternal life in the beyond.

●

Unverhofftes Wiedersehen is based on a contemporary newspaper account that Hebel read in a magazine, where it appeared as an excerpt from Gotthilf Schubert's *Views about the Night Side of the Natural Sciences* (*Ansichten von der Nachtseite der Naturwissenschaften*, 1808). The event was a great sensation in its day and was widely reported in prose and song. Hebel transformed it into "the most beautiful story in the world" (Ernst Bloch). The theme of fidelity in love is developed on the background of world events with unmatched skill. Hebel's version was first published in 1810 in *Der Rheinländische Hausfreund* and appeared in book form the following year in the *Schatzkästlein*. The motif has also been used by E. T. A. Hoffman in a novella and by Hugo von Hofmannsthal in a drama. Hofmannsthal's text became the libretto for an opera by R. Wagner-Regeny (1961).

Title page for the *Rhineland Family Friend*

Unverhofftes Wiedersehen

In Falun in Schweden küßte vor guten fünfzig Jahren und mehr ein junger Bergmann seine junge hübsche Braut[1] und sagte zu ihr: »Auf Sankt Luciä[2] wird unsere Liebe von des Priesters Hand gesegnet. Dann sind wir Mann und Frau und bauen uns ein eigenes Nestlein.« »Und Friede und Liebe soll darin wohnen«, sagte die schöne Frau mit holdem Lächeln, »denn du bist mein Einziges und Alles, und ohne dich möchte ich lieber im Grab sein als an einem anderen Ort.« Als sie aber vor Sankt Luciä der Pfarrer zum zweitenmal in der Kirche ausgerufen hatte: »So[3] nun jemand Hindernis wüßte anzuzeigen, warum diese Personen nicht möchten ehelich zusammenkommen«, da meldete sich[4] der Tod. Denn als der Jüngling den anderen Morgen in seiner schwarzen Bergmannskleidung an ihrem Haus vorbeiging, der Bergmann hat sein Totenkleid immer an, da klopfte er zwar noch einmal an ihrem Fenster und sagte ihr guten Morgen, aber keinen guten Abend mehr. Er kam nimmer aus dem Bergwerk zurück, und sie saumte vergeblich selbigen[5] Morgen ein schwarzes Halstuch mit rotem Rand für ihn zum Hochzeitstag, sondern[6] als er nimmer kam, legte sie es weg und weinte um ihn und vergaß ihn nie. Unterdessen[7] wurde die Stadt Lissabon in Portugal durch ein Erdbeben zerstört, und der siebenjährige Krieg ging vorüber, und Kaiser Franz der Erste starb, und der Jesuiten-Orden wurde aufgehoben und Polen geteilt, und die Kaiserin Maria Theresia starb, und der Struensee wurde hingerichtet, Amerika wurde frei, und die vereinigte französische und spanische Macht konnte Gibraltar nicht erobern. Die Türken schlossen den General Stein in der Veteraner Höhle in Ungarn ein, und der Kaiser Joseph starb auch. Der König Gustav von Schweden

An Unexpected Reunion

In Falun in Sweden a good fifty years ago and more, a young miner kissed his pretty fiancée and said to her: "On St. Lucia's Day our love will be blessed by the priest's hand. Then we shall be man and wife and will build ourselves a little nest of our own." "And peace and love shall dwell in it," said the lovely woman with a sweet smile, "for you are my One and All and without you I would rather be in the grave than in another place." But when the clergyman had read the banns in church for the second time before St. Lucia's Day: "If any of you can show just cause why these two may not lawfully be joined together in holy matrimony," Death spoke up. For when the youth walked past her house next day in his black miner's garb (the miner always wears his shroud), he knocked on her window once more and said good morning to her but never again good evening. He never returned from the mine, and on that same morning she hemmed a black kerchief for him with a red border for their wedding—in vain. But when he did not come, she laid it aside and wept for him and never forgot him. Meanwhile the city of Lisbon in Portugal was destroyed by an earthquake, and the Seven Years' War passed by, and the emperor Francis I died, and the Jesuit order was abolished, and Poland was partitioned, and the empress Maria Theresa died, and Struensee was executed, America became free, and the combined French and Spanish power could not capture Gibraltar. The Turks locked up General Stein in the Veterani Cave in Hungary, and the emperor Joseph died too. King Gustav of Sweden conquered Russian Finland, and the French Revolution and the long war began, and emperor Leopold II went to his grave too. Napoleon conquered Prussia and the English bombarded

eroberte russisch Finnland, und die französische Revolution und der lange Krieg fing an, und der Kaiser Leopold der Zweite ging auch ins Grab. Napoleon eroberte Preußen, und die Engländer bombardierten Kopenhagen, und die Ackerleute säeten und schnitten. Der Müller mahlte, und die Schmiede hämmerten, und die Bergleute gruben nach den Metalladern in ihrer unterirdischen Werkstatt. Als aber die Bergleute in Falun im Jahre 1809 etwas vor oder nach Johannis[8] zwischen zwei Schachten eine Öffnung durchgraben wollten, gute dreihundert Ellen[9] tief unter dem Boden, gruben sie aus dem Schutt und Vitriolwasser[10] den Leichnam eines Jünglings heraus, der ganz mit Eisenvitriol[11] durchdrungen, sonst aber unverwest und unverändert war; also daß man seine Gesichtszüge und sein Alter noch völlig erkennen konnte, als wenn er erst vor einer Stunde gestorben und ein wenig eingeschlafen wäre an der Arbeit. Als man ihn aber zu Tag ausgefördert hatte, Vater und Mutter, Gefreundete[12] und Bekannte waren schon lange tot, kein Mensch wollte[13] den schlafenden Jüngling kennen oder etwas von seinem Unglück wissen, bis die ehemalige Verlobte des Bergmannes kam, der eines Tages auf die Schicht gegangen war und nimmer zurückkehrte. Grau und zusammengeschrumpft kam sie an einer Krücke an den Platz und erkannte ihren Bräutigam; und mehr mit freudigem Entzücken als mit Schmerz sank sie auf die geliebte Leiche nieder, und erst als sie sich von einer langen heftigen Bewegung des Gemüts erholt hatte, »es ist mein Verlobter«, sagte sie endlich, »um den ich fünfzig Jahre lang getrauert hatte und den mich Gott noch einmal sehen läßt vor meinem Ende. Acht Tage vor der Hochzeit ist er auf die Grube gegangen und nimmer gekommen.« Da wurden die Gemüter aller Umstehenden von Wehmut und Tränen ergriffen, als sie sahen die ehemalige Braut jetzt in der Gestalt des hingewelkten kraftlosen Alters und den Bräutigam noch in seiner jugendlichen Schöne,[14] und wie in ihrer Brust nach fünfzig Jahren die Flamme der jugendlichen Liebe noch einmal erwachte; aber er öffnete den Mund nimmer zum Lächeln oder die Augen zum Wiedererkennen; und wie sie ihn endlich von den Bergleuten in ihr Stüblein tragen ließ, als die einzige, die ihm angehöre und ein Recht an ihn habe, bis sein Grab gerüstet sei auf dem Kirchhofe. Den anderen Tag, als

Copenhagen, and the farmers sowed and harvested. The miller milled and the blacksmiths hammered, and the miners dug for metal veins in their underground workshops. But when in the year 1809, shortly before or after Midsummer Day, the miners of Falun wanted to dig through an opening between two shafts, a good three hundred ells deep under the earth, they dug out of the rubble and vitriol water the corpse of a youth completely saturated with iron sulphate but otherwise showing no sign of decomposition and completely unaltered, so that one could still fully recognize his facial features and his age, as if he had died only an hour ago and had fallen into a light sleep at his work. But when he was brought up into the light of day, no one cared to recognize the sleeping youth or to know anything about his accident (his father and mother, friends, and acquaintances had long been dead) until the former fiancée of the miner appeared, the one who had one day gone down into the shaft and never returned. Gray and shriveled she came on a crutch to the public square and recognized her betrothed; and more in joyful rapture than in pain she sank down upon the beloved corpse; and only after she had recovered from a long, severe emotional crisis she finally said: "He is my betrothed, for whom I have mourned for fifty long years and whom God is letting me see once more before my end. A week before our wedding he went down into the pit and never came up again." Then the spirits of all the bystanders were moved to sadness and tears when they saw the former bride in the form of withered, feeble age and the bridegroom still in his youthful beauty, and how after fifty years the flame of youthful love awakened again in her breast; but he did not open his mouth to smile or his eyes in recognition; and how she finally had him carried by the miners to her small room, as the only person who belonged to him and who had a claim on him, till his grave was prepared at the cemetery. The following day when his grave in the cemetery was prepared and the miners fetched him, she unlocked a little box, tied the black silken kerchief with the red border around his neck, and accompanied him in her Sunday dress as if it were her wedding day and not the day of his burial. For when he was laid in his grave in the cemetery, she said: "Now sleep well for another day or ten in your cool wedding bed and don't

das Grab gerüstet war auf dem Kirchhlof und ihn die Bergleute holten, schloß sie ein Kästlein auf, legte ihm das schwarzseidene Halstuch mit roten Streifen um und begleitete ihn in ihrem Sonntagsgewand, als wenn es ihr Hochzeitstag und nicht der Tag seiner Beerdigung wäre. Denn als man ihn auf dem Kirchhof ins Grab legte, sagte sie: »Schlafe nun wohl, noch einen Tag oder zehn im kühlen Hochzeitbett, und laß dir die Zeit nicht lang werden.[15] Ich habe nur noch ein wenig zu tun und komme bald, und bald wird's wieder Tag.« — »Was die Erde einmal wiedergegeben hat, wird sie zum zweitenmal auch nicht behalten«, sagte sie, als sie fortging und noch einmal umschaute.

Notes: Hebel, *Unverhofftes Wiedersehen*

1. *Braut* and *Bräutigam* mean both betrothed and bride and groom.
2. *Sankt Lucia,* December 13.
3. *so,* older form for *wenn.*
4. *sich melden,* announce oneself, report [for an appointment]; *anderen = folgenden.*
5. *selbigen = am selben.*
6. *sondern = aber.*
7. The historical events alluded to in the following passage are (1) the severe earthquake in Lisbon, Portugal, in 1755; (2) the Seven Years' War 1756–63; (3) the death of Francis I (1708–65), husband of the empress Maria Theresa of the Habsburg Empire; (4) the suppression of the Jesuit order by Pope Clement XIV in 1773; (5) the first partition of Poland (1772); (6) the death of the empress Maria Theresa in 1780; (7) the trial and execution of Count Johann Friedrich Struensee (1737–72) for treason; (8) the independence of the United States in 1776; (9) the siege of Gibraltar (1779–82); (10) *Türken:* This incident occurred in the war between Austria and Turkey (1714–18); a Major (not General) Stein held out for twenty-one days against the Turks with part of a batallion in the Veterani Cave, located on the left bank of the Danube River; (11) the death of the emperor Joseph II, son of Maria Theresa, in 1790; (12) the conquest of Finland by King Gustavus III in a war against Russia (1788–90); (13) the French Revo-

let time hang heavy on your hands. I have only a little more left to do and will come soon, and soon it will be day again."—"What the earth has given back once, it will not keep for a second time," she said, as she went away and looked back once more.

lution, which began in 1789; (14) the Revolutionary and Napoleonic Wars (the "long war") that dragged on until 1815 when Napoleon was finally overthrown; (15) the death of emperor Leopold II, brother of Joseph II, in 1792; (16) Napoleon's conquest of Prussia in 1806; (17) the siege of Copenhagen in 1807 by the English.

8. *Johannis*, June 24, the longest day in the year.

9. *Ellen.* The ell is an old cloth measure, varying in length between twenty and eighty centimeters. In Germany alone it had more than a hundred lengths.

10. *Vitriol,* sulphate of metals (copper, iron, zinc).

11. *Eisenvitriol,* iron sulphate.

12. *Gefreundete* = *Befreundete.*

13. *wollte,* wanted to, i.e., cared to, ventured.

14. *Schöne* = *Schönheit.*

15. *lang werden.* The German word for boredom is *Langweile.*

Heinrich von Kleist
1777–1811

It took a century for the literate world to assess Heinrich von Kleist's true stature. Today he is recognized as a major figure in world literature. "Perhaps the greatest literary genius the Germans possess," the novelist Jakob Wassermann said of him. "The greatest of all psychologists," wrote the literary scholar Curt Hohoff. Franz Kafka spoke of Kleist with veneration, loved to recite from the master novella *Michael Kohlhaas*, and studied the art of writing from Kleist's prose. Thomas Mann, Arnold and Stefan Zweig, and many other German, English, and French writers and scholars have paid tribute to Kleist's greatness. E. L. Doctorow adapted the plot of *Michael Kohlhaas* as the basis of his novel *Ragtime* (1975). The centennial of Kleist's birth was celebrated by international scholarship, and the year 1982 produced a flurry of literary activity in the United States which is reminiscent of the Kleist vogue in France immediately after the end of the Second World War.

It was not always so. Kleist's life was embittered by his repeated failure to gain recognition, although there were, even in his lifetime, a few choice spirits who appreciated him for the

genius that he was. But his idol Goethe was repelled by the "pathological" element in his plays, and the rejection wounded the young poet deeply.

Kleist's short life was one long torment, relieved by a few sunny spots of happiness. He was born in Frankfurt on the Oder in Prussia into a military family of the minor Prussian aristocracy. After the death of his father Kleist was sent to Berlin at the age of eleven to continue his schooling. In 1792 he joined a guards regiment in Potsdam as a cadet; five years later he was commissioned as a second lieutenant. Finding the military life boring and intellectually stultifying, he resigned his commission in 1799 and returned to his native Frankfurt, where he enrolled at the university as a student of philosophy, mathematics, economics, and law. He became engaged to Wilhelmine von Zenge, the daughter of a general, a wholesome girl but intellectually his inferior. At this time (c. 1800) he began to write seriously, planning some of his later plays. And he set out on that nomadic life that took him through Germany, Austria, Switzerland, Italy, and France, for long stretches on foot, alone or in the company of a friend or of his loyal half-sister Ulrike.

The two principal intellectual influences in Kleist's formative years were Rousseau and Kant. The former nourished his idealist strain, his Utopian character, whereas Kant's rejection of metaphysical speculation and his sober criticism of the limits imposed on our knowledge of the outside world were misinterpreted by Kleist as a destructive blow to his need to attain absolute truth. His extremist mind was driven to near despair; he contemplated suicide but recovered sufficiently to begin a bourgeois career in the civil service. He could not, however, submit permanently to a bureaucratic existence. At one point Rousseau's ideal of the simple life inspired in him the wish to abjure civilization and to retire with Wilhelmine to an island on a Swiss lake and there lead a rustic existence in emulation of Rousseau. But his fiancée was reluctant to undertake the experiment, so he gave it up and broke the engagement.

Kleist was driven by ambition to achieve fame, either as a writer or as a soldier suffering heroic death on the field of battle. An enthusiastic supporter of the French Revolution, he

tried to join Napoleon's army that was to invade Britain. The defeat of Austria and then Prussia by Napoleon's forces (1805–06) aroused Kleist, as it did many other Germans, to a sense of patriotism and a hatred of the Corsican. In Kleist's case there was the added factor of personal humiliation, for in 1807 he was arrested by the French army in Germany on suspicion of being a Prussian spy and held a prisoner for six months in France. He thought of joining a group of conspirators who were plotting to assassinate the emperor.

Meanwhile, throughout these turbulent years, in the midst of his Odyssean wanderings, in spite of illness, a nervous breakdown, dire poverty, frustration, and failure, Kleist had been writing. He had spent over a year in Dresden in the company of writers and intellectuals, who recognized his merit. Here he coedited the literary journal *Phoebus,* in which he published some of his own work.

Kleist's patriotic fervor expressed itself through propaganda that preached hatred of the French and advocated the destruction of the enemy by trickery, deceit, and the fabrication of atrocities. After further wandering over German lands Kleist returned to Berlin in 1810 and there founded Germany's first daily newspaper, which enjoyed popular success for a few months but got into difficulties with the government censor and ceased publicaton in March 1811. Nevertheless, Kleist made some good and influential friends in the Prussian capital, literary people and statesmen, and he even received financial support from the royal family.

But Kleist thought of himself as an utter failure, a judgment that was pointedly corroborated by his family. As early as 1803 he had seriously thought of suicide. Twice he had proposed a double suicide to close friends. In the summer of 1811 he met a young woman who was suffering from terminal cancer; they agreed to die together. The plan was carried out with some deliberation. Like Werther in his last days, Kleist felt that in taking his life he was leaving an unhappy world for a better one and exchanging "the most tormented existence that ever man has experienced" for one in which "we shall embrace each other with the love of angels."

●

In less than a decade Kleist produced eight dramas,[1] an equal
number of novellas, some poetry, a small body of reflective
prose, and a considerable amount of journalism.[2] Among these
writings there are half a dozen masterpieces of drama and
fiction and one brilliant piece of discursive thinking, the essay
"On the Puppet Theater" (Über das Marinonettentheater).
The intellectual world in which Kleist grew up was in transition from Enlightenment to romanticism. The rationalist
ideology of the Enlightenment, which had its roots in the
Renaissance and had developed slowly and organically through
the seventeenth and eighteenth centuries, had been superseded
by the cult of feeling and irrationalism, which (strangely
enough) originated in Britain and whose prophet was Rousseau.
But the ideas for which the Enlightenment stood—political and
social equality, cosmopolitanism, religion without dogma and
ritual, free inquiry, natural law and natural rights, the right to
"life, liberty, and the pursuit of happiness"—that is, the fruits
of the American and French revolutions—these ideas were by
no means dead. The romantic rebellion was at first a literary
and artistic revolt against the Augustan-classicist-rationalist
spirit as it manifested itself in the arts. Under the banner of
feeling the rebels fought for nature, freedom, original genius,
unshackled imagination (as against intellectual measure and
control), and subjective sovereignty in art. An ironic paradox:
the apostles of feeling rebelled in the name of freedom against
a movement that for over two centuries had fought for freedom
against authoritarianism. The paradox is resolved by the historical fact that German romanticism, at least in its later stage,
developed a conservative ideology. Under the influence of
Herder and other later Enlightenment thinkers, the German
romantics rediscovered "the people" (das Volk) and popular
culture; they romanticized the Middle Ages, favoring the restoration of the "organic" medieval state and society. So from 1750
to 1830 there was a conflict in Western thought between the
two views of life, with the ideas of the Englightenment in tem-

---

[1]Only nine scenes of the drama *Robert Guiskard* have survived because Kleist
destroyed the completed manuscript in a fit of melancholy.

[2]He also completed a novel in two volumes, but the manuscript was lost.

porary eclipse, only to reemerge after 1830 and develop throughout the nineteenth century into our own time.

Western thought around 1800 was as much in ferment as the political world at that time. And Kleist's mental world was a microcosm of this intellectual effervescence. He subscribed to the ideology of the Englightenment, he was a "liberal" thinker, as was Rousseau himself. But he was also drawn by his passionate nature to the new emotional wave that produced the literature of romanticism. Kleist's letters around the year 1800 contain passionate tributes to Rousseau and the cult of feeling. And his early writings too show the influence of Rousseau's thought. There are some interpreters who see him as a Rousseauist to the end of his life. But this reading of his work is not supported by the texts. His development shows a gradual retreat from romanticism to a "classical" search for harmony, for a synthesis between reason and emotion.[3] This view is supported by the late works: *Michael Kohlhaas, Der Prinz von Homburg*, and the essay "On the Puppet Theatre."

Kleist was deeply conscious of "the frailty of the world" (*die Gebrechlichkeit der Welt*); he could not forget that life in society falls far short of what it should be. His life was a passionate search for truth and justice, and he found too much downright evil for his taste. Who is responsible for the evil in the world? Religious people have always absolved God of this responsibility, and this is theoretically Kleist's position too. The late essay "Zoroaster's Prayer" (1810) is penetrated by the feeling for the misery that afflicts this age, resulting from the wretchedness, inadequacy, untruthfulness, and hyprocrisy that prevail everywhere. But this is not God's doing, for the essay begins: "God, my Father in Heaven, Thou hast destined man to live a life so free, glorious, and abundant . . . " And it ends with the prayer: "But may love for Thee, Lord, keep watch over everything, for without love nothing succeeds, not even the most trivial thing, so that Thy kingdom may be glorified and expanded through all space and time." Kleist's private thinking

---

[3]Of course the early German romantics, Friedrich Schlegel in particular, also advocated a synthesis of reason and emotion, poetry and prose, a mixture of genres. But the synthesis described here is not usually associated with the romantic movement.

was not so positive. In August 1806 he wrote to a friend: "It is true that the Divinity cannot be an evil spirit, but it may well be one that we don't understand." And to another friend: "It can't be an evil spirit that rules the world; it's only a spirit that we don't understand. Don't we too laugh when children cry?" The implicaton of the last sentence is a cynicism that is not characteristic of Kleist.

The later writings end with what may be called a faint theodicy, reminiscent of Peer Gynt's rueful conclusion: "God is a Father to me after all; but economical he certainly is not." In *Michael Kohlhaas* justice does triumph, but at the price of tremendous suffering, and in *Der Prinz von Homburg* both the strict law and the human will that flies in the face of law are reconciled. And the essay on puppets does envision a reconciliation between intellect and instinct, but only if intellect is carried to infinity, where it becomes an all-encompassing wisdom, that is, when man reaches the stage of becoming like God, which is not likely to happen in the near future.

But the early writings mirror no such theodicy. In them Kleist shows only the fragility of the world. He depicts radical evil, naked corruption, blind passion that leads to destruction, misunderstanding, confusion of feeling, and the inadequacy of language to establish communication.

Even when Kleist was a disciple of the early Rousseau and shared his cultural pessimism, he was not an uncritical adherent. He saw the paradox that weakened the primitivist myth;[4] and his sojourn in Paris in 1801 brought him face to face with the

---

[4]In a letter of August 15, 1801 Kleist writes to Wilhelmine:

> Assuming that Rousseau was right in answering no to the question whether science has made men better, what strange contradictions would follow from this truth! For many millennia would have to pass before so much knowledge would have to be gathered as is necessary to realize that we need have none. And how we would have to forget all our knowledge in order to rectify our error, and with that our misery would begin all over again. For man has an incontestable need to enlighten himself. Without enlightenment he is little more than a beast. His moral need impels him toward knowledge even if there were no such physical need. He would therefore be, like Ixion, condemned to roll a wheel up a mountain which would roll down again when it was half way up. If ignorance secures our simplicity,

fruits of the Rousseau ideology. In a letter to Wilhelmine he writes: "Every fourth word in the mouths of the French is Rousseau; but how ashamed he would be if he were told that this was his work."

●

The Earthquake in Chile (*Das Erdbeben in Chili*) is in fact an examination of Rousseau's social myth that civilization or intellect is the cause of all our woes and that we can only escape from this corruption by rejecting culture and returning to a state of innocent nature in which man, like the beast, is guided by his instincts. Like Goethe's tale of the *Attorney*, Kleist's story is a "moral tale," a *conte philosophique*, although it is told with such realism that the philosophical basis has escaped Kleist interpreters. The opening section clearly does not present a credible sequence of events but a contrived situation, such as one finds in Voltaire's *contes*, designed to demonstrate a philosophical or sociological thesis. And although the story becomes more credible as it develops, sober reflection leads to the conclusion that we are dealing here with an *exemplum*, a religious tale used for a didactic purpose. We are shown three stages of human history: (1) a society in the state of corrupt high "culture"; (2) the destruction of that society by an act of God, followed by a return to an Edenic state of "nature"; (3) the inevitable retrogression to corrupt "culture," human nature being what it is.

The narrator of the story is, like Kleist, a liberal rationalist who is sharply critical of the established order. The events he has chosen to illustrate his thesis, the subtle gradation of characters, representing all social and psychological nuances found in a community, his apportionment of guilt and responsibility for the misdeeds that are committed—all deserve the most careful study because they reveal Kleist's greatness as a storyteller.

A word about Kleist's style. It can only be described as baroque. Kleist constructs intricate, convoluted Miltonic periods

---

our innocence and all our enjoyment of peaceful nature, it opens the gates to all the horrors of superstition.

The argument continues for another page.

that are ingenious but hardly elegant. As an example take the
opening sentence of the novella *The Foundling* (*Der Findling*):

> Duke Wilhelm von Breisach who, since his secret union with a
> countess named Katharina von Heersbruck of the House of Alt-
> Hüningen, who seemed to be beneath him in rank, had been living
> in enmity with his half-brother Count Jacob the Redbeard, was
> returning toward the end of the fourteenth century at dusk on the
> Eve of St. Remigius from a conference held in Worms with the
> German emperor, at which he had obtained from his sovereign, in
> default of legitimate offspring, all of whom had died, the legitima-
> tion of a natural son, Count Philip von Hüningen, engendered
> premaritally with his spouse.

The opening sentence of *The Earthquake in Chile* is a somewhat
attenuated example of the same style. Kleist scholars express
unanimous admiration for these Pisan constructs. But in their
heart of hearts many admirers of Kleist must have felt that he
is a great writer in spite of his style. So, because Kleist has
so much to say to the modern reader, I have committed the
sacrilege of breaking up his linguistic colossi into more normal English periods. I firmly believe that God and Kleist will
forgive me.

●

Kleist may have written *Das Erdbeben in Chili* during his
months of captivity in France in 1807. It appeared in September
of that year in a literary journal under the title *Jeronimo und
Josepha.* It was revised for inclusion in Kleist's first volume of
Erzählungen, which was published in 1810. Kleist's sources, if
he had any, are not known. The earthquake of 1647 in Santiago
is historical. Kleist may have remembered chapters 5 and 6 of
Voltaire's *Candide,* in which reference is made to the famous
earthquake of 1755 at Lisbon. The narrator writes that after
that devastating catastrophe the wise men of the country had
been unable to find a more efficacious way of preventing total
ruination than to give the people a splendid *auto-da-fé:* "The
doctors at the University of Coimbre decided that the spectacle
of several people burned over a slow fire in a grand ceremony
is an infallible secret for preventing earthquakes." This may

have suggested to Kleist the church scene that ends the story. But in the absence of hard facts it is sensible to assume that Kleist had enough native wit to invent the plot.

Das Erdbeben in Chili

In St. Jago, der Hauptstadt des Königreichs Chili, stand gerade in dem Augenblicke der großen Erderschütterung vom Jahre 1647, bei welcher viele tausend Menschen ihren Untergang fanden, ein junger, auf ein Verbrechen angeklagter Spanier, namens Jeronimo Rugera, an einem Pfeiler des Gefängnisses, in welches man ihn eingesperrt hatte, und wollte sich erhenken. Don Henrico Asteron, einer der reichsten Edelleute der Stadt, hatte ihn ungefähr ein Jahr zuvor aus seinem Hause, wo er als Lehrer angestellt war, entfernt, weil er sich mit Donna Josephe, seiner einzigen Tochter, in einem zärtlichen Einverständnis befunden hatte. Eine geheime Bestellung, die dem alten Don, nachdem er die Tochter nachdrücklich gewarnt hatte, durch die hämische Aufmerksamkeit seines stolzen Sohnes verraten worden war, entrüstete ihn dergestalt, daß er sie in dem Karmeliterkloster unsrer lieben Frauen[1] vom Berge daselbst unterbrachte.

Durch einen glücklichen Zufall hatte Jeronimo hier die Verbindung von neuem anzuknüpfen gewußt, und in einer verschwiegenen Nacht den Klostergarten zum Schauplatze seines vollen Glückes gemacht. Es war am Fronleichnamsfeste,[2] und die feierliche Prozession der Nonnen, welchen die Novizen folgten, nahm eben ihren Anfang, als die unglückliche Josephe, bei dem Anklange der Glocken, in Mutterwehen auf den Stufen der Kathedrale niedersank.

Dieser Vorfall machte außerordentliches Aufsehn; man brachte die junge Sünderin, ohne Rücksicht auf ihren Zustand, sogleich in ein Gefängnis, und kaum war sie aus den Wochen erstanden, als ihr schon, auf Befehl des Erzbischofs, der ge-

The Earthquake in Chile

In the year 1647 the city of Santiago, capital of the kingdom of Chile, was shaken by a great earthquake in which many thousands perished. At the moment when the earthquake occurred a young Spaniard named Jeronimo Rugera was standing beside a pillar of the prison into which he had been thrown for a crime with which he was charged. He was on the point of hanging himself. About a year before, this young Spaniard had been dismissed from his post as tutor to the family of Don Henrico Asteron, one of the wealthiest noblemen in the city, because he was involved in an amorous relationship with Dona Josepha, the nobleman's only daughter. A clandestine meeting between the two young people had been betrayed to the father by his proud, spiteful son, who had spied on them. Don Henrico had given his daughter ample warning to break off relations with Jeronimo; the news brought by his son made him so indignant that he had his daughter locked up in the Carmelite convent of Our Dear Lady of the Mountain.

Through a lucky chance Jeronimo had been able to renew relations with the girl here, and on a silent night he had made the convent garden the setting for his complete bliss. On Corpus Christi Day, just as the nuns, followed by the novices, were beginning the solemn procession, just when the bells began to peal, the unhappy Josepha collapsed on the steps of the cathedral in the pangs of childbirth.

This incident caused an extraordinary sensation. The young sinner was at once thrown into prison without consideration for her condition. She had hardly risen from her childbed when she was subjected to a most rigorous trial on orders from the

schärfteste Prozeß gemacht ward.[3] Man sprach in der Stadt mit
einer so großen Erbitterung von diesem Skandal, und die
Zungen fielen so scharf über das ganze Kloster her, in welchem
er sich zugetragen hatte, daß weder die Fürbitte der Familie
Asteron, noch auch sogar der Wunsch der Äbtissin selbst,
welche das junge Mädchen wegen ihres sonst untadelhaften
Betragens lieb gewonnen hatte, die Strenge, mit welcher das
klösterliche Gesetz sie bedrohte, mildern konnte. Alles, was
geschehen konnte, war, daß der Feuertod, zu dem sie verurteilt
wurde, zur großen Entrüstung der Matronen und Jungfrauen
von St. Jago, durch einen Machtspruch des Vizekönigs, in eine
Enthauptung verwandelt ward.

Man vermietete in den Straßen, durch welche der Hinrich-
tungszug gehen sollte, die Fenster, man trug die Dächer der
Häuser ab, und die frommen Töchter der Stadt luden ihre
Freundinnen ein, um dem Schauspiele, das der göttlichen
Rache gegeben wurde, an ihrer schwesterlichen Seite bei-
zuwohnen.

Jeronimo, der inzwischen auch in ein Gefängnis gesetzt worden war, wollte die Besinnung verlieren, als er diese ungeheure
Wendung der Dinge erfuhr. Vergebens sann er auf Rettung:
überall, wohin ihn auch der Fittich[4] der vermessensten Gedanken trug, stieß er auf Riegel und Mauern, und ein Versuch,
die Gitterfenster zu durchfeilen, zog ihm, da er entdeckt ward,
eine nur noch engere Einsperrung zu. Er warf sich vor dem
Bildnisse der heiligen Mutter Gottes nieder, und betete mit
unendlicher Inbrunst zu ihr, als der einzigen, von der ihm jetzt
noch Rettung kommen könnte.

Doch der gefürchtete Tag erschien, und mit ihm in seiner
Brust die Überzeugung von der völligen Hoffnungslosigkeit
seiner Lage. Die Glocken, welche Josephen zum Richtplatze
begleiteten, ertönten, und Verzweiflung bemächtigte sich seiner Seele. Das Leben schien ihm verhaßt, und er beschloß, sich
durch einen Strick, den ihm der Zufall gelassen hatte, den Tod
zu geben. Eben stand er, wie schon gesagt, an einem Wandpfei-
ler, und befestigte den Strick, der ihn dieser jammervollen Welt
entreißen sollte, an eine Eisenklammer, die an dem Gesimse
derselben eingefugt war; als plötzlich der größte Teil der Stadt,
mit einem Gekrache, als ob das Firmament einstürzte, versank,

archbishop. This scandal caused so much bitterness in the city, and the convent in which it occurred became the object of such savage attacks, that neither the intercession of the Asteron family nor even the wishes of the abbess herself, who had become fond of Josepha because of her otherwise exemplary conduct, could soften the severity with which the ecclesiastical laws threatened the young girl. The best that could be done for her was to commute her sentence of death by fire to decapitation, and this by executive order of the viceroy, to the great indignation of the matrons and virgins of Santiago.

In the streets through which the procession was to pass on the way to the place of execution, windows were rented out to spectators; roofs were removed from houses; the virtuous daughters of the city invited their friends to witness the spectacle of divine retribution at their sisterly side.

Meanwhile Jeronimo, who had also been thrown into prison, nearly lost his reason when he learned of the monstrous turn that events had taken. In vain he planned ways of rescuing Josepha; wherever he was borne on the wings of his boldest thoughts, he always found himself thwarted by walls and bolts, and an attempt to file through the bars of his prison window was discovered and only brought him closer confinement. He prostrated himself before the image of the Holy Mother of God and prayed to her in boundless fervor as the sole source from whom salvation might yet come to him.

But the dreaded day appeared, and with it the conviction in his heart that his situation was utterly hopeless. The bells that accompanied Josepha to the place of execution began to toll, and despair took possession of his soul. Life seemed odious to him, and he resolved to end it with a rope that chance had thrown into his hands. As we have already mentioned, he was just standing beside a pillar, fastening the rope that was to snatch him out of this wretched world to an iron hook attached to a cornice, when the biggest part of the city suddenly collapsed with a crash, as if the firmament itself were falling, burying all living things beneath its ruins. Jeronimo Rugera stood there

und alles, was Leben atmete, unter seinen Trümmern begrub.
Jeronimo Rugera war starr vor Entsetzen; und gleich[5] als ob
sein ganzes Bewußtsein zerschmettert worden wäre, hielt er
sich jetzt an dem Pfeiler, an welchem er hatte sterben wollen,
um nicht umzufallen. Der Boden wankte unter seinen Füßen,
alle Wände des Gefängnisses rissen, der ganze Bau neigte sich,
nach der Straße zu[6] einzustürzen, und nur der, seinem langsamen Fall begegnende, Fall des gegenüberstehenden Gebäudes[7]
verhinderte, durch eine zufällige Wölbung, die gänzliche
Zubodenstreckung desselben. Zitternd, mit sträubenden Haaren, und Knieen, die unter ihm brechen wollten, glitt Jeronimo
über den schiefgesenkten Fußboden hinweg, der Öffnung zu,
die der Zusammenschlag beider Häuser in die vordere Wand
des Gefängnisses eingerissen hatte.

Kaum befand er sich im Freien,[8] als die ganze, schon erschüt-
terte Straße auf eine zweite Bewegung der Erde völlig zusam-
menfiel. Besinnungslos, wie er sich aus diesem allgemeinen
Verderben retten würde, eilte er über Schutt und Gebälk hinweg, indessen der Tod von allen Seiten Angriffe auf ihn machte,
nach einem der nächsten Tore der Stadt. Hier stürzte noch ein
Haus zusammen, und jagte ihn, die Trümmer weit umher-
schleudernd, in eine Nebenstraße; hier leckte die Flamme
schon, in Dampfwolken blitzend, aus allen Giebeln, und trieb
ihn schreckenvoll in eine andere; hier wälzte sich, aus seinem
Gestade gehoben, der Mapochofluß auf ihn heran, und riß ihn
brüllend in eine dritte. Hier lag ein Haufen Erschlagener, hier
ächzte noch eine Stimme unter dem Schutte, hier schrieen
Leute von brennenden Dächern herab, hier kämpften Menschen und Tiere mit den Wellen, hier war ein mutiger Retter
bemüht, zu helfen; hier stand ein anderer, bleich wie der Tod,
und streckte sprachlos zitternde Hände zum Himmel. Als
Jeronimo das Tor erreicht, und einen Hügel jenseits desselben
bestiegen hatte, sank er ohnmächtig auf demselben nieder.

Er mochte[9] wohl eine Viertelstunde in der tiefsten Bewußt-
losigkeit gelegen haben, als er endlich wieder erwachte, und
sich, mit nach der Stadt gekehrtem Rücken, halb auf dem Erdboden erhob. Er befühlte sich Stirn und Brust, unwissend, was
er aus seinem Zustande machen sollte, und ein unsägliches
Wonnegefühl ergriff ihn, als ein Westwind, vom Meere her,

frozen with horror; the next moment, as if his conscious mind
had been shattered, he was clinging to the pillar at which he
had wanted to die, to save himself from falling. The ground
swayed under his feet; all the walls of the prison cracked; the
whole building bent forward into the street, preparing to collapse; it escaped total destruction only because, as it fell, it met
the falling building from across the street so as to form an
accidental arch. Trembling, his hair on end, and his knees ready
to give under him, Jeronimo slid down the sloping floor toward
the opening that had been torn in the prison's outside wall by
the collision of the two buildings.

He had barely reached the open air when a second quake
caused the whole street, which was already badly torn up, to
collapse. At his wits' end how to save himself from this general
destruction, Jeronimo hurried along over rubble and fallen
beams toward one of the nearby city gates, pursued by death
from every direction. At one point another house was collapsing, hurling its debris in a wide circle and driving him into a
side street; at another, the flames were already licking at all
the gables, flashing through the clouds of smoke, driving him
in terror into another street. At one spot the raging Mapocho
river, bursting its banks, rolled toward him, so that he had to
run into a third street; at another, a heap of dead bodies was
piled up, with an occasional voice still groaning under the rubble; at another, people were screaming from the burning roof-
tops, men and beasts were battling the waves; here a brave man
was busy rescuing others; here another man stood pale as death,
his trembling hands raised mutely to Heaven. When Jeronimo
reached the city gate and climbed a hill beyond it, he fell down
in a faint.

He had been lying completely unconscious for about a quarter
of an hour when he awoke and rose to his knees with his back
to the city. He felt his forehead and chest, not knowing what
to make of his condition. An indescribable feeling of bliss came
over him when a west wind, blowing from the sea, fanned him
back to life; his eye roamed over the whole blooming landscape

sein wiederkehrendes Leben anwehte, und sein Auge sich nach allen Richtungen über die blühende Gegend von St. Jago hinwandte. Nur die verstörten Menschenhaufen, die sich überall blicken ließen, beklemmten sein Herz; er begriff nicht, was ihn und sie hiehergeführt haben konnte, und erst, da er sich umkehrte, und die Stadt hinter sich versunken sah, erinnerte er sich des schrecklichen Augenblicks,[10] den er erlebt hatte. Er senkte sich so tief, daß seine Stirn den Boden berührte, Gott für seine wunderbare Errettung zu danken; und gleich, als ob der eine entsetzliche Eindruck, der sich seinem Gemüt eingeprägt hatte, alle früheren daraus verdrängt hätte, weinte er vor Lust, daß er sich des lieblichen Lebens,[11] voll bunter Erscheinungen, noch erfreue.

Drauf, als er eines Ringes an seiner Hand gewahrte, erinnerte er sich plötzlich auch Josephens; und mit ihr seines Gefängnisses, der Glocken, die er dort gehört hatte, und des Augenblicks, der dem Einsturze desselben[12] vorangegangen war. Tiefe Schwermut erfüllte wieder seine Brust; sein Gebet fing ihn zu reuen an, und fürchterlich schien ihm das Wesen, das über den Wolken waltet. Er mischte sich unter das Volk, das überall, mit Rettung des Eigentums beschäftigt, aus den Toren stürzte, und wagte schüchtern nach der Tochter Asterons, und ob die Hinrichtung an ihr vollzogen worden sei, zu fragen; doch niemand war, der ihm umständliche Auskunft gab. Eine Frau, die auf einem fast zur Erde gedrückten Nacken eine ungeheure Last von Gerätschaften und zwei Kinder, an der Brust hängend, trug, sagte im Vorbeigehen, als ob sie es selbst angesehen hätte: daß sie enthauptet worden sei. Jeronimo kehrte sich um; und da er, wenn er die Zeit berechnete, selbst an ihrer[13] Vollendung nicht zweifeln konnte, so setzte er sich in einem einsamen Walde nieder, und überließ sich seinem vollen Schmerz. Er wünschte, daß die zerstörende Gewalt der Natur von neuem über ihn einbrechen möchte. Er begriff nicht, warum er dem Tode, den seine jammervolle Seele suchte, in jenen Augenblicken, da er ihm freiwillig von allen Seiten rettend erschien, entflohen sei. Er nahm sich fest vor, nicht zu wanken, wenn auch jetzt die Eichen entwurzelt werden, und ihre Wipfel über ihn zusammenstürzen sollten. Darauf nun, da er sich ausgeweint hatte, und ihm, mitten unter den heißesten Tränen, die

around Santiago. Only the heaps of perishing humanity, visible
everywhere, oppressed his heart. He could not comprehend
what could have brought them or him out here; it was not until
he turned around and saw the city in ruins that he recalled the
terrible moment he had experienced. He bent down till his
forehead touched the ground and thanked God for his miracu-   .
lous rescue; the next moment, as if the one frightful impression
that had imprinted itself on his mind had driven out all others,
he wept for joy because he still savored the beauty of life in all
its varied manifestations.

Then, catching sight of a ring on his finger, he suddenly
remembered Josepha; with her came the memory of his impris-
onment, the bells he had heard in his cell, and the moment
before the collapse of the building. A profound melancholy
filled his heart again; he began to regret his thanksgiving prayer,
and the Being that rules above the clouds seemed terrible to
him. He mingled with the people who were streaming out of
their gateways, busying themselves with the rescue of their chat-
tels. He ventured a few timid questions about Asteron's daughter and whether the execution had taken place; there was no
one who could give him any details about the matter. A woman
with a monstrous load on her shoulders and two babies clinging
to her breast so that she was almost bowed to the ground said
in passing, as if she had been an eyewitness to the affair, that
the girl had been beheaded. Jeronimo turned back; when he
judged the time of day, he realized that there could be no
reasonable doubt that she had already been executed. So he
sat down in a solitary wood and gave free rein to his grief. He
yearned for the destructive power of nature to strike him anew.
He could not understand why he had fled from the death that
his wretched soul sought, at those moments when it had appeared to him from all sides voluntarily, offering him release.
He made a firm resolve not to waver again, even if oaks should
now be uprooted and their crowns fall on him. When he could
weep no more and found that amidst his hottest tears hope
had once more arisen in his heart, he stood up and began to

Hoffnung wieder erschienen war, stand er auf, und durch-
streifte nach allen Richtungen das Feld. Jeden Berggipfel, auf
dem sich die Menschen versammelt hatten, besuchte er; auf
allen Wegen, wo sich der Strom der Flucht noch bewegte, begegnete er ihnen; wo nur irgend ein weibliches Gewand im
Winde flatterte, da trug ihn sein zitternder Fuß hin: doch keines
deckte die geliebte Tochter Asterons. Die Sonne neigte sich,
und mit ihr seine Hoffnung schon wieder zum Untergange,
als er den Rand eines Felsens betrat, und sich ihm die Aussicht
in ein weites, nur von wenig Menschen besuchtes Tal eröffnete.
Er durchlief, unschlüssig, was er tun sollte, die einzelnen Gruppen derselben,[14] und wollte sich schon wieder wenden, als er
plötzlich an einer Quelle, die die Schlucht bewässerte, ein
junges Weib erblickte, beschäftigt, ein Kind in seinen Fluten
zu reinigen. Und das Herz hüpfte ihm bei diesem Anblick; er
sprang voll Ahndung[15] über die Gesteine herab, und rief: O
Mutter Gottes, du Heilige! und erkannte Josephen, als sie sich
bei dem Geräusche schüchtern umsah. Mit welcher Seligkeit
umarmten sie sich, die Unglücklichen, die ein Wunder des
Himmels gerettet hatte!

Josephe war, auf ihrem Gang zum Tode, dem Richtplatze
schon ganz nahe gewesen, als durch den krachenden Einsturz
der Gebäude plötzlich der ganze Hinrichtungszug auseinander
gesprengt ward. Ihre ersten entsetzensvollen Schritte trugen
sie hierauf dem nächsten Tore zu; doch die Besinnung kehrte
ihr bald wieder, und sie wandte sich, um nach dem Kloster zu
eilen, wo ihr kleiner, hilfloser Knabe zurückgeblieben war. Sie
fand das ganze Kloster schon in Flammen, und die Äbtissin, die
ihr in jenen Augenblicken, die ihre letzten sein sollten, Sorge
für den Säugling angelobt hatte, schrie eben, vor den Pforten
stehend, nach Hilfe, um ihn zu retten. Josephe stürzte sich,
unerschrocken durch den Dampf, der ihr entgegenqualmte, in
das von allen Seiten schon zusammenfallende Gebäude, und
gleich, als ob alle Engel des Himmels sie umschirmten, trat sie
mit ihm unbeschädigt wieder aus dem Portal hervor. Sie wollte
der Äbtissin, welche die Hände über ihr Haupt zusammen-
schlug,[16] eben in die Arme sinken, als diese, mit fast allen ihren
Klosterfrauen, von einem herabfallenden Giebel des Hauses,
auf eine schmähliche Art erschlagen ward. Josephe bebte bei

wander over the fields at random. He climbed to the peak of every mountain on which people had gathered; on every road where he met a stream of refugees; wherever a woman's dress fluttered in the breeze, his trembling steps carried him to that spot; but none clothed the body of Asteron's beloved daughter. The sun was already setting, and with it Jeronimo's hopes, when he came to the edge of a cliff. Before him lay a broad valley on which only a few people were visible. He examined the individual groups, undecided about what to do. He was just on the point of turning back when he suddenly caught sight of a young woman who was washing an infant in a spring that watered the gorge. At this sight his heart leaped within him; filled with hope, he leaped down over the rocks and cried: "O holy Mother of God!" and recognized Josepha timidly looking around when she heard the noise. With what bliss they embraced, these two unlucky people, who had been rescued by a miracle from Heaven!

Josepha had already been quite close to the place of execution on her death march when the roar of the collapsing buildings suddenly scattered the whole procession of executioners. Her first steps, filled with dread, then led her to the nearest city gate. But she soon regained her senses and hastened back to the convent, where her helpless little boy had been left behind. She found the whole convent already in flames. The abbess was standing in front of the gate, crying for someone to help rescue the child, which she had promised Josepha in what were to be her last moments to care for. Undismayed by the smoke that poured out toward her, Josepha rushed into the building, which was collapsing from all sides. Almost immediately she appeared in the gateway, bearing the child uninjured, as if all the angels of Heaven were protecting her. She was about to throw herself into the arms of the abbess, who stood there with her hands raised in astonishment, when a falling gable of the building crushed the abbess and nearly all the inmates of the convent in a shameful death. At this dreadful sight Josepha fell back trembling with horror; hurriedly closing the eyes of

diesem entsetzlichen Anblicke zurück; sie drückte der Äbtissin flüchtig die Augen zu, und floh, ganz von Schrecken erfüllt, den teuern Knaben, den ihr der Himmel wieder geschenkt hatte, dem Verderben zu entreißen.

Sie hatte noch wenig Schritte getan, als ihr auch schon die Leiche des Erzbischofs begegnete, die man soeben zerschmettert aus dem Schutt der Kathedrale hervorgezogen hatte. Der Palast des Vizekönigs war versunken, der Gerichtshof, in welchem ihr das Urteil gesprochen worden war, stand in Flammen, und an die Stelle, wo sich ihr väterliches Haus befunden hatte, war ein See getreten, und kochte rötliche Dämpfe aus. Josephe raffte alle ihre Kräfte zusammen, sich zu halten. Sie schritt, den Jammer von ihrer Brust entfernend, mutig mit ihrer Beute von Straße zu Straße, und war schon dem Tore nah, als sie auch das Gefängnis, in welchem Jeronimo geseufzt hatte, in Trümmern sah. Bei diesem Anblicke wankte sie, und wollte besinnungslos an einer Ecke niedersinken; doch in demselben Augenblick jagte sie der Sturz eines Gebäudes hinter ihr, das die Erschütterungen schon ganz aufgelöst hatten, durch das Entsetzen gestärkt, wieder auf; sie küßte das Kind, drückte sich die Tränen aus den Augen, und erreichte, nicht mehr auf die Greuel, die sie umringten, achtend, das Tor. Als sie sich im Freien sah, schloß sie bald, daß nicht jeder, der ein zertrümmertes Gebäude bewohnt hatte, unter ihm notwendig müsse zerschmettert worden sein.

An dem nächsten Scheidewege stand sie still, und harrte, ob nicht einer, der ihr, nach dem kleinen Philipp, der liebste auf der Welt war, noch erscheinen würde. Sie ging, weil niemand kam, und das Gewühl der Menschen anwuchs, weiter, und kehrte sich wieder um, und harrte[17] wieder; und schlich, viel Tränen vergießend, in ein dunkles, von Pinien beschattetes Tal, um seiner Seele, die sie entflohen glaubte, nachzubeten; und fand ihn hier, diesen Geliebten, im Tale, und Seligkeit, als ob es das Tal von Eden gewesen wäre.

Dies alles erzählte sie jetzt voll Rührung dem[18] Jeronimo, und reichte ihm, da sie vollendet hatte, den Knaben zum Küssen dar. Jeronimo nahm ihn, und hätschelte ihn in unsäglicher Vaterfreude, und verschloß ihm, da er das fremde Antlitz anweinte, mit Liebkosungen ohne Ende den Mund. Indessen war

the dead abbess, she fled in terror, bent on saving from destruction the precious child that Heaven had given back to her.

She had taken only a few steps when she passed the archbishop's mangled corpse, which had just been dug out from the rubble of the cathedral. The viceroy's palace had been leveled; the courthouse in which sentence had been passed on her was in flames; and on the spot where her parental home had stood, a lake was bubbling up reddish vapor. Josepha made a supreme effort to control her senses. Banishing the misery from her heart, she strode courageously from street to street, carrying her booty. Near the city gate she perceived the ruins of the prison in which Jeronimo had languished. At this sight her knees gave way under her and she was about to fall senseless at a street corner; but at that moment a building behind her, which had been badly weakened by the tremors, caved in; her terror gave her new strength to push on. She kissed the child, wiped the tears from her eyes, and, disregarding the horrors that surrounded her, reached the city gate. When she saw that she was in open country, she concluded that not everyone who lived in the buildings now lying in ruins had necessarily been crushed beneath them.

At the next crossroads she stopped and waited to see whether one who, next to little Philip, was the most precious person in the world to her, might yet appear. But as no one came and the throng of people swelled, she went on and turned round again, then waited once more. Shedding many tears, she crept into a dark valley, shaded by pines, where she intended to offer up a prayer for his soul, which she believed to have gone to Heaven. And here in the valley she found him, her beloved; here she found bliss, as if it were the Vale of Eden.

She now related this whole tale to her Jeronimo, moved by deep feeling. When she had finished, she handed him the child to kiss. Jeronimo took the boy and fondled him with infinite fatherly tenderness. As the child cried in fear at the sight of the strange face, he closed its lips with endless caresses. Mean-

die schönste Nacht herabgestiegen, voll wundermilden Duftes,
so silberglänzend und still, wie nur ein Dichter davon träumen
mag. Überall, längs der Talquelle, hatten sich, im Schimmer
des Mondscheins, Menschen niedergelassen, und bereiteten
sich sanfte Lager von Moos und Laub, um von einem so qual-
vollen Tage auszuruhen. Und weil die Armen immer noch
jammerten; dieser, daß er sein Haus, jener, daß er Weib und
Kind, und der dritte, daß er alles verloren habe: so schlichen
Jeronimo und Josephe in ein dichteres Gebüsch, um durch das
heimliche Gejauchz ihrer Seelen niemand zu betrüben. Sie fanden einen prachtvollen Granatapfelbaum, der seine Zweige,
voll duftender Früchte, weit ausbreitete; und die Nachtigall
flötete im Wipfel ihr wollüstiges Lied. Hier ließ sich Jeronimo
am Stamme nieder, und Josephe in seinem, Philipp in
Josephens Schoß, saßen sie, von seinem Mantel bedeckt, und
ruhten. Der Baumschatten zog, mit seinen verstreuten
Lichtern, über sie hinweg, und der Mond erblaßte schon wieder
vor der Morgenröte, ehe sie einschliefen. Denn Unendliches
hatten sie zu schwatzen vom Klostergarten und den Gefängnis-
sen, und was sie um einander gelitten hätten; und waren sehr
gerührt, wenn sie dachten, wie viel Elend über die Welt kommen mußte, damit sie glücklich würden!

Sie beschlossen, sobald die Erderschütterungen aufgehört
haben würden, nach La Conception[19] zu gehen, wo Josephe
eine vertraute Freundin hatte, sich mit einem kleinen Vorschuß,
den sie von ihr zu erhalten hoffte, von dort nach Spanien einzuschiffen, wo Jeronimos mütterliche Verwandten wohnten,
und daselbst ihr glückliches Leben zu beschließen. Hierauf,
unter vielen Küssen, schliefen sie ein.

●

Als sie erwachten, stand die Sonne schon hoch am Himmel,
und sie bemerkten in ihrer Nähe mehrere Familien, beschäftigt,
sich am Feuer ein kleines Morgenbrot zu bereiten. Jeronimo
dachte eben auch, wie er Nahrung für die Seinigen herbei-
schaffen sollte, als ein junger wohlgekleideter Mann, mit einem
Kinde auf dem Arm, zu Josephen trat, und sie mit Bescheidenheit fragte: ob sie diesem armen Wurme,[20] dessen Mutter dort
unter den Bäumen beschädigt liege, nicht auf kurze Zeit ihre
Brust reichen wolle? Josephe war ein wenig verwirrt, als sie in

while the most beautiful night had settled over the country, filled with a wonderfully mild fragrance, so still and gleaming with silver, as only a poet's fancy could dream of. Everwhere along the spring that ran through the valley, people had settled down in the shimmering moonlight and were spreading soft beds of moss and foliage to rest on after such a harrowing day. And because these poor people were still lamenting: one because he had lost his home, another his wife and child, a third because he had lost everything, Jeronimo and Josepha stole away into a denser clump of bushes so that they might sadden no one through the secret exultation of their souls. They found a gorgeous pomegranate tree that spread its branches wide, laden with fragrant fruit, while in its crest the nightingale warbled its voluptuous song. Jeronimo sat down by the trunk of this tree, Josepha sat in his lap, holding Phillip in hers; and so they sat there resting, wrapped in Jeronimo's cloak. The shadow of the tree crossed over them with its wavering light, and the moon was already paling at the approaching dawn before they could find sleep. For they had an infinite variety of themes to talk about, of the convent garden and the prisons, and of what they had endured for each other. And they were deeply moved by the thought that so much misery had to come over the world in order that they might find happiness.

They decided that as soon as the earthquake was definitely over they would go to Conception, where Josepha had a close friend, from whom she hoped to borrow a little money to pay for their passage to Spain, where Jeronimo's maternal relatives lived and where they could live happily to the end of their days. After this they fell asleep amid many kisses.

●

When they awoke the sun was already high in the sky and they noticed several families near them, busy preparing a little breakfast beside a fire. Jeronimo was just wondering how to procure food for his dear ones when a young, well-dressed man with a child on his arm came up to Josepha and asked her deferentially whether she would be good enough to give the poor creature her breast for a short time, as its mother lay injured over there among the trees. Josepha recognized the man as an acquaintance and showed some confusion on her

ihm einen Bekannten erblickte; doch da er, indem er ihre Verwirrung falsch deutete, fortfuhr: »Es ist nur auf wenige Augenblicke, Donna Josephe, und dieses Kind hat, seit jener
Stunde, die uns alle unglücklich gemacht hat, nichts genossen«;
so sagte sie: »Ich schwieg—aus einem andern Grunde, Don
Fernando; in diesen schrecklichen Zeiten weigert sich niemand,
von dem, was er besitzen mag, mitzuteilen«: und nahm den
kleinen Fremdling, indem sie ihr eigenes Kind dem Vater gab,
und legte ihn an ihre Brust. Don Fernando war sehr dankbar
für diese Güte, und fragte: ob sie sich nicht mit ihm zu jener
Gesellschaft verfügen wollten, wo eben jetzt beim Feuer ein
kleines Frühstück bereitet werde? Josephe antwortete, daß sie
dies Anerbieten mit Vergnügen annehmen würde, und folgte
ihm, da auch Jeronimo nichts einzuwenden hatte, zu seiner
Familie, wo sie auf das innigste und zärtlichste von Don Fernandos beiden Schwägerinnen, die sie als sehr würdige junge
Damen kannte, empfangen ward.

Donna Elvire, Don Fernandos Gemahlin, welche schwer an
den Füßen verwundet auf der Erde lag, zog Josephen, da sie
ihren abgehärmten Knaben an der Brust derselben sah, mit
vieler Freundlichkeit zu sich nieder. Auch Don Pedro, sein
Schwiegervater, der an der Schulter verwundet war, nickte ihr
liebreich mit dem Haupte zu.

In Jeronimos und Josephens Brust regten sich Gedanken
von seltsamer Art. Wenn sie sich mit so vieler Vertraulichkeit
und Güte behandelt sahen, so wußten sie nicht, was sie von der
Vergangenheit denken sollten, vom Richtplatze, von dem Ge-
fängnisse, und der Glocke; und ob sie bloß davon geträumt
hätten? Es war, als ob die Gemüter, seit dem fürchterlichen
Schlage, der sie durchdröhnt hatte, alle versöhnt wären. Sie
konnten in der Erinnerung gar nicht weiter, als bis auf ihn,
zurückgehen. Nur Donna Elisabeth, welche bei einer Freundin,
auf das Schauspiel des gestrigen Morgens, eingeladen worden
war, die Einladung aber nicht angenommen hatte, ruhte zuweilen mit träumerischem Blicke auf Josephen; doch der Be-
richt, der über irgend ein neues gräßliches Unglück erstattet
ward, riß ihre, der Gegenwart kaum entflohene Seele[21] schon
wieder in dieselbe zurück.

face. Misconstruing the cause of her embarrassment, he continued: "It's only for a few moments, Dona Josepha; the child has had no nourishment since that hour which made us all unhappy." "I was silent—for another reason, Don Fernando," she replied; "in these terrible times no one refuses to share whatever one possesses." And handing her own child to its father, she took the little stranger and laid him to her breast. Don Fernando was very grateful for this kindness and asked whether they would not like to join the group, which was now preparing a small breakfast around a fire. Josepha replied that she would accept the invitation with pleasure; as Jeronimo made no objection either, she followed Don Fernando to his family circle, where she was welcomed by his two sisters-in-law, whom she knew to be very worthy young ladies.

Upon seeing her unwell child at Josepha's breast, Dona Elvira, Don Fernando's wife, who was lying on the ground with severe wounds in her feet, drew the young woman down to her with much warmth. Fernando's father-in-law, Don Pedro, who was wounded in one shoulder, also nodded graciously to her.

Strange thoughts now stirred in the minds of Jeronimo and Josepha. Seeing themselves treated with so much kindness and intimacy, they did not know what to make of the past, the execution square, the prison, and the bell; had it all been a mere dream? It seemed as if all these spirits were reconciled since the fearful blow had struck them. Their memories refused to go back beyond this event. Only Dona Elizabeth, who had been invited by a friend to witness the spectacle of the previous morning but had declined the invitation, cast a dreamy look on Josepha from time to time. But a report that came in about some ghastly new misfortune immediately drew her mind back to the present, from which it had momentarily escaped.

Man erzählte, wie die Stadt gleich nach der ersten Haupter-
schütterung von Weibern ganz voll gewesen, die vor den Augen
aller Männer niedergekommen seien; wie die Mönche darin,
mit dem Kruzifix in der Hand, umhergelaufen wären, und
geschrieen hätten: das Ende der Welt sei da! wie man einer
Wache, die auf Befehl des Vizekönigs verlangte, eine Kirche
zu räumen, geantwortet hätte: es gäbe keinen Vizekönig von
Chili mehr! wie der Vizekönig in den schrecklichsten Augenblicken hätte müssen Galgen aufrichten lassen, um der Dieberei
Einhalt zu tun;[22] und wie ein Unschuldiger, der sich von hinten
durch ein brennendes Haus gerettet, von dem Besitzer aus
Übereilung ergriffen, und sogleich auch aufgeknüpft worden
wäre. Donna Elvire, bei deren Verletzungen Josephe viel beschäftigt war, hatte in einem Augenblick, da gerade die Erzählungen sich am lebhaftesten kreuzten, Gelegenheit genommen,
sie zu fragen: wie es denn ihr an diesem fürchterlichen Tag
ergangen sei? Und da Josephe ihr, mit beklemmtem Herzen,
einige Hauptzüge davon angab, so ward ihr die Wollust, Tränen
in die Augen dieser Dame treten zu sehen; Donna Elvire ergriff
ihre Hand, und drückte sie, und winkte ihr, zu schweigen.
Josephe dünkte sich unter den Seligen.[23] Ein Gefühl, das sie
nicht unterdrücken konnte, nannte den verfloßnen Tag, so viel
Elend er auch über die Welt gebracht hatte, eine Wohltat,[24] wie
der Himmel noch keine über sie verhängt hatte. Und in der
Tat schien, mitten in diesen gräßlichen Augenblicken, in welchen alle irdischen Güter der Menschen zu Grunde gingen,
und die ganze Natur verschüttet zu werden drohte, der menschliche Geist selbst, wie eine schöne Blume, aufzugehn. Auf
den Feldern, so weit das Auge reichte, sah man Menschen von
allen Ständen durcheinander liegen, Fürsten und Bettler, Matronen und Bäuerinnen, Staatsbeamte und Tagelöhner, Klo-
sterherren und Klosterfrauen: einander bemitleiden, sich
wechselseitig Hilfe reichen, von dem, was sie zur Erhaltung
ihres Lebens gerettet haben mochten, freudig mitteilen, als ob
das allgemeine Unglück alles, was ihm entronnen war, zu *einer*
Familie gemacht hätte.

Statt der nichtssagenden Unterhaltungen, zu welchen sonst
die Welt an den Teetischen den Stoff hergegeben hatte, erzählte
man jetzt Beispiele von ungeheuern Taten: Menschen, die man

They were telling how, right after the first main quake, the city had been full of women giving birth to babies before the eyes of all the men; how the monks had rushed about, crucifix in hand, shrieking that the end of the world was at hand; how, when a guard had attempted to clear a church by order of the viceroy, they had been told that there no longer was a viceroy of Chile; how, during the most frightful moments, the viceroy had been compelled to have gallows erected in order to curb the looting; and how an innocent man, who had run out from the rear of a burning house to save his life, had been seized precipitously by the owner of the house and instantly strung up. During a moment when the stories were being exchanged with animation, Dona Elvira had seized the opportunity of asking Josepha, who was very busy tending Dona Elvira's wounds, what had happened to her on that frightful day. Josepha related the main outlines of her story with a feeling of oppression, and she had the satisfaction of seeing tears in the lady's eyes. Dona Elvira took her hand, pressed it, and motioned to her to be silent. Josepha thought she was in Paradise. A feeling she was unable to suppress forced her to regard the day that had just passed, for all the misery it had brought into the world, as a blessing, the like of which Heaven had never yet bestowed on her. And indeed, during these gruesome moments when all earthly goods were destroyed and all nature threatened with disintegration, the human spirit itself seemed to open up like a beautiful flower. In the fields, as far as the human eye could reach, one saw people of all social classes lying indiscriminately beside one another. Princes and beggars, matrons and peasant women, government officials and day laborers, monks and nuns showed pity for one another, helped one another, joyfully shared what they had rescued for the preservation of their lives, as if the general catastrophe had fused all those who had escaped it into *one* family.

Instead of the insignificant topics that society normally offered for conversation at the tea table, extraordinary deeds were now related: people who had formerly been of little

sonst in der Gesellschaft wenig geachtet hatte, hatten Römergröße gezeigt; Beispiele zu Haufen von Unerschrockenheit,
von freudiger Verachtung der Gefahr, von Selbstverleugnung
und der göttlichen Aufopferung, von ungesäumter Wegwerfung des Lebens, als ob es, dem nichtswürdigsten Gute gleich,
auf dem nächsten Schritte schon wiedergefunden würde. Ja,
da nicht einer war, für den nicht an diesem Tage etwas
Rührendes geschehen wäre, oder der nicht selbst etwas Großmütiges getan hätte, so war der Schmerz in jeder Menschenbrust mit so viel süßer Lust vermischt, daß sich, wie sie meinte,
gar nicht angeben ließ, ob die Summe des allgemeinen Wohlseins nicht von der einen Seite um ebenso viel gewachsen war,
als sie von der anderen abgenommen hatte.

Jeronimo nahm Josephen, nachdem sich beide in diesen Betrachtungen stillschweigend erschöpft hatten, beim Arm, und
führte sie mit unaussprechlicher Heiterkeit unter den schattigen Lauben des Granatwaldes auf und nieder. Er sagte ihr,
daß er, bei dieser Stimmung der Gemüter[25] und dem Umsturz
aller Verhältnisse, seinen Entschluß, sich nach Europa einzuschiffen, aufgebe; daß er vor dem Vizekönig, der sich seiner
Sache immer günstig gezeigt, falls er noch am Leben sei, einen
Fußfall[26] wagen würde; und daß er Hoffnung habe (wobei er
ihr einen Kuß aufdrückte), mit ihr in Chili zurückzubleiben.
Josephe antwortete, daß ähnliche Gedanken in ihr aufgestiegen
wären; daß auch sie nicht mehr, falls ihr Vater nur noch am
Leben sei, ihn zu versöhnen zweifle; daß sie aber statt des Fußfalles lieber nach La Conception zu gehen, und von dort aus
schriftlich das Versöhnungsgeschäft mit dem Vizekönig zu betreiben rate, wo man auf jeden Fall in der Nähe des Hafens
wäre, und für den besten, wenn das Geschäft die erwünschte
Wendung nähme, ja leicht wieder nach St. Jago zurückkehren
könnte. Nach einer kurzen Überlegung gab Jeronimo der
Klugheit dieser Maßregel seinen Beifall, führte sie noch ein
wenig, die heitern Momente der Zukunft überfliegend, in den
Gängen umher, und kehrte mit ihr zur Gesellschaft zurück.

Inzwischen war der Nachmittag herangekommen, und die
Gemüter der herumschwärmenden Flüchtlinge hatten sich, da
die Erdstöße nachließen, nur kaum wieder ein wenig beruhigt,
als sich schon die Nachricht verbreitete, daß in der Domini

account in society had displayed a Roman grandeur; numerous examples of steadfastness, of joyful contempt for danger, of self-denial and divine self-sacrifice, of unhesitating readiness to throw away one's life as if it were some worthless bauble that could be recovered one step ahead. Indeed, there was not a single person for whom something touching had not been done that day or who had not himself done something generous. Hence the pain in every human heart was mixed with so much pleasure that, Josepha felt, it was impossible to say whether the sum of general welfare had not grown on the one side by just as much as it had diminished on the other.

After they had exhausted themselves in such silent reflections, Jeronimo took Josepha by the arm and led her with indescribable happiness up and down under the shaded arbors of the pomegranate grove. He told her that in view of the new spirit that had taken possession of people and because of the complete reversal of the order of things, he was giving up his intention of sailing to Europe. He would venture to prostrate himself before the viceroy (if he were still alive), who had always been favorably inclined toward him. He hoped to stay on with her in Chile; and in saying this, he imprinted a kiss on her lips. Josepha replied that she had been nursing similar thoughts; she too no longer had any doubt that she could bring about a reconciliation with her father if he were still alive; but that instead of prostrating herself before the viceroy, she preferred to go to Conception and from there initiate the reconciliation by writing to him. They would be near the harbor there, ready for any eventuality; if things took a turn for the better, they could easily return to Santiago. After brief reflection Jeronimo approved the wisdom of this course. They strolled a while longer on the walks, dreaming of the serene future, then rejoined the company.

Meanwhile afternoon had come and the emotions of the roaming refugees had hardly had time to calm down, once the tremors had ceased, when the news spread that a solemn mass would be said in the Dominican church—the only one spared

kanerkirche, der einzigen, welche das Erdbeben verschont
hatte, eine feierliche Messe von dem Prälaten des Klosters selbst
gelesen werden würde, den Himmel um Verhütung ferneren
Unglücks anzuflehen.

Das Volk brach schon aus allen Gegenden auf, und eilte in
Strömen zur Stadt. In Don Fernandos Gesellschaft ward die
Frage aufgeworfen, ob man nicht auch an dieser Feierlichkeit
Teil nehmen, und sich dem allgemeinen Zuge anschließen solle?
Donna Elisabeth erinnerte, mit einiger Beklemmung, was für
ein Unheil gestern in der Kirche vorgefallen sei; daß solche
Dankfeste ja[27] wiederholt werden würden, und daß man sich
der Empfindung alsdann,[28] weil die Gefahr schon mehr vorüber
wäre, mit desto größerer Heiterkeit und Ruhe überlassen
könnte. Josephe äußerte, indem sie mit einiger Begeisterung
sogleich aufstand, daß sie den Drang, ihr Antlitz[29] vor dem
Schöpfer in den Staub zu legen, niemals lebhafter empfunden
habe, als eben jetzt, wo er seine unbegreifliche und erhabene
Macht so entwickle.[30] Donna Elvire erklärte sich mit Lebhaftigkeit für Josephens Meinung. Sie bestand darauf, daß man
die Messe hören sollte, und rief Don Fernando auf, die Gesellschaft zu führen, worauf sich alles,[31] Donna Elisabeth auch,
von den Sitzen erhob. Da man jedoch letztere, mit heftigarbei-
tender Brust, die kleinen Anstalten zum Aufbruche zaudernd
betreiben sah, und sie, auf die Frage: was ihr fehle? antwortete:
sie wisse nicht, welch eine unglückliche Ahndung in ihr sei? so
beruhigte sie Donna Elvire, und forderte sie auf, bei ihr und
ihrem kranken Vater zurückzubleiben. Josephe sagte: »So werden Sie mir wohl, Donna Elisabeth, diesen kleinen Liebling
abnehmen, der sich schon wieder, wie Sie sehen, bei mir eingefunden hat.« »Sehr gern«, antwortete Donna Elisabeth, und
machte Anstalten ihn zu ergreifen; doch da dieser über das
Unrecht, das ihm geschah, kläglich schrie, und auf keine Art
darein[32] willigte, so sagte Josephe lächelnd, daß sie ihn nur
behalten wolle, und küßte ihn wieder still. Hierauf bot Don
Fernando, dem die ganze Würdigkeit und Anmut ihres Betragens sehr gefiel, ihr den Arm; Jeronimo, welcher den kleinen
Philipp trug, führte Donna Constanzen; die übrigen Mitglieder,
die sich bei der Gesellschaft eingefunden hatten, folgten; und
in dieser Ordnung ging der Zug nach der Stadt.

by the earthquake—by the prelate of the monastery himself,
who would implore Heaven to preserve them from further
calamity.

People were already on the move from every quarter, streaming toward the city. In Don Fernando's group the question was
raised whether they too ought not to take part in this celebration
and join the general concourse of humanity. Dona Elizabeth
reminded them, with some anxiety, of the unhappy event that
had occurred in the church yesterday; such festivals of
thanksgiving would be repeated; they could then abandon
themselves to their emotions with greater calm and serenity
because the danger would be further removed. Josepha jumped
to her feet with a measure of enthusiasm and said that she had
never before felt a keener urge to prostrate her face in the
dust before her Creator than at this moment when he was
manifesting his sublime and incomprehensible power in this
way. Don Elvira vigorously supported Josepha's opinion. She
insisted that they should attend the mass and urged Don
Fernando to lead the group; whereupon everyone, including
Dona Elizabeth, stood up. But when they noticed that the latter
was carrying out the trifling preparations for the trip with hesitation and with heaving breast, they asked her what was wrong.
She replied that she didn't know but had a premonition of
disaster. Dona Elvira soothed her and urged her to stay behind
with her and her sick father. Josepha said: "Will you then take
this little darling from me, Dona Elizabeth? You see, he's found
his way to me again." "Gladly," replied Dona Elizabeth and
prepared to take the child. But as the infant set up a wail at
the injustice that was being done him and in no way consented
to the plan, Josepha said with a smile that she would just keep
him and subdued him into silence with kisses. Don Fernando,
who was very much taken by the charm and dignity of Josepha's
behavior, offered her his arm. Jeronimo, with little Philip on
his arm, escorted Dona Constanza; the other members of the
company followed. In this order the procession moved toward
the city.

Sie waren kaum fünfzig Schritte gegangen, als man Donna
Elisabeth, welche inzwischen heftig und heimlich mit Donna
Elvire gesprochen hatte:»Don Fernando!« rufen hörte, und
dem Zuge mit unruhigen Tritten nacheilen sah. Don Fernando
hielt, und kehrte sich um; harrte ihrer, ohne Josephen loszu-
lassen, und fragte, da sie, gleich als ob sie auf sein Entgegen-
kommen wartete, in einiger Ferne stehen blieb: was sie wolle?
Donna Elisabeth näherte sich ihm hierauf, obschon, wie es
schien, mit Widerwillen, und raunte ihm, doch so, daß Josephe
es nicht hören konnte, einige Worte ins Ohr.»Nun?« fragte
Don Fernando:»und das Unglück, das daraus entstehen kann?«
Donna Elisabeth fuhr fort, ihm mit verstörtem Gesicht ins Ohr
zu zischeln. Don Fernando[33] stieg eine Röte des Unwillens ins
Gesicht; er antwortete: es wäre gut! Donna Elvire möchte sich
beruhigen; und führte seine Dame weiter.

Als sie in der Kirche der Dominikaner ankamen, ließ sich
die Orgel schon mit musikalischer Pracht hören, und eine unermeßliche Menschenmenge wogte darin. Das Gedränge er-
streckte sich bis weit vor den Portalen auf den Vorplatz der
Kirche hinaus, und an den Wänden hoch, in den Rahmen der
Gemälde, hingen Knaben, und hielten mit erwartungsvollen
Blicken ihre Mützen in der Hand. Von allen Kronleuchtern
strahlte es herab, die Pfeiler warfen, bei der einbrechenden
Dämmerung, geheimnisvolle Schatten, die große von gefärb-
tem Glas gearbeitete Rose in der Kirche[34] äußerstem Hintergrunde glühte, wie die Abendsonne selbst, die sie erleuchtete,
und Stille herrschte, da die Orgel jetzt schwieg, in der ganzen
Versammlung, als hätte keiner einen Laut in der Brust. Niemals
schlug aus einem christlichen Dom eine solche Flamme der
Inbrunst gen[35] Himmel, wie heute aus dem Dominikanerdom
zu St. Jago; und keine menschliche Brust gab wärmere Glut
dazu her, als Jeronimos und Josephens!

Die Feierlichkeit fing mit einer Predigt an, die der ältesten
Chorherren einer,[36] mit dem Festschmuck angetan, von der
Kanzel hielt. Er begann gleich mit Lob, Preis und Dank,
seine zitternden, vom Chorhemde weit umflossenen Hände
hoch gen Himmel erhebend, daß noch Menschen seien, auf
diesem, in Trümmer zerfallenden Teile der Welt, fähig, zu
Gott empor zu stammeln. Er schilderte, was auf den Wink

They had scarcely taken fifty steps when Dona Elizabeth, who had been conferring secretly and excitedly with Dona Elvira, was heard to call "Don Fernando!" and seen hurrying after the procession with uneasy steps. Don Fernando stopped and turned around. Without letting go of Josepha's arm, he waited for her; since she halted at some distance from them, as if expecting him to come to her, he asked what she wanted. Dona Elizabeth approached him, though with seeming reluctance, and whispered a few words in his ear so that Josepha might not hear what she said. "Well," asked Fernando, "what misfortune can come from that?" Dona Elizabeth continued to whisper into his ear with a look of distress on her face. Don Fernando turned red with displeasure. It was all right, he replied; she could set her mind at rest; and he continued to escort his lady.

When they arrived at the Dominican church, the organ was already sending forth its splendid tones, and a countless mass of humanity surged within its walls. The throng extended far beyond the portals into the square in front of the church. High up on the walls, in the frames of the paintings, boys were perched, cap in hand, with a look of expectancy in their eyes. Light streamed from all the chandeliers; the pillars cast mysterious shadows in the approaching twilight. The great stained-glass rose window in the background of the church glowed like the evening sun by which it was illuminated. When the organ stopped, silence reigned in the whole congregation, as if everyone there had been deprived of speech. Never before had such a flame of devotion leaped toward Heaven from a Christian cathedral as it did today from the Dominican church at Santiago; and no human heart added warmer fire to this flame than Jeronimo's and Josepha's.

The service began with a sermon, delivered by one of the senior canons attired in festive robes. Raising his trembling hands to Heaven, extending them out of the ample sleeves of his surplice, he began by offering praise and thanks to God that there were still human beings in this crumbling section of the world who were capable of stammering praise to God. He described what had happened at the bidding of the Almighty;

des Allmächtigen geschehen war; das Weltgericht kann nicht
entsetzlicher sein; und als er das gestrige Erdbeben gleichwohl,
auf einen Riß, den der Dom erhalten hatte, hinzeigend, einen
bloßen Vorboten davon nannte, lief ein Schauder über die
ganze Versammlung. Hierauf kam er, im Flusse priesterlicher
Beredsamkeit, auf das Sittenverderbnis der Stadt; Greuel, wie
Sodom und Gomorrha sie nicht sahen, straft'[37] er an ihr; und
nur der unendlichen Langmut Gottes schrieb er es zu, daß sie
noch nicht gänzlich vom Erdboden vertilgt worden sei.

Aber wie dem Dolche gleich fuhr es durch die von dieser
Predigt schon ganz zerrissenen Herzen unserer beiden Un-
glücklichen, als der Chorherr bei dieser Gelegenheit umständ-
lich des Frevels erwähnte, der in dem Klostergarten der
Karmeliterinnen verübt worden war; die Schonung, die er bei
der Welt gefunden hatte, gottlos nannte, und in einer von
Verwünschungen erfüllten Seitenwendung, die Seelen der
Täter, wörtlich genannt, allen Fürsten der Hölle übergab!
Donna Constanze rief, indem sie an Jeronimos Armen zuckte:
»Don Fernando!« Doch dieser antwortete so nachdrücklich
und doch so heimlich, wie sich beides verbinden ließ: »Sie
schweigen, Donna, Sie rühren auch den Augapfel nicht, und
tun,[38] als ob Sie in eine Ohnmacht versänken; worauf wir die
Kirche verlassen.« Doch, ehe Donna Constanze diese sinnreiche
zur Rettung erfundene Maßregel noch ausgeführt hatte, rief
schon eine Stimme, des Chorherrn Predigt laut unterbrechend,
aus: »Weichet[39] fern hinweg, ihr Bürger von St. Jago, hier stehen diese gottlosen Menschen!« Und als eine andere Stimme
schreckenvoll, indessen sich ein weiter Kreis des Entsetzens um
sie bildete, fragte: »Wo?«—»Hier!« versetzte ein Dritter, und
zog, heiliger Ruchlosigkeit voll, Josephen bei den Haaren
nieder, daß sie mit Don Fernandos Sohne zu Boden getaumelt
wäre, wenn dieser sie nicht gehalten hätte. »Seid ihr wahnsinnig?« rief der Jüngling, und schlug den Arm um Josephen:
»ich bin Don Fernando Ormez, Sohn des Kommandanten der
Stadt, den ihr alle kennt.« »Don Fernando Ormez?« rief, dicht
vor ihn hingestellt, ein Schuhflicker, der für Josephen gear-
beitet hatte, und diese wenigstens so genau kannte, als ihre
kleinen Füße. »Wer ist der Vater zu diesem Kinde?« wandte

Judgment Day could not be more terrible. Pointing to the one crack that the cathedral had received in yesterday's earthquake, he referred to the catastrophe as a mere precursor of worse to come. At this a shudder ran through the whole congregation. Carried away by the torrent of ecclesiastical eloquence, he went on to speak of the moral corruption in the city; he lashed out at horrors, the like of which were unknown even in Sodom and Gomorrah. That the city had not suffered total annihilation from the face of the earth could only be ascribed to the infinite mercy of a long-suffering God.

But when the canon seized the occasion to refer in detail to the sacrilege that had been committed in the convent garden of the Carmelite nuns, the already lacerated hearts of our two unfortunates were pierced as if by a dagger. The indulgence with which the crime had been treated by society he branded as godless. In an aside filled with imprecations, he consigned the souls of the perpetrators, whom he singled out by name, to all the princes of hell. Dona Constanza, tugging at Jeronimo's arm, cried: "Don Fernando!" The latter replied, as emphatically as he could without raising his voice, "Not a word, Dona, not a move of your eyeballs; pretend you've fainted and we'll leave the church." But even before Dona Constanza could carry out this clever stratagem for saving themselves, a loud voice interrupted the canon's sermon: "Make room, citizens of Santiago, here stand these godless people!" A wide circle of horror formed about them and another frightened voice asked: "Where?" "Here," replied a third person; and, filled with a holy malice, he pulled Josepha down by the hair, so that she would have struck the floor with Don Fernando's son if Fernando had not caught her. "Are you mad?" the youth shouted to the crowd, as he put his arm around Josepha. "I am Don Fernando Ormez, the son of the Commandant of the city, known to you all." "Don Fernando Ormez?" cried a cobbler who was standing near him and who had worked for Josepha and knew her as well as he knew her dainty feet. "Who is the father of this child?" he shouted to Asteron's daughter with insolent defiance. At this question Don Fernando turned pale. He first looked uncertainly at Jeronimo, then he scanned the congregation for someone who might know him. Josepha, tormented by the horror of the

er sich mit frechem Trotz zur Tochter Asterons. Don Fernando erblaßte bei dieser Frage. Er sah bald den Jeronimo schüchtern an, bald überflog er die Versammlung, ob nicht einer sei, der ihn kenne? Josephe rief, von entsetzlichen Verhältnissen gedrängt: »Dies ist nicht mein Kind, Meister Pedrillo, wie Er[40] glaubt«; indem sie, in unendlicher Angst der Seele, auf Don Fernando blickte. »Dieser junge Herr ist Don Fernando Ormez, Sohn des Kommandanten der Stadt, den ihr alle kennt!« Der Schuster fragte: »Wer von euch, ihr Bürger, kennt diesen jungen Mann?« Und mehrere der Umstehenden wiederholten: »Wer kennt den Jeronimo Rugera? Der trete vor!« Nun traf es sich, daß in demselben Augenblicke der kleine Juan, durch den Tumult erschreckt, von Josephens Brust weg Don Fernando[41] in die Arme strebte. Hierauf: »Er *ist* der Vater!« schrie eine Stimme; und: »Er *ist* Jeronimo Rugera!« eine andere: und: »Sie *sind* die gotteslästerlichen Menschen!« eine dritte; und: »Steinigt sie! steinigt sie!« die ganze im Tempel Jesu versammelte Christenheit! Drauf jetzt Jeronimo: »Halt! Ihr Unmenschlichen! Wenn ihr den Jeronimo Rugera sucht: hier ist er! Befreit jenen Mann, welcher unschuldig ist!«

Der wütende Haufen, durch die Äußerung Jeronimos verwirrt, stutzte; meherere Hände ließen Don Fernando los; und da in demselben Augenblick ein Marine-Offizier von bedeutendem Rang herbeieilte, und, indem er sich durch den Tumult drängte, fragte: »Don Fernando Ormez! Was ist Euch widerfahren?« so antwortete dieser, nun völlig befreit, mit wahrer heldenmütiger Besonnenheit: »Ja, sehen Sie, Don Alonzo, die Mordknechte! Ich wäre verloren gewesen, wenn dieser würdige Mann sich nicht, die rasende Menge zu beruhigen, für Jeronimo Rugera ausgegeben hätte. Verhaften Sie ihn, wenn Sie die Güte haben wollen, nebst dieser jungen Dame, zu ihrer beiderseitigen Sicherheit; und diesen Nichtswürdigen«, indem er Meister Pedrillo ergriff, »der den ganzen Aufruhr angezettelt hat!« Der Schuster rief: »Don Alonzo Onoreja, ich frage Euch auf Euer Gewissen, ist dieses Mädchen nicht Josephe Asteron?« Da nun Don Alonzo, welcher Josephen sehr genau kannte, mit der Antwort zauderte, und mehrere Stimmen, dadurch von neuem zur Wut entflammt, riefen: »Sie ists, sie ists!« und: »Bringt

situation, cried: "This is not my child, Master Pedrillo, as you seem to think," looking at Don Fernando in the infinite anguish of her soul. "This young gentleman is Don Fernando Ormez, son of the Commandant of the city, whom you all know." The cobbler asked: "Who among you, citizens, knows this young man?" Several of the crowd repeated: "Who knows Jeronimo Rugera? Let him come forward." Now it happened that at this moment little Juan, frightened by the uproar, strained away from Josepha toward Don Fernando. Whereupon a voice shrieked: "He *is* the father!" and another: "He *is* Jeronimo Rugera!" and a third: "They *are* the blasphemers!" And then all of Christendom assembled in the temple of Jesus screamed: "Stone them! stone them!" At this point Jeronimo shouted: "Stop! you inhuman people. If you are looking for Jeronimo Rugera, here he is. Free that man, who is innocent."

Confused by Jeronimo's words, the raging mob hesitated; several hands released Don Fernando; at that moment a naval officer of high rank forced his way through the crowd and hastened to the little group. "Don Fernando Ormez," he asked, "what has happened?" Don Fernando, now completely free, replied with truly heroic calm: "Why, look at these assassins, Don Alonzo. I would have been lost if this worthy man, to calm the raving mob, had not identified himself as Jeronimo Rugera. Arrest him, if you will be good enough, together with this young lady, for their own security; and this villain too," seizing Master Pedrillo, "who instigated the whole uproar." The cobbler cried: "Don Alonzo Onoreja, I ask you on your conscience, is this girl not Josepha Asteron?" Don Alonzo, who knew Josepha very well, hestitated, and several voices, stirred to new fury, cried: "She is! she is!" and "kill her!" Josepha therefore handed little Philip, whom Jeronimo had until now held on his arm, and little Juan to Don Fernando and said: "Go, Don Fernando, save your two children and leave us to our fate."

sie zu Tode!« so setzte Josephe den kleinen Philipp, den Je-
ronimo bisher getragen hatte, samt dem kleinen Juan, auf Don
Fernandos Arm, und sprach: »Gehn Sie, Don Fernando, retten
Sie Ihre beiden Kinder, und überlassen Sie uns unserm
Schicksale!«

Don Fernando nahm die beiden Kinder und sagte: er wolle
eher umkommen, als zugeben, daß seiner Gesellschaft etwas
zu Leide geschehe. Er bot Josephen, nachdem er sich den
Degen des Marine-Offiziers ausgebeten[42] hatte, den Arm, und
forderte das hintere Paar auf, ihm zu folgen. Sie kamen auch
wirklich, indem man ihnen, bei solchen Anstalten, mit hin-
länglicher Ehrerbietigkeit Platz machte, aus der Kirche heraus,
und glaubten sich gerettet. Doch kaum waren sie auf den von
Menschen gleichfalls erfüllten Vorplatz derselben[43] getreten,
als eine Stimme aus dem rasenden Haufen, der sie verfolgt
hatte, rief: »Dies ist Jeronimo Rugera, ihr Bürger, denn ich
bin sein eigner Vater!« und ihn an Donna Constanzens Seite
mit einem ungeheuren Keulenschlage zu Boden streckte. »Jesus
Maria!« rief Donna Constanze, und floh zu ihrem Schwager;
doch: »Klostermetze!« erscholl es schon, mit einem zweiten
Keulenschlage, von einer andern Seite, der sie leblos neben
Jeronimo niederwarf. »Ungeheuer!« rief ein Unbekannter:
»Dies war Donna Constanze Xares!« »Warum belogen sie uns!«
antwortete der Schuster; »sucht die rechte auf, und bringt sie
um!« Don Fernando, als er Constanzens Leichnam erblickte,
glühte vor Zorn; er zog und schwang das Schwert, und hieb,[44]
daß er ihn gespalten hätte, den fanatischen Mordknecht, der
diese Greuel veranlaßte, wenn derselbe nicht, durch eine Wendung, dem wütenden Schlag entwichen wäre. Doch da er die
Menge, die auf ihn eindrang, nicht überwältigen konnte:
»Leben Sie wohl, Don Fernando mit den Kindern!« rief
Josephe—und: »Hier mordet mich, ihr blutdürstenden Tiger!«
und stürzte sich freiwillig unter sie, um dem Kampf ein Ende
zu machen. Meister Pedrillo schlug sie mit der Keule nieder.
Darauf ganz mit ihrem Blute bespritzt: »Schickt ihr den Bastard zur Hölle nach!« rief er, und drang, mit noch ungesättig-
ter Mordlust, von neuem vor.

Don Fernando, dieser göttliche Held, stand jetzt, den Rücken
an die Kirche gelehnt; in der Linken hielt er die Kinder, in

Don Fernando took the two children and said he would sooner perish than allow his companions to be harmed. Borrowing the naval officer's sword, he offered his arm to Josepha and ordered the couple to follow behind him. They did manage to get out of the church, as these maneuvers secured them a respectable distance from the bystanders, and they thought they were saved. But they had scarcely reached the square in front of the church, which was likewise teeming with people, when a voice from the fanatical band that had followed them cried: "This is Jeronimo Rugera, citizens, for I'm his own father!" A terrific blow from a club struck Jeronimo down at Dona Constanza's side. "Jesus and Mary!" cried Dona Constanza as she ran to her brother-in-law. But already a second voice roared from another quarter: "Convent whore!" and another blow from a club stretched her lifeless at Jeronimo's side. "Monster!" cried an unknown man. "That was Dona Constanza Xares!" "Why did they lie to us?" replied the cobbler. "Seek out the right one and kill her." At the sight of Dona Constanza's corpse Don Fernando burned with anger. He drew his sword, swung it, and lunged at the fanatical murderous slave who had caused these horrors. He would have split the fellow in two if the cobbler had not avoided the furious thrust by a deft turn. But as Fernando could not cope with the mob that was pressing in on him, Josepha cried: "Farewell, Don Fernando, farewell children. Here, murder me, you bloodthirsty tigers!" and rushed deliberately into their midst so as to put an end to the fighting. Master Pedrillo felled her with his club. Then, covered with her blood, he screamed: "Send her bastard to hell after her!" and rushed forward again, his lust to kill still unsated.

Don Fernando, that divine hero, now stood with his back to the church. In his left arm he held the children, in his right

der Rechten das Schwert. Mit jedem Hiebe wetterstrahlte[45] er
einen zu Boden; ein Löwe wehrt sich nicht besser. Sieben
Bluthunde lagen tot vor ihm, der Fürst der satanischen Rotte
selbst war verwundet. Doch Meister Pedrillo ruhte nicht eher,
als bis er der Kinder eines bei den Beinen von seiner Brust
gerissen, und, hochher im Kreise geschwungen, an eines Kirch-
pfeilers Ecke zerschmettert hatte. Hierauf ward es still, und
alles entfernte sich. Don Fernando, als er seinen kleinen Juan
vor sich liegen sah, mit aus dem Hirne vorquellendem Mark,
hob, voll namenlosen Schmerzes, seine Augen gen Himmel.

Der Marine-Offizier fand sich wieder bei ihm ein, suchte ihn
zu trösten, und versicherte ihn, daß seine Untätigkeit bei diesem
Unglück, obschon durch mehrere Umstände gerechtfertigt,
ihn reue; doch Don Fernando sagte, daß ihm nichts vorzuwer-
fen sei, und bat ihn nur, die Leichname jetzt fortschaffen zu
helfen. Man trug sie alle, bei der Finsternis der einbrechenden
Nacht, in Don Alonzos Wohnung, wohin Don Fernando ihnen,
viel über das Antlitz des kleinen Philipp weinend, folgte. Er
übernachtete auch bei Don Alonzo, und säumte lange, unter
falschen Vorspiegelungen, seine Gemahlin von dem ganzen
Umfang des Unglücks zu unterrichten; einmal, weil sie krank
war, und dann, weil er auch nicht wußte, wie sie sein Verhalten
bei dieser Begebenheit beurteilen würde; doch kurze Zeit
nachher, durch einen Besuch zufällig von allem, was geschehen
war, benachrichtigt, weinte diese treffliche Dame im Stillen
ihren mütterlichen Schmerz aus, und fiel ihm mit dem Rest
einer erglänzenden Träne eines Morgens um den Hals und
küßte ihn. Don Fernando und Donna Elvire nahmen hierauf
den kleinen Fremdling zum Pflegesohn an; und wenn Don
Fernando Philippen mit Juan verglich, und wie er beide erworben hatte, so war es ihm fast, als müßt' er sich freuen.

hand the sword. With every blow that he gave, he struck down a victim; a lion does not protect himself better. Seven of the bruisers lay dead before him, the prince of the satanic pack himself was wounded. But Master Pedrillo did not rest until he had snatched one of the children by the legs from Don Fernando's arm and, swinging it high above his head, dashed its body against the edge of a church pillar. Then silence reigned and the mob dispersed. Seeing his little Juan lying before him with marrow flowing from his brain, Don Fernando raised his eyes to Heaven, overcome by inexpressible pain.

The naval officer appeared again, sought to comfort him and assured him that he repented of his passive role in this calamity, though it could be justified by several circumstances. Don Fernando told him that he had nothing to reproach himself with and only asked his help in removing the corpses. In the dusk of the approaching night they carried the bodies into Don Alonzo's house, followed by Don Fernando shedding many tears, which fell on little Philip's face. He spent the night at Don Alonzo's and for a long time, under spurious pretexts, he hesitated to inform his wife of the total extent of the catastrophe; first because she was ill, and then because he did not know how she would judge his conduct in this event. But a short time later she learned by chance from a visitor all that had happened. The excellent lady silently cried out her motherly grief; then one morning she threw her arms around her husband's neck and kissed him, the remnant of a glistening tear in her eyes. Don Fernando and Dona Elvira then adopted the little stranger as their son; and whenever Fernando compared Philip with Juan and thought of the way he had acquired them both, it almost seemed as though he must rejoice.

Notes: Kleist, *Das Erdbeben in Chili*

1. *Frauen*, obsolete genitive singular.

2. *Fronleichnamsfest*, Corpus Christi festival, celebrated in the Roman Catholic church in honor of the Eucharist on the Thursday after Trinity Sunday, which is the Sunday after Pentecost, which is the seventh Sunday after Easter, which is the first Sunday after full moon after the vernal equinox, which falls on or after March 21.

3. *ward*, older form of *wurde*.

4. *Fittich* = *pinion*, poetical synonym for *Flügel*.

5. *gleich*, literally: at once.

6. *nach der Straße zu*, toward the street.

7. *der . . . Gebäudes*, a long adjectival phrase; literally: the fall of the opposing building (i.e., on the opposite side of the street) meeting the slow fall of the first building.

8. *im Freien*, in the open [air].

9. *mochte gelegen haben*, may have lain.

10. *sich erinnern*, generally with *an* and the accusative; older usage: with the genitive.

11. *sich erfreuen*, with the genitive case.

12. *desselben*, refers to *Gefängnisses*.

13. *ihrer*, refers to *Hinrichtung*.

14. *derselben*, refers to *Menschen*.

15. *Ahndung*, punishment, retribution; here used for *Ahnung* presentiment.

16. *die Hände . . . zusammenschlagen*, a sign of astonishment or grief.

17. *harren* = modern *warten*.

18. The definite article before a name indicates endearment or admiration but also contempt. Here it probably denotes endearment, indicated in the English by *her*.

19. *Conception*, a provincial capital on the coast of Chile, south of Santiago.

20. *Wurm*, an affectionate designation for a child: tot, mite.

21. *Seele* = *soul*, psyche; often used in German for mind or heart.

22. *Einhalt tun*, put a stop.

23. *Seligen*, the blessed.

24. *Wohltat*, literally: beneficence, kindness.

25. *bei . . . Gemüter*, literally: in view of this mood of the spirits. *Gemüt* is a multifaceted word meaning spirit, soul, heart, feeling, state of mind, temperament, disposition.

26. *Fußfall*, prostration.

27. *ja*, indeed, of course, no doubt.

28. *alsdann* = *dann.*
29. *Antlitz,* countenance.
30. *entwickeln,* develop.
31. *alles,* everyone.
32. *darein,* literally: into it.
33. *Don Fernando,* a dative; the subject of the sentence is *eine Röte des Unwillens.*
34. *der Kirche* a genitive depending on *Hintergrunde.*
35. *gen* = *gegen.*
36. *einer,* inversion of *einer der ältesten Chorherren.*
37. *straft'* = *strafte* literally: punished.
38. *tun,* act.
39. *weichen,* yield, retreat, make way.
40. *Er,* older form of address used to both superiors and inferiors.
41. *Don Fernando,* dative case, as above in note 33.
42. *sich ausbitten,* to request and obtain.
43. *derselben* refers to *Kirche.*
44. *hieb,* past tense of *hauen* (participle: *gehauen*), strike, hew.
45. *wetterstrahlen,* a Kleistian invention; to strike with the speed of lightning (*Wetterstrahl*).

Ernst Theodor Amadeus Hoffmann

1776–1822

Hoffmann took the middle name Amadeus out of admiration for the genius of Mozart. Hoffmann himself was a man of many talents: a writer of fiction, a painter, a singer, a composer, a theater director, an orchestra conductor, a music critic; he was also a capable and enlightened judge and civil servant. He came from a family of jurists, studied law himself, and embarked on a career in the law. His fortunes suffered from the turmoil caused by the Napoleonic Wars and his own satirical bent. For some years he made his living as music director in theaters at Hamburg and Dresden and as a journalist. At the same time he composed music and wrote fiction. In 1814 he was appointed Councillor of the Court of Appeals in Berlin, a post he held for the rest of his life.

Like so many of the romantic writers, Hoffmann was a divided soul. He was a Utopian dreamer, imbued with a lofty idealism, seeking the Infinite; but he was also tragically conscious of the downward pull that reality exerts on the dreamer. This conflict is central in his work. It takes two forms: the

perpetual war waged in society between the artist and the philistine and the conflict in the soul of the artist himself, who is
torn between his urge to live for the ideal and the counterurge
to enjoy the life of the senses. This theme is set on the background of the supernatural, the fairy-tale, the grotesque and
macabre. He was known as "Spuk" Hoffmann because he filled
his novels and tales with occult phenomena: magnetism, mes-
merism, telepathy, *Doppelgänger*, robots, ghosts. He brought
into German literature the theme *die Tücke des Objekts*, the malice
practiced by inanimate objects which thwart and frustrate
people, especially those of high intellect.[1] It was through this
dark side of romanticism that Hoffmann's influence on world
literature has been greatest.

●

Don Juan, written in 1812 and published the following year,
is one of Hoffmann's earliest tales. It deals with a subject that
was dear to the romantics: the nature of the artistic process,
the total domination of life by art, and the position of the
misunderstood artist in bourgeois society. At the story's core is
a highly original interpretation of Mozart's opera *Don Giovanni*,
conceived with a depth that was unknown in music criticism at
the time. Don Juan is seen as a great Luciferian idealist under
the influence of the devil; he is a cousin to Milton's Satan and
later satanic figures like Byron's Manfred, Oscar Wilde's Dorian
Gray, and Thomas Mann's Adrian Leverkühn. He also has
certain affinities with Goethe's Faust. Like Faust, Don Juan is
a restless seeker, wanderer, a dynamic soul possessed by the
demon of Infinity, which he seeks to attain through erotic
experience.

The letter that the narrator writes to his friend is an essay
in literary interpretation. As Don Juan stands out above the
people who surround him by virtue of his tragic, though evil,
greatness, so Donna Anna is presented as a rare, noble soul, a
pure, loving woman who recognizes Don Juan's heroic stature
and suffers from the knowledge that for all his greatness he is
a damned soul. Her mission is to save him from his demonic

[1]See page 411, 3.

possession, but she comes into his life too late to accomplish this. The story hints that after her relationship with the titan Juan, a life with the philistine Ottavio will destroy her. This total devotion to the service of greatness and beauty is represented also by the Italian actress who plays the role of Donna Anna in the opera. At the very moment when she appears in a vision to the narrator-artist, she makes the ultimate sacrifice for her love of art. The final scene brings us back to the world of banality, characterized by the vapid talk of the philistines. But the tale is pervaded by the ideal spirit of art, by Mozart's incomparable music and his profound vision of the tragic aspect of life.

Drawing by E.T.A. Hoffmann

Don Juan

Eine fabelhafte Begebenheit
die sich mit einem reisenden Enthusiasten zugetragen

Ein durchdringendes Läuten, der gellende Ruf: „Das Theater
fängt an!" weckte mich aus dem sanften Schlaf, in den ich
versunken war; Bässe brummen durcheinander—ein Pauken-
schlag—Trompetenstöße—ein klares A, von der Hoboe ausge-
halten—Violinen stimmen ein: ich reibe mir die Augen. Sollte
der allezeit geschäftige Satan mich im Rausche—? Nein! ich
befinde mich in dem Zimmer des Hotels, wo ich gestern abend
halb gerädert abgestiegen. Gerade über meiner Nase hängt die
stattliche Troddel der Klingelschnur; ich ziehe sie heftig an,
der Kellner erscheint.

„Aber was, ums Himmelswillen, soll die konfuse Musik da
neben mir bedeuten? gibt es denn ein Konzert hier im Hause?"

„Ew.[1] Exzellenz"—(ich hatte mittags an der Wirtstafel[2] Cham-
pagner getrunken!)—„Ew. Exzellenz wissen vielleicht noch
nicht, daß dieses Hotel mit dem Theater verbunden ist. Diese
Tapetentür führt auf einen kleinen Korridor, von dem Sie
unmittelbar in Nr. 23 treten: das ist die Fremdenloge."

„Was?—Theater?—Fremdenloge?"

„Ja, die kleine Fremdenloge zu zwei, höchstens drei Per-
sonen—nur so für vornehme Herren, ganz grün tapeziert, mit
Gitterfenstern, dicht beim Theater! Wenn's Ew. Exzellenz ge-
fällig ist—wir führen heute den 'Don Juan' von dem berühmten
Herrn Mozart aus Wien auf. Das Legegeld, einen Taler[3] acht
Groschen, stellen wir in Rechnung."[4]

Das Letzte sagte er, schon die Logentür aufdrückend, so
rasch war ich bei dem Worte Don Juan durch die Tapetentür
in den Korridor geschritten. Das Haus war für den mittel-

Don Juan

A Fabulous Incident
That Happened to a Traveling Enthusiast

A penetrating peal, the shrill cry: "The show is beginning!" woke me out of the gentle sleep into which I had sunk. Bass fiddles rumble in confusion—a bass drum beats—trumpets blare—a clear A, sustained by the oboe—violins tune up: I rub my eyes. Can it be that Satan, ever busy, has caught me in a state of intoxication? No, I am in the room of the hotel where I put up last night, half dead from exhaustion. Right above my nose hangs the elegant tassel of the bell rope; I give it a violent tug, the waiter appears.

"What in Heaven's name can be the meaning of the confused music near me? Is there a concert here in the house?"

"Your Excellency!" (I had drunk champagne in the inn at noon!) "Perhaps Your Excellency doesn't know yet that this hotel is connected with the theater. This door covered with wallpaper leads to a small hallway, out of which you step directly into No. 23: that is the visitors' box."

"What?—theater?—a visitors' box?"

"Yes, the small visitors' box for two or, at the most, three people—only for gentlemen of quality, decorated all in green, with latticed windows, close to the stage. If it please Your Excellency—today we're performing *Don Juan* by the famous Herr Mozart from Vienna. The entrance fee, a thaler and eight groschen, can be added to the bill."

He spoke the last words as he was already pushing open the loge door, so swiftly had I stepped into the hall through the papered door at the sound of the words "Don Juan." For this

mäßigen Ort geräumig, geschmackvoll verziert und glänzend erleuchtet. Logen und Parterre waren gedrängt voll. Die ersten Akkorde der Ouvertüre überzeugten mich, daß ein ganz vortreffliches Orchester, sollten die Sänger auch nur im mindesten etwas leisten, mir den herrlichsten Genuß des Meisterwerks verschaffen würde. In dem Andante ergriffen mich die Schauer des furchtbaren, unterirdischen *regno all pianto;*[5] grausenerregende Ahnungen des Entsetzlichen erfüllten mein Gemüt. Wie ein jauchzender Frevel klang mir die jubelnde Fanfare im siebenten Takte des Allegro; ich sah aus tiefer Nacht feurige Dämonen ihre glühenden Krallen ausstrecken—nach dem Leben froher Menschen, die auf des bodenlosen Abgrunds dünner Decke lustig tanzten. Der Konflikt der menschlichen Natur mit den unbekannten, gräßlichen Mächten, die ihn, sein Verderben erlauernd, umfangen, trat klar vor meines Geistes Augen. Endlich beruhigt sich der Sturm; der Vorhang fliegt auf. Frostig und unmutvoll in seinen Mantel gehüllt, schreitet Leporello in finstrer Nacht vor dem Pavillon einher: *"Notte e giorno faticar."*[6]—Also italienisch?—Hier am deutschen Ort italienisch? *Ah che piacere!*[7] ich werde alle Rezitative, alles so hören, wie es der große Meister in seinem Gemüt empfing und dachte! Da stürzt Don Juan heraus; hinter ihm Donna Anna, bei dem Mantel den Frevler festhaltend. Welches Ansehen! Sie könnte höher, schlanker gewachsen, majestätischer im Gange sein: aber welch ein Kopf!—Augen, aus denen Liebe, Zorn, Haß, Verzweiflung, wie aus e i n e m Brennpunkt eine Strahlenpyramide blitzender Funken werfen, die wie griechisches Feuer unauslöschlich das Innerste durchbrennen! Des dunklen Haares aufgelöste Flechten wallen in Wellenringeln den Nakken hinab. Das weiße Nachtkleid enthüllt verräterisch nie gefahrlos belauschte Reize. Von der entsetzlichen Tat umkrallt, zuckt das Herz in gewaltsamen Schlägen.—Und nun—welche Stimme *"Non sperar se non m'uccidi."*[8]—Durch den Sturm der Instrumente leuchten, wie glühende Blitze, die aus ätherischem Metall gegossenen Töne!—Vergebens sucht sich Don Juan loszureißen.—Will er es denn? Warum stößt er nicht mit kräftiger Faust das Weib zurück und entflieht? Macht ihn die böse Tat kraftlos, oder ist es der Kampf von Haß und Liebe im Innern, der ihm Mut und Stärke raubt?—Der alte Papa hat seine

moderate-sized town the house was spacious, decorated in good taste and brilliantly illuminated. Boxes and orchestra were filled to overflowing. The first chords of the overture convinced me that if the singers gave even a minimum performance, a very excellent orchestra would afford me the most splendid enjoyment of the masterpiece. During the andante I was gripped by the horrors of the terrible, infernal *regno al pianto;* horror inspiring premonitions of the terrible filled my mind. The jubilant fanfare in the seventh bar of the allegro sounded to me like an exultation in crime; out of the deep night I saw fiery demons stretch out their glowing claws for the lives of happy people who were dancing merrily on the thin cover of the bottomless abyss. The conflict of man's nature with the unknown, gruesome powers that surround him, waiting to destroy him, stood clearly before my mind's eye. Finally the storm calms down; the curtain rises quickly. Frosty and peevish, wrapped in his cloak, Leporello paces in front of the pavilion in the dark night: "*Notte e giorno faticar.*"—In Italian then?—Italian here in this German town? *Ah che piacere!* I shall hear all the recitatives, everything just as the great master conceived and created it in his mind! Then Don Juan rushes out; behind him Donna Anna, holding the villain tightly by his cloak. What a sight! She could be taller, slimmer in build, more majestic in her walk; but what a head!—Eyes out of which love, anger, hatred, despair hurl flashing sparks, as from the focus of a pyramid of light; eyes that burn inextinguishably through to the core, like Greek fire. The loosened tresses of her dark hair flow down the nape of her neck in waved ringlets. The white nightdress treacherously reveals charms that are never espied without danger. Clawed by the horrible deed, her heart quivers with powerful beats.—And now—what a voice! "*Non sperar se non m'uccidi.*" Through the storm of the instruments the notes, cast of ethereal metal, shine like glowing flashes of lightning.—In vain Don Juan seeks to tear himself loose.—Does he really want to? Why does he not beat the woman back with his powerful fist and flee? Does the evil deed make him powerless, or is it the conflict between hatred and love within him which robs him of his courage and strength?—The old papa has paid with his life for the folly of attacking his powerful opponent in the dark; Don

Torheit, im Finstern den kräftigen Gegner anzufallen, mit dem
Leben gebüßt; Don Juan und Leporello treten im rezitierenden
Gespräch weiter vor ins Proszenium.[9] Don Juan wickelt sich
aus dem Mantel und steht da in rotem, gerissenen Sammet mit
silberner Stickerei, prächtig gekleidet. Eine kräftige, herrliche
Gestalt: das Gesicht ist männlich schön; eine erhabene Nase,
durchbohrende Augen, weich geformte Lippen; das sonder-
bare Spiel eines Stirnmuskels über den Augenbrauen bringt
sekundenlang etwas vom Mephistopheles[10] in die Physio-
gnomie, das, ohne dem Gesicht die Schönheit zu rauben, einen
unwillkürlichen Schauer erregt. Es ist, als könne er die ma-
gische Kunst der Klapperschlange üben; es ist, als könnten die
Weiber, von ihm angeblickt, nicht mehr von ihm lassen, und
müßten, von der unheimlichen Gewalt gepackt, selbst ihr Verderben vollenden.—Lang und dürr, in rot- und weißgestreif-
ter[11] Weste, kleinem roten Mantel, weißem Hut mit roter Feder,
trippelt Leporello um ihn her. Die Züge seines Gesichts mischen
sich seltsam zu dem Ausdruck von Gutherzigkeit, Schelmerei,
Lüsternheit und ironisierender Frechheit; gegen das grauliche
Kopf- und Barthaar stechen seltsam die schwarzen Augenbrauen ab. Man merkt es, der alte Bursche verdient, Don Juans
helfender Diener zu sein.—Glücklich sind sie über die Mauer
geflüchtet.—Fackeln—Donna Anna und Don Ottavio erscheinen: ein zierliches, geputztes, gelecktes Männlein von einund-
zwanzig Jahren höchstens. Als Annas Bräutigam wohnte er, da
man ihn so schnell herbeirufen konnte, wahrscheinlich im
Hause; auf den ersten Lärm, den er gewiß hörte, hätte er her-
beieilen und den Vater retten können: er mußte sich aber erst
putzen, und mochte überhaupt nachts nicht gern sich heraus-
wagen.—*"Ma qual mai s'offre, o dei, spettacolo funesto agli occhi
miei!"*[12] Mehr als Verzweiflung über den grausamsten Frevel
liegt in den entsetzlichen, herzzerschneidenden Tönen dieses
Rezitativs und Duetts. Don Juans gewaltsames Attentat, das ihr
Verderben nur drohte, dem Vater aber den Tod gab, ist es
nicht allein, was diese Töne der beängsteten Brust[13] entreißt:
nur ein verderblicher, tötender Kampf im Innern kann sie
hervorbringen.—
    Eben schalt die lange, hagere Donna Elvira mit sichtlichen
Spuren großer, aber verblühter Schönheit den Verräter, Don

Juan and Leporello advance farther onto the proscenium in
spoken conversation. Don Juan unwraps his cloak and there
he stands splendidly dressed in a suit of red slashed velvet with
silver embroidery. A powerful, splendid figure: his face has a
masculine beauty; a prominent nose, piercing eyes, softly
formed lips; the strange play of a muscle in the forehead above
the eyebrows brings something Mephistophelian into his
physiognomy for a few seconds; without depriving the face of
its beauty, it makes one involuntarily shudder. It is as if he
were able to practice the magic art of the rattlesnake; it is as if
women, once he has looked at them, could no longer let him
go and, gripped by his uncanny power, were forced to complete
their own destruction.—Tall and lean, in his waistcoat with red
and white stripes, his little red coat, white hat with a red plume,
Leporello skips around him. The features of his face inter-
mingle strangely in an expression of good nature, roguishness,
sensuality, and ironical insolence; his black eyebrows contrast
strangely with the grayish hair on his head and in his beard.
One feels it—the old fellow deserves to be Don Juan's helpful
servant.—They have successfully escaped over the wall.—
Torches—Donna Anna and Don Ottavio appear: a dainty,
foppish, dapper little man, twenty-one years old at most. As
Anna's fiancé he probably lived in the house, since they were
able to summon him so quickly; at the first alarm, which he
had certainly heard, he could have hurried over and saved the
father: but he had to get all dressed up first, and he did not
like to venture out at night at all.—"*Ma qual mai s'offre, o dei,
spettacolo funesto agli occhi miei!*" More than despair at the most
brutal crime lies in the terrible, heartrending tones of this recitative and duet. It is not only Don Juan's violent attack, which
only threatened her with ruin but caused the death of her
father, that tears these notes from her anguished heart: only
a destructive, murderous inner struggle can produce them.—

Tall, thin Donna Elvira, with visible traces of great but faded
beauty, was just scolding the betrayer Don Juan, "*Tu nido

Juan: *"Tu nido d'inganni"*,[14] und der mitleidige Leporello bemerkte ganz klug: *"Parla come un libro stampato"*,[15] als ich jemand
neben oder hinter mir zu bemerken glaubte. Leicht konnte
man die Logentür hinter mir geöffnet haben und hineinge-
schlüpft sein—das fuhr mir wie ein Stich durchs Herz. Ich war
so glücklich, mich allein in der Loge zu befinden, um ganz
ungestört das so vollkommen dargestellte Meisterwerk mit allen
Empfindungsfasern, wie mit Polypenarmen, zu umklammern,
und in mein Selbst hineinzuziehn! ein einziges Wort, das
obendrein albern sein konnte, hätte mich auf eine schmerzhafte
Weise herausgerissen aus dem herrlichen Moment der poetisch-
musikalischen Begeisterung! Ich beschloß, von meinem Nachbar gar keine Notiz zu nehmen, sondern, ganz in die Darstellung vertieft, jedes Wort, jeden Blick zu vermeiden. Den Kopf
in die Hand gestützt, dem Nachbar den Rücken wendend,
schaute ich hinaus.—Der Gang der Darstellung entsprach dem
vortrefflichen Anfange. Die kleine, lüsterne, verliebte Zerlina
tröstete mit gar lieblichen Tönen und Weisen den gutmütigen
Tölpel Masetto. Don Juan sprach sein inneres, zerrissenes
Wesen, den Hohn über die Menschlein um ihn her, nur aufgestellt zu seiner Lust, in ihr mattliches Tun und Treiben ver-
derbend einzugreifen, in der wilden Arie: *"Fin ch'han dal
vino"*[16]—ganz unverhohlen aus. Gewaltiger als bisher zuckte
hier der Stirnmuskel.—Die Masken erscheinen. Ihr Terzett[17]
ist ein Gebet, das in rein glänzenden Strahlen zum Himmel
steigt.—Nun fliegt der Mittelvorhang auf. Da geht es lustig
her; Becher erklingen, in fröhlichem Gewühl wälzen sich die
Bauern und allerlei Masken umher, die Don Juans Fest her-
beigelockt hat.—Jetzt kommen die drei zur Rache Verschwo-
renen. Alles wird feierlicher, bis der Tanz angeht. Zerlina wird
gerettet, und in dem gewaltig donnernden Finale tritt mutig
Don Juan mit gezogenem Schwert seinen Feinden entgegen.
Er schlägt dem Bräutigam den stählernen Galanteriedegen aus
der Hand, und bahnt sich durch das gemeine Gesindel, das er,
wie der tapfere Roland[18] die Armee des Tyrannen Cymork,
durcheinander wirft, daß alles gar possierlich übereinander
purzelt, den Weg ins Freie.—
　　Schon oft glaubte ich dicht hinter mir einen zarten, warmen
Hauch gefühlt, das Knistern eines seidenen Gewandes gehört

d'inganni," and the sympathetic Leporello remarked quite clev-
erly, "*Parla come un libro stampato,*" when I thought I noticed
someone near or behind me. Someone could easily have opened
the loge door behind me and slipped in—this thought went
through my heart like a needle. I was so happy to be alone in
the box, so that I could embrace the masterpiece that was being
performed so perfectly, with every sensory fiber as with the
tentacles of an octopus, and to absorb it into my inner being;
a single word, which might moreover be a silly one, would have
torn me painfully out of the glorious moment of poetic-musical
ecstasy! I resolved to take no notice whatever of my neighbor
but, wholly engrossed in the performance, to avoid every word,
every look. With my head in my hand, my back turned to my
neighbor, I looked out.—The sequel of the performance bore
out the excellent beginning. Sensual, infatuated little Zerlina
consoled the good-natured bumpkin Masetto, in very lovely
tones and airs. In the wild aria "*Fin ch'han dal vino,*" Don Juan
frankly expressed his inner torn soul, his scorn of the petty
people around him, existing only for his pleasure, so that he
may bring ruin into their insipid doings and dealings.—The
masks appear. Their terzetto is a prayer that rises to heaven in
pure and shining rays.—Now the central curtain rises quickly.
There is a merry scene; cups ring, in a merry throng peasants
and all sorts of masks whirl about, attracted by Don Juan's
party.—Now the three conspirators appear, sworn to vengeance. Everything becomes more solemn until the dance begins. Zerlina is rescued, and in the powerfully thundering finale
Don Juan bravely goes to meet his enemies with drawn sword.
He knocks the steel dress sword out of the fiancé's hand and
makes a way for himself into the open through the common
rabble, throwing them into a confusion such as the gallant
Roland caused among the host of the tyrant Cymork, so that
they all fall over one another in very comical disorder.—

A number of times I thought I felt close behind me a gentle,
warm breath and heard the rustle of a silk dress: this naturally

zu haben: das ließ mich wohl die Gegenwart eines Frauenzimmers[19] ahnen, aber ganz versunken in die poetische Welt, die
mir die Opera aufschloß, achtete ich nicht darauf. Jetzt, da der
Vorhang gefallen war, schaute ich nach meiner Nachbarin.—
Nein—keine Worte drücken mein Erstaunen aus: Donna Anna,
ganz in dem Kostüme, wie ich sie eben auf dem Theater gesehen, stand hinter mir, und richtete auf mich den durchdringenden Blick ihres seelenvollen Auges.—Ganz sprachlos starrte ich
sie an; ihr Mund (so schien es mir) verzog sich zu einem leisen,
ironischen Lächeln, in dem ich mich spiegelte und meine alberne Figur erblickte. Ich fühlte die Notwendigkeit, sie anzureden, und konnte doch die durch das Erstaunen, ja ich möchte
sagen, wie durch den Schreck gelähmte Zunge nicht bewegen.
Endlich, endlich fuhren mir beinahe unwillkürlich die Worte
heraus: „Wie ist es möglich, Sie hier zu sehen?" worauf sie
sogleich in dem reinsten Toskanisch[20] erwiderte, daß, verstände
und spräche ich nicht Italienisch, sie das Vergnügen meiner
Unterhaltung entbehren müsse, indem sie keine andere als nur
diese Sprache rede.—Wie Gesang lauteten die süßen Worte.
Im Sprechen erhöhte sich der Ausdruck des dunkelblauen
Auges, und jeder daraus leuchtende Blitz goß einen Glutstrom
in mein Inneres, von dem alle Pulse stärker schlugen und alle
Fibern erzuckten.—Es war Donna Anna unbezweifelt. Die Möglichkeit abzuwägen, wie sie auf dem Theater und in meiner
Loge habe zugleich sein können, fiel mir nicht ein. So wie
der glückliche Traum das Seltsamste verbindet, und dann ein
frommer Glaube das Übersinnliche versteht und es den sogenannten natürlichen Erscheinungen des Lebens zwanglos
anreiht: so geriet ich auch in der Nähe des wunderbaren
Weibes in eine Art Somnambulismus, in dem ich die geheimen
Beziehungen erkannte, die mich so innig mit ihr verbanden,
daß sie selbst bei ihrer Erscheinung auf dem Theater nicht
hatte von mir weichen können.—Wie gern setzte ich dir, mein
Theodor,[21] jedes Wort des merkwürdigen Gesprächs her, das
nun zwischen der Signora und mir begann: allein, indem ich
das, was sie sagte, deutsch hinschreiben will, finde ich jedes
Wort steif und matt, jede Phrase[22] ungelenk, das auszudrücken,
was sie leicht und mit Anmut Toskanisch sagte.

led me to suspect the presence of a woman; but, wholly engrossed in the world of poetry which the opera opened before
me, I paid no attention to it. Now, after the curtain had fallen,
I looked at my neighbor.—No—no words can express my
astonishment: Donna Anna, in the very costume in which I had
just seen her on the stage, stood behind me, fixing the penetrating glance of her soulful eyes on me.—I stared at her utterly
speechless; her lips (so it seemed to me) were pursed in a gentle,
ironical smile in which I was reflected and perceived the silly
figure I cut. I felt the necessity of addressing her, and yet I
could not move my tongue, which was paralyzed by astonishment, yes, I might even say by terror. Finally, finally, almost
against my will, these words escaped me: "How is it possible to
see you here?" to which she promptly replied in the purest
Tuscan that if I did not understand or speak Italian she would
have to forgo the pleasure of conversing with me, as she spoke
no other tongue but this.—These sweet words sounded like
music. As she spoke, the expression in her dark blue eyes was
heightened and every flash of lightning that came from them
poured a stream of fire into my soul, making my pulse beat
faster and all my fibers quiver.—It was Donna Anna, without
a doubt. It did not occur to me to weigh the possibility how
she could have been on the stage and in my loge at the same
time. Just as a happy dream combines the strangest things, and
as a pious faith understands the supernatural, and then fits it
without effort into the so-called natural phenomena of life, so
too, in the presence of the amazing woman, I fell into a kind
of somnambulism in which I recognized the mysterious bonds
that united me so intimately with her, so that she had not been
able to keep away from me even when she was on the stage.—
How I would like, my dear Theodor, to put down for you every
word of the remarkable conversation that now began between
the signora and myself; but when I want to write down in
German what she said, I find every word stiff and pale, every
phrase too clumsy to express what she said in Tuscan with
lightness and grace.

Indem sie über den ‚Don Juan', über ihre Rolle sprach, war es, als öffneten sich mir nun erst die Tiefen des Meisterwerks, und ich konnte hell hineinblicken und einer fremden Welt phantastische Erscheinungen deutlich erkennen. Sie sagte, ihr ganzes Leben sei Musik, und oft glaube sie manches im Innern geheimnisvoll Verschlossene, was keine Worte aussprächen, singend zu begreifen. „Ja, ich begreife es dann wohl", fuhr sie mit brennendem Auge und erhöhter Stimme fort, „aber es bleibt tot und kalt um mich, und indem man eine schwierige Roulade,[23] eine gelungene Manier beklatscht, greifen eisige Hände in mein glühendes Herz!—Aber du—du verstehst mich, denn ich weiß, daß auch d i r das wunderbare, romantische Reich aufgegangen,[24] wo die himmlischen Zauber der Töne wohnen!"—

„Wie, du herrliche, wundervolle Frau—du—du solltest mich kennen?"

„Ging nicht der zauberische Wahnsinn ewig sehnender Liebe in der Rolle der * * * in deiner neuesten Oper aus deinem Innern hervor?—Ich habe dich verstanden: dein Gemüt hat sich im Gesange mir aufgeschlossen!—Ja" (hier nannte sie meinen Vornamen), „ich habe d i c h gesungen, sowie deine Melodien i c h sind."

Die Theaterglocke läutete: eine schnelle Blässe entfärbte Donna Annas ungeschminktes Gesicht; sie fuhr mit der Hand nach dem Herzen, als empfände sie einen plötzlichen Schmerz, und indem sie leise sagte: „Unglückliche Anna, jetzt kommen deine fürchterlichsten Momente"—war sie aus der Loge verschwunden.

Der erste Akt hatte mich entzückt, aber nach dem wunderbaren Ereignis wirkte jetzt die Musik auf eine ganz andere, seltsame Weise. Es war, als ginge eine lang verheißene Erfüllung der schönsten Träume aus einer andern Welt wirklich in das Leben ein; als würden die geheimsten Ahnungen der entzückten Seele in Tönen festgebannt und müßten sich zur wunderbarsten Erkenntnis seltsamlich gestalten.—In Donna Annas Szene fühlte ich mich von einem sanften, warmen Hauch, der über mich hinwegglitt, in trunkener Wollust erbeben; unwillkürlich schlossen sich meine Augen, und ein glü-

As she spoke about *Don Juan* and about her role, it seemed as if the depth of the masterpiece opened up before me only now; I could look into it brightly and recognize clearly the fantastic phenomena of a strange world. She said that her whole life was music, and she often thought she understood in song what was mysteriously locked up in her mind, what no words could express. "Yes, I understand it well then," she continued with burning eyes and raising her voice; "but it remains dead and cold about me, and when they applaud a difficult roulade or a successful mannerism, icy hands clutch at my glowing heart!—But you—you understand me, for I know that the marvelous, romantic realm in which the heavenly magic of the tones dwells has been opened for you, too."—

"What, you glorious, wonderful woman—you—can you possibly know me?"

"Did not the magic madness of eternally yearning love, in the role of * * * in your most recent opera, come from the depths of your soul?—I understood you; your soul revealed itself to me in song.—Yes (here she called me by my first name) I sang *you*, just as *I* am your melodies."

The intermission bell rang; a swift pallor spread over Donna Anna's unpainted face. She put her hand to her heart as if she felt a sudden pain there, and with the words: "Unhappy Anna, now your most terrible moments are coming", spoken softly— she had vanished from the box.—

The first act had enthralled me, but after the remarkable experience the music now affected me in an entirely different, strange way. It was a if a long-promised fulfillment of the most beautiful dreams from another world were really entering into life; as though the most secret premonitions of my enraptured soul were being captured in music and must assume strange shape in the most wonderful revelations.—In Donna Anna's scene I felt myself quiver with an intoxicated voluptuousness from a gentle, warm breath that floated over me. Involuntarily my eyes closed and a glowing kiss seemed to burn on my lips;

hender Kuß schien auf meinen Lippen zu brennen; aber
der Kuß war ein wie von ewig dürstender Sehnsucht lang
ausgehaltener Ton.

Das Finale war in frevelnder Lustigkeit angegangen: *"Già la
mensa è preparata!"*[25]—Don Juan saß kosend zwischen zwei
Mädchen und lüftete einen Kork nach dem andern, um den
brausenden Geistern,[26] die hermetisch verschlossen, freie Herrschaft über sich zu verstatten. Es war ein kurzes Zimmer mit
einem großen gotischen Fenster im Hintergrunde, durch das
man in die Nacht hinaussah. Schon während Elvira den Unge-
treuen an alle Schwüre erinnert, sah man es oft durch das
Fenster blitzen und hörte das dumpfe Murmeln des heranna-
henden Gewitters. Endlich das gewaltige Pochen. Elvira, die
Mädchen entfliehen, und unter den entsetzlichen Akkorden
der unterirdischen Geisterwelt tritt der gewaltige Marmorkoloß,[27] gegen den Don Juan pygmäisch[28] dasteht, ein. Der
Boden erbebt unter des Riesen donnerndem Fußtritt.—Don
Juan ruft durch den Sturm, durch den Donner, durch das
Geheul der Dämonen sein fürchterliches: *"No!"* die Stunde des
Untergangs ist da. Die Statue verschwindet, dicker Qualm erfüllt das Zimmer, aus ihm entwickeln sich fürchterliche Larven.
In Qualen der Hölle windet sich Don Juan, den man dann und
wann unter den Dämonen erblickt. Eine Explosion, wie wenn
tausend Blitze einschlügen—: Don Juan, die Dämonen, sind
verschwunden, man weiß nicht wie! Leporello liegt ohnmächtig
in der Ecke des Zimmers.—Wie wohltätig wirkt nun die
Erscheinung der übrigen Personen, die den Juan, der von
unterirdischen Mächten irdischer Rache entzogen, vergebens
suchen. Es ist, als wäre man nun erst dem furchtbaren Kreise
der höllischen Geister entronnen.—Donna Anna erschien ganz
verändert: eine Totenblässe überzog ihr Gesicht, das Auge
war erloschen, die Stimme zitternd und ungleich: aber eben
dadurch in dem kleinen Duett mit dem süßen Bräutigam, der
nun, nachdem ihn der Himmel des gefährlichen Rächeramts
glücklich überhoben hat, gleich Hochzeit machen will, von
herzzereißender Wirkung.

Der fugierte Chor hatte das Werk herrlich zu einem Ganzen
gerundet, und ich eilte, in der exaltiertesten Stimmung, in der
ich mich je befunden, in mein Zimmer. Der Kellner rief mich

but the kiss was a long note that seemed sustained by an eternally
thirsty yearning.

The finale had begun in outrageous merriment: "*Già la mensa
è preparata!*"—Don Juan sat chatting between two girls, drawing
one cork after the other, to permit the effervescent spirits,
hitherto hermetically locked in, free reign over himself. It was
a short room with a large Gothic window in the background
through which one looked out into the night. Even while Elvira
reminds the unfaithful man of all his vows, one often saw flashes
of lightning through the window and heard the muffled mur-
mur of the approaching storm. Finally the tremendous pound-
ing. Elvira and the girls flee, and amidst the horrifying chords
of the infernal spirit world, the enormous marble colossus enters; beside him Don Juan stands there like a pygmy. The
ground shakes under the thundering footsteps of the giant.—
Don Juan shouts through the storm, through the thunder,
through the howling of the demons, his terrible "*No!*"The hour
of his destruction has come. The statue vanishes, thick smoke
fills the room, out of it horrible masks emerge. Don Juan writhes
in the torments of hell; from time to time one catches sight of
him among the demons. An explosion, as though a thousand
bolts of lightning struck—: Don Juan and the demons have
vanished, one does not know how! Leporello lies unconscious
in the corner of the room.—How beneficial is the effect produced by the appearance of the other persons who look in vain
for Don Juan who has been removed from earthly vengeance
by the infernal powers.It is as if one had only now escaped
from the fearful circle of the hellish spirits.—Donna Anna
seemed quite changed: a deathlike pallor covered her face, her
eyes were dull, her voice trembling and uneven; but for this
very reason the effect is heartrending in the little duet she sings
with her sweet fiancé who, now that Heaven has happily absolved him from his dangerous vow of vengeance, wants to
celebrate the marriage at once.

The fugal chorus had rounded the work into a splendid
whole, and I hurried to my room in the most exalted frame of
mind which I had ever experienced. The waiter called me to

zur Wirtstafel, und ich folgte ihm mechanisch.—Die Gesellschaft war, der Messe wegen, glänzend, und die heutige Darstellung des ‚Don Juan' der Gegenstand des Gesprächs. Man
pries im allgemeinen die Italiener und das Eingreifende ihres
Spiels: doch zeigten kleine Bemerkungen, die hier und da ganz
schalkhaft hingeworfen wurden, daß wohl keiner die tiefere
Bedeutung der Oper aller Opern auch nur ahnte.—Don Ottavio hatte sehr gefallen. Donna Anna war einem zu leidenschaft-
lich gewesen. Man müsse, meinte er, auf dem Theater sich
hübsch mäßigen und das zu sehr Angreifende vermeiden. Die
Erzählung des Überfalls habe ihn ordentlich konsterniert.[29]
Hier nahm er eine Prise Tabak und schaute ganz unbeschreib-
lich dummklug seinen Nachbar an, welcher behauptete: Die
Italienerin sei aber übrigens eine recht schöne Frau, nur zu
wenig besorgt um Kleidung und Putz; eben in jener Szene sei
ihr eine Haarlocke aufgegangen und habe das Demiprofil des
Gesichts beschattet! Jetzt fing ein anderer ganz leise zu intonie-
ren an: *"Fin ch'han dal vino"*—worauf eine Dame bemerkte: am
wenigsten sei sie mit dem Don Juan zufrieden: der Italiener
sei viel zu finster, viel zu ernst gewesen und habe überhaupt
den frivolen, lustigen Charakter nicht leicht genug genommen.—Die letzte Explosion wurde sehr gerühmt. Des Ge-
wäsches satt, eilte ich in mein Zimmer.

In der Fremdenloge Nr. 23

Es war mir so eng, so schwül in dem dumpfen Gemach!—
Um Mitternacht glaubte ich deine Stimme zu hören, mein
Theodor! Du sprachst deutlich meinen Namen aus, und es
schien an der Tapetentür zu rauschen. Was hält mich ab, den
Ort meines wunderbaren Abenteuers noch einmal zu betreten?—Vielleicht sehe ich dich und sie, die mein ganzes Wesen
erfüllt!—Wie leicht ist es, den kleinen Tisch hineinzutragen—
zwei Lichter—Schreibzeug! Der Kellner sucht mich mit dem
bestellten Punsch; er findet das Zimmer leer, die Tapetentür
offen: er folgt mir in die Loge und sieht mich mit zweifelndem
Blick an. Auf meinen Wink setzt er das Getränk auf den Tisch
und entfernt sich, mit einer Frage auf der Zunge noch einmal

a meal and I followed him mechanically.—The company was brilliant because of the fair, and the topic of conversation was tonight's performance of *Don Juan.* There was general praise for the Italians and the incisive nature of their playing; but little remarks, rather facetiously thrown in here and there, showed that probably no one had any idea of the deeper significance of this opera of all operas.—They had all liked Don Ottavio. Donna Anna had been too passionate for one. He felt that in the theater one had to observe a nice moderation and avoid all excess of emotion. The narration of the attack had caused him real consternation. At this point he took a pinch of snuff and looked with an indescribably stupid-sly expression at his neighbor, who asserted, however, that the Italian was in other respects a really beautiful woman, only too little concerned about her dress and jewelry; in that very scene one of her curls had come loose and had cast a shadow on the semi-profile of her face. Now another man began to intone very softly: *"Fin ch'han dal vino"*—at which a lady remarked, that she was least satisfied with Don Juan; the Italian had been much too sinister, much too serious, and in general had not interpreted the frivolous, jovial character lightly enough.—The final explosion was highly praised. Tired of this rubbish I hurried to my room.

In Visitors' Box No. 23

I felt so constricted, so oppressed in the musty room!—At midnight I thought I heard your voice, my Theodor! You uttered my name clearly, and there seemed to be a rustling at the tapestried door. What prevents me from entering the site of my wonderful adventure once more?—Perhaps I will see you and her who fills my whole being!—How easy it is to carry in the little table—two candles—writing materials! The waiter looks for me with the punch I had ordered; he finds the room empty, the tapestried door stands open; he follows me into the box and looks at me with a doubtful eye. At a sign from me he puts the beverage on the table and goes away with a question on his tongue, looking back at me again. Turning my back to

sich nach mir umschauend. Ich lehne mich, ihm den Rücken
wendend, über der Loge Rand und sehe in das verödete Haus,
dessen Architektur, von meinen beiden Lichtern magisch be-
leuchtet, in wunderlichen Reflexen fremd und feenhaft hervor-
springt. Den Vorhang bewegt die das Haus durchschneidende
Zugluft.—Wie wenn er hinaufwallte? wenn Donna Anna, ge-
ängstet von gräßlichen Larven, erschiene?—„Donna Anna!"
rufe ich unwillkürlich: der Ruf verhallt in dem öden Raum,
aber die Geister der Instrumente im Orchester werden wach—
ein wunderbarer Ton zittert herauf; es ist, als säusle in ihm der
geliebte Name fort!—Nicht erwehren kann ich mich des heimlichen Schauers, aber wohltätig durchbebt er meine Nerven.—

Ich werde meiner Stimmung Herr und fühle mich aufgelegt,
dir, mein Theodor, wenigstens anzudeuten, wie ich jetzt erst
das herrliche Werk des göttlichen Meisters in seiner tiefen
Charakteristik richtig aufzufassen glaube.—Nur der Dichter
versteht den Dichter; nur ein romantisches Gemüt kann eingehen in das Romantische; nur der poetisch exaltierte Geist,
der mitten im Tempel die Weihe empfing, das verstehen, was
der Geweihte in der Begeisterung ausspricht.—Betrachtet man
das Gedicht (den ‚Don Juan'), ohne ihm eine tiefere Bedeutung
zu geben, so daß man nur das Geschichtliche in Anspruch
nimmt: so ist es kaum zu begreifen, wie Mozart eine solche
Musik dazu denken und dichten konnte. Ein Bonvivant, der
Wein und Mädchen über die Maßen liebt, der mutwilligerweise
den steinernen Mann als Repräsentanten des alten Vaters, den
er bei Verteidigung seines eigenen Lebens niederstach, zu
seiner lustigen Tafel bittet—wahrlich, hierin liegt nicht viel
Poetisches, und ehrlich gestanden, ist ein solcher Mensch es
wohl nicht wert, daß die unterirdischen Mächte ihn als ein ganz
besonderes Kabinettstück[30] der Hölle auszeichnen; daß der
steinerne Mann, von dem verklärten Geiste beseelt, sich bemüht vom Pferde zu steigen, um den Sünder vor dem letzten
Stündlein[31] zur Buße zu ermahnen; daß endlich der Teufel
seine besten Gesellen ausschickt, um den Transport in sein
Reich auf die gräßlichste Weise zu veranstalten.—Du kannst es
mir glauben, Theodor, den Juan stattete die Natur, wie ihrer
Schoßkinder liebstes,[32] mit alle dem aus, was den Menschen, in
näherer Verwandtschaft mit dem Göttlichen, über den gemei-

him, I lean over the railing of the box and look into the deserted auditorium, the architecture of which, magically illuminated by my two candles, stands out weird and fairylike in the strange reflections. The curtain is stirred by the draft that cuts through the house.—Suppose it were to go up? Suppose Donna Anna were to appear, frightened by gruesome monsters?—"Donna Anna!" I cry involuntarily; my cry dies away in the deserted house, but the spirits of the instruments in the orchestra become alive—a wonderful tone quivers up to me; it is as if the beloved name kept whispering through it.—I cannot escape a mysterious shudder that sends a pleasant tremor through my nerves.

I become master of my mood and feel inclined, my dear Theodor, at least to indicate to you that I believe I really grasp the glorious work of the divine master in its profound spirit only now.—Only a poet understands a poet; only a romantic disposition can enter into the romantic spirit; only the poetically exalted spirit, which received its consecration in the center of the temple, can understand what the initiated expresses under inspiration.—If one studies the poem (Don Juan), without giving it a deeper significance so that one considers only the story element in itself, it is scarcely understandable how Mozart could imagine and compose such music for it. A bon vivant, who likes wine and girls to excess, who arrogantly invites the stone man to his gay dinner table, as the representative of the old father whom he stabbed to death in defense of his own life—really there is not much poetry in this; and to tell the truth such a man is really not worth being singled out by the infernal powers as a special specimen of hell; that the stone man, animated by his transfigured spirit, should take the trouble to descend from his horse to urge the sinner to repentance before his last hour on earth; nor, finally, the devil should send out his best helpers to arrange for the transport into his kingdom in the most gruesome fashion.—You may believe me, Theodor, Nature equipped Juan, as the dearest of her bosom children, with everything that elevates a man, in his closer affinity with the divine, above the common throng, above the factory products that are discarded from the workshop like zeros in front of which some integer must take up its position if they are to have

nen Troß, über die Fabrikarbeiten, die als Nullen, vor die,
wenn sie gelten sollen, sich erst ein Zähler stellen muß, aus der
Werkstätte geschleudert werden, erhebt; was ihn bestimmt zu
besiegen, zu herrschen. Ein kräftiger, herrlicher Körper, eine
Bildung, woraus der Funke hervorstrahlt, der, die Ahnungen
des Höchsten entzündend, in die Brust fiel; ein tiefes Gemüt,
ein schnell ergreifender Verstand.—Aber das ist die entsetzliche Folge des Sündenfalls,[33] daß der Feind die Macht behielt,
dem Menschen aufzulauern und ihm selbst in dem Streben
nach dem Höchsten, worin er seine göttliche Natur ausspricht,
böse Fallstricke zu legen. Dieser Konflikt der göttlichen und
der dämonischen Kräfte erzeugt den Begriff des irdischen,
sowie der erfochtene Sieg den Begriff des überirdischen Lebens.—Den[34] Juan begeisterten die Ansprüche auf das Leben,
die seine körperliche und geistige Organisation herbeiführte,
und ein ewiges brennendes Sehnen, von dem sein Blut siedend
die Adern durchfloß, trieb ihn, daß er, gierig und ohne Rast
alle Erscheinungen der irdischen Welt aufgriff, in ihnen vergebens Befriedigung hoffend!—Es gibt hier auf Erden wohl
nichts, was den Menschen in seiner innigsten Natur so hinauf-
steigert als die Liebe; sie ist es, die so geheimnisvoll und so
gewaltig wirkend, die innersten Elemente des Daseins zerstört
und verklärt; was Wunder also, daß Don Juan in der Liebe die
Sehnsucht, die seine Brust zerreißt, zu stillen hoffte, und daß
der Teufel hier ihm die Schlinge über den Hals warf? In Don
Juans Gemüt kam durch des Erbfeindes List der Gedanke, daß
durch die Liebe, durch den Genuß des Weibes, schon auf Erden
das erfüllt werden könne, was bloß als himmlische Verheißung
in unserer Brust wohnt und eben jene unendliche Sehnsucht
ist, die uns mit dem Überirdischen in unmittelbaren Rapport
setzt. Vom schönen Weibe zum schönern rastlos fliehend; bis
zum Überdruß, bis zur zerstörenden Trunkenheit ihrer Reize
mit der glühendsten Inbrunst genießend; immer in der Wahl
sich betrogen glaubend, immer hoffend, das Ideal endlicher
Befriedigung zu finden, mußte doch Juan zuletzt alles irdische
Leben matt und flach finden, und indem er überhaupt den
Menschen verachtete, lehnte er sich auf gegen die Erscheinung, die, ihm als das Höchste im Leben geltend, so bitter ihn
getäuscht hatte. Jeder Genuß des Weibes war nun nicht mehr

any value; and this destined him to conquer and to command. A vigorous, splendid physique, a personality from which a spark radiated that, kindling premonitions of the highest powers, reached the heart; a profound sensibility, a swift, alert intellect.—But this is the horrible result of the Fall, that the Evil One retained the power of lying in wait for man and setting wicked snares for him even in his striving for the highest in which he expresses his divine nature. This conflict between divine and demonic powers creates the concept of life, just as triumphant victory creates that of life beyond.—Juan was inspired by those claims on life which were produced by his physical and mental organization, and an eternal burning longing, which made his blood course through his veins at boiling point, impelled him to grasp avidly and relentlessly at the manifestations of the earthly world, hoping in vain for satisfaction in them.—There is probably nothing here on earth that elevates man in his innermost nature as much as love; it is love that, working so mysteriously and so powerfully, destroys and transfigures the innermost elements of existence. What wonder then that Don Juan hoped to still in love the longing that was tearing his heart asunder and that the devil here slipped the noose around his neck? Through the archfiend's trickery the thought came into Don Juan's mind that through love, through the enjoyment of woman there could be fulfilled even on earth what dwells in our hearts merely as a promise of heaven, and is that very infinite longing that puts us into immediate rapport with the supernatural. Restlessly fleeing from a beautiful woman to a more beautiful one; enjoying their charms with the most burning ardor, to the point of surfeit, to the point of destructive intoxication; always believing he had been deceived in his choice; always hoping to find the ideal of eventual satisfaction—Juan was finally bound to find all earthly life insipid and flat; and while he despised man in general he rebelled against the manifestation that, valued by him as the highest thing in life, had so bitterly deceived him. Every enjoyment of a woman was now no longer the satisfaction of his senses but a blasphemous mocking of nature and the Creator. A profound contempt for the common aspects of life, which he felt were beneath him; a bitter scorn of people who were able to expect,

Befriedigung seiner Sinnlichkeit, sondern frevelnder Hohn gegen die Natur und den Schöpfer. Tiefe Verachtung der gemeinen Ansichten des Lebens, über die er sich erhoben fühlte, und bitterer Spott über Menschen, die in der glücklichen Liebe, in der dadurch herbeigeführten bürgerlichen Vereinigung auch nur im mindesten die Erfüllung der höheren Wünsche, die die Natur feindselig in unsere Brust legte, erwarten konnten, trieben ihn an, da vorzüglich sich aufzulehnen und, Verderben bereitend, dem unbekannten, schicksallenkenden Wesen, das ihm wie ein schadenfrohes, mit den kläglichen Geschöpfen seiner spottenden Laune ein grausames Spiel treibendes Ungeheuer erschien, kühn entgegenzutreten, wo von einem solchen Verhältnis die Rede war.—Jede Verführung einer geliebten Braut, jedes durch einen gewaltigen, nie zu verschmerzendes Unheil bringenden Schlag gestörte Glück der Liebenden ist ein herrlicher Triumph über jene feindliche Macht, der ihn immer mehr hinaushebt aus dem beengenden Leben—über die Natur—über den Schöpfer!—Er will auch wirklich immer mehr aus dem Leben, aber nur um hinabzustürzen in den Orkus.[35] Annas Verführung mit den dabei eingetretenen Umständen ist die höchste Spitze, zu der er sich erhebt.—

Donna Anna ist, rücksichtlich der höchsten Begünstigungen der Natur, dem Don Juan entgegengestellt. So wie Don Juan ursprünglich ein wunderbar kräftiger, herrlicher Mann war, so ist sie ein göttliches Weib, über deren reines Gemüt der Teufel nichts vermochte. Alle Kunst der Hölle konnte nur sie irdisch verderben.—Sowie der Satan dieses Verderben vollendet hat, durfte auch nach der Fügung des Himmels die Hölle die Vollstreckung des Rächeramts nicht länger verschieben.— Don Juan ladet den erstochenen Alten höhnend im Bilde ein zum lustigen Gastmahl, und der verklärte Geist, nun erst den gefallnen Menschen durchschauend und sich um ihn betrübend, verschmäht es nicht, in furchtbarer Gestalt ihn zur Buße zu ermahnen. Aber so verderbt, so zerrissen ist sein Gemüt, daß auch des Himmels Seligkeit keinen Strahl der Hoffnung in seine Seele wirft und ihn zum bessern Sein entzündet!—

Gewiß ist es dir, mein Theodor, aufgefallen, daß ich von Annas Verführung gesprochen; und so gut ich es in dieser

in happy love and in the bourgeois union that it produced, even the slightest fulfillment of the higher aspirations that Nature has spitefully implanted in our hearts;—all this impelled him to rebel especially in this area and, whenever there was talk of such a relationship, boldly to challenge (by his acts of destruction) that unknown power which guides our destiny, and which seemed to him to be a malicious monster playing a cruel game with the wretched creatures of its mocking whim.— Every seduction of a beloved bride, every happiness of lovers destroyed by a blow so powerful that it caused an irreparable catastrophe is a glorious triumph over that hostile power, lifting him ever higher above the constraints of life—above Nature— above the Creator!—He really wants more and more to leave life, but only to plunge into Orcus. The seduction of Anna, with the attendant circumstances, is the highest pinnacle to which he rises.—

With respect to the highest favors on Nature, Donna Anna is the counterpart to Don Juan. Just as Don Juan was originally a wonderfully vigorous, splendid man, so she is a divine woman, over whose pure mind the devil had no power. All the arts of hell could destroy her only physically.—As soon as Satan has completed this ruin, hell dared no longer postpone the execution of the act of vengeance that had been decreed by Heaven.— Don Juan mockingly invites the effigy of the stabbed old man to his gay banquet and the transfigured spirit, only now recognizing in him the fallen man, and grieving for him, does not disdain, in his awesome shape, to urge him to repentance. But so corrupt, so rent is his soul that even the bliss of Heaven casts no ray of hope into his soul nor does it inspire him to a better existence!—

It must certainly have surprised you, my Theodor, to hear me speak of Anna's seduction; and to the best of my ability at

Stunde, wo tief aus dem Gemüt hervorgehende Gedanken und
Ideen die Worte überflügeln, vermag, sage ich dir mit wenigen
Worten, wie mir in der Musik, ohne alle Rücksicht auf den
Text, das ganze Verhältnis der beiden im Kampf begriffenen
Naturen (Don Juan und Donna Anna) erscheint.—Schon oben
äußerte ich, daß Anna dem Juan gegenübergestellt ist. Wie,
wenn Donna Anna vom Himmel dazu bestimmt gewesen wäre,
den Juan in der Liebe, die ihn durch des Satans Künste
verdarb, die ihm inwohnende göttliche Natur erkennen zu lassen und ihn der Verzweiflung seines nichtigen Strebens zu
entreißen?—Zu spät, zur Zeit des höchsten Frevels, sah er sie,
und da konnte ihn nur die teuflische Lust erfüllen, sie zu verderben.—Nicht gerettet wurde sie! Als er hinausfloh, war die
Tat geschehen. Das Feuer einer übermenschlichen Sinnlichkeit, Glut aus der Hölle, durchströmte ihr Innerstes und machte
jeden Widerstand vergeblich. Nur E r, nur Don Juan konnte
den wollüstigen Wahnsinn in ihr entzünden, mit dem sie ihn
umfing, der mit der übermächtigen, zerstörenden Wut höl-
lischer Geister im Innern sündigte. Als er nach vollendeter Tat
entfliehen wollte, da umschlang wie ein gräßliches, giftigen Tod
sprühendes Ungeheuer sie der Gedanke ihres Verderbens mit
folternden Qualen.—Ihres Vaters Fall durch Don Juans Hand,
die Verbindung mit dem kalten, unmännlichen, ordinären Don
Ottavio, den sie einst zu lieben glaubte—selbst die im Innersten
ihres Gemüts in verzehrender Flamme wütende Liebe, die in
dem Augenblick des höchsten Genusses aufloderte und nun
gleich der Glut des vernichtenden Hasses brennt: Alles dieses
zerreißt ihre Brust. Sie fühlt, nur Don Juans Untergang kann
der von tödlichen Martern beängsteten Seele Ruhe verschaffen; aber diese Ruhe ist ihr eigner irdischer Untergang.—Sie
fordert daher unablässig ihren eiskalten Bräutigam zur Rache
auf, sie verfolgt selbst den Verräter, und erst als ihn die unterirdischen Mächte in den Orkus hinabgezogen haben, wird sie
ruhiger—nur vermag sie nicht dem hochzeitlustigen Bräutigam nachzugeben: *"lascia, o caro, un anno ancora, allo sfogo del
mio cor!"*[36] Sie wird dieses Jahr nicht überstehen; Don Ottavio
wird niemals d i e umarmen, die ein frommes Gemüt davon
rettete, des Satans geweihte Braut zu bleiben.

this hour, when thoughts and ideas that come from the depths of my mind, outdistance my words, I will tell you in few words how the music, without any regard for the text, seems to me to reflect the whole relationship of the two natures locked in combat (Don Juan and Donna Anna).—I have already said above that Anna is the counterpart of Juan. Suppose Donna Anna had been destined by Heaven to let Juan recognize the divine nature that is innate in him, in the love which destroyed him through the wiles of Satan, and to snatch him from the despair of his worthless ambition?—Too late, at the time of his supreme crime he saw her, and then he could only be filled with the devilish desire to destroy her.—She was not saved. When he fled, the deed had been done. The fire from a superhuman sensuality, a fire from hell, streamed through her innermost being and made all resistance vain. *He* alone, only Don Juan could kindle in her the voluptuous frenzy with which she embraced him, he who sinned with the superhuman, destructive fury of hellish spirits within him. When, after doing the deed, he wanted to flee, the thought of her ruin ensnared her with tormenting pains like a horrible monster spewing poisonous death.—Her father's death at Don Juan's hand, her union with the cold, unmanly, common Don Ottavio whom she once thought she loved, even the love that was raging in her heart with a consuming flame, flaring up at the moment of supreme enjoyment and is now burning life the fire of destructive hatred—all this is tearing her heart to shreds. She feels that only Don Juan's destruction can bring peace to her soul, which is a prey to mortal torment; but this peace is her own earthly destruction.—She therefore incessantly spurs her ice-cold fiancé to vengeance, she herself pursues her betrayer, and she grows calmer only when the infernal powers have dragged him down to Orcus—only she cannot yield to her bridegroom who is eager for marriage: "*lascia, o caro, un anno ancora, allo sfogo del mio cor!*" She will not outlive this year; Don Ottavio will never embrace the woman who was saved by her pious soul from remaining Satan's consecrated bride.

Wie lebhaft im Innersten meiner Seele fühlte ich alles dieses
in den die Brust zerreißenden Akkorden des ersten Rezitativs
und der Erzählung von dem nächtlichen Überfall!—Selbst die
Szene der Donna Anna im zweiten Akt: *"Crudele"*,[37] die, ober-
flächlich betrachtet, sich nur auf den Don Ottavio bezieht,
spricht in geheimen Anklängen, in den wunderbarsten Beziehungen jene innere, alles irdische Glück verzehrende Stimmung der Seele aus. Was soll selbst in den Worten der sonder-
bare, von dem Dichter vielleicht unbewußt, hingeworfene
Zusatz: *"forse un giorno il cielo ancora sentira pietà di me!"*[38]—
Es schlägt zwei Uhr!—Ein warmer elektrischer Hauch gleitet
über mich her—ich empfinde den leisen Geruch feinen italienischen Parfüms, der gestern zuerst mich die Nachbarin vermu-
ten ließ; mich umfängt ein seliges Gefühl, das ich nur in Tönen
aussprechen zu können glaube. Die Luft streicht heftiger durch
das Haus—die Saiten des Flügels im Orchester rauschen—
Himmel! wie aus weiter Ferne, auf den Fittichen schwellender
Töne eines luftigen Orchesters getragen, glaube ich Annas
Stimme zu hören: *"Non mi dir bell' idol mio!"*[39]—Schließe dich
auf, du fernes, unbekanntes Geisterreich—du Dschinnistan[40]
voller Herrlichkeit, wo ein unaussprechlicher, himmlischer
Schmerz wie die unsäglichste Freude der entzückten Seele alles
auf Erden Verheißene über alle Maßen erfüllt! Laß mich eintreten in den Kreis deiner holdseligen Erscheinungen! Mag
der Traum, den du bald zum Grausen erregenden, bald zum
freundlichen Boten an den irdischen Menschen erkoren[41]—
mag er meinen Geist, wenn der Schlaf den Körper in bleiernen
Banden festhält, den ätherischen Gefilden zuführen!—

GESPRÄCH DES MITTAGS AN DER WIRTSTAFEL,
ALS NACHTRAG

KLUGER MANN (mit der Dose, stark auf den Deckel derselben
schnippend): Es ist doch fatal, daß wir nun so bald keine or-
dentliche Oper mehr hören werden! aber das kommt von dem
häßlichen Übertreiben!
MULATTENGESICHT: Ja ja! hab's ihr oft genug gesagt! Die
Rolle der Donna Anna griff sie immer ordentlich an!—Gestern

How vividly I felt all this in my innermost soul in the heart-rending chords of the first recitative and the narrative of the nocturnal attack!—Even Donna Anna's scene in the second act, "*Crudele*," which on a superficial view refers only to Don Ottavio, expresses in hidden harmonies, in the most wonderful relationships, the inner mood of the soul that consumes all earthly happiness. What meaning is there even in the words of the strange passage added by the author perhaps unconsciously: "*forse un giorno il cielo ancora sentirà pietà di me!*"—

The clock strikes two!—A warm, electric breath glides over me—I smell the faint fragrance of fine Italian perfume that yesterday gave me the first inkling of the presence of my neighbor; I am enveloped by a feeling of bliss, which I think I can express only in tones. The air stirs more violently through the house—the strings of the grand piano in the orchestra sound—Heavens! I think I hear Anna's voice as though from a great distance, borne on the pinions of swelling tones of an ethereal orchestra: "*Non mi dir bell' idol mio!*"—Open up, you distant, unknown spirit realm—you jinnestan full of glory in which an inexpressible, celestial pain, akin to the most ineffable joy, fulfills for the enraptured soul, beyond all measure, everything that was promised it on earth! Let me enter the circle of your lovely apparitions! May the dream that you have chosen, either to arouse horror or to serve as a friendly messenger to earthly man—may it lead my spirit to the ethereal fields when sleep holds the body fast in bonds of lead!—

CONVERSATION AT NOON IN THE DINING ROOM,
BY WAY OF AN EPILOGUE

CLEVER MAN (snuffbox in hand, tapping vigorously on the lid): It's really unfortunate that we won't get to hear a decent opera for some time to come. But that's what comes of these hideous exaggerations.

MULATTO-FACE: Yes, yes. I've told her often enough. The part of Donna Anna always affected her deeply. Yesterday she

war sie vollends gar wie besessen. Den ganzen Zwischenakt
hindurch soll sie in Ohnmacht gelegen haben und in der Szene
im zweiten Akt hatte sie gar Nervenzufälle—

UNBEDEUTENDER: O sagen Sie—!

MULATTENGESICHT: Nun ja! Nervenzufälle, und war doch
wahrlich nicht vom Theater zu bringen.

ICH: Um des Himmels willen—die Zufälle sind doch nicht
von Bedeutung? wir hören doch Signora bald wieder?

KLUGER MANN (mit der Dose, eine Prise nehmend): Schwer-
lich, denn Signora ist heute morgen Punkt zwei Uhr gestorben.

Notes: Hoffmann, *Don Juan*

1. *Ew* = *Eure.*
2. *Wirtstafel,* table d'hôte; here: dining room of the inn.
3. *Taler,* three marks; *Groschen,* about a dime.
4. *stellen* . . . , add to the bill.
5. *regno all pianto,* reign of lamentation; Hoffmann's own words
to describe the character of this section of the overture.
6. *Notte* . . . , Night and day I slave; the first words of the opera,
spoken by Leporello.
7. *Ah che piacere,* Ah, what a delight; Hoffmann's own phrase.
8. *Non sperar* . . . , There's no hope, unless you kill me; Donna
Anna's first words.
9. The proscenium is the front part of the stage that is still visible
when the curtain is lowered.
10. *Mephistopheles:* the devil in Goethe's *Faust.*
11. *rot* . . . , of red and white stripes.
12. *Ma qual* . . . , But what fateful spectacle presents itself to my
eyes; sung by Donna Anna as she discovers her father's corpse.
13. *Brust,* often used in German where we would say *heart.*
14. *Tu nido d'inganni,* you nest of deception; spoken by Donna Elvira
to Don Juan.
15. *parla* . . . , she speaks like a printed book; spoken by Leporello
after Donna Elvira's tirade against Don Juan.
16. *Fin* . . . , Now that the wine has heated their heads; Don Juan's
aria toward the end of Act 1.
17. *Terzett,* tercet; a song for three voices.

was altogether like a woman possessed. Throughout the entr'
acte she's said to have been unconscious, and in the scene in
the second act she even had nervous attacks—
INSIGNIFICANT PERSON: Oh, I say—!
MULATTO-FACE:Really. Nervous attacks, and they just couldn't
get her out of the theater.
I: For Heaven's sake—I hope the attacks weren't serious? We
shall hear the signora again soon, won't we—?
CLEVER MAN (with his snuffbox, taking a pinch): Hardly, for
the signora died this morning at two o'clock sharp.

18. Roland and Cymork are characters in the medieval French epic
Chanson de Roland and in Ariosto's *Orlando Furioso*.
19. *Frauenzimmer*, see note 13 of Goethe's *Der Prokurator*.
20. *Toskanisch*, the Italian dialect spoken in Tuscany.
21. *Theodor*, a fictitious character to whom Hoffmann addresses
some of his stories.
22. *Phrase*, usually: empty, pompous talk; here used in the sense of
phrase or *sentence*.
23. *Roulade*, a rapid succession of notes sung to one syllable.
24. *aufgegangen*, supply *ist:* has opened up.
25. *Già* . . . , the table is already prepared; the opening aria of the
finale, sung by Don Juan.
26. *brausende Geister*, effervescent spirits; i.e., bubbling champagne.
27. *Marmorkoloß*, marble colossus; the statue of the Commandatore,
Donna Anna's dead father.
28. *pygmäisch*, as small as a pygmy.
29. *konsterniert*, the French word gives the gentleman's speech an
air of affectation and snobbery and is used with satirical intent.
30. *Kabinettstück*, a choice artifact displayed in a cabinet.
31. *Stündlein* = short hour. The diminutive indicates the small span
of time still left him.
32. *ihrer Schoßskinder*, a genitive case after *liebstes*.
33. *Sündenfall*, the Fall of man (Genesis II).
34. For the force of the article see note 18 for Kleist's *Das Erdbeben
in Chili*.

35. Orcus is the underworld in Greek mythology.

36. *lascia* . . . , allow, o dear one, another year for the relief of my heart.

37. *Crudele*, cruel one.

38. *forse* . . . , perhaps some day Heaven may yet have pity on me.

39. *non mi dir* . . . , do not tell me, my handsome lover.

40. Jinnestan is the ideal region in which the jinn and peris reside (Oriental mythology).

41. *erkoren*, archaic past participle of *kiesen* = *wählen* choose.

Adalbert Stifter

1805–68

Stifter was born of peasant and artisan stock in a village in the Bohemian forest. He lost his father at an early age and was brought up by his mother, to whom he owed much. His studies at the University of Vienna ranged over the fields of law, mathematics, and the physical sciences; but he was drawn especially to painting and literature. Disappointed in love, he married a woman to whom he was emotionally indifferent but with whom he lived an exemplary life.

Stifter's writings began to appear and to attract attention while he was a private tutor in aristocratic families. In 1840 he achieved a marked success with the publication of his story *Der Condor* in a Viennese periodical. From then on he published steadily for ten years. He turned away from the liberal ideals of *Das junge Deutschland*[1] and its program of making literature

[1] *Das junge Deutschland* is the literary movement (c. 1830–c. 1850) that succeeded German romanticism. It was oriented towards bringing literature closer to contemporary life and promoting liberal ideals in politics, religion, and in dealing with social problems. It was anything but a close-knit school, but there was a common ideological basis in the writings of Heine, Gutzkow, Laube, and

the instrument for political and social reform; but he also
distanced himself from the romanticism of Jean Paul and
E. T. A. Hoffmann. During this decade he published six volumes of novellas, all of which are concerned with the development of free and responsible personalities living harmoniously
in a world governed by law and order, in a society in which
individuals can find a useful (not utilitarian) existence: to be
helpful to others, learning through misfortune, serene in resignation, entrusting their fate to a higher wisdom. Stifter was
little interested in metaphysical problems; his concern was
wholly ethical and this-worldly: how to live the good life as a
member of a just and humane society.

Stifter was a moderate conservative or a conservative human-
ist, like Grillparzer.[2] They were both liberals in the spirit of the
eighteenth rather than the nineteenth century. Both were embittered by the excesses of the Revolution of 1848. Stifter
moved to Linz, where he edited a newspaper for a short time.
He had written a series of essays on educational reform. They
were noticed and Stifter was given a senior post in the ministry
of education. He was also made school inspector for Upper
Austria and curator of its architectural monuments. He retired
in 1865. His last years were saddened by domestic tragedy and
by his own fatal illness, thought to be cancer. Unable to endure
the pain, he took his own life.

Stifter's weltanschauung is the liberal humanity of the Enlightenment and the German classicism of Herder, Goethe,
Schiller, and Wilhelm von Humboldt. These intellectual leaders, Goethe especially, placed particular emphasis on the idea
of Bildung, education, self-cultivation. Goethe propagated this
educational ideal through the Bildungsroman[3] Wilhelm Meister's

the minor writers who are associated with the movement. Aesthetically, the
writers of Das junge Deutschland were moving in the direction of European
realism.

[2]Franz Grillparzer (1791–1872), Austrian dramatist and prose writer.

[3]Bildungsroman (also called Erziehungsroman, Entwicklungsroman) a work of
fiction that traces the development of a central character as he learns to meet
the problems of life and grows into a mature man. Forerunners of the genre
include Wolfram von Eschenbach's epic poem Parzival (early thirteenth century)
and Grimmelshausen's Simplizissimus (1669). The first Bildungsroman proper is

Apprenticeship (*Wilhelm Meisters Lehrjahre*, 1795–96) and its sequel *Wilhelm Meisters Years of Travel* (*Wilhelm Meisters Wanderjahre*, 1829). Stifter, too, wrote a *Bildungsroman*: *Indian Summer* (*Der Nachsommer*, 1857),[4] a Utopian novel in which the rather passive hero is subjected to a series of experiences: private tutors, extensive travel, the study of science, building homes, laying out gardens, buying jewelry and objects of art. He marries an ideal woman and comes under the benign influence of a wealthy landowner and former high civil servant, who becomes a second father to him.

Stifter's basic belief in *Bildung* has as its goal the development of character, which will express itself as integrity, resolution, simplicity, thrift, humaneness. The end of life is to achieve self-discipline and self-reliance, to avoid passion and extremes. It is Winckelmann's metaphor of the calm surface of the sea, no matter how violent the churning underneath.[5] Material success is by no means despised, but ideologically it is no more than a by-product of an existence that seeks to integrate the practical with the ideal, to fuse body, mind, and soul by achieving a synthesis of science, ethics, art, and practical life. Passion is the radical evil, and passion in the sense of suffering is to be avoided. We need to bring about a restoration of an orderly humane society.

Stifter's Utopian novel is a theodicy. It assumes that this is "the best of all possible worlds," for God has so ordered it that each social class—workers, managers, business and professional

---

Wieland's *Agathon* (1765–66), which was followed by Goethe's *Wilhelm Meister*. Other important examples are Tieck's *Franz Sternbalds Wanderungen* (1798), Keller's *Der grüne Heinrich* (1854), Stifter's *Der Nachsommer* (1857), Raabe's *Der Hungerpastor* (1864), Thomas Mann's *Der Zauberberg* (1924), and his *Joseph* tetralogy (1933–42).

[4] In the year 1857 Flaubert's classic of realism *Madame Bovary* appeared. A sharper contrast between the worlds depicted in these two works is hard to imagine.

[5] Johann Joachim Winckelmann (1717–68), noted art historian, indeed the founder of this discipline, may be regarded as the father of German classicism. His emphasis on simplicity, serenity, calm, and nobility excludes passion from art. The metaphor of the calm sea occurs in *Thoughts on the Imitation of Greek Works in Painting and Sculpture* (*Gedanken über die Nachahmung der griechischen Werke in der Malerei und Bildhauerkunst*, 1755).

people, leaders—can contribute to its smooth functioning. The latter, the elite few, enjoy the bounty that Fortune has bestowed on them, but enjoy it with a sense of obligation, with fairness and justice. But an integral part of the social order is the assurance that the business class will get an appreciation on its investments and a steady increase in the value of its real-estate holdings. Children will obey their parents, who know what is best for them. The ideal marriage is one that is free from passion.

The critical mind will ask itself how it was possible for a thinking human being living in 1850 to ignore the repeated cataclysms that had occurred in Europe since the Thirty Years' War as a result of dynastic ambitions, oppression of the common people by the aristocracy, and merciless exploitation of the masses, first by the aristocracy, then by the middle class, which became the ruling class after the French and Industrial revolutions. The answer is that such blindness *was* possible; it happened again and again that artists and intellectuals had little feeling for the social forces that direct human events and little faith in the power of political institutions to solve economic and social problems. The legacy of the eighteenth century, of Adam Smith, was the dogma of laissez-faire: If the individual citizen, of whatever station in life, will order his private economy on the principle of enlightened self-interest, society will run smoothly. As Goethe, quoting an old German proverb, put it: "Es kehre jeder vor seiner Tür" (Let everyone sweep in front of his own door). Big government will not save us, but individual effort will—it has a familiar ring to us in the 1980s. Man needs not politics and economics but religion to live the good life. Heinrich Heine came around to this belief after "herding swine with the Hegelians."[6] After the socially committed naturalists came the neoromantics and symbolists, who likewise rejected politics. The expressionists were divided among themselves: some were descendants of the Enlightenment, that is, politically committed; others sought salvation through religion or surro-

---

[6]Heine uses this metaphor in the afterword to his collection of poems *Romanzero* (1851). He regards the Hegelian philosophy as advocating atheism, glorifying man as a god who needs no God. In his youth he had been a disciple of Hegel; now he has returned to his Father, like the prodigal son of Scripture.

gate religions. Many twentieth-century writers preferred even an orthodox church affiliation to the thralldom of a political ideology.

Stifter's aversion to passion extends to his view of nature, as he expounds it in the celebrated preface to *Colored Stones* (*Bunte Steine*, 1853). He states there that he is not impressed by the violent perturbations in nature, its storms, volcanoes, earthquakes, but by the manifestations of the gentle law of nature, the regular day-to-day workings of God's creation. So it is also in human nature:

> A life filled with justice, simplicity, self-control, rationality, benign interaction with one's fellow humans, admiration of beauty, ending in a serene and calm death such a life I regard as great; powerful mental disturbances, fearful waves of anger, the desire for vengeance, an inflamed mind that strives for activity, for change, for destruction, and out of excitement often throws away its own life— this I do not regard as great but as smaller, since these things are merely the products of individual and one-sided forces, such as storms, fire-belching mountains, earthquakes. We will seek to discover the gentle law by which the human race is governed.

How unacceptable Stifter's ideal society is to us is perhaps best illustrated by the fact that Heinrich Böll, himself infected with the Utopian bacillus, was moved to write a parody of it: *Epilog zu Stifters Nachsommer* (1970). But in fact when Stifter's novel first appeared, voices were already raised against it as old-fashioned, irrelevant to the world of the mid-nineteenth century with its complex industrial society, warring nationalisms, competing empires, and Marxian class struggle. In the late twentieth century, after two world wars and the atomic arms race, with intensified economic rivalries, it is even more out of line with the mainstream of political, social, and religious thinking. The Utopias of this century (those of Wells, Shaw, Skinner, and Hesse) and the dystopias (those of Huxley

[7]H. G. Wells, *A Modern Utopia* (1904); George Bernard Shaw, *Back to Methuselah* (1921); B. F. Skinner, *Walden II* (1948); Hermann Hesse, *The Glass Bead Game* (*Das Glasperlenspiel*, translated as *Magister Ludi*, 1943); Aldous Huxley, *Brave New World* (1932); George Orwell, *Nineteen Eighty-Four* (1949).

and Orwell) show a humanity so corrupt that the very idea of setting up an ideal society seems ludicrous.

And yet, as a dream of what might have been if. . ., Stifter's program is not so naive as it appears. At the end of the Second World War an officer of the American army of occupation in Berlin discovered the eminent theologian Theodor Litt,[8] now a very old man. In an interview the officer asked Litt what he thought Germany must do to recover from the moral catastrophe of Nazism. The old man replied: "We must go back to the Ten Commandments." He meant that we must relearn basic ethics. Isn't this a program that the whole world needs today? Isn't this perhaps what Stifter is saying to his contemporaries? Reform must come out of a religious impulse; not from church-going but from a veneration for life as a noble enterprise that must not be sullied by base conduct. True, sweeping in front of your own door is not enough, but it is the first logical step in the spiritual rebirth of society.

After World War I a sort of Stifter cult arose in the German-speaking world. Stifter was recognized as a great German writer, and he remains so to this day. The same Heinrich Böll who satirized the naiveté and the sanctimoniousness of the *Nachsommer* admires Stifter as a great writer.

●

Bergkristall tells us why. This simple, rustic tale of two children who are lost on a mountain on Christmas Eve and found the next day is pervaded by the Stifter spirit of self-reliance, responsibility, natural authority, and a belief in the ultimate rightness of God's world. The theology may not appeal to us, but we must surely be gripped by Stifter's power of narration.

Bergkristall was first published in 1845 under the title *Christmas Eve* (*Der heilige Abend*). It was later rewritten and incorporated into the collection *Bunte Steine* under its present title because the glasslike clarity of rock crystal is a fitting symbol of the spirit that pervades the tale.

---

[8]Theodor Litt (1880–1962), professor at the University of Bonn and author of works on philosophy, sociology, and education.

Bergkristall

Unsere Kirche feiert verschiedene Feste, welche zum Herzen dringen. Man kann sich kaum etwas Liebreicheres denken als Pfingsten und kaum etwas Ernsteres und Heiligeres als Ostern. Das Traurige und Schwermütige der Charwoche und darauf das Feierliche des Sonntags begleiten uns durch das Leben. Eines der schönsten Feste feiert die Kirche fast mitten im Winter, wo beinahe die längsten Nächte und kürzesten Tage sind, wo die Sonne am schiefsten gegen unsere Gefilde steht, und Schnee alle Fluren deckt, das Fest der Weihnacht. Wie in vielen Ländern der Tag vor dem Geburtsfeste des Herrn der Christabend heißt, so heißt er bei uns der Heilige Abend, der darauf folgende Tag der Heilige Tag und die dazwischen liegende Nacht die Weihnacht. Die katholische Kirche begeht den Christtag als den Tag der Geburt des Heilandes mit ihrer allergrößten kirchlichen Feier, in den meisten Gegenden wird schon die Mitternachtstunde als die Geburtsstunde des Herrn mit prangender Nachtfeier geheiligt, zu der die Glocken durch die stille, finstere winterliche Mitternachtluft laden, zu der die Bewohner mit Lichtern oder auf dunkeln, wohlbekannten Pfaden aus schneeigen Bergen an bereiften Wäldern vorbei und durch knarrende Obstgärten zu der Kirche eilen, aus der die feierlichen Töne kommen, und die aus der Mitte des in beeiste Bäume gehüllten Dorfes mit den langen beleuchteten Fenstern emporragt.

Mit dem Kirchenfeste ist auch ein häusliches verbunden. Es hat sich fast in allen christlichen Ländern verbreitet, daß man den Kindern die Ankunft des Christkindleins—auch eines Kindes, des wunderbarsten, das je auf der Welt war—als ein heiteres, glänzendes, feierliches Ding zeigt, das durch das ganze

Rock Crystal

Our church celebrates various holidays that affect the heart deeply. One can scarcely imagine anything more charming than Whitsuntide or anything more earnest and sacred than Easter. The sad and melancholy character of Holy Week, followed by the solemnity of Easter Sunday, accompanies us through life. One of the most beautiful holidays is celebrated by the church almost in the middle of winter, when the nights are virtually longest and days shortest, when the sun shines most obliquely on our fields and snow covers them all—the feast of Christmas. In many countries the day preceding the birthday celebration of our Lord is called Christmas Eve; we call it Holy Eve; the day following, Holy Day; and the night that falls between them, the Night of Consecration. The Catholic Church celebrates Christmas day, the day on which our Savior was born, with the very greatest ecclesiastical solemnity. In most regions the hour of Our Lord's birth is sanctified from midnight on with a splendid nocturnal celebration, to which the church bells invite us through the silent, dark, wintry midnight air. The residents hasten to church with lanterns, or on dark, familiar paths from the snow-covered mountains, past frost-covered forests and through creaking orchards, to the church from which the solemn tones come and which, with its high, lighted windows, stands out in the midst of the village shrouded by ice-covered trees.

The church holiday is tied up with a domestic one. In almost all Christian countries the custom has spread of showing children the arrival of the Christ child—He too was a child, the most wonderful that ever was on earth—as a happy, splendid, solemn thing, which continues to affect us throughout our

Leben fortwirkt und manchmal noch spät im Alter bei trüben,
schwermütigen oder rührenden Erinnerungen gleichsam als
Rückblick in die einstige Zeit mit den bunten schimmernden
Fittichen durch den öden, traurigen und ausgeleerten Nacht-
himmel fliegt. Man pflegt den Kindern die Geschenke zu geben,
die das heilige Christkindlein gebracht hat, um ihnen Freude
zu machen. Das tut man gewöhnlich am Heiligen Abende, wenn
die tiefe Dämmerung eingetreten ist. Man zündet Lichter und
meistens sehr viele an, die oft mit den kleinen Kerzlein auf den
schönen grünen Ästen eines Tannen- oder Fichtenbäumchens
schweben, das mitten in der Stube steht. Die Kinder dürfen
nicht eher kommen, als bis das Zeichen gegeben wird, daß der
Heilige Christ zugegen gewesen ist und die Geschenke, die er
mitgebracht, hinterlassen hat. Dann geht die Tür auf, die
Kleinen dürfen hinein, und bei dem herrlichen schimmernden
Lichterglanze sehen sie Dinge auf dem Baume hängen oder
auf dem Tische herumgebreitet, die alle Vorstellungen ihrer
Einbildungskraft weit übertreffen, die sie sich nicht anzurüh-
ren getrauen und die sie endlich, wenn sie sie bekommen
haben, den ganzen Abend in ihren Ärmchen herumtragen und
mit sich in das Bett nehmen. Wenn sie dann zuweilen in ihre
Träume hinein die Glockentöne der Mitternacht hören, durch
welche die Großen in die Kirche zur Andacht gerufen werden,
dann mag es ihnen sein,[1] als[2] zögen jetzt die Englein durch den
Himmel oder als kehre der Heilige Christ nach Hause, welcher
nunmehr bei allen Kindern gewesen ist und jedem von ihnen
ein herrliches Geschenk hinterbracht hat.

Wenn dann der folgende Tag, der Christtag, kommt, so ist
er ihnen so feierlich, wenn sie früh morgens mit ihren schönsten Kleidern angetan in der warmen Stube stehen, wenn der
Vater und die Mutter sich zum Kirchgange schmücken, wenn
zu Mittage ein feierliches Mahl ist, ein besseres als in jedem
Tage des ganzen Jahres, und wenn nachmittags oder gegen
den Abend hin Freunde und Bekannte kommen, auf den
Stühlen und Bänken herumsitzen, miteinander reden und be-
haglich durch die Fenster in die Wintergegend hinausschauen
können, wo entweder die langsamen Flocken niederfallen oder
ein trübender Nebel um die Berge steht oder die blutrote kalte

whole lives; and sometimes, even in our old age, in the midst of troubled, melancholy, or touching memories, it flies on bright, glittering wings through the desolate, sad, and empty night sky like a backward glance into a time now past. It is customary to give children the gifts that the holy Christ child has brought, to give them happiness. This is usually done on Christmas Eve, when deep twilight has settled. Lights are lit— usually a great many—which often sway beside the little candles on the beautiful green branches of a fir or spruce tree that stands in the middle of the living room. The children are not permitted to come until the sign is given that the Holy Christ has been there and has left behind the gifts which He has brought. Then the door is opened, the little ones are permitted to enter, and in the splendid, glittering glow of the lights they see things hanging on the tree or spread out on the table which far surpass all the conceptions of their imagination, which they do not dare to touch, and which they finally, when they have been presented to them, carry about in their little arms all evening and take to bed with them. Sometimes they hear in their dreams the tones of the midnight bells which call the grown-ups to worship in church; then they imagine that the little angels are now moving through heaven or the Holy Christ is returning home after visiting all children and leaving each of them a splendid gift.

When the following day comes, Christmas day, it is a most solemn occasion for them. In the early morning they stand in the warm living room, dressed in their best clothes, while father and mother are dressing for church. At noon there is a formal meal, better than on any other day in the whole year. In the afternoon or toward evening friends and acquaintances come, sit about on chairs and benches and can talk to each other and comfortably look through the windows at the wintry countryside without, where either snowflakes are falling slowly, or a darkening mist clings to the mountains, or the blood-red, cold sun is setting. In various parts of the living room, on a chair or on

Sonne hinabsinkt. An verschiedenen Stellen der Stube, entweder auf einem Stühlchen oder auf der Bank oder auf dem
Fensterbrettchen, liegen die zaubrischen, nun aber schon be-
kannteren und vertrauteren Geschenke von gestern abend
herum.

Hierauf vergeht der lange Winter, es kommt der Frühling
und der unendlich dauernde Sommer—und wenn die Mutter
wieder vom Heiligen Christe erzählt, daß nun bald sein Festtag
sein wird und daß er auch diesmal herabkommen werde, ist es
den Kindern, als sei seit seinem letzten Erscheinen eine ewige
Zeit vergangen und als liege die damalige Freude in einer weiten
nebelgrauen Ferne.

Weil dieses Fest so lange nachhält, weil sein Abglanz so hoch
in das Alter hinaufreicht, so stehen wir so gerne dabei, wenn
die Kinder dasselbe begehen und sich darüber freuen.—

In den hohen Gebirgen unsers Vaterlandes steht ein Dörfchen mit einem kleinen, aber sehr spitzigen Kirchturme, der
mit seiner roten Farbe, mit welcher die Schindeln bemalt sind,
aus dem Grün vieler Obstbäume hervorragt und wegen derselben roten Farbe in dem duftigen und blauen Dämmern der
Berge weithin ersichtlich ist. Das Dörfchen liegt gerade mitten
in einem ziemlich weiten Tale, das fast wie ein länglicher Kreis[3]
gestaltet ist. Es enthält außer der Kirche eine Schule, ein
Gemeindehaus und noch mehrere stattliche Häuser, die einen
Platz gestalten, auf welchem vier Linden stehen, die ein
steinernes Kreuz in ihrer Mitte haben. Diese Häuser sind nicht
bloße Landwirtschaftshäuser, sondern sie bergen auch noch
diejenigen Handwerke in ihrem Schoße,[4] die dem menschlichen
Geschlechte unentbehrlich sind und die bestimmt sind, den
Gebirgsbewohnern ihren einzigen Bedarf an Kunsterzeugnis-
sen zu decken. Im Tale und an den Bergen herum sind noch
sehr viele zerstreute Hütten, wie das in Gebirgsgegenden sehr
oft der Fall ist, welche alle nicht nur zur Kirche und Schule
gehören, sondern auch jenen Handwerken, von denen gesprochen wurde, durch Abnahme der Erzeugnisse ihren Zoll ent-
richten. Es gehören sogar noch weitere Hütten zu dem Dörfchen, die man von dem Tale aus[5] gar nicht sehen kann, die
noch tiefer in den Gebirgen stecken, deren Bewohner selten
zu ihren Gemeindemitbrüdern herauskommen und die im

the bench or on the window sill, last night's presents lie about, by now better and more intimately known.

Then the long winter passes, spring comes and the endless summer. When mother tells them again of the Holy Christ, that His holiday is coming soon and that He will come down this time too, the children feel that an eternity has passed since His last appearance and that the joy of that time lies in the far, foggy gray distance.

Because this holiday has such a lasting effect, because its reflected light reaches so far into our old age, we like to be present when children celebrate it and rejoice in it.

In the high mountains of our country there is a little village with a small but very pointed church steeple that stands out from the green of many fruit trees because of the red color of its shingles; and because of this same red color it can be seen for a great distance in the delicate blue haze of the mountains. The little village is situated right in the center of a fairly wide valley, which has almost the shape of an ellipse. Besides the church it has a school, a community hall, and a few other stately houses which form a square on which there are four linden trees with a stone cross in their center. These houses are no mere farmhouses; they also harbor those handicrafts that are indispensable to the human species and which serve to provide the mountain dwellers' sole needs in manufactured products. In the valley and the mountains round about there are scattered many more huts, as is very often the case in mountain regions; not only do they all belong to the church and the school, but their inhabitants pay tribute to the crafts mentioned above by buying the products. Even more distant huts belong to the village; these cannot even be seen from the valley; they lie even deeper in the mountains. Their inhabitants rarely leave them to join their fellow parishioners, and in winter they often have to keep their dead until they can bring them down for burial after the snow has melted. The greatest man whom the villagers get to see in the course of the year is the priest. They venerate

Winter oft ihre Toten aufbewahren müssen, um sie nach dem
Wegschmelzen des Schnees zum Begräbnisse bringen zu können. Der größte Herr, den die Dörfler im Laufe des Jahres zu
sehen bekommen, ist der Pfarrer. Sie verehren ihn sehr, und
es geschieht gewöhnlich, daß derselbe durch längeren Aufent-
halt im Dörfchen ein der Einsamkeit gewöhnter Mann wird,
daß er nicht ungerne bleibt und einfach fortlebt. Wenigstens
hat man seit Menschengedenken nicht erlebt, daß der Pfarrer
des Dörfchens ein auswärtssüchtiger oder seines Standes un-
würdiger Mann gewesen wäre.

Es gehen keine Straßen durch das Tal, sie haben ihre zwei-
gleisigen Wege, auf denen sie ihre Felderzeugnisse mit ein-
spännigen Wäglein nach Hause bringen, es kommen daher
wenig Menschen in das Tal, unter diesen manchmal ein einsamer Fußreisender, der ein Liebhaber der Natur ist, eine Weile
in der bemalten Oberstube des Wirtes wohnt und die Berge
betrachtet, oder gar ein Maler, der den kleinen spitzen Kirchturm und die schönen Gipfel der Felsen in seine Mappe
zeichnet. Daher bilden die Bewohner eine eigene Welt, sie kennen einander alle mit Namen und mit den einzelnen Geschichten von Großvater und Urgroßvater her, trauern alle, wenn
einer stirbt, wissen, wie er heißt, wenn einer geboren wird,
haben eine Sprache, die von der der Ebene draußen abweicht,
haben ihre Streitigkeiten, die sie schlichten, stehen einander
bei und laufen zusammen, wenn sich etwas Außerordentliches
begibt.

Sie sind sehr stetig, und es bleibt immer beim alten.[6] Wenn
ein Stein aus einer Mauer fällt, wird derselbe wieder hinein-
gesetzt, die neuen Häuser werden wie die alten gebaut, die
schadhaften Dächer werden mit gleichen Schindeln ausgebes-
sert, und wenn in einem Hause scheckige Kühe sind, so werden
immer solche Kälber aufgezogen, und die Farbe bleibt bei dem
Hause.

Gegen Mittag[7] sieht man von dem Dorfe einen Schneeberg,
der mit seinen glänzenden Hörnern fast oberhalb der Haus-
dächer zu sein scheint, aber in der Tat doch nicht so nahe ist.
Er sieht das ganze Jahr, Sommer und Winter, mit seinen vor-
stehenden Felsen und mit seinen weißen Flächen in das Tal
herab. Als das Auffallendste, was sie in ihrer Umgebung haben,

him deeply, and it usually happens that he becomes accustomed to the isolation as a result of his lengthy stay in the village; and so he remains there not unwillingly and just lives on. At least as far as human memory can reach, it has never happened that the priest of the little village was anxious to leave it or was unworthy of his calling.

No highways pass through the valley; they have their double-track roads on which they bring their field products home on one-horse carts. Accordingly, few people come into the valley; among these few an occasional solitary pedestrian who is a lover of nature lives for a while in the painted upstairs room of the inn and contemplates the mountains, or even a painter, who sketches the small, pointed church steeple and the beautiful peaks of the rocks in his portfolio. And so the inhabitants form a world of their own; they all know one another by name and by the individual stories handed down from grandfather and great-grandfather. They all mourn when one of them dies, know what name is given to the newborn, have a language that deviates from that of the plains beyond, have their quarrels, which they settle, help one another, and flock together when something unusual happens.

They are very conservative and things always remain the same. When a stone falls out of a wall it is put in again, the new houses are built like the old, the damaged roofs are repaired with the same type of shingle, and if there are spotted cows on a farm, the same type of calf is always reared and the color stays with the farm.

Toward the south of the village one sees a snowy mountain whose gleaming horns seem to be almost directly above the house tops but are in fact not so near. All year, summer and winter, it looks down into the valley with its projecting rocks and its white surfaces. As the most striking sight they have in the region, the mountain is the object of contemplation for the

ist der Berg der Gegenstand der Betrachtung der Bewohner,
und er ist der Mittelpunkt vieler Geschichten geworden. Es lebt
kein Mann und Greis in dem Dorfe, der nicht von den Zacken
und Spitzen des Berges, von seinen Eisspalten und Höhlen,
von seinen Wässern und Geröllströmen etwas zu erzählen
wüßte, was er entweder selbst erfahren oder von andern erzählen gehört hat. Dieser Berg ist auch der Stolz des Dorfes,
als hätten sie ihn selber gemacht, und es ist nicht so ganz
entschieden, wenn man auch die Biederkeit und Wahrheitsliebe
der Talbewohner hoch anschlägt, ob sie nicht zuweilen zur
Ehre und zum Ruhme des Berges lügen. Der Berg gibt den
Bewohnern außer dem, daß er ihre Merkwürdigkeit ist, auch
wirklichen Nutzen; denn wenn eine Gesellschaft von Gebirgs-
reisenden hereinkommt, um von dem Tale aus den Berg zu
besteigen, so dienen die Bewohner des Dorfes als Führer, und
einmal Führer gewesen zu sein, dieses und jenes erlebt zu
haben, diese und jene Stelle zu kennen, ist eine Auszeichnung,
die jeder gerne von sich darlegt. Sie reden oft davon, wenn
sie in der Wirtsstube beieinander sitzen, und erzählen ihre
Wagnisse und ihre wunderbaren Erfahrungen und versäumen
aber auch nie zu sagen, was dieser oder jener Reisende gesprochen habe und was sie von ihm als Lohn für ihre Bemühungen empfangen hätten. Dann sendet der Berg von seinen
Schneeflächen die Wasser ab, welche einen See in seinen Hoch-
wäldern speisen und den Bach erzeugen, der lustig durch das
Tal strömt, die Brettersäge, die Mahlmühle und andere kleine
Werke treibt, das Dorf reinigt und das Vieh tränkt. Von den
Wäldern des Berges kommt das Holz, und sie halten die Lawi-
nen auf. Durch die innern[8] Gänge und Lockerheiten der Höhen
sinken die Wasser durch, die dann in Adern durch das Tal
gehen und in Brünnlein und Quellen hervorkommen, daraus[9]
die Menschen trinken und ihr herrliches, oft belobtes Wasser
dem Fremden reichen. Allein an letzteren Nutzen denken sie
nicht und meinen, das sei immer so gewesen.

   Wenn man auf die Jahresgeschichte des Berges sieht, so sind
im Winter die zwei Zacken seines Gipfels, die sie Hörner
heißen,[10] schneeweiß und stehen, wenn sie an hellen Tagen
sichtbar sind, blendend in der finstern Bläue der Luft; alle
Bergfelder, die um diese Gipfel herumlagern, sind dann weiß;

inhabitants and has become the focus of many stories. There
is not a man or oldster in the village who could not tell some
story about the crags and peaks of the mountain, of its crevasses
and caves, its waters and rock slides—something he has either
experienced himself or heard others tell. This mountain is also
the pride of the village, as if they had made it themselves; and
it is by no means certain, even if one puts a high value on the
honesty and veracity of the valley dwellers, that they do not
occasionally lie for the honor and fame of the mountain. Apart
from being their main object of interest, the mountain is also
actually useful; for when a party of mountain tourists arrives
to climb the mountain from the valley, the inhabitants of the
village serve as guides; and to have once served as a guide, to
have had this or that experience, to know this or that spot, is
a distinction that everyone is glad to claim for himself. They
often talk about it when they sit together in the taproom; they
narrate their acts of daring and their remarkable experiences;
but they also never fail to tell what this or that tourist had said
and how much they got from him as a reward for their efforts.
Moreover, from its snow fields the mountain sends down the
waters that feed a lake in its forests and make the brook that,
streaming merrily through the valley, drives the sawmill, the
gristmill, and other small works, cleans the village, and waters
the cattle. The mountain forests provide them with timber and
break the force of the avalanches. Through the underground
channels and loose soil on the heights the waters filter, then go
through the valley in veins and emerge in little fountains and
springs from which people drink and offer strangers their marvelous, much lauded water. Yet they do not think of its useful-
ness but believe it has always been so.

When one considers the seasonal history of the mountain,
the two crags of its peak, which they call horns, are snow white
in winter and, when they are visible on bright days, they stand
out in the dark blue of the air with dazzling brilliance. All the
mountain fields that lie about these peaks are then white; all

alle Abhänge sind so; selbst die steilrechten Wände, die die
Bewohner Mauern heißen, sind mit einem angeflogenen weißen
Reife bedeckt und mit zartem Eise wie mit einem Firnisse
belegt, so daß die ganze Masse wie ein Zauberpalast aus dem
bereiften Grau der Wälderlast emporragt, welche schwer um
ihre Füße herum ausgebreitet ist. Im Sommer, wo Sonne und
warmer Wind den Schnee von den Steilseiten wegnimmt, ragen
die Hörner nach dem Ausdrucke der Bewohner schwarz in
den Himmel und haben nur schöne weiße Äderchen und
Sprenkeln auf ihrem Rücken, in der Tat aber sind sie zart
fernblau, und was sie Äderchen und Sprenkeln heißen, das ist
nicht weiß, sondern hat das schöne Milchblau des fernen
Schnees gegen das dunklere der Felsen. Die Bergfelder um die
Hörner aber verlieren, wenn es recht heiß ist, an ihren höheren Teilen wohl den Firn nicht, der gerade dann recht weiß
auf das Grün der Talbäume herabsieht, aber es weicht von
ihren unteren Teilen der Winterschnee, der nur einen Flaum
machte, und es wird das unbestimmte Schillern von Bläulich
und Grünlich sichtbar, das das Geschiebe[11] von Eis ist, das dann
bloßliegt und auf die Bewohner unten hinabgrüßt. Am Rande
dieses Schillerns, wo es von ferne wie ein Saum von Edelstein-
splittern aussieht, ist es in der Nähe ein Gemenge wilder,
riesenhafter Blöcke, Platten und Trümmer, die sich drängen
und verwirrt ineinandergeschoben sind. Wenn ein Sommer gar
heiß und lang ist, werden die Eisfelder weit hinauf entblößt,
und dann schaut eine viel größere Fläche von Grün und Blau
in das Tal, manche Kuppen und Räume werden entkleidet,
die man sonst nur weiß erblickt hatte, der schmutzige Saum
des Eises wird sichtbar, wo es Felsen, Erde und Schlamm
schiebt, und viel reichlichere Wasser als sonst fließen in das
Tal. Dies geht fort, bis es nach und nach wieder Herbst wird,
das Wasser sich verringert, zu einer Zeit einmal ein grauer
Landregen die ganze Ebene des Tales bedeckt, worauf, wenn
sich die Nebel von den Höhen wieder lösen, der Berg seine
weiche Hülle abermals umgetan hat und alle Felsen, Kegel und
Zacken in weißem Kleide dastehen.

     So spinnt es sich ein Jahr um das andere mit geringen Ab-
wechslungen ab und wird sich fortspinnen, solange die Natur
so bleibt und auf den Bergen Schnee und in den Tälern

the slopes are so; even the perpendicular walls, which the people call stone walls, are covered with a coating of white hoarfrost and overlaid with delicate ice as with a varnish, so that the whole mass towers like an enchanted palace above the frosty gray of the huge forest that is spread out thickly about its feet. In the summer, when the sun and the warm wind remove the snow from the steep mountain sides, the horns, as the inhabitants say, jut out black into the sky and have only beautiful little white veins and speckles on their backs. But actually they are a delicate, distant blue, and what they call little veins and speckles are not white but possess the beautiful milk blue of the distant snow in contrast to the darker blue of the rocks. Even when it is really hot, the mountain fields around the horns do not lose their old snow in the higher regions; it looks down just then in all its whiteness on the green trees in the valley. But from the lower regions the recent winter snow, which merely formed a down, recedes and a vague iridescence of blue and green becomes visible; this is the glacial striation that is exposed and sends its greetings to the inhabitants below. At the edge of this iridescence, where from a distance it looks like a border of broken jewels, it is, from close up, a mixture of wild, gigantic blocks, slabs, and debris, crowded together and piled in confusion over one another. When a summer is very hot and long, the ice fields are bared for a great distance up, and then a much greater expanse of green and blue looks down into the valley; many knolls and spaces, which had formerly been seen as white, are stripped bare; the dirty border of the ice becomes visible, there where it shoves rocks, earth, and mud; and water flows into the valley much more plentifully than is usual. This continues until it gradually becomes autumn again; the water supply decreases; at some time a gray, steady rain covers the whole plain and then, when the mists lift from the heights again, the mountain has put on its soft wrap once more, and all the rocks, cones, and crags stand there in a white cloak. This goes on year after year with slight variations and will go on as long as Nature remains what she is and there are snow on the mountains and people in the valleys. The inhabitants of the valley call the slight variations great ones, note them well, and calculate the progress of the year by them. They

Menschen sind. Die Bewohner des Tales heißen die geringen
Veränderungen große, bemerken sie wohl und berechnen
an ihnen den Fortschritt des Jahres. Sie bezeichnen an den
Entblößungen die Hitze und die Ausnahmen der Sommer.
Was nun noch die Besteigung des Berges betrifft, so geschieht dieselbe von dem Tale aus. Man geht nach der Mit-
tagsrichtung zu auf einem guten, schönen Wege, der über einen
sogenannten Hals in ein anderes Tal führt. Hals heißen sie
einen mäßig hohen Bergrücken, der zwei größere und bedeu-
tendere Gebirge miteinander verbindet und über den man
zwischen den Gebirgen von einem Tale in ein anderes gelangen
kann. Auf dem Halse, der den Schneeberg mit einem gegen-
überliegenden großen Gebirgszuge verbindet, ist lauter[12] Tan-
nenwald. Etwa auf der größten Erhöhung desselben, wo nach
und nach sich der Weg in das jenseitige Tal hinabzusenken
beginnt, steht eine sogenannte Unglückssäule.[13] Es ist einmal
ein Bäcker, welcher Brot in seinem Korbe über den Hals trug,
an jener Stelle tot gefunden worden. Man hat den toten Bäcker
mit dem Korbe und mit den umringenden Tannenbäumen auf
ein Bild gemalt, darunter eine Erklärung und eine Bitte um
ein Gebet geschrieben, das Bild auf eine rot angestrichene höl-
zerne Säule getan und die Säule an der Stelle des Unglückes
aufgerichtet. Bei dieser Säule biegt man von dem Wege ab und
geht auf der Länge des Halses fort, statt über seine Breite in
das jenseitige Tal hinüberzuwandern. Die Tannen bilden dort
einen Durchlaß, als ob eine Straße zwischen ihnen hin ginge.
Es führt auch[14] manchmal ein Weg in dieser Richtung hin, der
dazu dient, das Holz von den höheren Gegenden zu der Unglücksäule herabzubringen, der aber dann wieder mit Gras
verwächst. Wenn man auf diesem Wege fortgeht, der sachte
bergan führt, so gelangt man endlich auf eine freie,[15] von
Bäumen entblößte Stelle. Dieselbe ist dürrer Heideboden, hat
nicht einmal[16] einen Strauch, sondern ist mit schwachem
Heidekraute, mit trockenen Moosen und Dürrbodenpflanzen
bewachsen. Die Stelle wird immer steiler, und man geht lange
hinan; man geht aber immer in einer Rinne, gleichsam wie in
einem ausgerundeten Graben, hinan, was den Nutzen hat, daß
man auf der großen, baumlosen und überall gleichen Stelle

measure the heat and the exceptional summers by the exposure
of the mountain.

Now as far as the ascent of the mountain is concerned, it is
undertaken from the valley. One walks in a southerly direction
on a good, beautiful road that leads into another valley by way
of a so-called "neck." By "neck" they mean a moderately high
mountain ridge that connects two bigger and more important
mountain ranges and over which one can get from one valley
to another between the ranges. The neck that connects the
snow mountain with a large mountain range that lies opposite
is covered with pine forest. At about the highest point of the
neck, where the road gradually begins to descend into the valley
on the other side, there stands a so-called "accident pillar." One
time a baker, who was carrying bread over the "neck" in his
basket, was found dead at that spot. A picture of the dead baker
with his basket and the surrounding pine trees was made; an
explanation and a request for a prayer were written under it;
the picture was attached to a wooden post painted red; and the
post was erected at the spot of the accident. At this pillar one
turns off from the road and continues along the length of the
neck, instead of going across the breadth of the ridge into the
valley beyond. The pines form an opening there, as if a highway
led between them. At times a road does actually lead in this
direction, serving to transport the timber from the higher regions to the accident pillar, but then it is overgrown with
grass. When one continues on this road, which leads gently
uphill, one finally reaches an open spot bare of trees. This area
is dry heath soil, with not even a shrub on it, but it is overgrown
with scant heather, dry mosses, and heath plants. The area
becomes steeper and steeper, and one climbs for a long time.
But one always keeps walking in a trench, a sort of rounded
ditch, which has the advantage that one cannot easily get lost
in that great, treeless, undifferentiated area. After a while rocks
appear which rise straight out of the grassy floor like churches,
and between these walls one can climb for quite a time. Then
bald ridges, almost bare of plants, appear again; these already

nicht leicht irren kann. Nach einer Zeit erscheinen Felsen, die wie Kirchen gerade aus dem Grasboden aufsteigen und zwischen deren Mauern man längere Zeit hinangehen kann. Dann erscheinen wieder kahle, fast pflanzenlose Rücken, die bereits in die Lufträume der höheren Gegenden ragen und gerade zu dem Eise führen. Zu beiden Seiten dieses Weges sind steile Wände, und durch diesen Damm hängt der Schneeberg mit dem Halse zusammen. Um das Eis zu überwinden, geht man eine geraume Zeit an der Grenze desselben, wo es von den Felsen umstanden ist, dahin, bis man zu dem ältesten Firn gelangt, der die Eisspalten überbaut und in den meisten Zeiten des Jahres den Wanderer trägt. An der höchsten Stelle des Firns erheben sich die zwei Hörner aus dem Schnee, wovon eines das höhere, mithin die Spitze des Berges ist. Diese Kuppen sind schwer zu erklimmen; da sie mit einem oft breiteren, oft engeren Schneegraben—dem Firnschrunde—umgeben sind, der übersprungen werden muß, und da ihre steilrechten Wände nur kleine Absätze haben, in welche der Fuß eingesetzt werden muß, so begnügen sich die meisten Besteiger des Berges damit, bis zu dem Firnschrunde gelangt zu sein und dort die Rundsicht, soweit sie nicht durch das Horn verdeckt ist, zu genießen. Die[17] den Gipfel besteigen wollen, müssen dies mit Hilfe von Steigeisen, Stricken und Klammern tun.

Außer diesem Berge stehen an derselben Mittagseite noch andere, aber keiner ist so hoch, wenn sie sich auch früh im Herbste mit Schnee bedecken und ihn bis tief in den Frühling hinein behalten. Der Sommer aber nimmt denselben immer weg, und die Felsen glänzen freundlich im Sonnenscheine, und die tiefer gelegenen Wälder zeigen ihr sanftes Grün von breiten blauen Schatten durchschnitten, die so schön sind, daß man sich in seinem Leben nicht satt daran sehen kann.

An den andern Seiten des Tales, nämlich von Mitternacht, Morgen und Abend[18] her, sind die Berge langgestreckt und niederer, manche Felder und Wiesen steigen ziemlich hoch hinauf, und oberhalb ihrer sieht man verschiedene Waldblößen, Alpenhütten und dergleichen, bis sie an ihrem Rande mit feingezacktem Walde am Himmel hingehen, welche Auszackung eben ihre geringe Höhe anzeigt, während die mittäg-

jut out into the atmosphere of the higher regions and lead directly to the ice. On both sides of this road there are steep walls and this defile connects the snow mountain with the neck. To scale the ice one walks for a considerable time along its border, where it is surrounded by rocks, until one reaches the oldest perpetual snow that bridges the crevasses and supports the traveler most of the year. At the highest level of the perpetual snow the two horns rise out of the snow; one of these is the higher and is therefore the peak of the mountain. These peaks are very difficult to climb; since they are surrounded by a snow ditch, the glacial cleft, now broader, now narrower, over which one must jump; and since its perpendicular walls have only small ledges into which the foot can be inserted, most of the mountain climbers are content to have reached the glacial cleft and to enjoy from there the panorama, in sofar as it is not cut off by the horn. Those who want to climb the summit must do so with the help of crampons, ropes, and clamps.

There are other mountains besides this one on the same southern side, but none is so high, though they are covered with snow early in autumn and keep the snow until late into the spring. But the summer always takes it away, and the rocks gleam friendly in the sunshine, and the forests lying lower down show a gentle green intersected by broad blue shadows that are so beautiful that one could not tire of looking at them all one's life.

On the other sides of the valley, that is, to the north, east, and west, the mountains stretch away at a lower level. Some fields and meadows climb to a fairly high level, and above them one sees various clearings, Alpine huts, and such like, until they merge with the sky at their border as a serrated forest. This serration indicates their lesser elevation, while the southern mountains, although they support even more magnificent

lichen Berge, obwohl sie noch großartigere Wälder hegen, doch mit einem ganz glatten Rande an dem glänzenden Himmel hinstreichen.

Wenn man so ziemlich mitten in dem Tale steht, so hat man die Empfindung, als ginge nirgends ein Weg in dieses Becken herein und keiner daraus hinaus; allein diejenigen, welche öfter im Gebirge gewesen sind, kennen diese Täuschung gar wohl: in der Tat führen nicht nur verschiedene Wege und darunter sogar manche durch die Verschiebungen der Berge fast auf ebenem Boden in die nördlichen Flächen hinaus, sondern gegen Mittag, wo das Tal durch steilrechte Mauern fast geschlossen scheint, geht sogar ein Weg über den obenbenannten Hals.

Das Dörflein heißt Gschaid, und der Schneeberg, der auf seine Häuser herabschaut, heißt Gars.

Jenseits des Halses liegt ein viel schöneres und blühenderes Tal, als das von Gschaid ist, und es führt von der Unglücksäule der gebahnte Weg hinab. Es hat an seinem Eingange einen stattlichen Marktflecken, Millsdorf, der sehr groß ist, verschiedene Werke hat und in manchen Häusern städtische Gewerbe und Nahrung treibt. Die Bewohner sind viel wohlhabender als die in Gschaid, und obwohl nur drei Wegstunden[19] zwischen den beiden Tälern liegen, was für die an große Entfernungen gewöhnten und Mühseligkeiten liebenden Gebirgsbewohner eine unbedeutende Kleinigkeit ist, so sind doch Sitten und Gewohnheiten in den beiden Tälern so verschieden, selbst der äußere Anblick derselben ist so ungleich, als ob eine große Anzahl Meilen zwischen ihnen läge. Das ist in Gebirgen sehr oft der Fall und hängt nicht nur von der verschiedenen Lage der Täler gegen die Sonne ab, die sie oft mehr oder weniger begünstigt, sondern auch von dem Geiste der Bewohner, der durch gewisse Beschäftigungen nach dieser oder jener Richtung gezogen wird. Darin stimmen aber alle überein, daß sie an Herkömmlichkeiten und Väterweise hängen, großen Verkehr[20] leicht entbehren, ihr Tal außerordentlich lieben und ohne demselben kaum leben können.

Es vergehen oft Monate, oft fast ein Jahr, ehe ein Bewohner von Gschaid in das jenseitige Tal hinüber kommt und den

forests, stretch along the gleaming sky with a quite smooth border.

When one stands in about the middle of the valley, one has the feeling that no road leads into this basin and none out of it; but those who have often been in the mountains are quite familiar with this illusion; in fact, not only do various roads lead into the northern plains, and among them some that lie almost on level ground because of the dislocation of the mountains, but toward the south, where the valley seems almost blocked by perpendicular walls, there is even a road over the above mentioned neck.

The little village is called Gschaid, and the snow mountain that looks down on its houses is called Gars.

On the other side of the neck there is a much more beautiful and more fertile valley than that of Gschaid, and the beaten road from the accident pillar leads down to it. At its entrance there is a stately market town, Millsdorf, which is very large, has various factories, and some houses in which the trades and professions of the city are carried on. Its inhabitants are much more prosperous than those of Gschaid; and although only three hours' walking distance lies between the two valleys, which is an insignificant trifle for mountain dwellers, who are used to great distances and love hardships, the customs and habits in the two valleys are so different and they are so unlike even in external appearance that one would think a great number of miles lay between them. This is very often the case in the mountains; it depends not only on the different position of the valleys with relation to the sun, which often favors them more or less, but also on the mentality of the inhabitants which is drawn in this or that direction by certain occupations. But they are all alike in this: that they cling to tradition and to the ways of their forefathers, easily dispense with outside communication, love their valley inordinately, and can scarcely live without it.

Months often pass, often almost a year, before an inhabitant of Gschaid crosses over into the valley beyond and visits the

großen Marktflecken Millsdorf besucht. Die Millsdorfer halten
es ebenso, obwohl sie ihrerseits doch Verkehr mit dem Lande
draußen pflegen und daher nicht so abgeschieden sind wie die
Gschaider. Es geht sogar ein Weg, der eine Straße heißen
könnte, längs ihres Tales, und mancher Reisende und mancher
Wanderer geht hindurch, ohne nur im geringsten zu ahnen,
daß mitternachtwärts seines Weges jenseits des hohen herab-
blickenden Schneebergs noch ein Tal sei, in dem viele Häuser
zerstreut sind und in dem das Dörflein mit dem spitzigen
Kirchturme steht.

Unter den Gewerben des Dorfes, welche bestimmt sind, den
Bedarf des Tales zu decken, ist auch das eines Schusters, das
nirgends entbehrt werden kann, wo die Menschen nicht in
ihrem Urzustande sind. Die Gschaider aber sind so weit über
diesem Stande, daß sie recht gute und tüchtige Gebirgsfußbe-
kleidung brauchen. Der Schuster ist mit einer kleinen Ausnahme der einzige im Tale. Sein Haus steht auf dem Platze in
Gschaid, wo überhaupt die besseren stehen, und schaut mit
seinen grauen Mauern, weißen Fenstersimsen und grün ange-
strichenen Fensterläden auf die vier Linden hinaus. Es hat im
Erdgeschosse die Arbeitsstube, die Gesellenstube, eine größere
und kleinere Wohnstube, ein Verkaufstübchen, nebst Küche
und Speisekammer und allen zugehörigen Gelassen; im ersten[21]
Stockwerke oder eigentlich im Raume des Giebels hat es die
Oberstube oder eigentliche Prunkstube. Zwei Prachtbetten,
schöne geglättete Kästen mit Kleidern stehen da, dann ein
Gläserkästchen mit Geschirren, ein Tisch mit eingelegter Arbeit, gepolsterte Sessel, ein Mauerkästchen mit den Ersparnis-
sen, dann hängen an den Wänden Heiligenbilder, zwei schöne
Sackuhren, gewonnene Preise im Schießen, und endlich sind
auch Scheibengewehre und Jagdbüchsen nebst ihrem Zugehöre
in einem eigenen, mit Glastafeln versehenen Kasten auf-
gehängt. An das Schusterhaus ist ein kleineres Häuschen, nur
durch den Einfahrtsschwibbogen getrennt, angebaut, welches
genau dieselbe Bauart hat und zum Schusterhause wie ein Teil
zum Ganzen gehört. Es hat nur eine Stube mit den dazu gehö-
rigen Wohnteilen. Es hat die Bestimmung, dem Hausbesitzer,
sobald er das Anwesen seinem Sohne oder Nachfolger überge-
ben hat, als sogenanntes Ausnahmstübchen zu dienen, in wel-

large market village of Millsdorf. The people of Millsdorf be-
have in the same way, although they for their part do associate
with the country outside and are therefore not as isolated as
the people of Gschaid. There is even a road that might be called
a highway stretching along their valley; and many a tourist and
many a wanderer traverses it without in the least suspecting
that to the north of his road, beyond the tall snow mountain
that looks down on him, there is another valley in which many
houses are scattered and in which the little village with the
pointed steeple is situated.

Among the trades of the village which are intended to supply
the needs of the valley there is also that of a shoemaker—a
trade that no place can dispense with where people do not live
in the primitive state. The people of Gschaid, however, are so
far above this state that they need really good and sturdy mountain footwear. The shoemaker is, with a small exception, the
only one in the valley. His house stands on the square in Gschaid
where in general the better houses stand and looks out at the
four linden trees with its gray walls, white window sills, and
green painted shutters. On its ground floor it has a work room,
the journeyman's room, a larger and a smaller living room, a
little sales room, besides the kitchen and pantry and all the little
rooms that go with these. On the second floor, which is really
under the gables, is the upper room or best room. Two handsome beds, beautiful polished wardrobes with clothes in them
stand in it, also a glass cabinet filled with china, an inlaid table,
upholstered easy chairs, a little wall safe containing his savings.
On the walls hang pictures of saints, two beautiful pocket
watches, trophies won in shooting. And finally, target and hunt-
ing rifles, together with their accessories, are hung in a special
cabinet with glass panels. A smaller house is built onto the
shoemaker's house, separated from it only by the arch over the
driveway; it is built in the same style of architecture exactly and
belongs to the cobbler's house as a part to the whole. It has
only one room and the requisite living accommodation. Its purpose is to serve as a so-called "old folks' room" for the owner
of the house after he has turned over his property to his son
or successor. He will live in it with his wife until both have died,
when the room will again stand empty awaiting a new occupant.

chem er mit seinem Weibe so lange haust, bis beide gestorben sind, die Stube wieder leer steht und auf einen neuen Bewohner wartet.

Das Schusterhaus hat nach rückwärts[22] Stall und Scheune; denn jeder Talbewohner ist, selbst wenn er ein Gewerbe treibt, auch Landbebauer und zieht hieraus seine gute und nachhaltige Nahrung. Hinter diesen Gebäuden ist endlich der Garten, der fast bei keinem besseren Hause in Gschaid fehlt und von dem sie ihre Gemüse, ihr Obst und für festliche Gelegenheiten ihre Blumen ziehen. Wie oft im Gebirge, so ist auch in Gschaid die Bienenzucht in diesen Gärten sehr verbreitet.

Die kleine Ausnahme, deren oben Erwähnung geschah, und die Nebenbuhlerschaft der Alleinherrlichkeit des Schusters ist ein anderer Schuster, der alte Tobias, der aber eigentlich kein Nebenbuhler ist, weil er nur mehr[23] flickt, hierin viel zu tun hat und es sich nicht im entferntesten beikommen läßt,[24] mit dem vornehmen Platzschuster in einen Wettstreit einzugehen, insbesondere, da der Platzschuster ihn häufig mit Lederflecken, Sohlenabschnitten und dergleichen Dingen unentgeltlich versieht. Der alte Tobias sitzt im Sommer am Ende des Dörfchens unter Holunderbüschen und arbeitet. Er ist umringt von Schuhen und Bundschuhen, die aber sämtlich alt, grau, kotig und zerrissen sind. Stiefel mit langen Röhren sind nicht da, weil sie im Dorfe und in der Gegend nicht getragen werden; nur zwei Personen haben solche, der Pfarrer und der Schullehrer, welche aber beides, flicken und neue Ware machen, nur bei dem Platzschuster lassen. Im Winter sitzt der alte Tobias in seinem Stübchen hinter den Holunderstauden und hat warm geheizt, weil das Holz in Gschaid nicht teuer ist.

Der Platzschuster ist, ehe er das Haus angetreten hat, ein Gemsewildschütze gewesen und hat überhaupt in seiner Jugend, wie die Gschaider sagen, nicht gut getan. Er war in der Schule immer einer der besten Schüler gewesen, hatte dann von seinem Vater das Handwerk gelernt, ist auf Wanderung[25] gegangen und ist endlich wieder zurückgekehrt. Statt, wie es sich für einen Gewerbsmann ziemt und wie sein Vater es zeitlebens getan, einen schwarzen Hut zu tragen, tat er einen grünen auf, steckte noch alle bestehenden Federn darauf und stolzierte mit ihm und mit dem kürzesten Lodenrocke,[26] den es im Tale

The shoemaker's house has a stable and barn at the rear; for every valley dweller, even when he has a trade, is a farmer too and derives a good and lasting sustenance from the soil. Behind these buildings there is finally the garden, which almost none of the better houses in Gschaid lacks and from which they obtain their vegetables, fruit, and flowers for festive occasions. As often in the mountains, so too in Gschaid bee-keeping is general in these gardens.

The small exception mentioned above, a rival of the unlimited monopoly of the shoemaker, is another shoemaker, old Tobias. He is, however, not a real competitor, because he now only mends, is kept busy at it, and has not the remotest intention of entering into competition with the elegant shoemaker on the square, especially as the latter frequently supplies him with scraps of leather, remnants of soles, and such things without charge. In the summer old Tobias sits at the end of the little village working under the elder bushes. He is surrounded by shoes and peasant boots, all of them old, gray, muddy, and torn. Boots with high tops are not there, because they are not worn in the village or in the region. Only two people have them, the priest and schoolteacher, but they have only the shoemaker on the square do both their mending and new work. In the winter old Tobias sits in his little room behind the elder bushes and keeps warm because wood is not expensive in Gschaid.

Before taking over the house, the shoemaker on the square was a chamois poacher; in his youth he was, as the people of Gschaid say, altogether a good-for-nothing. He had always been one of the best pupils in school, had then learned the trade from his father, had gone on the road as a journeyman, and had finally come home again. Instead of wearing a black hat as befits a tradesman and as his father had done all his life, he put on a green one, put every possible kind of feather on it, and strutted about in this hat and in the shortest Loden jacket in the valley, whereas his father always wore a jacket of dark,

gab, herum, während sein Vater immer einen Rock von dunkler, womöglich schwarzer Farbe hatte, der auch, weil er einem Gewerbsmanne angehörte, immer sehr weit herabgeschnitten sein mußte. Der junge Schuster war auf allen Tanzplätzen und Kegelbahnen zu sehen. Wenn ihm jemand eine gute Lehre gab, so pfiff er ein Liedlein. Er ging mit seinem Scheibengewehre zu allen Schießen der Nachbarschaft und brachte manchmal einen Preis nach Hause, was er für einen großen Sieg hielt. Der Preis bestand meistens aus Münzen, die künstlich[27] gefaßt waren und zu deren Gewinnung der Schuster mehr gleiche Münzen ausgeben mußte, als der Preis enthielt, besonders da er wenig haushälterisch mit dem Gelde war. Er ging auf alle Jagden, die in der Gegend abgehalten wurden, und hatte sich den Namen eines guten Schützen erworben. Er ging aber auch manchmal allein mit seiner Doppelbüchse und mit Steigeisen fort, und einmal sagte man, daß er eine schwere Wunde im Kopfe erhalten habe.

In Millsdorf war ein Färber, welcher gleich am Anfange des Marktfleckens, wenn man auf dem Wege von Gschaid hinüber kam, ein sehr ansehnliches Gewerbe hatte, mit vielen Leuten und sogar, was im Tale etwas Unerhörtes war, mit Maschinen arbeitete. Außerdem besaß er noch eine ausgebreitete Feldwirtschaft. Zu der Tochter dieses reichen Färbers ging der Schuster über das Gebirge, um sie zu gewinnen. Sie war wegen ihrer Schönheit weit und breit[28] berühmt, aber auch wegen ihrer Eingezogenheit, Sittsamkeit und Häuslichkeit belobt. Dennoch, hieß es,[29] soll der Schuster ihre Aufmerksamkeit erregt haben. Der Färber ließ ihn nicht in sein Haus kommen; und hatte die schöne Tochter schon früher keine öffentlichen Plätze und Lustbarkeiten besucht und war selten außer dem Hause ihrer Eltern zu sehen gewesen: so ging sie jetzt schon gar nirgends mehr hin als in die Kirche oder in ihren Garten oder in den Räumen des Hauses herum.

Einige Zeit nach dem Tode seiner Eltern, durch welchen ihm das Haus derselben zugefallen war, das er nun allein bewohnte, änderte sich der Schuster gänzlich. So wie er früher getollt hatte, so saß er jetzt in seiner Stube und hämmerte Tag und Nacht an seinen Sohlen. Er setzte prahlend einen Preis darauf,

if possible black, color and which also had to be very long because it was worn by a tradesman. The young shoemaker could be seen on every dance floor and bowling alley. When anyone tried to give him good advice, he whistled a little song. He went to every shooting match in the neighborhood with his target rifle and sometimes brought home a prize, which he considered a great triumph. The prize consisted mostly of coins in an artistic setting, but to win them the shoemaker had to spend more coins of the same kind than the prize amounted to, especially as he was not economical with money. He went to every hunt that was held in the region and had gained the name of a good marksman. But sometimes he went away alone with his double-barreled shotgun and climbing irons, and once, it was said, he had received a serious wound in his head.

In Millsdorf there was a dyer who had a considerable business right at the entrance to the market village, where one came over on the road from Gschaid. He employed many people and even used machinery, which was something unheard of in the valley. Besides, he owned an extensive farm. To win the daughter of this rich dyer the shoemaker crossed the range. She was noted for her beauty far and wide, but she was also praised for her modesty, virtue, and domesticity. Nevertheless, it was said, the shoemaker had attracted her attention. The dyer would not admit him to his house; if the beautiful daughter had, even before this, never gone to public places of amusement and had rarely been seen outside her parents' house, she now went absolutely nowhere except to church or she walked about in her garden or in the rooms of her home.

Some time after the death of his parents, whereby he had acquired their house in which he now lived alone, the shoemaker changed completely. As he had formerly led a wild life, so he now sat in his room, hammering away at his soles day and night. He boastingly offered a prize to anyone who

wenn es jemand gäbe, der bessere Schuhe und Fußbekleidungen machen könne. Er nahm keine andern Arbeiter als die besten und trillte[30] sie noch sehr herum, wenn sie in seiner Werkstätte arbeiteten, daß sie ihm folgten und die Sache so einrichteten, wie er befahl. Wirklich brachte er es jetzt auch dahin, daß nicht nur das ganze Dorf Gschaid, das zum größten Teile die Schusterarbeit aus benachbarten Tälern bezogen hatte, bei ihm arbeiten ließ, daß das ganze Tal bei ihm arbeiten ließ und daß endlich sogar einzelne von Millsdorf und anderen Tälern herein kamen und sich ihre Fußbekleidungen von dem Schuster in Gschaid machen ließen. Sogar in die Ebene hinaus verbreitete sich sein Ruhm, daß manche, die in die Gebirge gehen wollten, sich die Schuhe dazu von ihm machen ließen.

Er richtete das Haus sehr schön zusammen, und in dem Warengewölbe glänzten auf den Brettern die Schuhe, Bundstiefel und Stiefel; und wenn am Sonntage die ganze Bevölkerung des Tales hereinkam und man bei den vier Linden des Platzes stand, ging man gerne zu dem Schusterhause hin und sah durch die Gläser in die Warenstube, wo die Käufer und Besteller waren.

Nach seiner Vorliebe zu den Bergen machte er auch jetzt die Gebirgsbundschuhe am besten. Er pflegte in der Wirtsstube zu sagen: es gäbe keinen, der ihm einen fremden Gebirgsbundschuh zeigen könne, der sich mit einem seinigen vergleichen lasse. „Sie wissen es nicht", pflegte er beizufügen, „sie haben es in ihrem Leben nicht erfahren, wie ein solcher Schuh sein muß, daß der gestirnte Himmel der Nägel recht auf der Sohle sitze und das gebührende Eisen enthalte, daß der Schuh außen hart sei, damit kein Geröllstein, wie scharf er auch sei, empfunden werde und daß er sich von innen doch weich und zärtlich wie ein Handschuh an die Füße lege."

Der Schuster hatte sich ein sehr großes Buch machen lassen, in welches er alle verfertigte Ware eintrug, die Namen derer beifügte, die den Stoff geliefert und die Ware gekauft hatten, und eine kurze Bemerkung über die Güte des Erzeugnisses beischrieb. Die gleichartigen Fußbekleidungen hatten ihre fortlaufenden Zahlen, und das Buch lag in der großen Lade seines Gewölbes.

could make better shoes and footwear than he. He employed
none but the best workmen and drilled away at them when
they worked in his shop until they obeyed him and did things
exactly as he ordered them to do. And really he now brought
matters to the point where not only the whole village of Gschaid,
which for the most part had had its shoe work done in neighboring valleys, now patronized him but that the whole valley
had him do their work and finally even some people from
Millsdorf and other valleys came over and had the shoemaker
of Gschaid make their footwear. His fame spread even to the
plain, so that some who wanted to go into the mountains had
him make their shoes for this purpose.

He fixed up the house handsomely, and in his salesroom the
shoes, laced boots, and high boots shone on the shelves. On
Sundays, when the whole population of the valley came in and
stood around at the four linden trees on the square, they liked
to go over to the shoemaker's house and look through the
windows into the salesroom in which shoes were being bought
and orders taken.

In accordance with his love for the mountains, his best work
was now his laced mountain shoes. He used to say in the taproom: no one could show him a laced mountain shoe made
elsewhere that could compare with his. "They don't know," he
would add, "they haven't had the practical experience in all
their lives how such a shoe should be made: so that the starry
heaven of nails should sit properly on the sole and that there
should be the necessary iron, that the shoe should be hard on
the outside, so that no loose stone, however sharp it might be,
would be felt, and that it would yet settle on the foot softly and
tenderly like a glove on the inside."

The shoemaker had had a very large book made into which
he entered all the goods he had finished, adding the names of
those who had supplied the material and bought the goods and
a brief remark about the quality of the product. Footwear of
the same type had serial numbers, and the book lay in the large
drawer of the shop.

Wenn die schöne Färberstochter von Millsdorf auch nicht
aus der Eltern Hause kam, wenn sie auch weder Freunde noch
Verwandte besuchte, so konnte es der Schuster von Gschaid
doch so machen, daß sie ihn von ferne sah, wenn sie in die
Kirche ging, wenn sie in dem Garten war und wenn sie aus
den Fenstern ihres Zimmers auf die Matten blickte. Wegen
dieses unausgesetzten Sehens hatte es die Färberin durch
langes, inständiges und ausdauerndes Flehen für ihre Tochter
dahin gebracht, daß der halsstarrige Färber nachgab und daß
der Schuster, weil er denn nun doch besser geworden, die
schöne, reiche Millsdorferin als Eheweib nach Gschaid führte.
Aber der Färber war desungeachtet auch ein Mann, der seinen
Kopf hatte.[31] Ein rechter Mensch, sagte er, müsse sein Gewerbe
treiben, daß es blühe und vorwärts komme, er müsse daher
sein Weib, seine Kinder, sich und sein Gesinde ernähren, Hof
und Haus im Stande des Glanzes halten und sich noch ein
Erkleckliches erübrigen, welches letztere doch allein imstande
sei, ihm Ansehen und Ehre in der Welt zu geben; darum erhalte
seine Tochter nichts als eine vortreffliche Ausstattung, das andere ist Sache des Ehemanns, daß er es mache und für alle
Zukunft es besorge. Die Färberei in Millsdorf und die Landwirtschaft auf dem Färberhause sei für sich ein ansehnliches
und ehrenwertes Gewerbe, das seiner Ehre willen[32] bestehen
und wozu alles, was da sei, als Grundstock dienen müsse, daher
er nichts weggebe. Wenn einmal er und sein Eheweib, die
Färberin, tot seien, dann gehöre Färberei und Landwirtschaft
in Millsdorf ihrer einzigen Tochter, nämlich der Schusterin in
Gschaid, und Schuster und Schusterin könnten dann damit
tun, was sie wollten; aber alles dieses nur, wenn die Erben es
wert wären, das Erbe zu empfangen; wären sie es nicht wert,
so ging das Erbe auf die Kinder derselben, und wenn keine
vorhanden wären, mit der Ausnahme des ledichlichen Pflicht-
teiles auf andere Verwandte über. Der Schuster verlangte auch
nichts, er zeigte im Stolze, daß es ihm nur um die schöne Färberstochter in Millsdorf zu tun gewesen[33] und daß er sie schon
ernähren und erhalten könne, wie sie zu Hause ernährt und
erhalten worden ist. Er kleidete sie als sein Eheweib nicht nur
schöner als alle Gschaiderinnen und alle Bewohnerinnen des
Tales, sondern auch schöner, als sie sich je zu Hause getragen

Even though the fair daughter of the dyer of Millsdorf did not leave her parents' house, even though she visited neither friends nor relatives, the shoemaker of Gschaid could yet bring it about that she saw him from a distance when she went to church, when she was in the garden, and when she looked out on the meadows from the windows of her room. Because of this constant looking, the dyer's wife had succeeded, through long, insistent, and persevering supplication on behalf of her daughter, in making the stiff-necked dyer yield, so that the shoemaker, because he had improved after all, led the beautiful rich girl from Millsdorf home to Gschaid as his wife. Neverthe less, the dyer was a headstrong man too. A real man, he said, must carry on his trade in such a way that it will flourish and progress; he must therefore support his wife, his children, himself, and his servants, maintain his house and farm in a prosperous state. He must besides lay aside a considerable sum, which alone will procure for him respect and honor in the world. For this reason his daughter would get nothing but an excellent trousseau; the rest was the concern of her husband, to look after her now and to provide for her future. The dyeworks in Millsdorf and the farm adjoining the house were in themselves a respectable and honorable business; they would have to continue for the sake of his honor and serve as the basis for everything else that was there; so he would give away nothing. Once he and his wife were dead, the dyeworks and the farm in Millsdorf would belong to their only daughter, that is the wife of the shoemaker of Gschaid, and they could both do what they pleased with it. But all this only if the heirs were worthy of receiving the inheritance; if they were not, the inheritance would go to their children, and if there were none, to other relatives, except for what was legally theirs. The shoemaker too asked for nothing; he demonstrated in his pride that his interest had been confined to the fair daughter of the dyer of Millsdorf and that he could certainly support and maintain her as she had been supported and maintained at home. He dressed her, as his wife, not only more handsomely than all the women of Gschaid and all the inhabitants of the valley but even more handsomely than she had ever dressed at home; and food, drink, and all other services had to be better and choicer than

hatte, und Speise, Trank und übrige Behandlung mußte besser
und rücksichtsvoller sein, als sie das gleiche im väterlichen
Hause genossen hatte. Und um dem Schwiegervater zu trotzen,
kaufte er mit erübrigten Summen nach und nach immer mehr
Grundstücke so ein, daß er einen tüchtigen Besitz beisammen
hatte.

Weil die Bewohner von Gschaid so selten aus ihrem Tale kommen und nicht einmal oft nach Millsdorf hinüber gehen, von
dem sie durch Bergrücken und durch Sitten geschieden sind,
weil ferner ihnen gar kein Fall vorkommt, daß ein Mann sein
Tal verläßt und sich in dem benachbarten ansiedelt (Ansied-
lungen in großen Entfernungen kommen öfter vor), weil endlich auch kein Weib oder Mädchen gerne von einem Tale in
ein anderes auswandert, außer in dem ziemlich seltenen Falle,
wenn sie der Liebe folgt und als Eheweib und zu dem Ehemann
in ein anderes Tal kommt: so geschah es, daß die schöne
Färberstochter von Millsdorf, da sie Schusterin in Gschaid
geworden war, doch immer von allen Gschaidern als Fremde
angesehen wurde, und wenn man ihr auch nichts Übles antat,
ja wenn man sie ihres schönen Wesens und ihrer Sitten wegen
sogar liebte, doch immer etwas vorhanden war, das wie Scheu
oder, wenn man will, wie Rücksicht aussah und nicht zu dem
Innigen und Gleichartigen kommen ließ,[34] wie Gschaiderinnen
gegen Gschaiderinnen, Gschaider gegen Gschaider hatten. Es
war so, ließ sich nicht abstellen und wurde durch die bessere
Tracht und durch das erleichterte häusliche Leben der Schusterin noch vermehrt.

Sie hatte ihrem Manne nach dem ersten Jahre einen Sohn
und in einigen Jahren darauf ein Töchterlein geboren. Sie
glaubte aber, daß er die Kinder nicht so liebe, wie sie sich
vorstellte, daß es sein solle, und wie sie sich bewußt war, daß
sie dieselben liebe; denn sein Angesicht war meistens ernsthaft
und mit seinen Arbeiten beschäftigt. Er spielte und tändelte
selten mit den Kindern und sprach stets ruhig mit ihnen,
gleichsam so, wie man mit Erwachsenen spricht. Was Nahrung
und Kleidung und andere äußere Dinge anbelangte, hielt er
die Kinder untadelig.

In der ersten Zeit der Ehe kam die Färberin öfter nach
Gschaid, und die jungen Eheleute besuchten auch Millsdorf

she had enjoyed in her father's house. And to spite his father-in-law he bought more and more land with sums of money that he had saved, so that he amassed a considerable estate.

Because the inhabitants of Gschaid so rarely leave their valley and do not even frequently go to Millsdorf, from which they are separated by mountains and customs; and because it never happens to them that a man leaves his valley and settles in the neighboring one (settlements in distant places occur more often); and finally because no wife or girl likes to emigrate from one valley to another, except in the fairly rare case when she follows the call of love and joins her husband as his wedded wife in another valley—it happened that the fair daughter of the dyer of Millsdorf was still regarded as a stranger by all the people of Gschaid even after she had become the wife of the shoemaker of Gschaid. And even though they did her no harm, indeed though they even loved her because of her beauty and good manners, there was always something present that looked like shyness or, if you will, deference and did not permit the development of that intimacy and equality that the men and women of Gschaid had for each other. It was so, could not be stopped, and was even increased by the better clothes the shoemaker's wife wore and the easier life she led at home.

After the first year she had borne her husband a son and a few years later a little daughter. But she felt that he did not love the children as she imagined he should and as she was conscious of loving them herself, for his countenance was mostly serious and he was busy with his work. He rarely played and dallied with the children and always spoke quietly to them, just as one speaks to grown-ups. But as far as food and clothing and other externals were concerned, he kept the children above reproach.

In the first period of the marriage the dyer's wife came to Gschaid fairly often, and the young couple visited Millsdorf at

zuweilen bei Kirchweihen oder anderen festlichen Gelegenheiten. Als aber die Kinder auf der Welt waren, war die Sache
anders geworden. Wenn schon Mütter ihre Kinder lieben und
sich nach ihnen sehnen, so ist dieses von Großmüttern öfter
noch in höherem Grade der Fall: sie verlangen zuweilen mit
wahrlich krankhafter Sehnsucht nach ihren Enkeln. Die Färberin kam sehr oft nach Gschaid herüber, um die Kinder zu
sehen, ihnen Geschenke zu bringen, eine Weile dazubleiben
und dann mit guten Ermahnungen zu scheiden. Da aber das
Alter und die Gesundheitsumstände der Färberin die öfteren
Fahrten nicht mehr so möglich machten, und der Färber aus
dieser Ursache Einsprache tat, wurde auf etwas anderes geson-
nen, die Sache wurde umgekehrt, und die Kinder kamen jetzt
zur Großmutter. Die Mutter brachte sie selber öfter in einem
Wagen, öfter aber wurden sie, da sie noch im zarten Alter
waren, eingemummt einer Magd mitgegeben, die sie in einem
Fuhrwerke über den Hals brachte. Als sie aber größer waren,
gingen sie zu Fuße entweder mit der Mutter oder mit einer
Magd nach Millsdorf, ja da der Knabe geschickt, stark und klug
geworden war, ließ man ihn allein den bekannten Weg über
den Hals gehen, und wenn es sehr schön war, und er bat,
erlaubte man auch, daß ihn die kleine Schwester begleite. Dies
ist bei den Gschaidern gebräuchlich, weil sie an starkes Fußge-
hen gewöhnt sind und die Eltern überhaupt, namentlich aber
ein Mann wie der Schuster, es gerne sehen und eine Freude
daran haben, wenn ihre Kinder tüchtig werden.

So geschah es, daß die zwei Kinder den Weg über den Hals
öfter zurücklegten als die übrigen Dörfler zusammengenom-
men, und da schon ihre Mutter in Gschaid gewissermaßen wie
eine Fremde behandelt wurde, so wurden durch diesen Um-
stand auch die Kinder fremd, sie waren kaum Gschaider und
gehörten halb nach Millsdorf hinüber.

Der Knabe Konrad hatte schon das ernste Wesen seines Vaters, und das Mädchen Susanna, nach ihrer Mutter so genannt,
oder, wie man es zur Abkürzung nannte, Sanna, hatte viel
Glauben zu seinen Kenntnissen, seiner Einsicht und seiner
Macht und gab sich unbedingt unter seine Leitung, gerade so
wie die Mutter sich unbedingt unter die Leitung des Vaters
gab, dem sie alle Einsicht und Geschicklichkeit zutraute.

times, at church fairs or on other festive occasions. But when
the children came, matters were different. Though mothers
may love their children and yearn for them, this is often the
case to an even higher degree with grandmothers; they sometimes yearn for their grandchildren with a truly morbid craving.
The dyer's wife came over to Gschaid very often to see the
children, to bring them gifts, to remain there a while, and then
to depart with some good advice to them. But since the age
and the health of the dyer's wife made the fairly frequent
visits impossible, and because the dyer raised objections on this
account, another plan was devised; the matter was reversed
and the children now came to the grandmother. Their mother
herself often brought them in a carriage; more frequently,
however, they were bundled up, because they were still of a
tender age, and handed over to a maid, who brought them
over the neck in a carriage. But when they were bigger, they
went to Millsdorf on foot either with their mother or with a
maid. Indeed, since the boy had become alert, strong, and
clever, he was allowed to take the familiar road over the neck
alone; and when the weather was very beautiful and he requested it, he was allowed to take his little sister with him.
This is customary with the people of Gschaid because they are
accustomed to a good deal of walking, and parents in general,
especially a man like the shoemaker, are glad and happy to see
their children growing to be capable.

So it happened that the two children took the road over the
neck more often than all the rest of the villagers taken together.
Since their mother was already treated more or less as a stranger
in Gschaid, the children too became strangers because of this
circumstance; they were scarcely Gschaid children and half
belonged to Millsdorf.

The boy Conrad already had the serious character of his
father, and the girl Susanna, named after her mother, or Sanna,
as she was called for short, had much faith in his knowledge,
judgment, and power and yielded absolutely to his leadership,
just as her mother yielded absolutely to the leadership of the
father, to whom she attributed unerring judgment and ability.

An schönen Tagen konnte man morgens die Kinder durch
das Tal gegen Mittag wandern sehen, über die Wiese gehen
und dort anlangen, wo der Wald des Halses gegen sie her-
schaut. Sie näherten sich dem Walde, gingen auf seinem Wege
allgemach über die Erhöhung hinan, und kamen, ehe der Mittag eingetreten war, auf den offenen Wiesen auf der anderen
Seite gegen Millsdorf hinunter. Konrad zeigte Sanna die Wiesen, die dem Großvater gehörten, dann gingen sie durch seine
Felder, auf denen er ihr die Getreidearten erklärte, dann sahen
sie auf Stangen unter dem Vorsprunge des Daches die langen
Tücher zum Trocknen herabhängen, die sich im Winde schlän-
gelten oder närrische Gesichter machten, dann hörten sie seine
Walkmühle[35] und seinen Lohstampf, die er an seinem Bache
für Tuchmacher und Gerber angelegt hatte, dann bogen sie
noch um eine Ecke der Felder und gingen in kurzem durch
die Hintertür in den Garten der Färberei, wo sie von der Großmutter empfangen wurden. Diese ahnte immer, wenn die
Kinder kamen, sah zu den Fenstern aus und erkannte sie von
weitem, wenn Sannas rotes Tuch recht in der Sonne leuchtete.

Sie führte die Kinder dann durch die Waschstube und Presse
in das Zimmer, ließ sie niedersetzen, ließ nicht zu, daß sie
Halstücher oder Jäckchen lüfteten, damit sie sich nicht ver-
kühlten,[36] und behielt sie beim Essen da. Nach dem Essen
durften sie sich lüften, spielen, durften in den Räumen des
großväterlichen Hauses herumgehen oder sonst tun, was sie
wollten, wenn es nur nicht unschicklich oder verboten war. Der
Färber, welcher immer bei dem Essen war, fragte sie um ihre
Schulgegenstände aus und schärfte ihnen besonders ein, was
sie lernen sollten. Nachmittags wurden sie von der Großmutter
schon, ehe die Zeit kam, zum Aufbruche getrieben, daß sie ja
nicht zu spät kämen. Obgleich der Färber keine Mitgift gegeben
hatte und vor seinem Tode von seinem Vermögen nichts weg-
zugeben gelobt hatte, glaubte sich die Färberin an diese Dinge
doch nicht so strenge gebunden, und sie gab den Kindern nicht
allein während ihrer Anwesenheit allerlei, worunter nicht selten
ein Münzstück und zuweilen gar von ansehnlichem Werte war,
sondern sie band ihnen auch immer zwei Bündelchen zusammen, in denen sich Dinge befanden, von denen sie glaubte,

On fine days one could see the children hiking in the morning southward through the valley, walking over the meadow and reaching the place where the forest of the neck looks down toward it. They would approach the forest, walk gradually up the slope on the road, and before noon were coming down the open meadows on the other side toward Millsdorf. Conrad showed Sanna the meadows that belonged to their grandfather; then they went through his fields, in which he explained to her the various kinds of grain; then they saw the long cloths hanging on poles under the projecting roof to dry, coiling snakelike in the wind or making comical faces; then they heard his fulling mill and his bark crusher that he had built beside his brook for cloth makers and tanners; then they turned another corner of the fields and in a short while entered the garden of the dyeworks by a back door, where they were received by their grandmother. She always had a premonition when the children were coming, looked out of the windows and recognized them from a distance when Sanna's red kerchief shone brightly in the sun.

She would then lead the children through the laundry and ironing room into the living room, made them sit down, would not let them loosen their kerchiefs or little jackets, so that they might not catch cold, and kept them there for dinner. After dinner they were allowed to undo their things, play, walk around in the rooms of grandfather's house or do whatever they wished, as long as it was not improper or forbidden. The dyer, who was always present at dinner, questioned them about their studies at school and especially impressed on them what they ought to learn. In the afternoon their grandmother would urge them, even before it was time, to start out so that they would not arrive too late. Although the dyer had given no dowry and had vowed to give away no part of his fortune before his death, his wife did not consider herself strictly bound to these vows, and she not only gave the children all sorts of things while they were present, often including coins of considerable value, but she always tied up two bundles for them in which there were things she thought they needed or which would give the children pleasure. And even if the same things were

daß sie notwendig wären oder daß sie den Kindern Freude machen könnten. Und wenn oft die nämlichen Dinge im Schusterhause in Gschaid in aller Trefflichkeit vorhanden waren, so gab sie die Großmutter in der Freude des Gebens doch, und die Kinder trugen sie als etwas Besonderes nach Hause. So geschah es nun, daß die Kinder am Heiligen Abende schon unwissend die Geschenke in Schachteln gut versiegelt und verwahrt nach Hause trugen, die ihnen in der Nacht einbeschert werden sollten.

Weil die Großmutter die Kinder immer schon vor der Zeit zum Fortgehen drängte, damit sie nicht zu spät nach Hause kämen, so erzielte sie hiedurch, daß die Kinder gerade auf dem Wege bald an dieser, bald an jener Stelle sich aufhielten. Sie saßen gerne an dem Haselnußgehege, das auf dem Halse ist, und schlugen mit Steinen Nüsse auf oder spielten, wenn keine Nüsse waren, mit Blättern oder mit Hölzlein oder mit den weichen, braunen Zäpfchen, die im ersten Frühjahre von den Zweigen der Nadelbäume herabfielen. Manchmal erzählte Konrad dem Schwesterchen Geschichten, oder wenn sie zu der roten Unglücksäule kamen, führte er sie ein Stück auf dem Seitenwege links gegen die Höhen hinan und sagte ihr, daß man da auf den Schneeberg gelange, daß dort Felsen und Steine seien, daß die Gemsen herumspringen und große Vögel fliegen. Er führte sie oft über den Wald hinaus, sie betrachteten dann den dürren Rasen und die kleinen Sträucher der Heidekräuter; aber er führte sie wieder zurück und brachte sie immer vor der Abenddämmerung nach Hause, was ihm stets Lob eintrug.

Einmal war am Heiligen Abende, da die erste Morgendämmerung in dem Tale von Gschaid in Helle übergegangen war, ein dünner, trockener Schleier über den ganzen Himmel gebreitet, so daß man die ohnedem schiefe und ferne Sonne im Südosten nur als einen undeutlichen roten Fleck sah, überdies war an diesem Tage eine milde, beinahe laulichte Luft unbeweglich im ganzen Tale und auch an dem Himmel, wie die unveränderte und ruhige Gestalt der Wolken zeigte. Da sagte die Schustersfrau zu ihren Kindern: „Weil ein so angenehmer Tag ist, weil es so lange nicht geregnet hat und die Wege fest sind, und weil es auch der Vater gestern unter der Bedingung

often in the shoemaker's house in Gschaid, and of excellent quality, the grandmother gave them nevertheless, for the joy of giving, and the children took them home as something special. And so it happened that on Christmas Eve the children would, without knowing it, carry home well-sealed and packed boxes containing the gifts that were to be presented to them that night.

Because their grandmother always urged the children to start for home sooner than was necessary, so that they might not arrive too late, all she achieved by this maneuver was that the children stopped on the way now at one spot, now at another. They liked to sit by the hazelnut bushes on the neck and they cracked the nuts open with stones, or, if there were no nuts, they played with leaves or little bits of wood or with the soft brown little cones that fell from the branches of the pine trees in the early spring. Sometimes Conrad told his little sister stories, or when they came to the red accident pillar he took her up a piece on the side road to the left toward the heights and told her that you got to the snow mountain that way, that there were rocks and stones there, that the chamois leaped about and the big birds flew there. He often took her beyond the forest; they would then gaze at the dry grass and the little shrubs of heather; but he led her back and always brought her home again before dark, which always earned him praise.

Once, on the day before Christmas, when the first dawn in the valley of Gschaid had changed into full day, a thin, dry veil was spread over the whole sky, so that the sun in the southeast, which in any case was low and distant, could only be seen as an indistinct red spot. On this day, moreover, the air in the whole valley and in the sky too was mild, almost tepid and motionless, as was proved by the unchanged and calm shape of the clouds. So the shoemaker's wife said to her children: "Since it is such a pleasant day, because it hasn't rained for such a long time, and the roads are firm, and because father gave permission for it on condition that today would be suitable

erlaubt hat, wenn der heutige Tag dazu geeignet ist, so dürft ihr zur Großmutter nach Millsdorf gehen; aber ihr müßt den Vater noch vorher fragen."

Die Kinder, welche noch in ihren Nachtkleidchen dastanden, liefen in die Nebenstube, in welcher der Vater mit einem Kunden sprach, und baten um die Wiederholung der gestrigen Erlaubnis, weil ein so schöner Tag sei. Sie wurde ihnen erteilt, und sie liefen wieder zur Mutter zurück.

Die Schustersfrau zog nun ihre Kinder vorsorglich an, oder eigentlich, sie zog das Mädchen mit dichten, gut verwahrenden Kleidern an; denn der Knabe begann sich selber anzukleiden und stand viel früher fertig da, als die Mutter mit dem Mädchen hatte ins reine kommen können.[37] Als sie dieses Geschäft vollendet hatte, sagte sie: „Konrad, gib wohl acht: weil ich dir das Mädchen mitgehen lasse, so müsset ihr beizeiten fort gehen, ihr müsset an keinem Platze stehen bleiben, und wenn ihr bei der Großmutter gegessen habt, so müsset ihr gleich wieder umkehren und nach Hause trachten; denn die Tage sind jetzt sehr kurz, und die Sonne geht gar bald unter."

„Ich weiß es schon, Mutter", sagte Konrad.

„Und siehe gut auf Sanna, daß sie nicht fällt oder sich erhitzt."

„Ja, Mutter."

„So, Gott behüte euch, und geht noch zum Vater und sagt, daß ihr jetzt fortgehet."

Der Knabe nahm eine von seinem Vater kunstvoll aus Kalbfellen genähte Tasche an einem Riemen um die Schulter, und die Kinder gingen in die Nebenstube, um dem Vater Lebewohl zu sagen. Aus dieser kamen sie bald heraus und hüpften, von der Mutter mit einem Kreuze[38] besegnet, fröhlich auf die Gasse.

Sie gingen schleunig längs des Dorfplatzes hinab und dann durch die Häusergasse und endlich zwischen den Planken der Obstgärten in das Freie hinaus. Die Sonne stand schon über dem mit milchigen Wolkenstreifen durchwobenen Wald der morgendlichen Anhöhen, und ihr trübes, rötliches Bild schritt durch die laublosen Zweige der Holzäpfelbäume mit den Kindern fort.

for it, you may go to grandmother's at Millsdorf; but you must first ask father again."

The children, who were still standing there in their night clothes, ran into the adjoining room in which the father was talking to a customer and asked for a repetition of yesterday's permission, because it was such a beautiful day. It was given them and they ran back again to their mother.

The shoemaker's wife now dressed her children carefully, or rather she dressed the girl in heavy, protective clothing; for the boy began to dress himself and stood all dressed much sooner than the mother could finish with the girl. When she had completed this task she said: "Pay attention, Conrad; because I'm letting the girl go along with you, you must set out in good time, you must not stop anywhere, and when you've had dinner at grandmother's, you must turn around at once and get home; for the days are very short now, and the sun sets soon."

"I know that, mother," said Conrad.

"And look after Sanna carefully, so that she doesn't fall or get overheated."

"Yes, mother."

"There, God protect you, and go to father first and tell him that you're leaving now."

The boy took a bag that his father had sewn together skillfully out of calfskins and slung it over his shoulder by a strap; and the children went into the adjoining room to say good-bye to their father. They soon emerged from it and skipped happily out into the street, blessed by their mother with a sign of the cross.

They quickly went down along the village square and then through the street of houses and finally between the board fences of the orchards out into the open. The sun already stood above the forest on the eastern heights, interlaced with milky strips of cloud, and its dull, reddish image accompanied the children through the leafless branches of the crab apple trees.

In dem ganzen Tale war kein Schnee, die größeren Berge,
von denen er schon viele Wochen herabgeglänzt hatte, waren
damit bedeckt, die kleineren standen in dem Mantel ihrer Tan-
nenwälder und im Fahlrot ihrer entblößten Zweige unbeschneit
und ruhig da. Der Boden war noch nicht gefroren, und er
wäre vermöge der vorhergegangenen langen regenlosen Zeit
ganz trocken gewesen, wenn ihn nicht die Jahreszeit mit einer
zarten Feuchtigkeit überzogen hätte, die ihn aber nicht schlüp-
frig, sondern eher fest und widerprallend machte, daß sie leicht
und gering darauf fortgingen. Das wenige Gras, welches noch
auf den Wiesen und vorzüglich an den Wassergräben derselben
war, stand in herbstlichem Ansehen. Es lag kein Reif und bei
näherem Anblicke nicht einmal ein Tau, was nach der Meinung
der Landleute baldigen Regen bedeutet.

Gegen die Grenzen der Wiesen zu war ein Gebirgsbach, über
welchen ein hoher Steg führte. Die Kinder gingen auf den Steg
und schauten hinab. Im Bache war schier kein Wasser, ein
dünner Faden von sehr stark blauer Farbe ging durch die
trockenen Kiesel des Gerölles, die wegen Regenlosigkeit ganz
weiß geworden waren, und sowohl die Wenigkeit als auch die
Farbe des Wassers zeigten an, daß in den größeren Höhen
schon Kälte herrschen müsse, die den Boden verschließe, daß
er mit seiner Erde das Wasser nicht trübe, und die das Eis
erhärte, daß es in seinem Innern nur wenige klare Tropfen
abgeben könne.

Von dem Stege liefen die Kinder durch die Gründe fort und
näherten sich immer mehr den Waldungen.

Sie trafen endlich die Grenze des Holzes und gingen in demselben weiter.

Als sie in die höheren Wälder des Halses hinaufgekommen
waren, zeigten sich die langen Furchen des Fahrweges nicht
mehr weich, wie es unten im Tale der Fall gewesen war, sondern
sie waren fest, und zwar nicht aus Trockenheit, sondern, wie
die Kinder sich bald überzeugten, weil sie gefroren waren. An
manchen Stellen waren sie so überfroren, daß sie die Körper
der Kinder trugen. Nach der Natur der Kinder gingen sie nun
nicht mehr auf dem glatten Pfade neben dem Fahrwege, sondern in den Gleisen, und versuchten, ob dieser oder jener
Furchenaufwurf sie schon trage. Als sie nach Verlauf einer

There was no snow in the whole valley; the larger mountains, which had been glistening with it for many weeks now, were covered by it; the smaller ones stood free from snow and calm, wrapped in the cloak of their pine forests and in the pale red of their bare branches. The ground was not frozen yet and it would have been quite dry because of the long time that had passed without rain if the season had not covered it with a delicate moisture that, however, did not make it slippery but rather firm and resilient, so that they walked lightly and easily on it. The little grass that was still on the meadows and especially in the water ditches had an autumnal look about it. There was no hoarfrost and, on closer inspection, not even a dew, which the country folk interpret as signifying imminent rain.

Toward the edges of the meadows there was a mountain brook that was crossed by a high footbridge. The children walked over the footbridge and looked down. There was almost no water in the brook; a thin thread of very strong blue color went through the dry pebbles of the gravel, which had turned quite white because of the lack of rain. Both the scantiness and color of the water indicated that at the greater heights there already prevailed a cold that sealed up the soil so that the earth would not make the water muddy and hardened the ice so that it could only give off a few clear drops at its core.

From the footbridge the children ran on across the lower ground and came closer and closer to the forests.
They finally met the edge of the forest and continued on in it.

When they had come up into the higher forests of the neck, the long ruts of the road were no longer soft as had been the case down below in the valley, but they were firm, and that not because of dryness but, as the children soon convinced themselves, because they were frozen. At some spots they were so frozen over that they could support the children's bodies. As was natural for children, they no longer walked on the smooth path beside the roadway but in the tracks, trying out whether this or that clump of earth would bear their weight. When, after the passing of an hour, they had come to the top of the

Stunde auf der Höhe des Halses angekommen waren, war der
Boden bereits so hart, daß er klang und Schollen wie Steine
hatte.

An der roten Unglücksäule des Bäckers bemerkte Sanna
zuerst, daß sie heute gar nicht dastehe. Sie gingen zu dem Platze
hinzu und sahen, daß der runde, rot angestrichene Balken, der
das Bild trug, in dem dürren Grase liege, das wie dünnes Stroh
an der Stelle stand und den Anblick der liegenden Säule verdeckte. Sie sahen zwar nicht ein, warum die Säule liege, und
ob sie umgeworfen worden oder ob sie von selber umgefallen
sei, das sahen sie, daß sie an der Stelle, wo sie in die Erde ragte,
sehr morsch war und daß sie daher sehr leicht habe umfallen
können; aber da sie einmal lag, so machte es ihnen Freude,
daß sie das Bild und die Schrift so nahe betrachten konnten,
wie es sonst nie der Fall gewesen war. Als sie alles—den Korb
mit den Semmeln, die bleichen Hände des Bäckers, seine ge-
schlossenen Augen, seinen grauen Rock und die umstehenden
Tannen—betrachtet hatten, als sie die Schrift gelesen und laut
gesagt hatten, gingen sie wieder weiter.

Abermals nach einer Stunde wichen die dunklen Wälder zu
beiden Seiten zurück, dünnstehende Bäume, teils einzelne
Eichen, teils Birken und Gebüschgruppen empfingen sie, gelei-
teten sie weiter, und nach kurzem liefen sie auf den Wiesen in
das Millsdorfer Tal hinab.

Obwohl dieses Tal bedeutend tiefer liegt als das von Gschaid
und auch um so viel wärmer war, daß man die Ernte immer
um vierzehn Tage früher beginnen konnte als in Gschaid, so
war doch auch hier der Boden gefroren, und als die Kinder
bis zu den Loh- und Walkwerken des Großvaters gekommen
waren, lagen auf dem Wege, auf dem die Räder oft Tropfen
herausspritzten, schöne Eistäfelchen. Den Kindern ist das gewöhnlich ein sehr großes Vergnügen.

Die Großmutter hatte sie kommen gesehen, war ihnen entgegen gegangen, nahm Sanna bei den erfrorenen Händchen und
führte sie in die Stube.

Sie nahm ihnen die wärmeren Kleider ab, sie ließ in dem
Ofen nachlegen und fragte sie, wie es ihnen im Herübergehen
gegangen sei.

neck, the soil was already so hard that it resounded and had clods as hard as stone.

Sanna was the first to notice, at the red accident pillar erected to the baker, that it wasn't there at all today. They went over to the place and saw that the round red post that supported the picture was lying in the dried grass, which was like thin straw and hid the pillar lying there from view. But they could not understand why the pillar was lying there, whether it had been knocked over or had fallen down by itself; this they saw, that it was very rotten at the spot where it projected from the ground and could therefore have fallen over easily. But because it was now lying on the ground they were glad to be able to study the picture and the writing from so close a distance as never before. When they had examined everything—the basket with rolls, the baker's pale hands, his closed eyes, his gray coat and the pines surrounding him—and when they had read the writing and spoken it out loud, they went on again.

After another hour the dark forests on both sides receded, thin stands of trees, partly individual oaks, partly birches, and groups of bushes, received them, led them on, and after a short while they ran down the meadows into the Millsdorf valley.

Although this valley lies appreciably deeper than that of Gschaid and was accordingly so much warmer that one could always begin harvesting about two weeks sooner than in Gschaid, the ground was frozen here too. When the children had reached their grandfather's tannery and fulling mill, there were beautiful little sheets of ice lying on the road, on which the wheels often splashed drops of water. This is often a great source of pleasure for children.

Their grandmother had seen them coming, had gone to meet them, took Sanna by her frozen little hands, and led her into the living room.

She took off their warmer clothes, had more wood put in the stove, and asked them how things had gone on their way over.

Als sie hierauf die Antwort erhalten hatte, sagte sie: „Das ist schon recht, das ist gut, es freut mich gar sehr, daß ihr wieder gekommen seid; aber heute müßt ihr bald fort, der Tag ist kurz, und es wird auch kälter, am Morgen war es in Millsdorf nicht gefroren."

„In Gschaid auch nicht", sagte der Knabe.

„Siehst du, darum müßt ihr euch sputen, daß euch gegen Abend nicht zu kalt wird", antwortete die Großmutter.

Hierauf fragte sie, was die Mutter mache,[39] was der Vater mache und ob nichts Besonderes in Gschaid geschehen sei.

Nach diesen Fragen bekümmerte sie sich um das Essen, sorgte, daß es früher bereitet wurde als gewöhnlich, und richtete selber den Kindern kleine Leckerbissen zusammen, von denen sie wußte, daß sie eine Freude damit erregen würde. Dann wurde der Färber gerufen, die Kinder bekamen an dem Tische aufgedeckt wie große Personen und aßen nun mit Großvater und Großmutter, und die letzte legte ihnen hiebei besonders Gutes vor. Nach dem Essen streichelte sie Sannas unterdessen sehr rot gewordene Wangen.

Hierauf ging sie geschäftig hin und her und steckte das Kalbfellränzchen des Knaben voll und steckte ihm noch allerlei in die Taschen. Auch in die Täschchen von Sanna tat sie allerlei Dinge. Sie gab jedem ein Stück Brot, es auf dem Wege zu verzehren, und in dem Ränzchen, sagte sie, seien noch zwei Weißbrote, wenn etwa der Hunger zu groß würde.

„Für die Mutter habe ich einen guten gebrannten Kaffee mitgegeben", sagte sie, „und in dem Fläschchen, das zugestopft und gut verbunden ist, befindet sich auch ein schwarzer Kaffeeaufguß, ein besserer, als die Mutter bei euch gewöhnlich macht, sie soll ihn nur kosten, wie er ist, er ist eine wahre Arznei, so kräftig, daß nur ein Schlückchen den Magen so wärmt, daß es den Körper in den kältesten Wintertagen nicht frieren kann. Die anderen Sachen, die in der Schachtel und in den Papieren im Ränzchen sind, bringt unversehrt nach Hause."

Da sie noch ein Weilchen mit den Kindern geredet hatte, sagte sie, daß sie gehen sollten.

„Habe acht, Sanna", sagte sie, „daß du nicht frierst, erhitze dich nicht; und daß ihr nicht über die Wiesen hinauf und unter

When she had received the answer, she said: "That's quite right, that's good, I'm very glad that you've come again; but today you must go back soon, the day is short and it's getting colder too; this morning there was no frost in Millsdorf."

"Nor in Gschaid," said the boy.

"You see? That's why you must hurry, so you don't feel too cold toward evening," the grandmother answered.

Then she asked them how their mother was, how their father was, and if anything special had happened in Gschaid.

After these questions she concerned herself with the meal, saw to it that it was prepared sooner than usual, and herself prepared little delicacies for the children which she knew would make them happy. Then the dyer was called, the children were served at the table like grown-ups, and now ate with their grandfather and grandmother, and the latter served them particularly good things. After dinner she patted Sanna's cheeks, which had meanwhile become very red.

After this she walked about busily and filled the boy's calfskin satchel and put all sorts of other things into his pockets. She also put all sorts of things in Sanna's little pockets. She gave each of them a piece of bread to eat on the way and told them that there were two more pieces of white bread in the satchel in case their hunger became too great.

"For mother I've sent along some good roasted coffee," she said, "and in the little bottle that is corked and tied there is some black liquid coffee, better than your mother usually makes at home; let her taste it just as it is, it's a real tonic, so strong that just one little sip warms the stomach, so that the body can't be chilled even on the coldest winter days. The other things there in the box and in the papers in the satchel you must bring home intact."

After talking to the children for a while longer she told them they should go.

"Be careful, Sanna," she said, "that you don't get chilled and don't get overheated; and that you don't run up over the

den Bäumen lauft. Etwa kommt gegen Abend ein Wind,[40] da
müßt ihr langsamer gehen, Grüßet Vater und Mutter, und sagt,
sie sollen recht glückliche Feiertage haben."

Die Großmutter küßte beide Kinder auf die Wangen und
schob sie durch die Tür hinaus. Nichtsdestoweniger ging sie
aber auch selber mit, geleitete sie durch den Garten, ließ sie
durch das Hinterpförtchen hinaus, schloß wieder und ging in
das Haus zurück.

Die Kinder gingen an den Eistäfelchen neben den Werken
des Großvaters vorbei, sie gingen durch die Millsdorfer Felder
und wendeten sich gegen die Wiesen hinan.

Als sie auf den Anhöhen gingen, wo, wie gesagt wurde, zerstreute Bäume und Gebüschgruppen standen, fielen äußerst
langsam einzelne Schneeflocken.

„Siehst du, Sanna", sagte der Knabe, „ich habe es gleich gedacht, daß wir Schnee bekommen; weißt du, da wir von Hause
weggingen, sahen wir noch die Sonne, die so blutrot war wie
eine Lampe bei dem Heiligen Grabe,[41] und jetzt ist nichts mehr
von ihr zu erblicken, und nur der graue Nebel ist über den
Baumwipfeln oben. Das bedeutet allemal Schnee."

Die Kinder gingen freudiger fort, und Sanna war recht froh,
wenn sie mit dem dunkeln Ärmel ihres Röckchens eine der
fallenden Flocken auffangen konnte und wenn dieselbe recht
lange nicht auf dem Ärmel zerfloß. Als sie endlich an dem
äußersten Rand der Millsdorfer Höhen angekommen waren,
wo es gegen die dunkeln Tannen des Halses hineingeht, war
die dichte Waldwand schon recht lieblich gesprenkelt von den
immer reichlicher herabfallenden Flocken. Sie gingen nunmehr in den dicken Wald hinein, der den größten Teil ihrer
noch bevorstehenden Wanderung einnahm.

Es geht von dem Waldrande noch immer aufwärts, und zwar
bis man zur roten Unglücksäule kommt, von wo sich, wie schon
oben angedeutet wurde, der Weg gegen das Tal von Gschaid
hinabwendet. Die Erhebung des Waldes von der Millsdorfer
Seite aus ist sogar so steil, daß der Weg nicht gerade hinangeht,
sondern daß er in sehr langen Abweichungen von Abend nach
Morgen und von Morgen nach Abend hinanklimmt. An der
ganzen Länge des Weges hinauf zur Säule und hinab bis zu
den Wiesen von Gschaid sind hohe, dichte, ungelichtete Wald-

meadows and under the trees. If a wind rises toward evening, you must walk slower. Give our love to father and mother and tell them to have a really happy holiday."

The grandmother kissed both children on the cheeks and pushed them out through the door. However, she accompanied them herself, led them through the garden, let them out by the little back gate, closed it again, and went into the house.

The children walked past their grandfather's factory on the little sheets of ice, walked through the Millsdorf fields, and turned toward the meadows.

When they were walking on the slopes where, as we have said, scattered trees and groups of bushes stood, individual snowflakes were falling very slowly.

"See, Sanna," said the boy, "I knew right away that we'd get snow. You know when we left the house we could still see the sun, which was blood-red like a lamp at the Holy Sepulcher, and now it can't be seen at all, and there is only the gray mist over the treetops above. That always means snow."

The children walked on more joyfully and Sanna was really happy when she could catch one of the falling flakes on the dark sleeve of her little frock and it did not melt on her sleeve for a long time. When they finally reached the outermost edge of the Millsdorf heights, where you enter the dark pines of the neck, the dense wall of forest was already beautifully speckled with the snowflakes, which were falling more and more plentifully. They now entered the dense forest, which made up the greatest part of the walk that was still before them.

The way from the edge of the forest is still steadily upward, indeed until one comes to the accident pillar, from which point, as has already been indicated above, the road turns down toward the valley of Gschaid. The ascent of the forest from the Millsdorf side is actually so steep that the road does not go straight up but climbs up in long turns from west to east and from east to west. Throughout the length of the road up to the pillar and down to the meadows of Gschaid there are high, dense, uncleared stands of forest, and they become a little thinner only

bestände, und sie werden erst ein wenig dünner, wenn man in die Ebene gelangt ist und gegen die Wiesen des Tales von Gschaid hinauskommt. Der Hals ist auch, wenn er gleich nur eine kleine Verbindung zwischen zwei großen Gebirgshäuptern abgibt, doch selbst so groß, daß er, in die Ebene gelegt, einen bedeutenden Gebirgsrücken abgeben würde.

Das erste, was die Kinder sahen, als sie die Waldung betraten, war, daß der gefrorne Boden sich grau zeigte, als ob er mit Mehl besät wäre, daß die Fahne manches dünnen Halmes des am Wege hin und zwischen den Bäumen stehenden dürren Grases mit Flocken beschwert war, und daß auf den verschiedenen grünen Zweigen der Tannen und Fichten, die sich wie Hände öffneten, schon weiße Fläumchen saßen.

„Schneit es denn jetzt bei dem Vater zu Hause auch?" fragte Sanna.

„Freilich", antwortete der Knabe, „es wird auch kälter, und du wirst sehen, daß morgen der ganze Teich gefroren ist."

„Ja, Konrad", sagte das Mädchen.

Es verdoppelte beinahe seine kleinen Schritte, um mit denen des dahinschreitenden Knaben gleichbleiben zu können.

Sie gingen nun rüstig in den Windungen fort, jetzt von Abend nach Morgen, jetzt von Morgen nach Abend. Der von der Großmutter vorausgesagte Wind stellte sich nicht ein, im Gegenteile war es so stille, daß sich nicht ein Ästchen oder Zweig rührte, ja sogar es schien im Walde wärmer, wie es in lockeren Körpern, dergleichen ein Wald auch ist immer im Winter zu sein pflegt, und die Schneeflocken fielen stets reichlicher, so daß der ganze Boden schon weiß war, daß der Wald sich grau zu bestäuben anfing und daß auf dem Hute und den Kleidern des Knaben sowie auf denen des Mädchens der Schnee lag.

Die Freude der Kinder war sehr groß. Sie traten auf den weichen Flaum, suchten mit dem Fuße absichtlich solche Stellen, wo er dichter zu liegen schien, um dorthin zu treten und sich den Anschein zu geben, als wateten sie bereits. Sie schüttelten den Schnee nicht von den Kleidern ab.

Es war große Ruhe eingetreten. Von den Vögeln, deren doch manche auch zuweilen im Winter in dem Walde hin und her fliegen und von denen die Kinder im Herübergehen sogar

when one has reached the plain and comes out to the meadows of the valley of Gschaid. Even though it forms only a small connection between two large summits, the neck itself is so large that, placed in the plain, it would form a considerable mountain ridge.

The first thing that the children saw when they entered the woods was that the frozen ground looked gray, as if someone had sown flour on it, that the heads of some of the thin blades of dried grass that stood along the road and between the trees were heavy with snowflakes, and that little bits of white fluff were already sitting on the different green branches of the spruces and firs which opened up like hands.

"Is it snowing at home now too, at father's?" asked Sanna.

"Of course," the boy replied, "it's getting colder too, and you'll see that tomorrow the whole pond will be frozen."

"Yes, Conrad," said the girl.

She almost doubled her short steps, to keep up with those of the boy, who was striding along.

They now walked briskly on the winding road, from west to east and from east to west. The wind that their grandmother had predicted did not appear; on the countrary, it was so still that not a twig or branch stirred; in fact it actually seemed to be warmer in the woods, as it always is in winter in rarer areas like forests. The snowflakes fell more and more plentifully, so that the whole ground was already white, the forest began to be covered with a gray dust, and the snow lay on the boy's hat and clothes as well as on those of the girl.

The joy of the children was very great. They stepped on the soft down, deliberately felt with their feet for places where it seemed to be lying thicker, walked on those spots and pretended that they were already wading through it. They did not shake the snow from their clothes.

A great peace had settled down. The birds, some of which fly about the forest even in the winter and several of which the children had actually heard twittering on their way over, could

mehrere zwitschern gehört hatten, war nichts zu vernehmen,
und sie sahen auch keine auf irgendeinem Zweige sitzen oder
fliegen, und der ganze Wald war gleichsam ausgestorben.

Weil nur die bloßen Fußstapfen der Kinder hinter ihnen blieben und weil vor ihnen der Schnee rein und unverletzt war,
so war daraus zu erkennen, daß sie die einzigen waren, die
heute über den Hals gingen.

Sie gingen in ihrer Richtung fort, sie näherten sich öfter den
Bäumen, öfter entfernten sie sich, und wo dichtes Unterholz
war, konnten sie den Schnee auf den Zweigen liegen sehen.

Ihre Freude wuchs noch immer; denn die Flocken fielen stets
dichter, und nach kurzer Zeit brauchten sie nicht mehr den
Schnee aufzusuchen, um in ihm zu waten, denn er lag schon
so dicht, daß sie ihn überall weich unter den Sohlen empfanden
und daß er sich bereits um ihre Schuhe zu legen begann; und
wenn es so ruhig und heimlich war, so war es, als ob sie das
Knistern des in die Nadeln herabfallenden Schnees vernehmen
könnten.

„Werden wir heute auch die Unglücksäule sehen?" fragte
das Mädchen, „sie ist ja umgefallen, und da wird es darauf
schneien, und da wird die rote Farbe weiß sein."

„Darum können wir sie doch sehen", antwortete der Knabe,
„wenn auch der Schnee auf sie fällt, und wenn sie auch weiß
ist, so müssen wir sie liegen sehen, weil sie eine dicke Säule ist
und weil sie das schwarze eiserne Kreuz auf der Spitze hat, das
doch immer herausragen wird."

„Ja, Konrad."

Indessen, da sie noch weiter gegangen waren, war der
Schneefall so dicht geworden, daß sie nur mehr die allernäch-
sten Bäume sehen konnten.

Von der Härte des Weges oder gar von den Furchenaufwer-
fungen war nichts zu empfinden, der Weg war vom Schnee
überall gleich weich und war überhaupt nur daran zu erkennen,
daß er als ein gleichmäßiger weißer Streifen in dem Walde
fortlief. Auf allen Zweigen lag schon die schöne weiße Hülle.

Die Kinder gingen jetzt mitten auf dem Wege, sie furchten
den Schnee mit ihren Füßlein und gingen langsamer, weil das
Gehen beschwerlicher ward. Der Knabe zog seine Jacke empor
an dem Halse zusammen, damit ihm nicht der Schnee in den

no longer be heard at all; they saw none sitting on any of the branches or flying, and the whole forest was as though dead.

Because only the footprints made by the children were left behind them and because the snow in front of them was pure and unbroken, it was clear that they were the only people who were walking over the neck today.

They continued in the same direction; they often approached trees, often went away from them, and where there was dense undergrowth they could see the snow lying on the branches.

Their joy kept increasing, for the flakes were falling more and more densely, and after a short time they no longer had to look for snow to wade in; for it already lay so thick that they felt it soft under their soles everywhere, and it even began to settle about their shoes. It was so peaceful and still that it seemed as if they could hear the crackling of the snow that was falling into the pine needles.

"Will we see the accident pillar today?" asked the girl. "It fell over, you know, so the snow will fall on it and so the red color will be white."

"We can see it just the same," replied the boy, "even though the snow falls on it, and even though it's white, we must see it lying there because it's a thick post and because it has the black iron cross at the top, which will always stick out."

"Yes, Conrad."

Meanwhile, when they had gone still further, the snowfall had become so dense that they could now see only the nearest trees.

They could feel nothing of the hardness of the road or of the earth thrown out of the ruts; everywhere the road was equally soft from the snow; it could only be distinguished by the fact that it ran on in the forest as an even, white strip. The beautiful white covering was already lying on all the branches.

The children now walked in the middle of the road; they plowed through the snow with their little feet and walked more slowly because the going was getting harder. The boy pulled his jacket up about his throat, so that the snow would not fall

Nacken falle, und er setzte den Hut tiefer in das Haupt, daß
er geschützter sei. Er zog auch seinem Schwesterlein das Tuch,
das ihm die Mutter um die Schulter gegeben hatte, besser
zusammen und zog es ihm mehr vorwärts in die Stirne, daß es
ein Dach bilde.

Der von der Großmutter vorausgesagte Wind war noch immer nicht gekommen, aber dafür wurde der Schneefall nach
und nach so dicht, daß auch nicht mehr die nächsten Bäume
zu erkennen waren, sondern daß sie wie neblige Säcke in der
Luft standen.

Die Kinder gingen fort. Sie duckten die Köpfe dichter in
ihre Kleider und gingen fort.

Sanna nahm den Riemen, an welchem Konrad die Kalbfelltasche um die Schulter hängen hatte, mit den Händchen, hielt
sich daran, und so gingen sie ihres Weges.

Die Unglücksäule hatten sie noch immer nicht erreicht. Der
Knabe konnte die Zeit nicht ermessen, weil keine Sonne am
Himmel stand und weil es immer gleichmäßig grau war.

„Werden wir bald zu der Unglücksäule kommen?" fragte
Sanna.

„Ich weiß es nicht", antwortete der Knabe, „ich kann heute
die Bäume nicht sehen und den Weg nicht erkennen, weil er
so weiß ist. Die Unglücksäule werden wir wohl gar nicht sehen,
weil so viel Schnee liegen wird, daß sie verhüllt sein wird und
daß kaum ein Gräschen oder ein Arm des schwarzen Kreuzes
hervorragen wird. Aber es macht nichts. Wir gehen immer
auf dem Wege fort, der Weg geht zwischen den Bäumen, und
wenn er zu dem Platze der Unglücksäule kommt, dann wird
er abwärts gehen, wir gehen auf ihm fort, und wenn er aus
den Bäumen hinausgeht, dann sind wir schon auf den Wiesen
von Gschaid, dann kommt der Steg, und dann haben wir nicht
mehr weit nach Hause."

„Ja, Konrad", sagte das Mädchen.

Sie gingen auf ihrem aufwärtsführenden Wege fort. Die
hinter ihnen liegenden Fußstapfen waren jetzt nicht mehr lange
sichtbar; denn die ungemeine Fülle des herabfallenden Schnees
deckte sie bald zu, daß sie verschwanden. Der Schnee knisterte
in seinem Falle nun auch nicht mehr in den Nadeln, sondern
legte sich eilig und heimlich auf die weiße, schon daliegende

into the back of his neck and he pulled his hat down over his head so that he would have more protection. He also pulled the kerchief, which his mother had given his little sister, tighter about her shoulders and pulled it further forward over her forehead so that it formed a roof.

The wind that their grandmother had predicted had still not come; but then the snowfall gradually became so dense that even the nearest trees could no longer be discerned but stood like misty sacks in the air.

The children went on. They thrust their heads deeper into their clothes and went on.

Sanna took the strap by which Conrad's calfskin bag hung about his shoulders in her little hands, clung to it, and so they continued their way.

They had still not reached the accident pillar. The boy could not judge the time because there was no sun in the sky and it remained uniformly gray.

"Will we soon come to the accident pillar?" asked Sanna.

"I don't know," the boy replied, "I can't see the trees today and I can't make out the road because it's so white. I don't suppose we'll see the accident pillar at all because there'll be so much snow that it will be covered up and scarcely a blade of grass or an arm of the black cross will stick out. But it doesn't matter. We'll continue on the road; the road leads between the trees and when it comes to the place of the accident pillar it will go downward; we'll continue on it and when it comes out of the trees we'll already be on the meadows of Gschaid; then comes the footbridge and then it won't be far till home."

"Yes, Conrad," said the girl.

They continued on the ascending road. The footprints they left behind them were now no longer visible, for the uncommon density of the falling snow soon covered them up so that they vanished. The snow no longer crackled as it fell into the needles but lay down hurriedly and stealthily on the white blanket that was already there. The children pulled their clothes even more

Decke, nieder. Die Kinder nahmen die Kleider noch fester, um das immerwährende allseitige Hineinrieseln abzuhalten.

Sie gingen sehr schleunig, und der Weg führte noch stets aufwärts.

Nach langer Zeit war noch immer die Höhe nicht erreicht, auf welcher die Unglücksäule stehen sollte und von wo der Weg gegen die Gschaider Seite sich hinunterwenden mußte.

Endlich kamen die Kinder in eine Gegend, in welcher keine Bäume standen.

„Ich sehe keine Bäume mehr", sagte Sanna.

„Vielleicht ist nur der Weg so breit, daß wir sie wegen des Schneiens nicht sehen können", antwortete der Knabe.

„Ja, Konrad", sagte das Mädchen.

Nach einer Weile blieb der Knabe stehen und sagte: „Ich sehe selber keine Bäume mehr, wir müssen aus dem Walde gekommen sein, auch geht der Weg immer bergan. Wir wollen ein wenig stehen bleiben und herumsehen, vielleicht erblicken wir etwas."

Aber sie erblickten nichts. Sie sahen durch einen trüben Raum in den Himmel. Wie bei dem Hagel über die weißen oder grünlich gedunsenen Wolken die finsteren fransenartigen Streifen herabstarren, so war es hier, und das stumme Schütten dauerte fort. Auf der Erde sahen sie nur einen runden Fleck Weiß und dann nichts mehr.

„Weißt du, Sanna", sagte der Knabe, „wir sind auf dem dürren Grase, auf welches ich dich oft im Sommer heraufgeführt habe, wo wir saßen und wo wir den Rasen betrachteten, der nacheinander hinaufgeht, und wo die schönen Kräuterbüschel wachsen. Wir werden da jetzt gleich rechts hinabgehen!"

„Ja, Konrad."

„Der Tag ist kurz, wie die Großmutter gesagt hat und wie du auch wissen wirst,[42] wir müssen uns daher sputen."

„Ja, Konrad", sagte das Mädchen.

„Warte ein wenig, ich will dich besser einrichten", erwiderte der Knabe.

Er nahm seinen Hut ab, setzte ihn Sanna auf das Haupt und befestigte ihn mit den beiden Bändchen unter ihrem Kinne. Das Tüchlein, welches sie umhatte, schützte sie zu wenig, während auf seinem Haupte eine solche Menge dichter Locken

tightly around them to keep out the constant trickle of snow from all sides.

They walked very rapidly and the road still kept leading upward.

After a long time they still had not reached the height on which the accident pillar was supposed to stand and from which the road had to turn downhill to the Gschaid side.

Finally the children came into a region in which there were no trees.

"I don't see any more trees," said Sanna.

"Perhaps the road has become so wide that we can't see them because of the snow," replied the boy.

"Yes, Conrad," said the girl.

After a while the boy stopped and said: "I don't see any trees myself now; we must have got out of the forest and the road keeps going uphill. We'll stop for a moment and look about, perhaps we'll see something."

But they saw nothing. They looked through dull space into the sky. Just as in a hailstorm the dark, fringelike strips stare down from the white or greenish bloated clouds, so it was here; and the silent downpour continued. On the ground they saw only a round spot of white and then nothing more.

"Do you know, Sanna," said the boy, "we're on the dried grass where I often brought you in summer, where we used to sit and where we looked at the grass that gradually slopes upward and where the beautiful clusters of herbs grow. We'll start going downhill to the right in a moment."

"Yes, Conrad."

"The day is short, as grandmother said and as you must know yourself, so we'll have to hurry."

"Yes, Conrad," said the girl.

"Wait a moment, I'll fix you up better," the boy replied.

He took off his hat, put it on Sanna's head and fastened it with the two little ribbons under her chin. The small kerchief she had on gave her too little protection, while he had such a thick mane of curls on his head that much more snow could

war, daß noch lange Schnee darauf fallen konnte, ehe Nässe
und Kälte durchzudringen vermochten. Dann zog er sein
Pelzjäckchen aus und zog dasselbe über die Ärmelein der
Schwester. Um seine eigenen Schultern und Arme, die jetzt
das bloße Hemd zeigten, band er das kleinere Tüchlein, das
Sanna über die Brust, und das größere, das sie über die Schultern gehabt hatte. Das sei für ihn genug, dachte er, wenn er
nur stark auftrete, werde ihn nicht frieren.

Er nahm das Mädchen bei der Hand, und so gingen sie jetzt
fort.

Das Mädchen schaute mit den willigen Äuglein in das ringsum herrschende Grau und folgte ihm gerne, nur daß es mit
den kleinen eilenden Füßlein nicht so nachkommen konnte,
wie er vorwärts strebte gleich einem, der es zur Entscheidung
bringen wollte.

Sie gingen nun mit der Unablässigkeit und Kraft, die Kinder
und Tiere haben, weil sie nicht wissen, wieviel ihnen beschieden
ist und wann ihr Vorrat erschöpft ist.

Aber wie sie gingen, so konnten sie nicht merken, ob sie über
den Berg hinabkämen oder nicht. Sie hatten gleich rechts nach
abwärts gebogen, allein sie kamen wieder in Richtungen, die
bergan führten, bergab und wieder bergan. Oft begegneten
ihnen Steilheiten, denen sie ausweichen mußten, und ein Graben, in dem sie fortgingen, führte sie in einer Krümmung
herum. Sie erklommen Höhen, die sich unter ihren Füßen
steiler gestalteten, als sie dachten, und was sie für abwärts hielten, war wieder eben, oder es war eine Höhlung, oder es ging
immer gedehnt fort.

„Wo sind wir denn, Konrad?" fragte das Mädchen.

„Ich weiß es nicht", antwortete er.

„Wenn ich nur mit diesen meinen Augen etwas zu erblicken
imstande wäre", fuhr er fort, „daß ich mich danach richten
könnte."

Aber es war rings um sie nichts als das blendende Weiß,
überall das Weiß, das aber selber nur einen immer kleineren
Kreis um sie zog und dann in einen lichten, streifenweise
niederfallenden Nebel überging, der jedes Weitere verzehrte
und verhüllte und zuletzt nichts anderes war als der unersättlich niederfallende Schnee.

fall on it before wetness and cold could penetrate through it.
Then he took off his little fur jacket and drew it over his sister's
little sleeves. On his own shoulders and arms, which now showed
his bare shirt, he tied the smaller kerchief that Sanna had worn
over her chest and the larger one she had had around her
shoulders. This was enough for him, he thought; if he only
walked briskly he would not be cold.

He took the girl by the hand and so they now went on.

With her willing eyes the girl looked into the prevailing gray
all around and gladly followed him; but her small hurrying
feet could not keep pace with his, as he strove forward like
someone who was bent on doing something decisive.

They now walked with the steadiness and energy that children
and animals possess because they do not know what is in store
for them and when their supply will run out.

But as they went on they could not make out whether they
were coming down across the mountain or not. They had at
once turned downhill to the right, but they again came to regions that led uphill, downhill, and then again uphill. Often
they met steep inclines that they were compelled to avoid; and
a ditch in which they were walking led them around in a curve.
They climbed heights that became steeper under their feet than
they had expected, and what they took to be downhill was level
ground, or it was a hollow, or it continued to stretch out.

"But where are we, Conrad?" asked the girl.

"I don't know," he replied.

"If only I could catch sight of something with these eyes of
mine," he continued, "so that I could guide myself by it."

But all about them there was nothing but the dazzling white;
everywhere the white that, however, drew an ever narrowing
circle about them and then changed into a bright mist that fell
down in streaks, consuming and enveloping everything, and
was in the end nothing but the insatiably falling snow.

„Warte, Sanna", sagte der Knabe, „wir wollen ein wenig stehen bleiben und horchen, ob wir nicht etwas hören können,
was sich im Tale meldet, sei es nun ein Hund oder eine Glocke
oder die Mühle, oder sei es ein Ruf, der sich hören läßt, hören
müssen wir etwas, und dann werden wir wissen, wohin wir zu
gehen haben."

Sie blieben nun stehen, aber sie hörten nichts. Sie blieben
noch ein wenig länger stehen, aber es meldete sich nichts, es
war nicht ein einziger Laut, auch nicht der leiseste, außer ihrem
Atem zu vernehmen, ja in der Stille, die herrschte, war es, als
sollten sie den Schnee hören, der auf ihre Wimpern fiel. Die
Voraussage der Großmutter hatte sich noch immer nicht erfüllt,
der Wind war nicht gekommen, ja, was in diesen Gegenden
selten ist, nicht das leiseste Lüftchen rührte sich an dem ganzen
Himmel.

Nachdem sie lange gewartet hatten, gingen sie wieder fort.

„Es tut auch nichts, Sanna", sagte der Knabe, „sei nur nicht
verzagt, folge mir, ich werde dich doch noch hinüberführen—
Wenn nur das Schneien aufhörte!"

Sie war nicht verzagt, sondern hob die Füßchen, so gut es
gehen wollte, und folgte ihm. Er führte sie in dem weißen,
lichten, regsamen undurchsichtigen Raume fort.

Nach einer Weile sahen sie Felsen. Sie hoben sich dunkel
und undeutlich aus dem weißen und undurchsichtigen Lichte
empor. Da die Kinder sich näherten, stießen sie fast daran. Sie
stiegen wie eine Mauer hinauf und waren ganz gerade, so daß
kaum ein Schnee an ihrer Seite haften konnte.

„Sanna, Sanna", sagte er, „da sind die Felsen, gehen wir nur
weiter, gehen wir weiter."

Sie gingen weiter, sie mußten zwischen die Felsen hinein und
unter ihnen fort. Die Felsen ließen sie nicht rechts und nicht
links ausweichen und führten sie in einem engen Wege dahin.
Nach einer Zeit verloren sie dieselben wieder und konnten sie nicht mehr erblicken. So wie sie unversehens unter sie
gekommen waren, kamen sie wieder unversehens von ihnen.
Es war wieder nichts um sie als das Weiß, und ringsum war
kein unterbrechendes Dunkel zu schauen. Es schien eine große
Lichtfülle zu sein, und doch konnte man nicht drei Schritte
vor sich sehen; alles war, wenn man so sagen darf, in eine

"Wait, Sanna," said the boy, "we'll stop for a while and listen; maybe we can hear something from the valley, whether it's a dog or a bell or the mill or a call that can be heard; we must hear something and then we'll know where we have to go."

They now stopped but they heard nothing. They stopped a while longer but they heard no report; there wasn't a single sound, not even the faintest, to be heard except their own breathing; in fact, in the silence that prevailed it seemed they could hear the snow that fell on their eyelashes. Their grandmother's forecast had still not come true: the wind had not come; in fact, what is rare in these regions, not the faintest breeze was stirring in the whole sky.

After waiting a long time they went on.

"It doesn't really matter, Sanna," said the boy, "don't lose heart, follow me, I'll get you over yet. . . . If only it would stop snowing!"

She was not despondent but lifted her little feet as best she could and followed him. He led her on in the white, bright, stirring, opaque space.

After a while they saw rocks. They stood out dark and indistinct from the white and opaque light. When the children approached, they almost ran into them. They rose up like a wall and were quite perpendicular, so that snow could scarcely cling to their sides.

"Sanna, Sanna," he said, "there are the rocks, let's go on, let's go on."

They went on; they had to move in between the rocks and along under them. The rocks did not permit them to turn right or left and led them on a narrow road. After a time they lost them again and could not see them any more. Just as they had come among them unexpectedly, so they came out of them unexpectedly. Again there was nothing around them except the whiteness and all round them no interrupting darkness could be seen. It seemed to be a great expanse of light and yet one could not see three paces ahead; everything was enveloped, if one may say so, in a single white darkness; and because there

einzige weiße Finsternis gehüllt, und weil kein Schatten war, so war kein Urteil über die Größe der Dinge, und die Kinder konnten nicht wissen, ob sie aufwärts oder abwärts gehen würden, bis eine Steilheit ihren Fuß faßte und ihn aufwärts zu gehen zwang.

„Mir tun die Augen weh", sagte Sanna.

„Schaue nicht auf den Schnee", antwortete der Knabe, „sondern in die Wolken. Mir tun sie schon lange weh; aber es tut nichts, ich muß doch auf den Schnee schauen, weil ich auf den Weg zu achten habe. Fürchte dich nur nicht, ich führe dich doch hinunter ins Gschaid."

„Ja, Konrad."

Sie gingen wieder fort; aber wie sie auch gehen mochten, wie sie auch wenden mochten, es wollte kein Anfang zum Hinabwärtsgehen kommen. An beiden Seiten waren steile Dachlehnen nach aufwärts, mitten gingen sie fort, aber auch immer aufwärts. Wenn sie den Dachlehnen entrannen und sie nach abwärts beugten, wurde es gleich so steil, daß sie wieder umkehren mußten, die Füßlein stießen oft auf Unebenheiten, und sie mußten häufig Büheln ausweichen.

Sie merkten auch, daß ihr Fuß, wo er tiefer durch den jungen Schnee einsank, nicht erdigen Boden unter sich empfand, sondern etwas anderes, das wie älterer gefrorner Schnee war; aber sie gingen immer fort, und sie liefen mit Hast und Ausdauer. Wenn sie stehen blieben, war alles still, unermeßlich still; wenn sie gingen, hörten sie das Rascheln ihrer Füße, sonst nichts; denn die Hüllen des Himmels sanken ohne Laut hernieder und so reich, daß man den Schnee hätte wachsen sehen können. Sie selber waren so bedeckt, daß sie sich von dem allgemeinen Weiß nicht hervorhoben und sich, wenn sie um ein paar Schritte getrennt worden wären, nicht mehr gesehen hätten.

Eine Wohltat war es, daß der Schnee so trocken war wie Sand, so daß er von ihren Füßen und den Bundschühlein und Strümpfen daran leicht abglitt und abrieselte, ohne Ballen und Nässe zu machen.

Endlich gelangten sie wieder zu Gegenständen.

Es waren riesenhaft große, sehr durcheinander liegende Trümmer, die mit Schnee bedeckt waren, der überall in die

was no shadow, there could be no judgment about the size of things, and the children could not know whether they would be going up or down until a steepness caught the foot and compelled it to go upward.

"My eyes hurt," said Sanna.

"Don't look at the snow," the boy replied, "but into the clouds. Mine have been hurting a long time, but it doesn't matter. I have to look down on the snow because I have to look out for the road. Just don't be afraid, I'll certainly bring you down to Gschaid."

"Yes, Conrad."

They went on again; but no matter how they went, how they might turn, the beginning of the descent would not come. On both sides there were steep cliffs slanting upward; they walked between them, but it was always upward. When they escaped the cliffs and turned downhill, it became so steep at once that they had to turn round again; they often stubbed their little feet on rough spots and they often had to avoid hills.

They noticed, too, that wherever their feet sank deeper through the fresh snow, they encountered not earthy soil but something else that was like older, frozen snow; but they kept on going and they walked with speed and persistence. When they stopped, everything was silent, boundlessly silent; when they walked, they heard the rustling of their feet, nothing else; for the veils of heaven sank down without a sound and so plentifully that one might have been able to see the snow grow. They themselves were so thickly covered that they did not stand out from the general whiteness and, if they had been separated by a few paces, would no longer have seen each other.

It was a blessing that the snow was as dry as sand so that it slid off and trickled easily from their little laced shoes and stockings without caking and soaking them.

Finally they reached objects again.

They were gigantic fragments of debris lying helter-skelter, covered with snow that trickled into the clefts everywhere; again

Klüfte hineinrieselte, und an die sie sich ebenfalls fast anstießen,
ehe sie sie sahen. Sie gingen ganz hinzu, die Dinge anzublicken.
Es war Eis—lauter Eis.

Es lagen Platten da, die mit Schnee bedeckt waren, an deren
Seitenwänden aber das glatte grünliche Eis sichtbar war, es
lagen Hügel da, die wie zusammengeschobener Schaum aussa-
hen, an deren Seiten es aber matt nach einwärts flimmerte und
glänzte, als wären Balken und Stangen von Edelsteinen durcheinander geworfen worden, es lagen ferner gerundete Kugeln
da, die ganz mit Schnee umhüllt waren, es standen Platten und
andere Körper auch schief oder gerade aufwärts, so hoch wie
der Kirchturm in Gschaid oder wie Häuser. In einigen waren
Höhlen eingefressen, durch die man mit einem Arme durch-
fahren konnte, mit einem Kopfe, mit einem Körper, mit einem
ganz großen Wagen voll Heu. Alle diese Stücke waren zusam-
men- oder emporgedrängt und starrten, so daß sie oft Dächer
bildeten oder Überhänge, über deren Ränder sich der Schnee
herüberlegte und herabgriff wie lange weiße Tatzen. Selbst ein
großer, schreckhaft schwarzer Stein, wie ein Haus, lag unter
dem Eise und war emporgestellt, daß er auf der Spitze stand,
daß kein Schnee an seinen Seiten liegen bleiben konnte. Und
nicht dieser Stein allein—noch mehrere und größere staken[43]
in dem Eise, die man erst später sah und die wie eine Trüm-
mermauer an ihm hingingen.

„Da muß recht viel Wasser gewesen sein, weil so viel Eis ist",
sagte Sanna.

„Nein, das ist von keinem Wasser", antwortete der Bruder,
„das ist das Eis des Berges, das immer oben ist, weil es so
eingerichtet ist."

„Ja, Konrad", sagte Sanna.

„Wir sind jetzt bis zu dem Eise gekommen", sagte der Knabe,
„wir sind auf dem Berge, Sanna, weißt du, den man von unserm
Garten aus im Sonnenscheine so weiß sieht. Merke gut auf, was
ich dir sagen werde. Erinnerst du dich noch, wie wir oft nachmittags in dem Garten saßen, wie es recht schön war, wie die
Bienen um uns summten, die Linden dufteten und die Sonne
von dem Himmel schien?"

„Ja, Konrad, ich erinnere mich."

they almost ran into them before seeing them. They walked right up to look at them.

It was ice—nothing but ice.

Slabs lay there, covered with snow, but on whose side walls the smooth greenish ice was visible; hills lay there which looked like compressed foam but whose sides had a faint inward glimmer and gloss, as if beams and poles of jewels had been thrown together; there were, moreover, round balls that were entirely enveloped in snow; there were slabs and other bodies there, standing slanting or upright, as high as the church tower or as houses in Gschaid. Into some of these, caves had been eaten, through which one could push an arm, a head, a body, or a big wagon loaded with hay. All these chunks were piled together or pushed up and frozen so as to form roofs or eaves over whose edges the snow spread and reached down like long, white paws. There was even a large, terrifyingly black stone, big as a house, lying under the ice, upright on its point so that no snow could cling to its sides. And not only this stone—several more and larger ones, which one did not notice until later, were set in the ice, forming a kind of wall of debris around it.

"There must have been a great deal of water here, because there's so much ice," said Sanna.

"No, that isn't from water," her brother replied, "that's the ice of the mountain; it's always up there because that's the way it's been arranged."

"Yes, Conrad," said Sanna.

"We have now got to the ice," said the boy, "we're on the mountain, Sanna, you know, the one we see from our garden looking so white in the sunshine. Now mark well what I'm going to tell you. Do you still remember how we often used to sit in the garden in the afternoon, how really beautiful it was, how the bees buzzed around us, the linden trees smelled sweet and the sun shone in the sky?"

"Yes, Conrad, I remember."

„Da sahen wir auch den Berg. Wir sahen, wie er so blau war, so blau wie das sanfte Firmament, wir sahen den Schnee, der oben ist, wenn auch bei uns Sommer war, eine Hitze herrschte und die Getreide reif wurden."

„Ja, Konrad."

„Und unten, wo der Schnee aufhört, da sieht man allerlei Farben, wenn man genau schaut, grün, blau, weißlich—das ist das Eis, das unten nur so klein ausschaut, weil man sehr weit entfernt ist, und das, wie der Vater sagte, nicht weggeht bis an das Ende der Welt. Und da habe ich oft gesehen, daß unterhalb des Eises die blaue Farbe noch fortgeht, das werden Steine sein, dachte ich, oder es wird Erde und Weidegrund sein, und dann fangen die Wälder an, die gehen herab und immer weiter herab, man sieht auch allerlei Felsen in ihnen, dann folgen die Wiesen, die schon grün sind, und dann die grünen Laubwälder, und dann kommen unsere Wiesen und Felder, die in dem Tale von Gschaid sind. Siehst du nun, Sanna, weil wir jetzt bei dem Eise sind, so werden wir über die blaue Farbe hinabgehen, dann durch die Wälder, in denen die Felsen sind, dann über die Wiesen und dann durch die grünen Laubwälder, und dann werden wir in dem Tale von Gschaid sein und recht leicht unser Dorf finden."

„Ja, Konrad", sagte das Mädchen.

Die Kinder gingen nun in das Eis henein, wo es zugänglich war.

Sie waren winzig kleine, wandelnde Punkte in diesen ungeheuren Stücken.

Wie sie so unter die Überhänge hineinsahen, gleichsam als gäbe ihnen ein Trieb ein, ein Obdach zu suchen, gelangten sie in einen Graben, in einen breiten, tiefgefurchten Graben, der gerade aus dem Eise hervorging. Er sah aus wie das Bett eines Stromes, der aber jetzt ausgetrocknet und überall mit frischem Schnee bedeckt war. Wo er aus dem Eise hervorkam, ging er gerade unter einem Kellergewölbe heraus, das recht schön aus Eis über ihn gespannt war. Die Kinder gingen in dem Graben fort und gingen in das Gewölbe hinein und immer tiefer hinein. Es war ganz trocken, und unter ihren Füßen hatten sie glattes Eis. In der ganzen Höhlung aber war es blau, so blau, wie gar nichts in der Welt ist, viel tiefer und viel schöner blau als das

"We saw the mountain then too. We saw how blue it was, as blue as the gentle firmament; we saw the snow that is at the top even when it was summer with us, it was very hot and the wheat was ripening."

"Yes, Conrad."

"And down below, where the snow stops, you see all kinds of colors if you look closely—green, blue, whitish—that's the ice that looks so small down below because we're so far away and that, as father said, doesn't go away till the world ends. And then I've often seen that the blue color continues even below the ice; they must be stones, I thought, or earth and pasture land; and then the woods begin; they go down and farther and farther down. You also see all sorts of rocks in them, then come the meadows, which are already green, and then the green leaf woods and then come our meadows and fields which are in the valley of Gschaid. Do you see now, Sanna, since we're at the ice now, we'll go down over the blue color, then through the forests where the rocks are, then over the meadows, then through the green leaf woods, and then we'll be in the valley of Gschaid and find our village easily."

"Yes, Conrad," said the girl.
The children now went into the ice where it was accessible.

They were tiny mobile points in these enormous chunks.

As they were looking in under the eaves, as if prompted by an instinct to seek shelter, they reached a ditch, a wide, deeply furrowed ditch, which came right out of the ice. It looked like the bed of a stream, which was now dried out and entirely covered with fresh snow. At the point where it came out of the ice, it extended right under a vaultlike cellar, which was quite beautifully stretched over it. The children walked on in the ditch and went into the vault and deeper and deeper into it. It was quite dry and they had smooth ice under their feet. But in the whole cavity it was blue, as blue as nothing else in the world, a much deeper and more beautiful blue than the firmament, something like sky-blue colored glass through which a

Firmament, gleichsam wie himmelblau gefärbtes Glas, durch welches lichter Schein hineinsinkt. Es waren dickere und dünnere Bogen, es hingen Zacken, Spitzen und Troddeln herab, der Gang wäre noch tiefer zurückgegangen, sie wußten nicht, wie tief, aber sie gingen nicht mehr weiter. Es wäre auch sehr gut in der Höhle gewesen, es war warm, es fiel kein Schnee, aber es war so schreckhaft blau, die Kinder fürchteten sich und gingen wieder hinaus. Sie gingen eine Weile in dem Graben fort und kletterten dann über seinen Rand hinaus.

Sie gingen an dem Eise hin, sofern es möglich war, durch das Getrümmer und zwischen den Platten durchzudringen.

„Wir werden jetzt da noch hinübergehen und dann von dem Eise abwärts laufen", sagte Konrad.

„Ja", sagte Sanna und klammerte sich an ihn an.

Sie schlugen von dem Eise eine Richtung durch den Schnee abwärts ein, die sie in das Tal führen sollte. Aber sie kamen nicht weit hinab. Ein neuer Strom von Eis, gleichsam ein riesenhaft aufgetürmter und aufgewölbter Wall, lag quer durch den weichen Schnee und griff gleichsam mit Armen rechts und links um sie herum. Unter der weißen Decke, die ihn verhüllte, glimmerte es seitwärts grünlich und bläulich und dunkel und schwarz und selbst gelblich und rötlich heraus. Sie konnten es nun auf weitere[44] Strecken sehen, weil das ungeheure und unermüdliche Schneien sich gemildert hatte und nur mehr wie an gewöhnlichen Schneetagen vom Himmel fiel. Mit dem Starkmute der Unwissenheit kletterten sie in das Eis hinein, um den vorgeschobenen Strom desselben zu überschreiten und dann jenseits weiter hinabzukommen. Sie schoben sich in die Zwischenräume hinein, sie setzten den Fuß auf jedes Körperstück, das mit einer weißen Schneehaube versehen war, war es Fels oder Eis, sie nahmen die Hände zu Hilfe, krochen, wo sie nicht gehen konnten, und arbeiteten sich mit ihren leichen Körpern hinauf, bis sie die Seite des Walles überwunden hatten und oben waren.

Jenseits wollten sie wieder hinabklettern.

Aber es gab kein Jenseits.

So weit die Augen der Kinder reichen konnten, war lauter Eis. Es standen Spitzen und Unebenheiten und Schollen empor wie lauter furchtbares überschneites Eis. Statt ein Wall zu sein,

bright light sinks. There were thicker and thinner arches, jagged ends, points and tassels hung down. The corridor would
have led back still farther, they did not know how deep, but
they did not go any farther. It would have been very good in
the cave too; it was warm, no snow fell; but it was so terrifyingly
blue, the children were afraid and went out again. They went
on for a while in the ditch and then climbed out over its edge.

They walked along the ice as far as it was possible to penetrate
through the debris and between the slabs.
"We'll go over to that spot now and then go downward from
the ice," said Conrad.
"Yes," said Sanna, clinging to him.
They took a direction away from the ice through the snow,
one that was to lead them into the valley. But they did not get
far down. A new river of ice, a sort of gigantic, towering, and
vaulted rampart, lay straight across the soft snow and, as it
were, sent out arms to the right and left of them. Under the
white cover that enveloped it, greenish and bluish and dark
and black and even yellowish and reddish sparks shot out side-
ward. They could now see it for distant stretches, because the
vast and tireless snowing had abated and now fell from the sky
as on ordinary snowy days. With the courage of ignorance they
climbed into the ice, in order to cross over the protruding river
and to get farther down on the other side. They pushed their
way into the interstices, they set their feet on every object that
was provided with a white hood of snow, whether it was rock
or ice; they used their hands, crawled where they could not
walk and worked their way up with their bodies until they had
overcome the side of the rampart and were at the top.

They intended to climb down again on the other side.
But there was no other side.
As far as the eyes of the children could reach there was
nothing but ice. Points and rough spots and clumps jutted out
like sheer terrible snow-covered ice. Instead of being a rampart

über den man hinübergehen könnte und der dann wieder von
Schnee abgelöst würde, wie sie sich unten dachten, stiegen aus
der Wölbung neue Wände von Eis empor, geborsten und ge-
klüftet, mit unzähligen blauen geschlängelten Linien versehen,
und hinter ihnen waren wieder solche Wände und hinter diesen
wieder solche, bis der Schneefall das Weitere mit seinem Grau
verdeckte.

„Sanna, da können wir nicht gehen", sagte der Knabe.

„Nein", antwortete die Schwester.

„Da werden wir wieder umkehren und anderswo hinabzukommen suchen."

„Ja, Konrad."

Die Kinder versuchten nun, von dem Eiswalle wieder da hinabzukommen, wo sie hinaufgeklettert waren, aber sie kamen
nicht hinab. Es war lauter Eis, als hätten sie die Richtung, in
der sie gekommen waren, verfehlt. Sie wandten sich hierhin
und dorthin und konnten aus dem Eise nicht herauskommen,
als wären sie von ihm umschlungen. Sie kletterten abwärts und
kamen wieder in Eis. Endlich, da der Knabe die Richtung immer
verfolgte, in der sie nach seiner Meinung gekommen waren,
gelangten sie in zerstreutere Trümmer, aber sie waren auch
größer und furchtbarer, wie sie gerne am Rande des Eises zu
sein pflegen, und die Kinder gelangten kriechend und kletternd
hinaus. An dem Eisessaume waren ungeheure Steine, sie waren
gehäuft, wie sie die Kinder ihr Leben lang nicht gesehen hatten.
Viele waren in Weiß gehüllt, viele zeigten die unteren schiefen
Wände sehr glatt und fein geschliffen, als wären sie darauf
geschoben worden, viele waren wie Hütten und Dächer gegeneinander gestellt, viele lagen aufeinander wie ungeschlachte
Knollen. Nicht weit von dem Standorte der Kinder standen
mehrere mit den Köpfen gegeneinander gelehnt, und über sie
lagen breite, gelagerte Blöcke wie ein Dach. Es war ein Häuschen, das gebildet war, das gegen vorne offen, rückwärts und
an den Seiten aber geschützt war. Im Innern war es trocken,
da der steilrechte Schneefall keine einzige Flocke hineingetra-
gen hatte. Die Kinder waren recht froh, daß sie nicht mehr in
dem Eise waren und auf ihrer Erde standen.

Aber es war auch endlich finster geworden.

that one could cross and that was then again replaced by snow, as they imagined below, new walls of ice rose up from the vaulting, burst and fissured, supplied with countless blue serpentine lines and behind them there were more such walls and behind these more still, until the snowfall concealed the rest with its gray.

"Sanna, we can't go there," said the boy.

"No," his sister replied.

"So we'll turn around again and try to go down somewhere else."

"Yes, Conrad."

The children now tried to get down from the rampart of ice at the same place where they had climbed up, but they did not get down. There was nothing but ice, as if they had missed the direction they had taken. They turned this way and that and could not get out of the ice, as if they were surrounded by it. They climbed downward and again came into more ice. Finally, since the boy kept following the direction that he thought they had taken, they reached a mass of scattered debris, which was, however, bigger and more terrible, as is normal at the edge of ice, and the children got out of it by crawling and climbing. At the rim of the ice there were enormous stones, piled up in a way the children had never seen in all their lives. Many were wrapped in white; many showed the lower, slanting walls very smoothly and finely polished, as if they had been shoved on that side; many were placed against each other like huts and roofs, many lay on each other like crude clumps. Not far from the spot where the children were standing several such stones stood with their heads leaning toward each other, and above them lay wide, flat blocks like a roof. A little house had been formed, open in front but protected at the sides and back. Inside it was dry, since the vertical snowfall had not carried in a single snowflake. The children were very glad that they were no longer on the ice but standing on their earth.

But it had finally become dark.

„Sanna", sagte der Knabe, „wir können nicht mehr hinabgehen, weil es Nacht geworden ist und weil wir fallen oder gar
in eine Grube geraten könnten. Wir werden da unter die Steine
hineingehen, wo es trocken und so warm ist, und da werden
wir warten. Die Sonne geht bald wieder auf, dann laufen wir
hinunter. Weine nicht, ich bitte dich recht schön, weine nicht,
ich gebe dir alle Dinge zu essen, welche uns die Großmutter
mitgegeben hat."

Sie weinte auch nicht, sondern, nachdem sie beide unter das
steinerne Überdach hineingegangen waren, wo sie nicht nur
bequem sitzen, sondern auch stehen und herumgehen konnten,
setzte sie sich recht dicht an ihn und war mäuschenstille.

„Die Mutter", sagte Konrad, „wird nicht böse sein, wir werden
ihr von dem vielen Schnee erzählen, der uns aufgehalten hat,
und sie wird nichts sagen; der Vater auch nicht. Wenn uns kalt
wird, weißt du, dann mußt du mit den Händen an deinen Leib
schlagen, wie die Holzhauer getan haben, und dann wird dir
wärmer werden."

„Ja, Konrad", sagte das Mädchen.

Sanna war nicht ganz so untröstlich, daß sie heute nicht mehr
über den Berg hinabgingen und nach Hause liefen, wie er etwa
glauben mochte; denn die unermeßliche Anstrengung, von der
die Kinder nicht einmal gewußt hatten, wie groß sie gewesen
sei, ließ ihnen das Sitzen süß, unsäglich süß erscheinen, und
sie gaben sich hin.

Jetzt machte sich auch der Hunger geltend. Beide nahmen
fast zu gleicher Zeit ihre Brote aus den Taschen und aßen sie.
Sie aßen auch die Dinge—kleine Stückchen Kuchen, Mandeln
und Nüsse und andere Kleinigkeiten—, die die Großmutter
ihnen in die Tasche gesteckt hatte.

„Sanna, jetzt müssen wir aber auch den Schnee von unsern
Kleidern tun", sagte der Knabe, „daß wir nicht naß werden."

„Ja, Konrad", erwiderte Sanna.

Die Kinder gingen aus ihrem Häuschen, und zuerst reinigte
Konrad das Schwesterlein von Schnee. Er nahm die Kleiderzip-
fel, schüttelte sie, nahm ihr den Hut ab, den er ihr aufgesetzt
hatte, entleerte ihn von Schnee, und was noch zurückgeblieben
war, das stäubte er mit einem Tuche ab. Dann entledigte er
auch sich, so gut es ging, des auf ihm liegenden Schnees.

"Sanna," said the boy, "we can't go down any more because night has come, and we might fall or even land in a pit. We'll go in there under the stones where it's so dry and so warm and we'll wait there. The sun will rise again soon, then we'll go down. Don't cry, please, don't cry, I'll give you all the things to eat which grandmother gave us to take with us."

And she did not cry, but when they had both gone in under the overhanging stone roof, where they could not only sit comfortably but could also stand up and walk about, she sat down quite close beside him and was as quiet as a mouse.

"Mother won't be angry," said Conrad; "we'll tell her about the heavy snow that held us up and she won't say anything; nor will father. If we get cold, you know, you must slap your hands against your body, the way the woodcutters did, and then you'll feel warmer."

"Yes, Conrad," said the girl.

Sanna was not so utterly disconsolate as he thought because they couldn't go down the mountain today and go home; for the enormous strain, the extent of which the children had not even realized, made sitting appear sweet, indescribably sweet, to them and they abandoned themselves to it.

But now hunger made itself felt too. Both of them took their bread out of their pockets almost at the same time and ate it. They also ate the things—little pieces of cake, almonds and nuts and other trifles—which their grandmother had put into their pockets.

"Sanna, but now we must also remove the snow from our clothes," said the boy, "so that we don't get wet."

"Yes, Conrad," replied Sanna.

The children left their little house and Conrad first cleaned the snow off his little sister. He held the clothes by their corners, shook them, took off the hat he had put on her head, emptied it of snow, and what had remained, he dusted off with a cloth. Then he also removed the snow that was on him as best he could.

Der Schneefall hatte zu dieser Stunde ganz aufgehört. Die
Kinder spürten keine Flocke.

Sie gingen wieder in die Steinhütte und setzten sich nieder.
Das Aufstehen hatte ihnen ihre Müdigkeit erst recht[45] gezeigt,
und sie freuten sich auf das Sitzen. Konrad legte die Tasche
aus Kalbfell ab. Er nahm das Tuch heraus, in welches die Großmutter eine Schachtel und mehrere Papierpäckchen gewickelt
hatte, und tat es zu größerer Wärme um seine Schultern. Auch
die zwei Weißbrote nahm er aus dem Ränzchen und reichte
sie beide an Sanna: das Kind aß begierig. Es aß eines der Brote
und von dem zweiten auch noch einen Teil. Den Rest reichte
es aber Konrad, da es sah, daß er nicht aß. Er nahm es und
verzehrte es.

Von da an saßen die Kinder und schauten.

So weit sie in der Dämmerung zu sehen vermochten, lag
überall der flimmernde Schnee hinab, dessen einzelne winzige
Täfelchen hie und da in der Finsternis seltsam zu funkeln begannen, als hätte er bei Tag das Licht eingesogen und gäbe es
jetzt von sich.

Die Nacht brach mit der in großen Höhen gewöhnlichen
Schnelligkeit herein. Bald war es rings herum finster, nur der
Schnee fuhr fort, mit seinem bleichen Lichte zu leuchten. Der
Schneefall hatte nicht nur aufgehört, sondern der Schleier an
dem Himmel fing auch an, sich zu verdünnen und zu verteilen;
denn die Kinder sahen ein Sternlein blitzen. Weil der Schnee
wirklich gleichsam ein Licht von sich gab und weil von den
Wolken kein Schleier mehr herabhing, so konnten die Kinder
von ihrer Höhle aus die Schneehügel sehen, wie sie sich in
Linien von dem dunklen Himmel abschnitten. Weil es in der
Höhle viel wärmer war, als es an jedem andern Platze im ganzen
Tage gewesen war, so ruhten die Kinder, enge aneinander
sitzend, und vergaßen sogar die Finsternis zu fürchten. Bald
vermehrten sich auch die Sterne, jetzt kam hier einer zum
Vorscheine, jetzt dort, bis es schien, als wäre am ganzen Himmel
keine Wolke mehr.

Das war der Zeitpunkt, in welchem man in den Tälern die
Lichter anzuzünden pflegte. Zuerst wird eines angezündet und
auf den Tisch gestellt, um die Stube zu erleuchten, oder es
brennt auch nur ein Span, oder es brennt das Feuer auf der

By this time the snow had ceased falling altogether. The children could not feel a single flake.

They went back into the stone hut and sat down. Getting up had proved to them how tired they really were and they looked forward to sitting down. Conrad put down his calfskin bag. He took out the cloth in which their grandmother had wrapped a box and several paper packages and put it about his shoulders for greater warmth. He also took the two white rolls from the satchel and handed them both to Sanna; the child ate them eagerly, first the one and then part of the second. The rest she handed to Conrad, since she saw that he wasn't eating. He took it and ate it.

From then on the children sat and looked.

As far as they were able to see in the half light, the glimmering snow lay around everywhere, and its individual tiny flakes began to sparkle strangely in the darkness as if it had absorbed the light by day and were now giving it off.

The night descended with the speed that is characteristic of great heights. Soon it was dark all around; only the snow continued to shine with its pale light. Not only had the snowfall ceased but the veil in the sky began to grow thinner and to divide, for the children saw a little star flash. Because the snow really gave off a sort of light and because there was no longer a veil hanging down from the clouds, the children could see from their cave the hills of snow and how they stood out in lines against the dark sky. Because it was much warmer in the cave than it had been in any other place that day, the children rested, sitting close beside each other, and they even forgot to be afraid of the dark. Soon the stars increased in number, now one appeared here, now another there, until it seemed as if there were not a cloud left in the whole sky.

This was the time when people in the valleys are accustomed to put on the lights. First one candle is lit and put on the table to light the room, or maybe it is only a chip of wood burning, or the fire burns in the lamp and all the windows of inhabited

Leuchte, und es erhellen sich alle Fenster von bewohnten Stuben und glänzen in die Schneenacht hinaus—aber heute erst[46]—am Heiligen Abende—, da wurden viel mehrere[47] angezündet, um die Gaben zu beleuchten, welche für die Kinder auf den Tischen lagen oder an den Bäumen hingen, es wurden wohl unzählige angezündet; denn beinahe in jedem Hause, in jeder Hütte, jedem Zimmer war eines oder mehrere Kinder, denen der Heilige Christ etwas gebracht hatte, und wozu man Lichter stellen mußte. Der Knabe hatte geglaubt, daß man sehr bald von dem Berge hinabkommen könne, und doch, von den vielen Lichtern, die heute in dem Tale brannten, kam nicht ein einziges zu ihnen herauf; sie sahen nichts als den blassen Schnee und den dunkeln Himmel, alles andere war ihnen in unsichtbare Ferne hinabgerückt. In allen Tälern bekommen die Kinder in dieser Stunde die Geschenke des Heiligen Christ: nur die zwei saßen oben am Rande des Eises, und die vorzüglichsten Geschenke, die sie heute hätten bekommen sollen, lagen in versiegelten Päckchen in der Kalbfelltasche im Hintergrunde der Höhle.

Die Schneewolken waren ringsum hinter die Berge hinabgesunken, und ein ganz dunkelblaues, fast schwarzes Gewölbe spannte sich um die Kinder voll von dichten brennenden Sternen, und mitten durch diese Sterne war ein schimmerndes breites milchiges Band gewoben, das sie wohl auch unten im Tale, aber nie so deutlich gesehen hatten. Die Nacht rückte vor. Die Kinder wußten nicht, daß die Sterne gegen Westen rücken und weiter wandeln, sonst hätten sie an ihrem Vorschreiten den Stand der Nacht erkennen können; aber es kamen neue und gingen die alten, sie aber glaubten, es seien immer dieselben. Es wurde von dem Scheine der Sterne auch lichter um die Kinder; aber sie sahen kein Tal, keine Gegend, sondern überall nur Weiß—lauter Weiß. Bloß ein dunkles Horn, ein dunkles Haupt, ein dunkler Arm wurde sichtbar und ragte dort und hier aus dem Schimmer empor. Der Mond war nirgends am Himmel zu erblicken, vielleicht war er schon frühe mit der Sonne untergegangen, oder er ist noch nicht erschienen.

Als eine lange Zeit vergangen war, sagte der Knabe: „Sanna, du mußt[48] nicht schlafen; denn weißt du, wie der Vater gesagt

rooms light up and shine out into the snowy night. But today especially, on Christmas Eve, far more lights were lit to illuminate the gifts that lay on the tables for the children or hung on the trees. Countless lights would be lit, for in almost every house, in every hut, in every room there were one or more children to whom the Holy Christ had brought something and for this purpose the lights had to be set out. The boy had thought that they could get down the mountain very soon, and yet not one of the many lights that shone below in the valley reached up to them. They saw nothing but the pale snow and the dark sky; everything else had moved down into an invisible distance for them. In all the valleys the children were at this time receiving the gifts from the Holy Christ; only these two sat up there at the edge of the ice, and the most excellent gifts that they were to have received today lay in sealed little packages in the calfskin satchel at the back of the cave.

All around, the clouds of snow had sunk behind the mountains, and a very dark blue, almost black, vault stretched about the children, full of dense burning stars; and in the midst of these stars a shimmering, broad, milky band was woven, which they had of course seen down in the valley too, but never so clearly. The night advanced. The children did not know that the stars move westward and go on, or they might have gauged the time of night by their progress; but new stars came and old ones went, and they thought they were always the same ones. It also became brighter around the children because of the starlight; but they saw no valley, no countryside, only whiteness everywhere, nothing but whiteness. Only a dark horn, a dark head, a dark arm became visible and jutted out of the faint light here and there. The moon was nowhere to be seen in the sky; perhaps it had gone down early with the sun or it had not appeared yet.

After a long time had passed the boy said: "Sanna, you mustn't sleep, for you know, as father said, if you sleep in the mountains

hat, wenn man im Gebirge schläft, muß man erfrieren, so wie
der alte Eschenjäger auch geschlafen hat und vier Monate tot
auf dem Steine gesessen ist,[49] ohne daß jemand gewußt hatte,
wo er sei."

„Nein, ich werde nicht schlafen", sagte das Mädchen matt.
Konrad hatte es an dem Zipfel des Kleides geschüttelt, um
es zu jenen Worten zu erwecken.

Nun war es wieder stille.

Nach einer Zeit empfand der Knabe ein sanftes Drücken
gegen seinen Arm, das immer schwerer wurde. Sanna war eingeschlafen und war gegen ihn herübergesunken.

„Sanna, schlafe nicht, ich bitte dich, schlafe nicht", sagte er.

„Nein", lallte sie schlaftrunken, „ich schlafe nicht."

Er rückte weiter von ihr, um sie in Bewegung zu bringen,
allein sie sank um und hätte auf der Erde liegend fortgeschla-
fen. Er nahm sie an der Schulter und rüttelte sie. Da er sich
dabei selber etwas stärker bewegte, merkte er, daß ihn friere
und daß sein Arm schwerer sei. Er erschrak und sprang auf.
Er ergriff die Schwester, schüttelte sie stärker und sagte:
„Sanna, stehe ein wenig auf, wir wollen eine Zeit stehen, daß
es besser wird."

„Mich friert nicht, Konrad", antwortete sie.

„Ja, ja, es friert dich, Sanna, stehe auf", rief er.

„Die Pelzjacke ist warm", sagte sie.

„Ich werde dir emporhelfen", sagte er.

„Nein", erwiderte sie und war stille.

Da fiel dem Knaben etwas anderes ein. Die Großmutter hatte
gesagt: Nur ein Schlückchen wärmt den Magen so, daß es den
Körper in den kältesten Wintertagen nicht frieren kann.

Er nahm das Kalbfellränzchen, öffnete es und griff so lange,
bis er das Fläschchen fand, in welchem die Großmutter der
Mutter einen schwarzen Kaffeeabsud schicken wollte. Er nahm
das Fläschchen heraus, tat den Verband weg und öffnete mit
Anstrengung den Kork. Dann bückte er sich zu Sanna und
sagte: „Da ist der Kaffee, den die Großmutter der Mutter
schickt, koste ihn ein wenig, er wird dir warm machen. Die
Mutter gibt ihn uns, wenn sie nur weiß, wozu wir ihn nötig
gehabt haben."

you're sure to freeze to death, just as old Eschenjäger slept and sat dead on a stone for four months without anyone knowing where he was."

"No, I'm not going to sleep," said the girl faintly.

Conrad had shaken her by the corner of her dress, to wake her so that she could hear his words.

Now it was quiet again.

After a while the boy felt a gentle pressure against his arm, getting heavier all the time. Sanna had fallen asleep and had settled against him.

"Sanna, don't sleep, please, don't sleep," he said.

"No," she mumbled, drunk with sleep, "I'm not sleeping."

He moved away from her to get her to move, but she fell over and would have continued to sleep lying on the earth. He took her by the shoulder and shook her. Since he moved a little more energetically as he did so, he noticed that he was cold and that his arm was numb. He was alarmed and jumped up. He seized his sister, shook her more strongly, and said: "Sanna, wake up for a while, we'll stand up a bit so that we'll feel better."

"I don't feel cold, Conrad," she replied.

"Yes, yes, you are cold, Sanna, get up," he cried.

"The fur jacket is warm," she said.

"I'll help you up," he said.

"No," she replied and was quiet.

Then the boy had another idea. Grandmother had said, one little sip warms the stomach so, that the body can't freeze even on the coldest winter days.

He took the calfskin satchel, opened it, and searched until he found the little flask in which their grandmother was sending mother the black liquid coffee. He took out the little bottle, removed the wrappings, and pulled out the cork with an effort. Then he bent down to Sanna and said: "There's the coffee that grandmother is sending to mother, taste a little of it, it will warm you. Mother will let us have it if she only knows why we needed it."

Das Mädchen, dessen Natur zur Ruhe zog,[50] antwortete:
„Mich friert nicht."

„Nimm nur etwas", sagte der Knabe, „dann darfst du schlafen."

Diese Aussicht verlockte Sanna, sie bewältigte sich so weit,
daß sie fast das eingegossene Getränk verschluckte. Hierauf
trank der Knabe auch etwas.

Der ungemein starke Auszug wirkte sogleich, und zwar um
so heftiger, da die Kinder in ihrem Leben keinen Kaffee gekostet hatten. Statt zu schlafen, wurde Sanna nun lebhafter und
sagte selber, daß sie friere, daß es aber von innen recht warm
sei und auch schon so in die Hände und Füße gehe. Die Kinder
redeten sogar eine Weile miteinander.

So tranken sie trotz der Bitterkeit immer wieder von dem Getränke, sobald die Wirkung nachzulassen begann, und steigerten ihre unschuldigen Nerven zu einem Fieber, das imstande
war, den zum Schlummer ziehenden Gewichten entgegenzuwirken.

Es war nun Mitternacht gekommen. Weil sie noch so jung
waren und an jedem Heiligen Abende in höchstem Drange der
Freude stets erst sehr spät entschlummerten, wenn sie nämlich
der körperliche Drang übermannt hatte, so hatten sie nie das
mitternächtliche Läuten der Glocken, nie die Orgel der Kirche
gehört, wenn das Fest[51] gefeiert wurde, obwohl sie nahe an der
Kirche wohnten. In diesem Augenblicke der heutigen Nacht
wurde nun mit allen Glocken geläutet, es läuteten die Glocken
in Millsdorf, es läuteten die Glocken in Gschaid, und hinter
dem Berge war noch ein Kirchlein mit drei hellen klingenden
Glocken, die läuteten. In den fernen Ländern draußen waren
unzählige Kirchen und Glocken, und mit allen wurde zu dieser
Zeit geläutet, von Dorf zu Dorf ging die Tonwelle, ja man
konnte wohl zuweilen von einem Dorfe zum andern durch die
blätterlosen Zweige das Läuten hören: nur zu den Kindern
herauf kam kein Laut, hier wurde nichts vernommen; denn
hier war nichts zu verkündigen. In den Talkrümmen gingen
jetzt an den Berghängen die Lichter der Laternen hin, und
von manchem Hofe tönte das Hausglöcklein, um die Leute zu
erinnern; aber dieses konnte um so weniger[52] herauf gesehen

The girl, whose constitution demanded rest, replied: "I'm not cold."

"Just take a little," said the boy, "then you may sleep."

This prospect tempted Sanna; she made enough of an effort to swallow the drink, almost all he had poured out for her. Then the boy drank some too.

The unusually powerful extract produced an immediate effect that was all the more violent because the children had never tasted coffee in their lives. Instead of sleeping, Sanna now became more animated and admitted that she was cold but that she felt really warm inside and that the warmth was already spreading to her hands and feet. The children even talked to each other for a while.

So, in spite of its bitterness, they kept drinking the beverage whenever its effect began to wear off and they stimulated their innocent nerves to fever pitch, which was able to counteract the weight that drew them toward slumber.

Midnight had now come. Because they were still so young and, in their ecstasy of joy, always fell asleep very late on Christmas Eve—that is, when physical weariness had overcome them—they had never heard the midnight pealing of the bells, nor the organ in church when Mass was celebrated, though they lived close to the church. At this moment tonight all the bells rang: the bells in Millsdorf rang, the bells in Gschaid rang, and behind the mountain there was another little church with three clear, resonant bells, which rang too. In the distant countryside beyond there were countless churches and bells, and they were all ringing at this time; from village to village the wave of sound went; at times one could even hear the chiming from one village to the next through the leafless branches. But no sound reached the children; they heard nothing, for there was nothing to herald here. In the windings of the valley and on the mountain slopes the lantern lights were now moving, and on many a farmyard the little house bell was ringing to remind the folk; but all this could scarcely be seen or heard up here; the stars alone shone and they calmly went on shining and twinkling.

und gehört werden, es glänzten nur die Sterne, und sie leuch-
teten und funkelten ruhig fort.

Wenn auch Konrad sich das Schicksal des erfrornen Eschen-
jägers vor Augen hielt, wenn auch die Kinder das Fläschchen
mit dem schwarzen Kaffee fast ausgeleert hatten, wodurch sie
ihr Blut zu größerer Tätigkeit brachten, aber gerade dadurch
eine folgende Ermattung herbeizogen: so würden sie den Schlaf
nicht haben überwinden können, dessen verführende Süßigkeit
alle Gründe überwiegt, wenn nicht die Natur in ihrer Größe
ihnen beigestanden wäre und in ihrem Innern eine Kraft aufge-
rufen hätte, welche imstande war, dem Schlafe zu widerstehen.

In der ungeheueren Stille, die herrschte, in der Stille, in der
sich kein Schneespitzchen zu rühren schien, hörten die Kinder
dreimal das Krachen des Eises. Was das Starrste scheint und
doch das Regsamste und Lebendigste ist, der Gletscher, hatte
die Töne hervorgebracht. Dreimal hörten sie hinter sich den
Schall, der entsetzlich war, als ob die Erde entzweigesprungen
wäre, der sich nach allen Richtungen im Eise verbreitete und
gleichsam durch alle Äderchen des Eises lief. Die Kinder blieben mit offenen Augen sitzen und schauten in die Sterne
hinaus.

Auch für die Augen begann sich etwas zu entwickeln. Wie
die Kinder so saßen, erblühte am Himmel vor ihnen ein bleiches
Licht mitten unter den Sternen und spannte einen schwachen
Bogen durch dieselben. Es hatte einen grünlichen Schimmer,
der sich sachte nach unten zog. Aber der Bogen wurde immer
heller und heller, bis sich die Sterne vor ihm zurückzogen und
erblaßten. Auch in andere Gegenden des Himmels sandte er
einen Schein, der schimmergrün sachte und lebendig unter die
Sterne floß. Dann standen Garben verschiedenen Lichtes auf
der Höhe des Bogens wie Zacken einer Krone und brannten.
Es floß helle durch die benachbarten Himmelsgegenden, es
sprühte leise und ging in sanftem Zucken durch lange Räume.
Hatte sich nun der Gewitterstoff des Himmels durch den un-
erhörten Schneefall so gespannt, daß er in diesen stummen,
herrlichen Strömen des Lichtes ausfloß, oder war es eine andere
Ursache der unergründlichen Natur? Nach und nach wurde
es schwächer und immer schwächer, die Garben erloschen

Even though Conrad kept the fate of the frozen Eschenjäger in mind, even though the children had almost emptied the little flask of black coffee—thus causing their blood to circulate more vigorously but by this very act bringing on a subsequent weariness—they could not have conquered sleep, whose seductive sweetness outweighs all reasoning, if Nature in her grandeur had not helped them and summoned up in their minds a power that was able to resist sleep.

In the vast stillness that prevailed, in the stillness in which not even a speck of snow seemed to stir, the children heard the ice crack three times. What seems to be the most rigid and is yet the most active and living of things, the glacier, had produced the sounds. Three times they heard behind them the sound that was horrifying, as if the earth had broken apart, spreading in the ice in all directions and running, as it were, through all the little veins of the ice. The children sat there with open eyes, looking out at the stars.

Something now began to unfold for their eyes too. As the children were sitting there, a pale light bloomed before them in the sky among the stars and stretched a weak arc through them. It had a greenish shimmer, which gently spread downward. But the arc became brighter and brighter until the stars withdrew before it and paled. It also sent a light into other regions of the sky, flowing gently and alive among the stars in a shimmering green. Then sheaves of varied light stood on the top of the arc like the jagged points of a crown, and were aflame. A brightness flowed through the adjacent celestial regions, it gave off a soft spray and went with a gentle quivering through the vast spaces. Had the electricity in the sky been so charged by the unprecedented snowfall that it discharged itself in these mute, glorious streams of light, or was it the result of some other cause in unfathomable nature? Gradually it grew weaker and ever weaker, the sheaves died out first, until it gradually and imperceptibly became slighter and once more

zuerst, bis es allmählich und ummerklich immer geringer wurde und wieder nichts am Himmel war als die tausend und tausend einfachen Sterne.

Die Kinder sagten keines zu dem andern ein Wort, sie blieben fort und fort sitzen und schauten mit offenen Augen in den Himmel.

Es geschah nun nichts Besonderes mehr. Die Sterne glänzten, funkelten und zitterten, nur manche schießende Schnuppe fuhr durch sie.

Endlich, nachdem die Sterne lange allein geschienen hatten und nie ein Stückchen Mond an dem Himmel zu erblicken gewesen war, geschah etwas anderes. Es fing der Himmel an, heller zu werden, langsam heller, aber doch zu erkennen;[53] es wurde seine Farbe sichtbar, die bleichsten Sterne erloschen, und die anderen standen nicht mehr so dicht. Endlich wichen auch die stärkeren, und der Schnee vor den Höhen wurde deutlicher sichtbar. Zuletzt färbte sich eine Himmelsgegend gelb, und ein Wolkenstreifen, der in derselben war, wurde zu einem leuchtenden Faden entzündet. Alle Dinge waren klar zu sehen, und die entfernten Schneehügel zeichneten sich scharf in die Luft.

„Sanna, der Tag bricht an", sagte der Knabe.

„Ja, Konrad", antwortete das Mädchen.

„Wenn es nur noch ein bißchen heller wird, dann gehen wir aus der Höhle und laufen über den Berg hinunter."

Es wurde heller, an dem ganzen Himmel war kein Stern mehr sichtbar, und alle Gegenstände standen in der Morgendämmerung da.

„Nun, jetzt gehen wir", sagte der Knabe.

„Ja, wir gehen", antwortete Sanna.

Die Kinder standen auf und versuchten ihre erst heute recht müden Glieder. Obwohl sie nicht geschlafen hatten, waren sie doch durch den Morgen gestärkt, wie das immer so ist. Der Knabe hing sich das Kalbfellränzchen um und machte das Pelzjäckchen an Sanna fester zu. Dann führte er sie aus der Höhle.

Weil sie nach ihrer Meinung nur über den Berg hinabzu-

there was nothing in the sky except the thousands upon thousands of simple stars.

The children did not say a word to each other, they kept sitting there, looking at the sky with wide open eyes.

Nothing special happened after this. The stars glittered, sparkled, and quivered, occasionally a shooting star went through them.

Finally, after the stars had shone alone for a long time without even a piece of the moon being visible in the sky, something else happened. The sky began to become brighter, slowly but still perceptibly brighter; its color became visible, the palest stars died away and the others no longer stood so close together. At last even the stronger ones vanished, and the snow in front of the heights became more clearly visible. Finally a region of the sky turned yellow and a strip of cloud in it was kindled into a glowing thread. Everything could be seen clearly and the distant hills of snow stood out sharply in the air.

"Sanna, day is breaking," said the boy.

"Yes, Conrad," the girl replied.

"When it gets just a bit lighter, we'll leave the cave and run down the mountain."

It became lighter; not a star was visible any longer in the whole sky and every object stood out in the faint morning light

"Well, let's go now," said the boy.

"Yes, we'll go," answered Sanna.

The children stood up and tried their limbs, which felt really tired today. Although they had not slept at all, they were strengthened by the morning, as is always the case. The boy hung the calfskin satchel over his shoulder and drew Sanna's little fur jacket tighter. Then he led her out of the cave.

Because they thought they need only run down the mountain,

laufen hatten, dachten sie an kein Essen und untersuchten das
Ränzchen nicht, ob noch Weißbrote oder andere Eßwaren da-
rinnen seien.

Von dem Berge wollte nun Konrad, weil der Himmel ganz
heiter war, in die Täler hinabschauen, um das Gschaider Tal
zu erkennen und in dasselbe hinunterzugehen. Aber er sah
gar keine Täler. Es war nicht, als ob sie sich auf einem Berge
befänden, von dem man hinabsieht, sondern in einer fremden,
seltsamen Gegend, in der lauter unbekannte Gegenstände sind.
Sie sahen auch heute in größerer[54] Entfernung furchtbare
Felsen aus dem Schnee emporstehen, die sie gestern nicht gesehen hatten, sie sahen das Eis, sie sahen Hügel und Schnee-
lehnen emporstarren, und hinter diesen war entweder der
Himmel, oder es ragte die blaue Spitze eines sehr fernen Berges
am Schneerande hervor.

In diesem Augenblicke ging die Sonne auf.

Eine riesengroße blutrote Scheibe erhob sich an dem Schnee-
saume in den Himmel, und in dem Augenblicke errötete der
Schnee um die Kinder, als wäre er mit Millionen Rosen über-
streut worden. Die Kuppen und die Hörner warfen sehr lange
grünliche Schatten längs des Schnees.

„Sanna, wir werden jetzt da weiter vorwärts gehen, bis wir
an den Rand des Berges kommen und hinuntersehen", sagte
der Knabe.

Sie gingen nun in den Schnee hinaus. Er war in der heiteren
Nacht noch trockener geworden und wich den Tritten noch
besser aus. Sie wateten rüstig fort. Ihre Glieder wurden sogar
geschmeidiger und stärker, da sie gingen. Allein sie kamen an
keinen Rand und sahen nicht hinunter. Schneefeld entwickelte
sich aus Schneefeld, und am Saume eines jeden stand alle Male[55]
wieder der Himmel.

Sie gingen desohngeachtet fort.

Da kamen sie wieder in das Eis. Sie wußten nicht, wie das
Eis daher gekommen sei, aber unter den Füßen empfanden
sie den glatten Boden, und waren gleich nicht[56] die fürchterlichen Trümmer, wie an jenem Rande, an dem sie die Nacht
zugebracht hatten, so sahen sie doch, daß sie auf glattem Eise
fortgingen, sie sahen hie und da Stücke, die immer mehr wur-

they did not think of food and did not examine the satchel to
see whether there were rolls or other food in it.

As the sky was now quite clear, Conrad wanted to look down
from the mountain into the valleys, to make out the Gschaid
valley and go down to it. But he saw no valleys at all. They did
not seem to be on a mountain from which one can look down,
but in a foreign strange region in which there are nothing but
unfamiliar objects. Today again they saw at some distance fearful rocks standing out from the snow, rocks they had not seen
yesterday. They saw the ice, they saw hills and snow-covered
slopes standing up rigidly, and behind these was either the sky,
or the blue point of a very distant mountain jutted out at the
edge of the snow.

At this moment the sun rose.
A gigantic blood-red disk rose up at the edge of the snow
into the sky, and at that moment the snow about the children
turned red, as if it had been strewn with millions of roses. The
knobs and horns cast very long, greenish shadows along the
snow.

"Sanna, we will now go on there some more until we come
to the edge of the mountain and can look down," said the boy.

They now went out into the snow. It had become even drier
in the clear night and yielded even more to their steps. They
waded on briskly. Their limbs became even more supple and
strong as they walked. But they came to no edge and could not
look down. Snowfield developed from snowfield, and at the
edge of each they found the sky every time.

They went on nevertheless.
Then they came to the ice again. They did not know where
the ice had come from, but under their feet they felt the smooth
ground, and even though there was none of the fearful debris
they had found at the rim where they had spent the night, they
saw nevertheless that they were walking on smooth ice; here
and there they saw chunks which kept increasing in number,

den, die sich näher an sie drängten und die sie wieder zu klettern zwangen.

Aber sie verfolgten doch ihre Richtung.

Sie kletterten neuerdings an Blöcken empor. Da standen sie wieder auf dem Eisfelde. Heute bei der hellen Sonne konnten sie erst erblicken, was es ist. Es war ungeheuer groß, und jenseits standen wieder schwarze Felsen empor, es ragte gleichsam Welle hinter Welle auf, das beschneite Eis war gedrängt, gequollen, emporgehoben, gleichsam als schöbe es sich noch vorwärts und flösse gegen die Brust der Kinder heran. In dem Weiß sahen sie unzählige vorwärtsgehende geschlängelte blaue Linien. Zwischen jenen Stellen, wo die Eiskörper gleichsam wie aneinandergeschmettert starrten, gingen auch Linien wie Wege, aber sie waren weiß und waren Streifen, wo sich fester Eisboden vorfand oder die Stücke doch nicht gar so sehr verschoben waren. In diese Pfade gingen die Kinder hinein, weil sie doch einen Teil des Eises überschreiten wollten, um an den Bergrand zu gelangen und endlich einmal hinunterzusehen. Sie sagten kein Wörtlein. Das Mädchen folgte dem Knaben. Aber es war auch heute wieder Eis, lauter Eis. Wo sie hinübergelangen wollten, wurde es gleichsam immer breiter und breiter. Da schlugen sie, ihre Richtung aufgebend, den Rückweg ein. Wo sie nicht gehen konnten, griffen sie sich durch die Mengen des Schnees hindurch, der oft dicht vor ihrem Auge wegbrach und den sehr blauen Streifen einer Eisspalte zeigte, wo doch früher alles weiß gewesen war; aber sie kümmerten sich nicht darum, sie arbeiteten sich fort, bis sie wieder irgendwo aus dem Eise herauskamen.

„Sanna", sagte der Knabe, „wir werden gar nicht mehr in das Eis hineingehen, weil wir in demselben nicht fortkommen. Und weil wir schon in unser Tal gar nicht hinabsehen können, so werden wir gerade über den Berg hinabgehen. Wir müssen in ein Tal kommen, dort werden wir den Leuten sagen, daß wir aus Gschaid sind, die werden uns einen Wegweiser nach Hause mitgeben."

„Ja, Konrad", sagte das Mädchen.

So begannen sie nun in dem Schnee nach jener Richtung abwärts zu gehen, welche sich ihnen eben darbot. Der Knabe

which pressed closer to them, and which compelled them to climb once more.

But they still pursued their direction.

They again climbed up blocks. There they were standing on the ice field again. Only today, in the bright sun, they were able to see what it was. It was enormously big, and on the other side black rocks stood out again, wave upon wave towered up as it were, the snow-covered ice was squeezed, swollen, lifted up as if it were still thrusting forward and flowing toward the children's chests. In the whiteness they saw countless serpentine blue lines advancing. Between those places where the ice blocks stood rigid, as if they had been smashed against each other, lines went like roads; but they were white and were stripes formed by a solid ice floor underneath or where the chunks were not too far out of place. The children entered these paths because they really wanted to cross a part of the ice to reach the edge of the mountain and to look down at long last. They did not speak a word. The girl followed the boy. But today too there was ice, nothing but ice. Where they wanted to cross, it seemed to become broader and broader. So, abandoning their direction, they turned back. Where they could not walk, they crawled through the masses of snow, which often broke away close before their eyes, showing the very blue stripe of a crevasse where everything had been white before; but they did not concern themselves about it, they worked their way forward, until they once more came out of the ice somewhere.

"Sanna," said the boy, "we won't go into the ice any more, because we aren't getting anywhere in it. And since we can't look down into our valley at all, we will go straight down over the mountain. We must get into a valley, there we'll tell the people that we're from Gschaid, and they'll give us a guide to take us home."

"Yes, Conrad," said the girl.

So they now began to walk down in the snow in the direction that happened to lie before them. The boy led the girl by the

führte das Mädchen an der Hand. Allein nachdem sie eine
Weile abwärts gegangen waren, hörte in dieser Richtung das
Gehänge auf, der Schnee stieg wieder empor. Also änderten
die Kinder die Richtung und gingen nach der Länge einer
Mulde hinab. Aber da fanden sie wieder Eis. Sie stiegen also
an der Seite der Mulde empor, um nach einer andern Richtung
ein Abwärts zu suchen. Es führte sie eine Fläche hinab, allein
die wurde nach und nach so steil, daß sie kaum noch einen
Fuß einsetzen konnten und abwärts zu gleiten fürchteten. Sie
klommen also wieder empor, um wieder einen andern Weg
nach abwärts zu suchen. Nachdem sie lange im Schnee empor-
geklommen und dann auf einem ebenen Rücken fortgelaufen
waren, war es wie früher: entweder ging der Schnee so steil
ab, daß sie gestürzt wären, oder er stieg wieder hinan, daß sie
auf den Berggipfel zu kommen fürchteten. Und so ging es
immerfort.

Da wollten sie die Richtung suchen, in der sie gekommen
waren, und zur roten Unglücksäule hinabgehen. Weil es nicht
schneit und der Himmel so helle ist, so würden sie, dachte der
Knabe, die Stelle schon erkennen, wo die Säule sein solle, und
würden von dort nach Gschaid hinabgehen können.

Der Knabe sagte diesen Gedanken dem Schwesterchen, und
diese folgte.

Allein auch der Weg auf den Hals hinab war nicht zu finden.

So[57] klar die Sonne schien, so schön die Schneehöhen dastanden und die Schneefelder dalagen, so konnten sie doch die
Gegenden nicht erkennen, durch die sie gestern heraufgegan-
gen waren. Gestern war alles durch den fürchterlichen Schneefall verhängt gewesen, daß sie kaum einige Schritte von sich
gesehen hatten, und da war alles ein einziges Weiß und Grau
durcheinander gewesen. Nur die Felsen hatten sie gesehen, an
denen und zwischen denen sie gegangen waren: allein auch
heute hatten sie bereits viele Felsen gesehen, die alle den nämlichen Anschein gehabt hatten wie die gestern gesehenen.
Heute ließen sie frische Spuren in dem Schnee zurück; aber
gestern sind alle Spuren von dem fallenden Schnee verdeckt
worden. Auch aus dem bloßen Anblicke konnten sie nicht erraten, welche Gegend auf den Hals führe, da alle Gegenden

hand. But after they had gone downhill a while, the slope stopped in this direction and the snow began to rise again. So the children changed their direction and went down the full length of a hollow. But there they found ice again. So they climbed up the side of the hollow to seek another road downhill. A flat surface led them down, but this gradually became so steep that they could hardly find footing and feared they would slip down. So they climbed up again, to seek another way down. After they had climbed in the snow for a long time and had then walked along a level ridge it was as it had been before: either the snow descended so steeply that they would have fallen or it rose again so that they were afraid they would get to the top of the mountain. And so it went, on and on.

Then they wanted to look for the direction from which they had come and go down to the red accident pillar. Because it isn't snowing, the boy thought, and the sky is so clear, they would easily recognize the spot where the pillar ought to be and would be able to go down to Gschaid from there.

The boy communicated this thought to his sister and she followed him.

But the road down the neck could not be found either.

Though the sun shone clearly, though the snowy heights stood and the fields of snow lay there so beautifully, they could not recognize the regions through which they had gone up yesterday. Yesterday everything had been obscured by the fearful snowfall, so that they had scarcely been able to see a few paces ahead of them, and everything had been a single confused mass of white and gray. They had seen only the rocks past and between which they had walked; but today too they had already seen many rocks, all of which had had the same appearance as those they had seen yesterday. Today they left fresh tracks behind them in the snow; but yesterday all their tracks were covered by the falling snow. Moreover, they could not tell from merely looking which region led to the neck, since all the regions were alike. Snow, nothing but snow. But they kept going for-

gleich waren. Schnee, lauter Schnee. Sie gingen aber doch immerfort und meinten, es zu erringen. Sie wichen den steilen Abstürzen aus und kletterten keine steilen Anhöhen hinauf.

Auch heute blieben sie öfter stehen, um zu horchen; aber sie vernahmen auch heute nichts, nicht den geringsten Laut. Zu sehen war auch nichts als der Schnee, der helle weiße Schnee, aus dem hie und da die schwarzen Hörner und die schwarzen Steinrippen emporstanden.

Endlich war es[58] dem Knaben, als sähe er auf einem fernen schiefen Schneefelde ein hüpfendes Feuer. Es tauchte auf, es tauchte nieder. Jetzt sahen sie es, jetzt sahen sie es nicht. Sie blieben stehen und blickten unverwandt auf jene Gegend hin. Das Feuer hüpfte immerfort, und es schien, als ob es näher käme; denn sie sahen es größer und sahen das Hüpfen deutlicher. Es verschwand nicht mehr so oft und nicht mehr auf so lange Zeit wie früher. Nach einer Weile vernahmen sie in der stillen blauen Luft schwach, sehr schwach, etwas wie einen lange anhaltenden Ton aus einem Hirtenhorne. Wie aus Instinkt schrien beide Kinder laut. Nach einer Zeit hörten sie den Ton wieder. Sie schrien wieder und blieben auf der nämlichen Stelle stehen. Das Feuer näherte sich auch. Der Ton wurde zum dritten Male vernommen und dieses Mal deutlicher. Die Kinder antworteten wieder durch lautes Schreien. Nach einer geraumen Weile erkannten sie auch das Feuer. Es war kein Feuer, es war eine rote Fahne, die geschwungen wurde. Zugleich ertönte das Hirtenhorn näher, und die Kinder antworteten.

„Sanna", rief der Knabe, „da kommen Leute aus Gschaid, ich kenne die Fahne, es ist die rote Fahne, welche der fremde Herr, der mit dem jungen Eschenjäger den Gars bestiegen hatte, auf dem Gipfel aufpflanzte, daß sie der Herr Pfarrer mit dem Fernrohre sähe, was als Zeichen gälte, daß sie oben seien, und welche Fahne damals der fremde Herr dem Herrn Pfarrer geschenkt hat. Du warst noch ein recht kleines Kind."

„Ja, Konrad."

Nach einer Zeit sahen die Kinder auch die Menschen, die bei der Fahne waren, kleine schwarze Stellen, die sich zu bewegen schienen. Der Ruf des Hornes wiederholte sich von Zeit zu Zeit und kam immer näher. Die Kinder antworteten jedesmal.

ward and thought they would make it. They avoided the steep drops and climbed up no steep slopes.

Today too they often stopped to listen; but they heard nothing today either, not the slightest sound. Nor could they see anything but the snow, the bright, white snow, from which the black horns and the black stone ribs stood out here and there.

Finally it seemed to the boy that he saw a skipping fire on a distant slanting snowfield. It bobbed up and it bobbed down. Now they saw it, now they didn't see it. They stopped and looked fixedly at that region. The fire kept skipping and it seemed to be coming nearer; for they saw it grow larger and saw the skipping more distinctly. It no longer vanished so often nor for so long a time as before. After a while they heard, in the silent blue air, faintly, very faintly, something like a long steady note from a shepherd's horn. As though by instinct both children cried aloud. After a while they heard the note again. They shouted again and stopped where they were. The fire was coming closer too. They heard the note a third time and this time more distinctly. The children replied again with a loud shout. After some time they recognized the fire. It wasn't fire, it was a red flag that was being swung. At the same time the shepherd's horn sounded closer and the children replied.

"Sanna," cried the boy, "there are people coming from Gschaid, I know that flag, it's the red flag that the foreign gentleman who had climbed the Gars with young Eschenjäger planted on the peak so that the pastor might see it with his telescope as a sign that they were at the top. The foreign gentleman gave the flag to the pastor at that time. You were still quite a little child."

"Yes, Conrad."

After a while the children also saw the people who were with the flag, little black spots that seemed to be moving. The call of the horn was repeated from time to time and came closer all the time. The children answered it every time.

Endlich sahen sie über den Schneehang gegen sich her mehrere Männer mit ihren Stöcken herabfahren, die die Fahne in
ihrer Mitte hatten. Da sie näher kamen, erkannten sie dieselben. Es war der Hirt Philipp mit dem Horne, seine zwei
Söhne, dann der junge Eschenjager und mehrere Bewohner
von Gschaid.

„Gebenedeit sei Gott", schrie Philipp, „da seid ihr ja. Der
ganze Berg ist voll Leute. Laufe doch einer gleich in die
Sideralpe hinab und läute die Glocke, daß die dort hören, daß
wir sie gefunden haben, und einer muß auf den Krebsstein
gehen und die Fahne dort aufpflanzen, daß sie dieselbe in dem
Tale sehen und die Pöller abschießen, damit die es wissen, die
im Millsdorfer Walde suchen, und damit sie in Gschaid die
Rauchfeuer anzünden, die in der Luft gesehen werden, und
alle, die noch auf dem Berge sind, in die Sideralpe hinabbedeu-
ten. Das sind Weihnachten!"[59]

„Ich laufe in die Alpe hinab", sagte einer.

„Ich trage die Fahne auf den Krebsstein", sagte ein anderer.

„Und wir werden die Kinder in die Sideralpe hinabbringen,
so gut wir es vermögen, und so gut uns Gott helfe", sagte
Philipp.

Ein Sohn Philipps schlug den Weg nach abwärts ein, und
der andere ging mit der Fahne durch den Schnee dahin.

Der Eschenjäger nahm das Mädchen bei der Hand, der Hirt
Philipp den Knaben. Die andern halfen, wie sie konnten. So
begann man den Weg. Er ging in Windungen. Bald gingen sie
nach einer Richtung, bald schlugen sie die entegegengesetzte
ein, bald gingen sie abwärts, bald aufwärts. Immer ging es
durch Schnee, immer durch Schnee, und die Gegend blieb sich
beständig gleich. Über sehr schiefe Flächen taten sie Steigeisen
an die Füße und trugen die Kinder. Endlich nach langer Zeit
hörten sie ein Glöcklein, das sanft und fein zu ihnen herauf-
kam und das erste Zeichen war, das ihnen die niederen Gegenden wieder zusandten. Sie mußten wirklich sehr tief herabge-
kommen sein, denn sie sahen ein Schneehaupt recht hoch und
recht blau über sich ragen. Das Glöcklein aber, das sie hörten,
war das der Sideralpe, das geläutet wurde, weil dort die Zusam-
menkunft verabredet war. Da sie noch weiter kamen, hörten sie

Finally they saw several men with sticks sliding down the snowy slope toward them, carrying the flag in their midst. When they came nearer they recognized them. It was Shepherd Philip with his horn, his two sons, then young Eschenjäger and several natives of Gschaid.

"God be praised!" cried Philip, "why, there you are. The whole mountain is full of people. One of you run down to the Sider meadow and ring the bell so that they may hear that we've found them, and one of you must go to the Krebsstein and plant the flag there, so that they'll see it in the valley and fire the small mortars so that the people who are searching in the Millsdorf forest may know and so that the people in Gschaid may light the smoke signals that will be seen in the air and bring all those who are still in the mountain down to the Sider meadow. What a Christmas!"

"I'll run down to the meadow," one said.

"I'll carry the flag to the Krebsstein," said another.

"And we'll bring the children down into the Sider meadow as best we can and with God's help," said Philip.

One of Philip's sons took the way downhill and the other went off through the snow with the flag.

Eschenjäger took the girl by the hand, the shepherd took the boy. The others helped in any way they could. So they started on their way. It led through many turns. Now they went in one direction, now in the opposite, now they went down, now up. Always they were walking through snow, always through snow and the scenery remained constantly the same. On very steep slopes they put climbing irons on their feet and carried the children. Finally, after a long time, they heard a little bell that came up to them softly and delicately and was the first sign sent to them by the lower regions. They must really have come down very far, for they saw a snowy head towering very high and very blue above them. But the little bell they heard was that of the Sider meadow, which was being rung because they had agreed to meet there. When they came farther still they faintly heard in the still air the reports of the small mortar;

auch schwach in die stille Luft die Böllerschüsse herauf, die infolge der ausgesteckten Fahne abgefeuert wurden, und sahen dann in die Luft feine Rauchsäulen aufsteigen.

Da sie nach einer Weile über eine sanfte schiefe Fläche abgingen, erblickten sie die Sideralphütte. Sie gingen auf sie zu. In der Hütte brannte ein Feuer, die Mutter der Kinder war da, und mit einem furchtbaren Schrei sank sie in den Schnee zurück, als sie die Kinder mit dem Eschenjäger kommen sah.

Dann lief sie herzu, betrachtete sie überall, wollte ihnen zu essen geben, wollte sie wärmen, wollte sie in vorhandenes Heu legen; aber bald überzeugte sie sich, daß die Kinder durch die Freude stärker seien, als sie gedacht hatte, daß sie nur einiger warmer Speise bedurften, die sie bekamen, und daß sie nur ein wenig ausruhen mußten, was ihnen ebenfalls zuteil werden sollte.

Da nach einer Zeit der Ruhe wieder eine Gruppe Männer über die Schneefläche herabkam, während das Hüttenglöcklein immerfort läutete, liefen die Kinder selber mit den andern hinaus, um zu sehen, wer es sei. Der Schuster war es, der einstige Alpensteiger, mit Alpenstock und Steigeisen, begleitet von seinen Freunden und Kameraden.

„Sebastian, da sind sie", schrie das Weib.

Er aber war stumm, zitterte und lief auf sie zu. Dann rührte er die Lippen, als wollte er etwas sagen, sagte aber nichts, riß die Kinder an sich und hielt sie lange. Dann wandte er sich gegen sein Weib, schloß es an sich und rief: „Sanna, Sanna!"

Nach einer Weile nahm er den Hut, der ihm in den Schnee gefallen war, auf, trat unter die Männer und wollte reden. Er sagte aber nur: „Nachbarn, Freunde, ich danke euch."

Da man noch gewartet hatte, bis die Kinder sich zur Beruhigung erholt hatten, sagte er: „Wenn wir alle beisammen sind, so können wir in Gottes Namen aufbrechen."

„Es sind wohl noch nicht alle", sagte der Hirt Philipp, „aber die noch abgehen, wissen aus dem Rauche, daß wir die Kinder haben, und sie werden schon nach Hause gehen, wenn sie die Alphütte leer finden."

Man machte sich zum Aufbruche bereit.

these were being fired because the flag had been hoisted, and
then they saw thin columns of smoke rising into the air.

When after a while they descended a gentle, slanting slope,
they caught sight of the Sider meadow hut. They went toward
it. In the hut a fire was burning, the mother of the children
was there, and when she saw the children coming with Eschenjäger, she sank back into the snow with a fearful cry.

Then she ran up to them, examined them from every side,
wanted to give them food, wanted to warm them, wanted to
bed them in the hay that was there. But she soon convinced
herself that joy had made the children stronger than she imagined, that they only needed some warm food, which they got,
and that they only needed a little rest, which they would likewise get.

After a period of quiet another group of men came down
over the snowy slope, while the little bell of the hut kept ringing.
The children ran out with the others to see who it was. It was
the shoemaker, the one-time Alpine climber, with his alpenstock
and climbing irons, accompanied by his friends and comrades.

"Sebastian, they're here," his wife cried.

But he was silent, he trembled and ran up to them. Then he
moved his lips as if he wanted to say something, but said nothing,
drew the children to him and held them a long time. Then he
turned to his wife, locked her in his arms and cried: "Sanna,
Sanna!"

After a while he picked up his hat, which had fallen into the
snow, stepped among the men, and wanted to speak. But all
he said was: "Neighbors, friends, I thank you."

They waited until the children had recovered their complete
calm, then he said: "If we are all here, we may start out in
God's name."

"I don't think they're all here," said the shepherd Philip, "but
those that are missing know from the smoke that we have found
the children and they'll go home when they find the meadow
hut empty."

They got ready to depart.

Man war auf der Sideralphütte nicht gar weit von Gschaid
entfernt, aus dessen Fenstern man im Sommer recht gut die
grüne Matte sehen konnte, auf der die graue Hütte mit dem
kleinen Glockentürmlein stand; aber es war unterhalb eine fall-
rechte Wand, die viele Klaftern hoch hinabging und auf der
man im Sommer nur mit Steigeisen, im Winter gar nicht hinabkommen konnte. Man mußte daher den Umweg zum Halse
machen, um von der Unglücksäule aus nach Gschaid hinabzukommen. Auf dem Wege gelangte man über die Siderwiese,
die noch näher an Gschaid ist, so daß man die Fenster des
Dörfleins zu erblicken meinte.

Als man über die Wiese ging, tönte hell und deutlich das
Glöcklein der Gschaider Kirche herauf, die Wandlung[60] des
heiligen Hochamtes verkündend.

Der Pfarrer hatte wegen der allgemeinen Bewegung, die am
Morgen in Gschaid war, die Abhaltung des Hochamtes verschoben, da er dachte, daß die Kinder zum Vorscheine kommen
würden. Allein endlich, da noch immer keine Nachricht eintraf,
mußte die heilige Handlung doch vollzogen werden.

Als das Wandlungsglöcklein[61] tönte, sanken alle, die über die
Siderwiese gingen, auf die Knie in den Schnee und beteten.
Als der Klang des Glöckleins aus war, standen sie auf und
gingen weiter.

Der Schuster trug meistens das Mädchen und ließ sich von
ihm alles erzählen.

Als sie schon gegen den Wald des Halses kamen, trafen sie
Spuren, von denen der Schuster sagte: „Das sind keine Fußstapfen von Schuhen meiner Arbeit."

Die Sache klärte sich bald auf. Wahrscheinlich durch die
vielen Stimmen, die auf dem Platze tönten, angelockt, kam
wieder eine Abteilung Männer auf die Herabgehenden zu. Es
war der aus Angst aschenhaft entfärbte Färber, der an der
Spitze seiner Knechte, seiner Gesellen und mehrerer Millsdorfer bergab kam.

„Sie sind über das Gletschereis und über die Schründe gegangen, ohne es zu wissen", rief der Schuster seinem Schwiegervater zu.

„Da sind sie ja—da sind sie ja—Gott sei Dank", antwortete
der Färber, „ich weiß es schon, daß sie oben waren, als dein

The Sider meadow hut was not very far from Gschaid, from whose windows the green meadow could be seen quite well in summer, with its gray hut and the little bell tower. But below it was a perpendicular wall, which went down many fathoms deep, and which could be descended in summer only with climbing irons and in winter not at all. They therefore had to make the detour to the neck to get down to Gschaid from the accident pillar. On the way they passed the Sider meadow, which is still closer to Gschaid, so that they thought they could see the windows of the little village.

As they were going over this meadow the little bell of the Gschaid church rang up to them bright and clear, announcing the transubstantiation at Holy Mass.

Because of the general commotion prevailing in Gschaid that morning, the pastor had postponed the celebration of High Mass, assuming that the children would be found. But finally, since there was still no news, High Mass had to be celebrated anyway.

When the little bell announcing transubstantiation rang, all those who were walking over the Sider meadow sank to their knees in the snow and prayed. When the bell stopped ringing, they stood up and went on.

The shoemaker carried the girl most of the way and had her tell him everything.

When they reached the forest of the neck, they met tracks of which the shoemaker remarked: "These footprints are not from shoes of my make."

The matter was soon cleared up. Probably attracted by the many voices that were heard on the square, another group of men came to meet those who were descending. It was the dyer, his face ashen white with anxiety, who was coming down the mountain at the head of his servants, his journeymen, and several people from Millsdorf.

"They went over the ice of the glacier and across the crevasses, without knowing it," the shoemaker called to his father-in-law.

"Why, there they are, there they are, thank God," the dyer replied. "I already know they were up there. When your mes-

Bote in der Nacht zu uns kam und wir mit Lichtern den ganzen Wald durchsucht und nichts gefunden hatten—und als dann das Morgengrau anbrach, bemerkte ich an dem Wege, der von der roten Unglücksäule links gegen den Schneeberg hinanführt, daß dort, wo man eben von der Säule weggeht, hin und wieder mehrere Reiserchen und Rütchen geknickt sind, wie Kinder gerne tun, wo sie eines Weges gehen—da wußte ich es—die Richtung ließ sie nicht mehr aus, weil sie in der Höhlung gingen, weil sie zwischen den Felsen gingen und weil sie dann auf dem Grat gingen, der rechts und links so steil ist, daß sie nicht hinabkommen konnten. Sie mußten hinauf. Ich schickte nach dieser Beobachtung gleich nach Gschaid, aber der Holzknecht Michael, der hinüberging, sagte bei der Rückkunft, da er uns fast am Eise oben traf, daß ihr sie schon habet, weshalb wir wieder heruntergingen."

„Ja", sagte Michael, „ich habe es gesagt, weil die rote Fahne schon auf dem Krebssteine steckt und die Gschaider dieses als Zeichen erkannten, das verabredet worden war. Ich sagte euch, daß auf diesem Wege da alle herabkommen müssen, weil man über die Wand nicht gehen kann."

„Und kniee nieder und danke Gott auf den Knieen, mein Schwiegersohn", fuhr der Färber fort, „daß kein Wind gegangen ist. Hundert Jahre werden wieder vergehen, daß ein so wunderbarer Schneefall niederfällt und daß er gerade niederfällt, wie nasse Schnüre von einer Stange hängen. Wäre ein Wind gegangen, so wären die Kinder verloren gewesen."

„Ja, danken wir Gott, danken wir Gott", sagte der Schuster.

Der Färber, der seit der Ehe seiner Tochter nie in Gschaid gewesen war, beschloß, die Leute nach Gschaid zu begleiten.

Da man schon gegen die rote Unglücksäule zu kam, wo der Holzweg begann, wartete ein Schlitten, den der Schuster auf alle Fälle[62] dahin bestellt hatte. Man tat[63] die Mutter und die Kinder hinein, versah sie hinreichend mit Decken und Pelzen, die im Schlitten waren, und ließ sie nach Gschaid vorausfahren.

Die andern folgten und kamen am Nachmittag in Gschaid an.

Die, welche noch auf dem Berge gewesen waren und erst durch den Rauch das Rückzugszeichen erfahren hatten, fanden sich auch nach und nach ein. Der letzte, welcher erst am Abend

senger came to us during the night and we hunted with lights
through the whole forest and found nothing, and when dawn
came I noticed by the road that leads from the red accident
pillar to the left toward the snow mountain that at the spot
where you leave the pillar several twigs and switches were broken here and there, as children are accustomed to do when
they walk along a road. Then I knew that this direction left
them no way out, because they were walking in the hollow
between the rocks and then on the ridge that is so steep both
to the right and to the left that they could not get down. They
had to go up. After noticing this I at once sent to Gschaid, but
Michael the lumberman, who went across, told me on returning
when he met us up there almost at the ice, that you already
had them, so we went down again."

"Yes," said Michael, "I said so because the red flag was already
planted on the Krebsstein and the people of Gschaid recognized
this as the sign that had been agreed on. I told you that they
all had to come down this way because you can't go over the
wall."

"And kneel down and thank God on your knees, my son-in-
law," the dyer continued, "that there was no wind stirring. It
will be a hundred years before another such strange snowfall
will come down, straight down as wet ropes hang down from
a pole. If there had been a wind the children would have been
lost."

"Yes, let us thank God, let us thank God," said the shoemaker.

The dyer, who had never been in Gschaid since his daughter's
marriage, decided to accompany the people to Gschaid.

When they were already approaching the red accident pillar
where the lumber road began, a sleigh was waiting which the
shoemaker had ordered to be sent there in case of emergency.
The mother and children were put into it, they were provided
with sufficient blankets and furs, which were in the sleigh, and
were sent ahead to Gschaid.

The others followed and arrived in Gschaid in the afternoon.

Those who had been on the mountain and had learned the
signal for retreat from the smoke, turned up gradually too.
The last man, who came only in the evening, was the son of

kam, war der Sohn des Hirten Philipp, der die rote Fahne auf den Krebsstein getragen und sie dort aufgepflanzt hatte.

In Gschaid wartete die Großmutter, welche herübergefahren war.

„Nie, nie", rief sie aus, „dürfen die Kinder in ihrem ganzen Leben mehr im Winter über den Hals gehen."

Die Kinder waren von dem Getriebe betäubt. Sie hatten noch etwas zu essen bekommen, und man hatte sie in das Bett gebracht. Spät gegen Abend, da sie sich ein wenig erholt hatten, da einige Nachbarn und Freunde sich in der Stube eingefunden hatten und dort von dem Ereignisse redeten, die Mutter aber in der Kammer an dem Bettchen Sannas saß und sie streichelte, sagte das Mädchen: „Mutter, ich habe heute nachts, als wir auf dem Berge saßen, den Heiligen Christ gesehen."

„O du mein geduldiges, du mein liebes, du mein herziges Kind", antwortete die Mutter, „er hat dir auch Gaben gesendet, die du bald bekommen wirst."

Die Schachteln waren ausgepackt worden, die Lichter waren angezündet, die Tür in die Stube wurde geöffnet, und die Kinder sahen von dem Bette auf den verspäteten, hell leuchtenden freundlichen Christbaum hinaus. Trotz der Erschöpfung mußte man sie noch ein wenig ankleiden, daß sie hinausgingen, die Gaben empfingen, bewunderten und endlich mit ihnen entschliefen.

In dem Wirtshause in Gschaid war es an diesem Abende lebhafter als je. Alle, die nicht in der Kirche gewesen waren, waren jetzt dort, und die andern auch. Jeder erzählte, was er gesehen und gehört, was er getan, was er geraten und was für Begegnisse und Gefahren er erlebt hatte. Besonders aber wurde hervorgehoben, wie man alles hätte anders und besser machen können.

Das Ereignis hat einen Abschnitt in die Geschichte von Gschaid gebracht, es hat auf lange den Stoff zu Gesprächen gegeben, und man wird noch nach Jahren davon reden, wenn man den Berg an heitern Tagen besonders deutlich sieht oder wenn man den Fremden von seinen Merkwürdigkeiten erzählt.

Die Kinder waren von dem Tage an erst recht das Eigentum des Dorfes geworden, sie wurden von nun an nicht mehr als

Shepherd Philip, who had carried the red flag to the Krebsstein and planted it there.

In Gschaid the grandmother, who had driven over, was waiting.

"Never, never in their whole lives," she exclaimed, "may the children again go over the neck in winter."

The children were bewildered by all the bustle. They had gotten something to eat and had been put to bed. Late toward evening, when they had somewhat recovered, a few neighbors and friends came into the living room and talked there about the event. The mother, however, was sitting in the bedroom beside Sanna's little bed, fondling her, and the girl said: "Mother, last night when we sat on the mountain, I saw the Holy Christ."

"Oh you patient, dear, beloved child," the mother replied, "He has also sent you gifts, which you will soon get."

The boxes had been unpacked, the lights were lit, the door to the living room was opened and the children looked from their beds on the belated, brightly lit, friendly Christmas tree. In spite of their exhaustion they had to be partially dressed, so that they might go out, receive their gifts, admire them, and finally fall asleep with them.

In the inn at Gschaid it was livelier than ever this evening. All those who had not been in church were there now, and the others too. Everyone told what he had seen and heard, what he had done, what he had advised, and what events and dangers he had experienced. But it was especially emphasized how everything could have been done differently and better.

The event created a chapter in Gschaid's history, it provided the material for conversation for a long time, and they will be talking about it for years to come, when the mountain is seen especially clearly on bright days or when strangers are told about its peculiarities.

The children had only from that day on really become the property of the village, from now on they were no longer

Auswärtige, sondern als Eingeborne betrachtet, die man sich von dem Berge herabgeholt hatte.

Auch ihre Mutter Sanna war nun eine Eingeborne von Gschaid.

Die Kinder aber werden den Berg nicht vergessen und werden ihn jetzt noch ernster betrachten, wenn sie in dem Garten sind, wenn wie in der Vergangenheit die Sonne sehr schön scheint, der Lindenbaum duftet, die Bienen summen und er so schön und so blau wie das sanfte Firmament auf sie herniederschaut.

Notes: Stifter, *Bergkristall*

1. *mag* . . . , they may feel.
2. *als* = *als ob*.
3. *länglicher Kreis*, i.e., ellipse.
4. *bergen in ihrem Schoße*, conceal in their lap; i.e., harbor.
5. *von dem Tale aus*, from the valley.
6. *es* . . . , they never change anything.
7. *Mittag*, south.
8. *inneren*, i.e., underground.
9. *daraus* = *woraus*.
10. *heißen* = *nennen*.
11. *Geschiebe*, *sérac*; a pointed mass or pinnacle of ice left among the crevasses of a glacier.
12. *lauter*, nothing but.
13. *Unglücksäule* a warning sign fastened to a post at a spot where there had been an accident.
14. *auch*, really *or* does indeed.
15. *frei*, open.
16. *nicht einmal*, not even.
17. *die* = *diejenigen, die*.
18. *Mitternacht* . . . , north, east and west.
19. *Wegstunden*. Germans often indicate distance by the time it takes to cover it.
20. *großen Verkehr*, communication with the outside world.
21. *ersten*, first; the ground floor does not count as a story in Europe; thus the floor above the ground floor is the first floor.
22. *nach rückwärts*, at the rear (lit.: backward).

regarded as outsiders but as natives who had been fetched down from the mountain.

Their mother Sanna too was now a native of Gschaid.

But the children will not forget the mountain and will now study it still more seriously when they are in the garden, when, as in the past, the sun shines very beautifully, the linden tree gives off its fragrance, the bees hum, and it looks down on them, as beautiful and as blue as the gentle firmament.

23. *nur mehr*, now only.

24. *sich . . . läßt*, hasn't the remotest intention.

25. *auf Wanderung*, i.e., the journeymen years—the years following the period of apprenticeship—spent on the road working for various masters.

26. *Lodenrock*, coat made of loden cloth; i.e., rough, unshorn wool.

27. *künstlich*, usually: artificially; here: artistically.

28. *weit und breit*, far and wide.

29. *hieß es*, it was said.

30. *trillen* = *drillen*.

31. *der . . .*, who had a mind of his own.

32. *seiner Ehre willen*, for the sake of his honor.

33. *daß es ihm zu tun gewesen*, that he had been interested.

34. *nicht . . .*, did not permit that intimacy and equality to develop.

35. *Walkmühle* a machine for cleaning, shrinking and thickening cloth.

36. *sich verkühlen*, South German and Austrian for *sich erkälten*.

37. *hatte . . .*, had been able to finish with the girl (lit.: come into the clear).

38. *Kreuze*, i.e., by making the sign of the Cross over them.

39. *was . . .*, how mother was.

40. *etwa . . .*, should a wind come toward evening.

41. *dem Heiligen Grabe*, the Holy Sepulchre, the grave in which Jesus was buried. The children had seen a painting of it at church.

42. *wissen wirst*: the future tense to express high probability.
43. *staken* = *steckten*.
44. *weitere*, fairly distant (absolute comparative).
45. *erst recht*, literally: more than ever.
46. *erst*, especially.
47. *mehrere*, several; here: *more*.
48. *mußt* colloquial for: *darfst*.
49. *ist*, South German and Austrian usage.
50. *zog*, i.e., needed.
51. *Fest*, Holy Mass.
52. *um so weniger*, literally: so much the less.
53. *zu erkennen*, perceptibly.
54. *größerer*, fairly great (absolute comparative).
55. *alle Male* = *immer*.
56. *waren gleich nicht*, though these were not.
57. *so*, however.
58. *war es*, it seemed.
59. *das* . . . , What a Christmas this is!
60. *Wandlung*, the change of the wine and wafer into the blood and flesh of Christ. This is the central mystery of the Mass and is known as *transubstantiation*.
61. *Wandlungsglöcklein*. The celebrating priest rings a handbell to indicate the moment at which the change occurs.
62. *auf alle Fälle*, to meet all contingencies.
63. *tat*, put.

Gottfried Keller

1819–90

Keller was born in Zurich, Switzerland, the son of a talented artisan of strong character. He lost his father at the age of five and was brought up by a stern but loving mother who raised her two children on very slender means. She enrolled the boy in a vocational school, from which he was expelled in his first year for leading a revolt by the pupils against a highly unpopular teacher, a charge which he stoutly denied. This brought an abrupt end to his education. He decided to become a painter, took lessons, and then went to the art academy in Munich, Germany, where he spent two futile years painting landscapes he could not sell. He received encouragement and slender financial support from his mother, but he lived in dire poverty, incurred heavy debts, and was finally driven to paint flagpoles. He therefore sold his pictures to a cheap dealer for a pittance and returned home.

During the turbulent forties Keller was caught up in the liberal movement, which brought German refugees like Herwegh, Freiligrath, and others to Zurich, where two mild uprisings occurred against the confederacy by a separatist Catholic

movement. Keller fought in both on the side of the government. He also wrote political poems in a liberal vein; a friend had his verse published in 1846 under the title *Poems* (*Gedichte*). The volume was well received and called attention to him as a promising writer.

Some prominent people persuaded the city administration to grant Keller a stipend to continue his education. In 1848 he went to Heidelberg, where he came under the decisive influence of Ludwig Feuerbach,[1] the radical philosopher of religion, and where he formed a lasting friendship with Hermann Hettner, who later became a prominent historian of literature. Feuerbach confirmed Keller's own pantheistic feelings and turned him into an idealistic materialist. He taught Keller to see religion and God as anthropomorphic creations invented by man out of a need to counteract his sense of helplessness and forlornness. Keller rejected Christian spirituality because it was a sublimation for man's fear of the senses. Such props he deemed unworthy of a thinking man. He denied all transcendence and put his faith in life on this earth; he espoused what the Germans call *Diesseitigkeit* (hitherworldliness).

> Hier fühl ich Zusammenhang
> Mit dem All und Einen
>
> [Here I feel a cohesion
> with the All and One.[2]]

he wrote in his poem "Among Stars" ("Unter Sternen").

Such a view of life Keller did not regard as an impoverishment but as an enhancement of life, which is not made more prosaic and commonplace by eschewing transcendence; on the con-

[1]Ludwig Feuerbach (1804–72) was a radical philosopher whose first publication was suppressed by the censor, as a result of which he was prevented from teaching at a German university. He lived as a free-lance writer and lectured in the city hall of Heidelberg, where Keller heard him and came under his profound influence.

[2]One and All, derived from the Greek formula *hen kai pan*, the core of a pantheist religion, according to which the whole universe is in God and God is dispersed in all creation.

trary, existence becomes clearer, sterner, more glowing and sensuous. Keller's humanism, directed from within rather than from above, matured in him an optimism that was not escapist and that is formulated in such poems as "A Springtime Faith" ("Frühlingsglaube") and "Evening Song" ("Abendlied") with its famous closing couplet:

> Trinkt, o Augen, was die Wimper hält,
> Von dem goldnen Überfluß der Welt.
>
> [Drink, o eyes, what the eyelash can hold
> Of the golden abundance of the world.]

In 1850 Keller went to Berlin on a second municipal stipend and spent five years there, planning literary works that were to come to fruition in the next two decades and writing the first version of his master work, the *Bildungsroman*[3] *Green Henry* (*Der grüne Heinrich*). Before leaving Berlin he had published two more volumes of verse, the novel *Green Henry* (1854), and had a book of short stories ready; the latter appeared in 1856 under the title of *The People of Seldwyla* (*Die Leute von Seldwyla*), which included the superb tragic novella *Romeo und Julia auf dem Dorfe*, a work that Edith Wharton translated into English as *A Village Romeo and Juliet*.

In 1861 Keller was appointed first secretary of the City of Zurich. He served loyally and efficiently for sixteen years, during which he published little. But he did bring out two important works during this period: *Seven Legends (Sieben Legenden)* (1872) and a second volume of novellas dealing with the people of Seldwyla (1874), and containing the delightful comic story *Clothes Make the Man (Kleider machen Leute)*. After his retirement in 1876 he kept on producing; his late work includes two more cycles of novellas and a social novel *Martin Salander* (1886).

His last years were serene and free from the suffering of his youth. He received many honors; when he died, the whole Swiss nation mourned him. He had never married, although he had fallen in love several times. He was too timid to press his suit.

[3]See note 3 of Stifter biography.

The description of Keller's Weltanschauung given above may suggest a solemn ideologue, a rather forbidding moralist and earnest do-gooder. It is true that Keller was a somewhat gruff person at times; but he was no owlish fanatic. On the contrary, he was a convivial man, with a delightful sense of humor, which comes out in his writing, with a strong satirical bent. His work is less burdened by heavy speculation than that of most German writers. When I read *Der grüne Heinrich* as an undergraduate, my professor, the great scholar Barker Fairley, asked me what I thought of it. I replied that I was disappointed in it. He wanted to know why. I told him that Keller didn't seem to have any philosophy of life. Professor Fairley replied: "Keller does have a philosophy. The trouble is that your philosophy is up here" (and he tapped his head), "Keller's is down there" (he patted his abdomen). That is a perfect description of Keller's Weltanschauung. His work deals with the daily commerce between people, with the dreams and foibles, the ambitions and follies of middle class folk and peasants. It presents a wide spectrum of moods from the tragic *Romeo und Julia auf dem Dorfe* to the near farcical *Kleider machen Leute,* and the grotesque *Die drei gerechten Kammacher.* His style is light and graceful, like Goethe's, free from brilliance and artifice.

●

The Little Dance Legend (Das Tanzlegendchen) is one of the *Sieben Legenden* that Keller published in 1872. The origin of the work goes back to his Berlin years, when he read Kosegarten's *Legenden* (1804), a devout, rather naive cycle of tales designed to glorify the medieval ideal of asceticism. By making slight changes in detail and shifts in motivation, Keller transformed these pious legends into a panegyric to earthly life and love. In them the Virgin Mary herself appears in the role of protectress of love and marriage and the enjoyment of a natural earthbound existence.

In this legend, as Keller has transformed it from what he found in Kosegarten, the conflict between the pagan and Christian views of life is succinctly presented with delicate irony. The artistic Musa must renounce all earthly pleasures, including the arts, on the promise that she will partake of heavenly pleasures in the afterlife, compared to which, King David the poet assures her, earthly dancing is as nothing. But when she gets to Heaven

she finds that Christian asceticism is the order of this realm too. True, the pagan Greek Muses have been invited to perform on this special holiday/holy day, but they are segregated at a separate table and shunned by the permanent residents, except for the attention paid to them by King David, Martha the sister of Lazarus, and the Virgin Mary herself, who befriend them and promise to secure a permanent visa for them. But Musa, the ascetic saint, is seated at the pagan table with the alien visitors from Hell. When they are invited to perform, the Greek Muses, out of gratitude for the invitation, try to bring an ascetic, Christian element into their song. Before their next visit to Heaven they rehearse a Christian melody in the underworld. And when they perform it, they out-herod Herod: the ascetic, spiritual gloom purveyed by their art is so potent that the Christian denizens of Paradise think themselves back on earth—but not as ascetic Christians, rather as nature and art loving pagans. Such is the power of pagan art. But this threat can obviously not be tolerated; so the Trinity itself steps in and forbids the subversive pagans from ever entering the gates of Heaven again.

Thus Keller, the disciple of Feuerbach joins the ranks of that coterie of German thinkers and artists (including Winckelmann, Goethe, Schiller, Hölderlin, Heine, Nietzsche, George, and Hauptmann) who have championed a pagan neo-Hellenism as a way of life for modern man. The *Tanzlegendchen* is a classic formulation of this Hellenic philosophy.

Das Tanzlegendchen

„Du Jungfrau Israel, du sollst noch
fröhlich pauken, und herausgehen an den
Tanz.—Alsdann werden die Jungfrauen
fröhlich am Reigen sein, dazu die junge
Mannschaft, und die Alten miteinander."
—Jeremia 31, 4, 13

Nach der Aufzeichnung des heiligen Gregorius[1] war Musa die
Tänzerin unter den Heiligen. Guter Leute Kind, war sie ein
anmutvolles Jungfräulein, welches der Mutter Gottes fleißig
diente, nur von *einer* Leidenschaft bewegt, nämlich von einer
unbezwinglichen Tanzlust, dermaßen, daß, wenn das Kind
nicht betete, es unfehlbar tanzte. Und zwar auf jegliche[2] Weise.
Musa tanzte mit ihren Gespielinnen, mit Kindern, mit den
Jünglingen und auch allein; sie tanzte in ihrem Kämmerchen,
im Saale, in den Gärten und auf den Wiesen, und selbst wenn
sie zum Altare ging, so war es mehr ein liebliches Tanzen als
ein Gehen, und auf den glatten Marmorplatten vor der Kir-
chentüre versäumte sie nie, schnell ein Tänzchen zu probieren.

Ja, eines Tages, als sie sich allein in der Kirche befand, konnte
sie sich nicht enthalten, vor dem Altar einige Figuren auszu-
führen und gewissermaßen der Jungfrau Maria ein niedliches
Gebet vorzutanzen. Sie vergaß sich dabei so sehr, daß sie bloß
zu träumen wähnte, als sie sah, wie ein ältlicher, aber schöner
Herr ihr entgegentanzte und ihre Figuren so gewandt ergänzte,
daß beide zusammen den kunstgerechtesten Tanz begingen.
Der Herr trug ein purpurnes Königskleid, eine goldene Krone
auf dem Kopf und einen glänzend schwarzen, gelockten Bart,
welcher vom Silberreif der Jahre wie von einem fernen Ster-
nenschein überhaucht war. Dazu ertönte eine Musik vom Chore
her, weil ein halbes Dutzend kleiner Engel auf der Brüstung
desselben stand oder saß, die dicken runden Beinchen darüber
hinunterhängen ließ und die verschiedenen Instrumente hand-

The Little Dance Legend

*"O virgin of Israel, thou shalt again be
adorned with thy tabrets, and shalt go
forth in the dances of them that make
merry.—Then shall the virgin rejoice
in the dance, both young men and old together."*   *—Jeremiah 31:4, 13*

According to a notation made by Saint Gregory, Musa was the
dancer among the saints. The child of good people, she was a
virgin full of grace serving the Mother of God diligently, swayed
by a single passion, namely, by an irresistible desire to dance;
so much so that when the child was not praying she unfailingly
danced. And indeed in every possible manner. Musa danced
with her playmates, with children, with youths, and even by
herself; she danced in her little room, in the large parlor, in
gardens, and on meadows; and even when she went to the altar,
it was more a graceful dancing than a walk, and on the smooth
marble blocks in front of the church door she never failed to
try a swift little dance.

Yes, one day, when she found herself alone in the church,
she could not restrain herself from executing several figures
in front of the altar and, so to speak, dancing a pretty prayer
to the Virgin Mary. In doing this she forgot herself so completely that she thought she was dreaming when she saw an
elderly but handsome gentleman dancing toward her and
complementing her figures so dexterously that the two of them
carried through the most artistic dance. The gentleman wore
a royal cloak of purple, a golden crown on his head, and a
shining black curly beard, touched by the silver rime of the
years as by the light of a distant star. They were accompanied
by music from the choir, because half a dozen little angels
were standing or sitting on the railing, letting their chubby
round little legs dangle and fingering or blowing on the various

[257]

habte oder blies. Dabei waren die Knirpse ganz gemütlich und praktisch und ließen sich die Notenhefte von ebensoviel steinernen Engelsbildern halten, welche sich als Zierat auf dem Chorgeländer fanden; nur der Kleinste, ein pausbäckiger Pfeifenbläser, machte eine Ausnahme, indem er die Beine übereinanderschlug und das Notenblatt mit den rosigen Zehen zu halten wußte. Auch war der am eifrigsten: die übrigen baumelten mit den Füßen, dehnten, bald dieser, bald jener, knisternd die Schwungfedern aus, daß die Farben derselben schimmerten wie Taubenhälse, und neckten einander während des Spieles.

Über alles dies sich zu wundern, fand Musa nicht Zeit, bis der Tanz beendigt war, der ziemlich lang dauerte; denn der lustige Herr schien sich dabei so wohl zu gefallen als die Jungfrau, welche im Himmel herumzuspringen meinte. Allein als die Musik aufhörte und Musa hochaufatmend dastand, fing sie erst an, sich ordentlich zu fürchten, und sah erstaunt auf den Alten, der weder keuchte noch warm hatte[3] und nun zu reden begann. Er gab sich als David, den königlichen Ahnherrn der Jungfrau Maria, zu erkennen[4] und als deren Abgesandten. Und er fragte sie, ob sie wohl Lust hätte, die ewige Seligkeit in einem unaufhörlichen Freudentanze zu verbringen, einem Tanze, gegen welchen der soeben beendigte ein trübseliges Schleichen zu nennen sei?

Worauf sie sogleich erwiderte, sie wüßte sich nichts Besseres zu wünschen! Worauf der selige König David wiederum sagte: So habe sie nichts anderes zu tun, als während ihrer irdischen Lebenstage aller Lust und allem Tanze zu entsagen und sich lediglich der Buße und den geistlichen[5] Übungen zu weihen, und zwar ohne Wanken und ohne allen Rückfall.

Diese Bedingung machte das Jungfräulein stutzig, und sie sagte: Also gänzlich müßte sie auf das Tanzen verzichten? Und sie zweifelte, ob denn auch im Himmel wirklich getanzt würde? Denn alles habe seine Zeit; dieser Erdboden schiene ihr gut und zweckdienlich, um darauf zu tanzen, folglich würde der Himmel wohl andere Eigenschaften haben, ansonst[6] ja der Tod ein überflüssiges Ding wäre.

Allein David setzte ihr auseinander, wie sehr sie in dieser Beziehung im Irrtum sei, und bewies ihr durch viele Bibelstel-

instruments. And the little urchins were quite nonchalant and practical about it all, using the stone angel figures that decorated the railing of the choirloft as supports for their sheet music. Only the smallest of them, a chubby-cheeked flutist, made an exception, crossing his legs and holding the sheet music between his pink toes. He was, moreover, the most zealous one among them; the rest let their feet dangle, and now one, now another stretched his wings with a crakling sound, so that their colors gleamed like the necks of doves, and they teased one another as they played.

Musa did not find time to wonder at all this until the dance was finished, and it lasted a fairly long time; for the merry gentleman seemed to be as pleased with it as the maiden, who thought she was hopping about in Heaven. But when the music stopped and Musa stood there breathing heavily, she really began to be afraid and looked in astonishment at the old gentleman, who was neither panting nor feeling warm and now began to talk. He identified himself as David, the royal ancestor of the Virgin Mary, and as her ambassador. And he asked her whether she wished to spend eternal bliss in an unceasing dance of joy, a dance compared with which the one they had just finished could only be called a sad crawl.

To which she replied promptly that she could wish nothing better. Whereupon the blessed King David said: then she need do nothing but renounce all pleasures and all dancing during her life on earth and consecrate herself solely to atonement and to spiritual exercises, and indeed without hesitation or backsliding.

This condition disconcerted the maiden and she said: so she must give up dancing wholly? And she expressed doubt whether there really was dancing in Heaven. For there was a time for everything; this earth seemed to her good and purposeful to dance on, so Heaven would probably have other properties, otherwise death would be a superfluous thing.

But David explained to her how very wrong she was in this regard, and proved to her by quoting many biblical passages

len sowie durch sein eigenes Beispiel, daß das Tanzen allerdings eine geheiligte Beschäftigung für Selige sei. Jetzt aber erfordere es einen raschen Entschluß, ja oder nein, ob sie durch zeitliche Entsagung zur ewigen Freude eingehen wolle oder nicht; wolle sie nicht, so gehe er weiter; denn man habe im Himmel noch einige Tänzerinnen vonnöten.

Musa stand noch immer zweifelhaft und unschlüssig und spielte ängstlich mit den Fingerspitzen am Munde; es schien ihr zu hart, von Stund an nicht mehr zu tanzen um eines unbekannten Lohnes willen.

Da winkte David, und plötzlich spielte die Musik einige Takte einer so unerhört glückseligen, überirdischen Tanzweise, daß dem Mädchen die Seele im Leibe hüpfte und alle Glieder zuckten; aber sie vermochte nicht eines[7] zum Tanze zu regen, und sie merkte, daß ihr Leib viel zu schwer und starr sei für diese Weise. Voll Sehnsucht schlug sie ihre Hand in diejenige des Königs und gelobte das, was er begehrte.

Auf einmal war er nicht mehr zu sehen, und die musizierenden Engel rauschten, flatterten und drängten sich durch ein offenes Kirchenfenster davon, nachdem sie in mutwilliger Kinderweise ihre zusammengerollten Notenblätter den geduldigen Steinengeln um die Backen geschlagen hatten, daß es klatschte.

Aber Musa ging andächtigen Schrittes nach Hause, jene himmlische Melodie im Ohr tragend, und ließ sich ein grobes Gewand anfertigen, legte alle Zierkleidung ab und zog jenes an. Zugleich baute sie sich im Hintergrunde des Gartens ihrer Eltern, wo ein dichter Schatten von Bäumen lagerte, eine Zelle, machte ein Bettchen von Moos darin und lebte dort von nun an abgeschieden von ihren Hausgenossen als eine Büßerin und Heilige. Alle Zeit brachte sie im Gebete zu, und öfter schlug sie sich mit einer Geißel; aber ihre härteste Bußübung bestand darin, die Glieder still und steif zu halten; sobald nur ein Ton erklang, das Zwitschern eines Vogels oder das Rauschen der Blätter in der Luft, so zuckten ihre Füße und meinten, sie müßten tanzen.

Als dies unwillkürliche Zucken sich nicht verlieren wollte, welches sie zuweilen, ehe sie sich dessen versah, zu einem kleinen Sprung verleitete, ließ sie sich die feinen Füßchen mit

as well as through his own example that dancing was indeed a consecrated occupation for the blessed. But now a swift decision must be made: yes or no, whether she was willing to enter eternal joy through temporal renunciation or not; if she didn't, he would go on; for several girl dancers were still needed in Heaven.

Musa was still standing in doubt and indecision, with the tips of her fingers playing nervously about her mouth; it seemed too hard to her to stop dancing henceforth for the sake of an unknown reward.

Then David made a sign and suddenly the music played a few bars of a dance tune, so ineffably blissful and ethereal that the girl's soul leaped in her body and all her limbs twitched; but she was unable to move any of them to dance, and she noted that her body was far too heavy and rigid for this tune. Filled with longing she put her hand into that of King David and vowed what he desired of her.

Suddenly he was no more to be seen and the music-making angels rustled, fluttered, and thronged out of sight through an open church window, after they had, in the mischievous way of children, slapped the patient stone angels about the cheeks with their rolled-up sheet music, thus producing a resounding noise.

But Musa went home with reverent step, hearing that heavenly melody in her ear, and had a coarse gown made for herself, laid aside all her pretty clothing, and put on that gown. At the same time she built herself a cell at the back of her parents' garden where a deep shadow was made by the trees; she made a little bed of moss in it and from now on she lived there as a penitent and saint, separated from her housemates. She spent all her time in prayer, and often she scourged herself with a whip; but her hardest act of penitence consisted in holding her limbs still and stiff; as soon as ever a note sounded, the twittering of a bird or the rustling of the leaves in the air, her feet twitched and felt they must dance.

When this involuntary twitching refused to disappear, seducing her at times, before she realized it, into a slight leap, she had her delicate little feet tied together with a light chain. Her

einer leichten Kette zusammenschmieden. Ihre Verwandten
und Freunde wunderten sich über die Umwandlung Tag und
Nacht, freuten sich über den Besitz einer solchen Heiligen und
hüteten die Einsiedelei unter den Bäumen wie einen Augapfel.
Viele kamen, Rat und Fürbitte zu holen. Vorzüglich brachte
man junge Mädchen zu ihr, welche etwas unbeholfen auf den
Füßen waren, da man bemerkt hatte, daß alle, welche sie be-
rührt, alsobald leichten und anmutvollen Ganges wurden.

So brachte sie drei Jahre in ihrer Klause zu; aber gegen das
Ende des dritten Jahres war Musa fast so dünn und durch-
sichtig wie ein Sommerwölklein geworden. Sie lag beständig
auf ihrem Bettchen von Moos und schaute voll Sehnsucht in
den Himmel, und sie glaubte schon die goldenen Sohlen der
Seligen durch das Blau hindurch tanzen und schleifen zu sehen.

An einem rauhen Herbsttage endlich hieß es,[8] die Heilige
liege im Sterben. Sie hatte sich das dunkle Bußkleid auszuziehen
und mit blendend weißen Hochzeitsgewändern bekleiden lassen. So lag sie mit gefalteten Händen und erwartete lächelnd
die Todesstunde. Der ganze Garten war mit andächtigen
Menschen angefüllt, die Lüfte rauschten, und die Blätter der
Bäume sanken von allen Seiten hernieder. Aber unversehens
wandelte sich das Wehen des Windes in Musik, in allen Baum-
kronen schien dieselbe zu spielen, und als die Leute emporsa-
hen, siehe, da waren alle Zweige mit jungem Grün bekleidet,
die Myrten und Granaten blühten und dufteten, der Boden
bedeckte sich mit Blumen, und ein rosenfarbiger Schein lagerte
sich auf die weiße zarte Gestalt der Sterbenden.

In diesem Augenblicke gab sie ihren Geist auf, die Kette an
ihren Füßen sprang mit einem hellen Klange entzwei, der Himmel tat sich auf weit in der Runde, voll unendlichen Glanzes,
und jedermann konnte hineinsehen. Da sah man viel tausend
schöne Jungfern und junge Herren im höchsten Schein, tanzend im unabsehbaren Reigen. Ein herrlicher König fuhr auf
einer Wolke, auf deren Rand eine kleine Extramusik von sechs
Engelchen stand, ein wenig gegen die Erde und empfing die
Gestalt der seligen Musa vor den Augen aller Anwesenden, die
den Garten füllten. Man sah noch, wie sie in den offenen Himmel sprang und augenblicklich tanzend sich in den tönenden
und leuchtenden Reihen verlor.

relatives and friends were astonished day and night at this transformation, rejoiced in the possession of such a saint, and kept guard over the hermitage under the trees as over the apple of their eye. Many came to obtain counsel and intercession. Young girls especially were brought to her, girls who were somewhat clumsy on their feet, since it had been noticed that all whom she touched at once became light and graceful in their walk.

In this way she spent three years in her cell; but toward the end of the third year Musa had become almost as thin and transparent as a little summer cloud. She lay constantly on her little bed of moss and, full of longing, looked into the sky; and she already thought she saw the golden soles of the blessed spirits dance and glide through the blue.

On a raw autumn day the news finally came that the saint lay dying. She had had her dark penitential gown taken off and dazzling white wedding clothes put on her. Thus she lay with folded hands awaiting the hour of her death with a smile. The whole garden was filled with devout people, there was a rustle in the air, and the leaves fell from the trees in all directions. But suddenly the blowing of the wind turned into music, which seemed to be playing in all the treetops; and when the people looked up, behold—all the branches were clothed in young green, the myrtle and the promegranates bloomed and gave off a fragrance, the ground was covered with flowers, and a pink halo settled on the white, delicate form of the dying woman.

At this moment she gave up the ghost, the chain at her feet burst in two with a shrill sound, the sky opened for a wide area, full of infinite radiance, and everyone was able to look into it. There one saw many thousands of beautiful virgins and young gentlemen in the brightest splendor, dancing a round-dance as far as eye could reach. On a cloud, at the rim of which a special orchestra of six little angels stood, a glorious king rode a short distance toward earth and received the form of the blessed Musa before the eyes of all who filled the garden. She was even seen leaping into the open sky and was lost as she danced in the singing and resplendent ranks.

Im Himmel war eben hoher Festtag; an Festtagen aber war es, was zwar vom heiligen Gregor von Nyssa bestritten, von demjenigen von Nazianz aber aufrechtgehalten wird, Sitte, die neun Musen, die sonst in der Hölle saßen, einzuladen und in den Himmel zu lassen, daß sie da Aushilfe leisteten. Sie bekamen gute Zehrung, mußten aber nach verrichteter Sache[9] wieder an den andern Ort gehen.

Als nun die Tänze und Gesänge und alle Zeremonien zu Ende und die himmlischen Heerscharen sich zu Tische setzten, da wurde Musa an den Tisch gebracht, an welchem die neun Musen bedient wurden. Sie saßen fast verschüchtert zusammengedrängt und blickten mit den feurigen schwarzen oder tiefblauen Augen um sich. Die emsige Martha[10] aus dem Evangelium sorgte in eigener Person für sie, hatte ihre schönste Küchenschürze umgebunden und einen zierlichen kleinen Rußfleck an dem weißen Kinn und nötigte den Musen alles Gute freundlich auf. Aber erst als Musa und auch die heilige Cäcilia[11] und noch andere kunsterfahrene Frauen herbeikamen und die scheuen Pierinnen[12] heiter begrüßten und sich zu ihnen gesellten, da tauten sie auf, wurden zutraulich, und es entfaltete sich ein anmutig fröhliches Dasein in dem Frauenkreise. Musa saß neben Terpsichore,[13] und Cäcilia zwischen Polyhymnien und Euterpen, und alle hielten sich bei den Händen. Nun kamen auch die kleinen Musikbübchen und schmeichelten den schönen Frauen, um von den glänzenden Früchten zu bekommen, die auf dem ambrosischen Tische strahlten. König David selbst kam und brachte einen goldenen Becher, aus dem alle tranken, daß holde Freude sie erwärmte; er ging wohlgefällig um den Tisch herum, nicht ohne der lieblichen Erato[14] einen Augenblick das Kinn zu streicheln im Vorbeigehen. Als es dergestalt hoch herging[15] an dem Musentisch, erschien sogar Unsere liebe Frau in all ihrer Schönheit und Güte, setzte sich auf ein Stündchen[16] zu den Musen und küßte die hehre Urania[17] unter ihrem Sternenkranze zärtlich auf den Mund, als sie ihr beim Abschiede zuflüsterte, sie werde nicht ruhen, bis die Musen für immer im Paradiese bleiben könnten.[18]

Es ist freilich nicht so gekommen. Um sich für die erwiesene Güte und Freundlichkeit dankbar zu erweisen und ihren guten Willen zu zeigen, ratschlagten die Musen untereinander und

It happened to be a high holiday in Heaven; and on holidays it was the custom—this is disputed by Saint Gregory of Nyssa but maintained by Saint Gregory of Nazianzus—to invite the nine Muses, who ordinarily lived in Hell, and admit them to Heaven to give temporary assistance. They got good food to eat but after they had done their stint had to go back to the other place.

Now when the dances and songs and all the ceremonies were over and the Heavenly Host sat down to dinner, Musa was brought to the table at which the nine Muses were being served. They sat squeezed together almost timidly, looking about with their fiery black or deep blue eyes. The eager Martha from the Gospel cared for them personally; she had put on her finest kitchen apron and showed a cute little soot spot on her white chin, and she amiably pressed all the delicacies on the Muses. But it was only when Musa and Saint Cecilia and other aesthetically experienced women came over and gaily greeted the shy Pierians and joined their company that they thawed out, became confidential, and a charming, cheerful social hour developed among the ladies. Musa sat beside Terpsichore, Cecilia between Polyhymnia and Euterpe, and they all held hands. And now the little music boys came too and flattered the beautiful ladies in order to get some of the shining fruit that lay in radiance on the ambrosial tables. King David himself came and brought a golden cup out of which they all drank, so that they were warmed with lovely joy. He walked around the table with satisfaction and did not fail to stroke the lovely Erato's chin for a moment as he passed. When things were at their height at the Muses' table even Our Dear Lady, in all Her Beauty and Goodness, appeared and sat down beside the Muses for a short while and tenderly kissed the sublime Urania on the lips beneath her crown of stars, whispering to her as she went that she would not rest until the Muses could remain in Paradise forever.

To be sure it did not turn out so. In order to show their gratitude for the kindness and friendliness that had been shown them and to demonstrate their good will the Muses held counsel

übten in einem abgelegenen Winkel der Unterwelt einen Lob-
gesang ein, dem sie die Form der im Himmel üblichen feierlichen Choräle zu geben suchten. Sie teilten sich in zwei Hälften
von je vier Stimmen, über welche Urania eine Art Oberstimme
führte, und brachten so eine merkwürdige Vokalmusik zuwege.
Als nun der nächste Festtag im Himmel gefeiert wurde und
die Musen wieder ihren Dienst taten, nahmen sie einen für ihr
Vorhaben günstig scheinenden Augenblick wahr, stellten sich
zusammen auf und begannen sänftlich ihren Gesang, der bald
gar mächtig anschwellte. Aber in diesen Räumen klang er so
düster, ja fast trotzig und rauh, und dabei so sehnsuchtsschwer
und klagend, daß erst eine erschrockene Stille waltete, dann
aber alles Volk von Erdenleid und Heimweh ergriffen wurde
und in ein allgemeines Weinen ausbrach.

Ein unendliches Seufzen rauschte durch die Himmel, bes-
türzt eilten alle Ältesten und Propheten herbei, indessen die
Musen in ihrer guten Meinung immer lauter und melancho-
lischer sangen und das ganze Paradies mit allen Erzvätern,
Ältesten und Propheten, alles, was je auf grüner Wiese gegangen oder gelegen, außer Fassung geriet.[19] Endlich aber kam
die allhöchste Trinität selber heran, um zum Rechten zu sehen
und die eifrigen Musen mit einem lang hinrollenden Don-
nerschlage zum Schweigen zu bringen.

Da kehrten Ruhe und Gleichmut in den Himmel zurück; aber
die armen neun Schwestern mußten ihn verlassen und durften
ihn seither nicht wieder betreten.

Notes: Keller, *Das Tanzlegendchen*

1. Later in the story Keller mentions two Gregories: St. Gregory
of Nazianzus (c.329–c.390), the rhetorician, and St. Gregory, Bishop
of Nyssa (c.331–c.396), the theologian and neoplatonic thinker. Both
were eminent fathers of the Eastern Church. Both are mentioned
on p. 264, ll. 2–3.
2. *jegliche = jede.*

among themselves and rehearsed, in a remote corner of the underworld, a hymn of praise to which they sought to give the form of those solemn chorales which were usual in Heaven. They divided into two groups of four voices each, with Urania acting as a kind of Overvoice, and thus produced a strange vocal music.

Now when the next holiday was celebrated in Heaven and the Muses once more performed their service, they seized a moment that seemed propitious for their plan, stood together, and softly began their song, which soon swelled to mighty volume. But in these halls it sounded so gloomy, indeed almost defiant and coarse, and at the same time so plaintive and heavy with longing, that at first a frightened silence prevailed; but then all the people were seized by an earthly sorrow and nostalgia and broke into a general weeping.

An infinite sighing rustled through the Heavens; in dismay the elders and the prophets hurried over, while the Muses, with the best of intentions, sang louder and with more melancholy all the time; and the whole of Paradise, with all the patriarchs, elders, and prophets, everyone who had ever walked or lain on a green meadow, lost control of themselves. But finally the All-highest Trinity Itself appeared to set things right and bring the eager Muses to silence with a long rolling thunderclap.

Then peace and equanimity returned to Heaven; but the poor nine sisters had to leave it and were not permitted to enter it since.

3. [es] warm hatte, felt warm.
4. gab sich zu erkennen, identified himself.
5. geistlich, properly: ecclesiastical; here: spiritual.
6. ansonst = sonst.
7. eines refers to Glied.
8. es hieß, it was said.

9. *nach . . . Sache,* when their job was finished.

10. Martha the sister of Lazarus and Mary of Bethany, in whose house Jesus was a frequent visitor. Martha served him and is therefore the patron of housewives (Luke 10:38 ff.).

11. St. Cecilia (†A.D. 230), Roman martyr, patron saint of music.

12. *Pierians,* the inhabitants of Pieria in Thessaly, the home of the Muses.

13. *Terpsichore,* the Muse of dancing; *Polyhymnia,* of sacred song; *Euterpe,* of flute playing.

14. *Erato,* Muse of the lyre; an allusion to the tradition that King David is the author of the Book of Psalms.

15. *es hoch herging,* things were going merrily.

16. *Stündchen,* (little hour) a short while.

17. *Urania,* Muse of astronomy.

18. The story originally ended here. The additional few paragraphs that follow lend it depth and subtlety.

19. *geriet außer Fassung,* lost control of himself.

Theodor Fontane

1819–98

Fontane was of Huguenot ancestry. His French parents settled in Prussia, where his father practiced as a pharmacist. After receiving a rather sketchy education at home, described with charm and humor in an autobiographical work, *My Childhood Years* (*Meine Kinderjahre*, 1894), young Fontane was apprenticed to a pharmacist and practiced this profession till age twenty-nine. He did a year of military service, worked as a free-lance journalist and civil servant, living in Berlin, Dresden, and Leipzig among other places.

Fontane first became known in literary circles as the author of two volumes of poetry (both published in 1850). In the fifties he lived in England, serving as a press agent to the German ambassador in London but also acting as foreign correspondent for German newspapers of diverse political persuasions. He traveled much in Britain and France and in his native Brandenburg-Prussia and wrote volumes of travel that describe the geography, history, and manners of the countries he visited. He participated as a war correspondent in the war between Prussia and Austria of 1866 and the Franco-German war of

1870–71. In the latter conflict he was taken prisoner by the French. His accounts of his experiences in these actions have historic importance.

After 1870 Fontane served as drama critic for the liberal Berlin newspaper *Vossische Zeitung*, in which he wrote favorably about the realist and naturalist literary drama and fiction. He was sixty years old when he began to publish fiction: a series of historical novels, followed by the social novels on which his fame in literature rests. Of the latter the best known is *Effi Briest* (1895), which was made into a fine film.

These novels about Prussian society show Germany in transition from the old order to a new one, in which much that was good had to give way before new social institutions that revealed questionable, even meretricious aspects. Fontane admired the best in both worlds; he felt a deep admiration for Emperor Wilhelm I but was ambivalent about Bismarck; and he welcomed some of the new social forms—with reservations. He was severely critical of the Prussian junkers as effete and decadent; yet he recognized and admired the Prussian virtues some of them possessed. In his Berlin novels he left a monument to the social forces that were churning in the new Germany. Although his personal sympathies were with the progressive left and he moved ever further in this direction, he was able to produce political and social articles that were acceptable to ultraconservative newspapers. He developed a formula to cover his position: he called it *heiteres Darüberstehen* (standing serenely above it all).

Fontane's outstanding literary quality is his gift for making people talk naturally. He has been called the most accomplished writer of dialogue among all German novelists. He described himself as a *causeur*; the reader feels that he is sitting opposite an elderly gentleman, listening to "mellow wisdom" (so wrote Thomas Mann, who was a great admirer of Fontane) about the interaction between human beings at all levels of sophistication. He shows a deep insight into character, again at all social levels; for he is a profound observer of the human comedy. His social criticism is gentle; even when it is severe, it never loses its urbanity. He is a master of irony, free from judgment, and of

course free from passion. In reading him one feels that sense of inevitability that one gets from the great masters.

•

The short story (or sketch) that represents Fontane in this collection, *Eine Frau in meinen Jahren* (*A Woman in My Years*), is a *causerie* in a cemetery between two old people who believe that their lives are over. This resignation is expressed in the two leitmotifs that run through the conversation between them: "a woman in my years" and "I have closed up shop." But as the sexton of the cemetery (one of those wise men of the people who reappear in Fontane's fiction) points out to them: only death can make one close up shop. And they are far from being dead. So they begin life over again. This trite theme, one of the most hackneyed in literature, is presented with Fontane's usual charm and irony, so that it becomes a literary experience. The reader with a sensitive ear for style will notice a formal quality about the diction used by the couple in this story. This is not stiffness or stuffiness; it is Victorian diction characteristic of the middle and upper class in the Western world before the realists transformed the vocabulary of human conversation.

The story was written in the 1880s and first published in 1887 in a magazine. It was incorporated into the miscellany *About, Before and After the Journey* (*Von, vor und nach der Reise*, 1894). Fontane called it a novelette. The historical event that serves as its background occurred during the Seven Weeks' War between Prussia and Austria in 1866, about which Fontane published a memoir: *Der deutsche Krieg von 1866.* On July 10, 1866, a Prussian brigade under the command of General Goeben attacked the health spa Bad Kissingen in southern Bavaria, which was allied with Austria against Prussia. The Prussians were victorious in the battle. The description of the fighting in the cemetery and the anecdote about Ruth Brown's grave are historical.

Eine Frau in meinen Jahren

»Erlauben Sie mir, meine gnädigste Frau,[1] Ihnen Ihren Becher zu präsentieren . . .«

Die Dame verneigte sich.

»Und Ihnen auf Ihrer Brunnenpromenade Gesellschaft zu leisten. Immer vorausgesetzt, daß ich keine Verlegenheiten schaffe.«

»Wie wäre das möglich, Herr Rat![2] Eine Frau in meinen Jahren . . .«

»Es gibt keine Jahre, die gegen die gute Meinung unserer Freunde sicherstellen. Am wenigsten hier in Kissingen.«

»Vielleicht bei den Männern.«

»Auch bei den Frauen. Und wie mir scheinen will, mit Recht. Ich erinnere mich eines kleinen anekdotischen Hergangs aus dem Leben der berühmten Schroeder[3] . . .«

»Der Mutter der Schroeder-Devrient?«

»Derselben.«

»Und was war es damit?«

»Eines Winters in Wien sprach sie von ihrem zurückliegenden Liebesleben und von dem unendlichen Glücksgefühl, all diese Torheit nun endlich überwunden und vor den Anfällen ihrer Leidenschaft Ruhe zu haben. Und einigermaßen indiskret gefragt, *wann* sie den letzten dieser Anfälle gehabt habe, seufzte sie: ›vor zwei Monaten.‹«

»Und wie alt war sie damals?«

»Dreiundsechzig.«

»Also mehr als nötig, um meine Mutter zu sein. Und doch bleib' ich bei meinem Ausspruch: ›eine Frau in meinen Jahren‹ . . . Aber wer war nur die stattliche Dame, der Sie sich gestern anschlossen, um Sie als *Cavaliere servente*[4] bis an den Finsterberg zu begleiten?«

A Woman in My Years

"Permit me, my dear lady, to present you with your cup . . . "

The lady bowed.
"And to accompany you on your promenade to the fountain, assuming that I cause you no embarrassment."

"How could you do that, Councillor? A woman in my years . . . "
"There are no years that protect us against the good opinion of our friends. Least of all here in Kissingen."
"Perhaps with men."
"With women too. And properly so, it seems to me. I remember a little anecdote from the life of the famous Frau Schröder . . . "
"The mother of Schröder-Devrient?"
"The same."
"And what was that?"
"One winter in Vienna she spoke of her past love life and of her boundless feeling of happiness at having finally overcome all this folly and being free from the attacks of her passion. And when someone asked her, rather indiscreetly, *when* she had had the last of these attacks, she sighed: "Two months ago."

"And how old was she at the time?"
"Sixty-three."
"Well, that's more than she needed to be my mother. And yet I'll stick to my words: 'a woman in my years' . . . But who was the imposing lady whom you attended yesterday as her *cavaliere servente* up to the Finsterberg?"

»Eine Freundin, Baronin Aßmannshausen, und seit vorgestern Großmutter, wie sie mir selbst mit Stolz erzählte.«

»Mit Stolz? Aber doch noch hübsch und lebhaft. Und dazu
der feurige[5] Name. Sehen Sie sich vor und gedenken Sie der
Schroeder.«

»Ach, meine Gnädigste, Sie belieben zu scherzen. Ich für
mein Teil, ich darf sagen, ich habe abgeschlossen.«

»Wer's Ihnen glaubt! Männer schließen nie ab und brauchen
es auch nicht und wollen es auch nicht. Soll ich Ihnen, bloß
aus meiner näheren Bekanntschaft, die Namen derer her-
zählen, die noch mit Siebzig in den glücklichsten Ehestand ein-
traten? Natürlich Kriegshelden, die den Zug eröffnen und
schließen . . . Aber hier ist schon der Brückensteg und die
Lindelsmühle. Wollen wir umkehren und denselben Weg, den
wir kamen, zurückmachen, oder gehen wir lieber um die Stadt
herum und besuchen den Kirchhof? Er ist so malerisch und
weckt der Erinnerungen so viele. Sonderbarerweise auch für
mich. Oder besuchen Sie nicht gerne Kirchhöfe?«

»Grabsteine lesen nimmt das Gedächtnis.«

»Dem ließe sich auf einfachste Weise vorbeugen: man liest
sie nicht. . . . Aber freilich, es gibt ihrer unter dem starken
Geschlecht so viele, die sich überhaupt nicht gerne daran erinnern lassen, daß alles einmal ein Ende nimmt, mit anderen
Worten, daß man stirbt.«

»Ich für meine Person zähle nicht zu diesen, mein Leben
liegt hinter mir, und ich darf Ihnen ruhig wiederholen: ich
habe abgeschlossen.«

Die Dame lächelte still vor sich hin und sagte: »Nun denn
also, zunächst um die Stadt und dann nach dem Kirchhof.«

Und dabei passierten sie den Lindelsmühlsteg und schlugen
einen Wiesen- und Feldweg ein. Über ihnen zog Gewölk im
Blauen, und beide freuten sich des frischen Luftzuges, der von
den Nüdlinger[6] Bergen her herüberwehte. Hart am Weg hin
blühte roter Mohn, und die Dame bückte sich danach und
begann die langen Stiele zusammenzuflechten. Als sie schon
eine Girlande davon in Händen hielt, sagte sie: »Der rote Mohn,
er ist so recht die Blume, die mir zukommt; bis Sechzehn blühen
einem die Veilchen, bis Zwanzig Rosen und um Dreißig herum
die Verbenen, an deren deutschem Namen[7] ich klüglich vor-

"A friend, Baroness Assmannshausen, and a grandmother as of the day before yesterday, as she herself told me with pride."

"With pride? Nevertheless, she is still attractive and vivacious. And then that fiery name. Watch out, and remember the Schröder case."

"Ah, my dearest lady, it is your pleasure to jest. I for my part dare to say I have closed up shop."

"Who would believe you? Men never close up shop, and they don't need to, and don't want to either. Shall I give you the names, drawn exclusively from my close acquaintances, of those who entered the state of most happy matrimony at seventy? War heroes of course, who open and close the offensive . . . But here we are already at the bridge path and the Lindel's mill. Shall we turn around and go back the same way we came, or shall we circle the city and visit the cemetery? It's so picturesque and awakens so many memories. For me too, strangely enough. Or don't you like to visit cemeteries?"

"Reading tombstones impairs one's memory."

"There's an easy way to prevent that: don't read them . . . But of course, there are so many members of the strong sex who don't like to be reminded that everything must come to an end some day, in other words, that we die."

"I personally am not one of these, my life lies behind me, and I may repeat serenely to you: I have closed up shop."

The lady silently smiled to herself and said: "Well then, first a walk around town and then to the cemetery."

On the way they passed the Lindel mill path and made for a meadow and field road. Above them clouds moved over the blue sky and they both enjoyed the cool breeze that blew from the Nüdling mountains. Close by the road the red poppies were in bloom and the lady bent down to them and began to twine the long stems together. When she held a garland of them in her hands, she said: "The red poppy is just the flower that suits me; till the age of sixteen the violets bloom for us, till twenty it's roses, around thirty verbenas, whose German name I wisely skip over. then it's all over, you pick only poppies, red ones

übergehe. Dann ist es vorbei, man pflückt nur noch Mohn,
heute roten und morgen vielleicht schon weißen Mohn, und
flicht sich Kränze daraus. Und so *soll* es auch sein. Denn Mohn
bedeutet Ruhe.«

●

So schritten sie weiter, bis der von ihnen eingeschlagene Feldweg wieder auf eine breite, dicht neben einem Parkgarten hin-
laufende Fahrstraße führte. Platanen und Ahorn streckten ihr
Gezweige weit über die Gitter hin, aus dem Parke selbst aber,
der einem großen Hotel zugehörte, rollten in ebendiesem
Augenblicke junge Sportsmen auf die fast tennenartige Chaus-
see hinaus, Radfahrer, Bicyclevirtuosen, die hoch oben[8] auf
ihrem Reitstuhl saßen und unter Gruß und Lachen vorüber-
sausten. Ihre kleinen Köpfe, dazu die hageren, im engsten
Trikot steckenden Figuren, ließen keinen Zweifel darüber, daß
es Fremde waren.

»Engländer?«

»Nein, Amerikaner«, sagte die Dame, »meine täglichen Vis-
avis[9] an der Table d'hote. Und sonderbar, mir lacht immer das
Herz, wenn ich sie sehe. Das frischere Leben ist doch da
drüben, und in nichts war ich mit meinem verstorbenen Manne,
der ein paar Jahre lang in New York und an den großen Seen
gelebt hatte, so einig wie in diesem Punkt, und wir schwärmten
oft um die Wette.[10] Die Wahrheit zu gestehen, ich begreife
nicht, daß nicht alles auswandert.«

»Und ich meinerseits teile diesen Enthusiasmus und habe
mich, eh' ich ins Amt trat, ernsthaft mit dem Plan einer Über-
siedelung beschäftigt. Aber das liegt nun zwanzig Jahre zurück
und ist ein für allemal begraben. Amerika, weil es selber jung
ist, ist für die Jugend. Und ich . . . «

» . . . habe abgeschlossen«, ergänzte sie lachend. »Freilich, je
mehr Sie mir's versichern, je weniger glaub' ich's. Sehen Sie,
dort ist der Finsterberg, nach dem Sie gestern Ihren langen
Spaziergang richteten und der Sie jetzt zu fragen scheint: ›Wo
haben Sie die Frau Baronin?‹ . . . Wie hieß sie doch?«

»Ich denke, wir lassen den Namen, und was den Finsterberg
angeht, er sieht mich *zu* gut aufgehoben,[11] um solche Fragen
zu tun.«[12]

●

today and tomorrow perhaps white ones, and make wreaths
out of them. And so it *should* be too. For poppy signifies peace."

●

So they went on, until the field road that they had chosen
led to a broad causeway that ran along beside a park. Plane
and maple trees thrust their branches far over the fences, but
from the park itself, which belonged to a large hotel, at that
very moment young sportsmen rolled out onto the causeway
that was almost as smooth as a threshing floor—cyclists, bicycle
virtuosi, who sat high up on their seats and whizzed by amidst
greetings and laughter. Their small heads, added to their lean
bodies wearing the tightest tricots, left no doubt that they were
foreigners.

"English?"

"No, Americans," the lady said, "my daily companions at the
table d'hôte. And strangely enough, my heart always rejoices
when I see them. After all, the livelier life is over there, and
there was nothing on which I and my late husband, who had
spent a couple of years in New York and had lived in the region
of the Great Lakes, agreed so thoroughly as on this point, and
we often raved about it, outdoing each other. To tell the truth,
I don't understand why we don't all emigrate."

"And I for my part share this enthusiasm, and before I entered the service I seriously considered a plan to emigrate. But
that's now twenty years in the past and has been buried for
good. America is for youth because it is young itself. And I . . . "

" . . . have closed up shop," she completed the sentence with
a laugh. "To be sure, the more you assure me of it, the less I
believe you. Look, there's the Fürstenberg, toward which you
directed your long walk yesterday and which now seems to be
asking you: 'Where is your baroness?' . . . What was her name,
by the way?"

"I think we'll skip the name, and as far as the Fürstenberg is
concerned, he sees me in *too* good hands to ask such questions."

●

Unter solchem Geplauder waren sie bis an ihr vorläufiges
Ziel gekommen und stiegen, an dem Bildstöckel[13] vorbei, die
Steintreppe zu dem Kirchhofe hinauf. In dem gleich links
gelegenen Mesnerhause standen alle Türen auf, und auf Dach
und Fensterbrett quirilierten die Spatzen.

»Ich übernehme nun die Führung«, sagte die Dame. »Grabsteine lesen, so bemerkten Sie, nimmt das Gedächtnis. Gut, es
soll wahr sein. Aber ganz kann ich es Ihnen nicht erlassen.
Sehen Sie hier . . . Kindergräber; eines neben dem andern.
Und nun lesen Sie.«

Der Begleiter der Dame säumte nicht zu gehorchen und las
mit halblauter Stimme: »Hier ruht das unschuldige Kind . . .«
Aber kaum, daß er bis zu diesem Wort gelesen hatte, so trat
er aus freien Stücken näher an den Grabhügel heran, um
neugierig den vom Regen halb verwaschenen Namen bequemer
entziffern zu können.

»O nicht doch«,[14] unterbrach sie lebhaft. »›Hier ruht das
unschuldige Kind‹, das reicht aus, das ist genug, und immer,
wenn ich es lese, gibt es mir einen Stich ins Herz, daß gerade
dies die Stelle war, wo die Preußen einbrachen, hier, durch
ebendieses Kirchhofstor, und das erste, was sie niedertraten
und umwarfen, das waren diese Kreuze mit ihrer schlichten,
so herzbeweglichen Inschrift . . . Aber kommen Sie, Kindergräber erzählen nicht viel und sind nur rührsam. Ich will lieber
zu Ruth Brown führen.«

»Zu Ruth Brown? Das klingt so englisch.«

»Und ist auch so. Generalin[15] Ruth Brown. Übrigens ist die
Geschichte, die sich an ihr Grab knüpft, und zwar ganz äußer-
lich an ihr Grab als solches, eigentlich die Hauptsache. Denken
Sie, die Generalin hat hier eine Art Mietsgrab bezogen, oder
wenigstens ein Grab aus zweiter Hand.«

»A second-hand grave?«

»Ja, so könnte man's beinah nennen. Dies Grab hier hatte
nämlich ursprünglich einen anderen Insassen und war die
leichtausgemauerte Behausung eines bei Kissingen gefallenen
Offiziers. Als dieser Offizier[16] aber in seine, wenn ich nicht irre,
westpreußische Heimat geschafft und die Gruft wieder leer
war, wurde sie neu gewölbt und neu gewandet, und nun erst
zog die Generalin ein. Es ist überhaupt ein Kirchhof mit bestän-

Amidst such talk they had reached their preliminary goal and climbed the stone steps past the memorial tablet to the cemetery. The sexton's house stood to the immediate left of the entrance, with all its doors open, and on its roof and windowsill the sparrows were chirping.

"I'll be the guide now," the lady said. "Reading tombstones, you remarked, impairs the memory. Good, we'll say it's so. But I can't accept it altogether. Look here . . . graves of children, one beside the other. And now read."

The lady's escort did not hesitate to obey and read in a low voice: "Here lies the innocent child . . . " But he had scarcely read so far when he stepped up to the mound spontaneously so that he could satisfy his curiosity and more easily decipher the name, which had been half washed away by rain.

"Oh don't," she interrupted with animation. "Here lies the innocent child, that's enough, and whenever I read it I feel a jab of pain in my heart, because this was the exact spot where the Prussians invaded, here through the cemetery gate, and the first thing they trampled on and knocked over were these crosses with their simple, moving inscriptions . . . But come, children's graves don't tell us much and are merely touching. I'd rather take you to Ruth Brown."

"To Ruth Brown? That sounds so English."

"And so it is, too. The wife of General Brown. Anyhow, the story connected with her grave, quite physically with her grave as such, is really the main thing. Just think, the general's wife moved into a sort of rental grave here, or at least a second-hand grave."

"A second-hand grave?"

"Yes, you could almost call it that. For this grave here, you should know, originally had another occupant; it was the home, lightly lined with masonry, of an officer who had been killed in the battle of Kissingen. But when this officer was transferred to his—if I'm not mistaken—West Prussian native city, and the grave was empty again, it was rebuilt with a new ceiling and new walls, and only then did the general's wife move in. All in

dig gestörter Ruhe, was niemand eindringlicher erfahren hat
als der hier . . . «

Und dabei war die Dame von dem Grabe der Generalin an
ein Nachbargrab herangetreten, aus dessen Inschrift ihr Begleiter unschwer entzifferte, daß der Sattlermeister Karl Teschner aus Großglogau[17] seine letzte Wohnung darin gefunden
habe.

»Haben Sie gelesen?«

»Ja. Was ist damit?«

»Nichts Besonderes . . . Und doch ein Grabstein, den ich nie
zu besuchen unterlasse. Sehen Sie schärfer hin, und Sie werden
erkennen, daß es ein zusammengeflickter Stein ist. Und das
kam so. Den 7. Juli 65 starb hier, denn leider auch Kurgäste
sterben, der Großsattlermeister,[18] dessen Namen Sie soeben
gelesen haben, und wurde den 10. desselben Monats an dieser
Stelle begraben. Und genau ein Jahr später, ja fast auf die
Stunde, schlug hier, vom Altenberg her, eine preußische Gra-
nate mitten auf den Grabstein und schleuderte die Stücke nach
allen Seiten hin auseinander. Etwas unheimlich. Aber das
Ganze hat doch, Gott sei Dank, ein versöhnliches Nachspiel
gehabt, denn kaum daß die Glogauer Bürgerschaft von dem
Grabsteinunglück ihres Großsattlermeisters gehört hatte, so
zeigte sie sich beflissen, für Remedur zu sorgen, und hat die
Grabsteinstücke wieder zusammenkitten und alles in gute
Wege bringen lassen. Eine Mosaik, die mehr sagt, als manche
Museumsmosaik. Aber nun bin ich matt und müde geworden,
und Sie müssen mich, ehe ich Sie freigebe, noch bis an meine
Lieblingsstelle begleiten.«

Es war dies eine von einer Traueresche[19] dicht überwachsene,
ziemlich in der Mitte des Kirchhofes gelegene Bank, in deren
unmittelbarer Nachbarschaft ein prächtiger und durch beson-
dere Schönheit ausgezeichneter Granitwürfel mit Helm und
Schwert hoch aufragte.

»Wem gilt es?«

»Einem Freunde. Ja, das war er mir. Und daß ich es gestehe,
mehr noch als das. Und dann kam das Leben, um uns zu trennen. Aber diese frühesten Eindrücke bleiben, wenigstens einem
Frauenherzen. Fast ein Menschenalter ist darüber hingegan-

all, this is a cemetery whose peace is being constantly disturbed, something that no one has experienced more intensely than this man here . . . "

In saying which the lady had walked from the grave of the general's wife to the next one, from whose inscription her escort easily deciphered that Karl Teschner, a prosperous saddle master from Glogau, had found his last home in it.

"Did you read it?"

"Yes, what about it?"

"Nothing special. And yet it's a tombstone I never fail to visit. If you look more closely you'll notice that it's a patched-up stone. This is how it happened. On July 7, '65, the prosperous saddle master whose name you have just read died here, for unfortunately visitors at watering places die too; he was buried on this spot on the tenth of the same month. And exactly one year later, almost to the hour, a Prussian grenade, fired from the Altenberg, struck the center of the tombstone and scattered the fragments in all directions. Somewhat uncanny. But thank Heaven, the whole matter had a conciliatory sequel, for scarcely had the citizens of Glogau heard of the accident to their saddle master's tombstone than they demonstrated a zealous care to remedy the situation; they had the tombstone fragments cemented together again and restored to their original form. A mosaic that tells us more than many a mosaic in a museum. But now I've grown faint and tired and you'll have to escort me to my favorite spot before I let you go."

This was a bench situated fairly close to the center of the cemetery, sheltered by a thick overgrowth of drooping ash branches; in its immediate vicinity a splendid cube of granite, distinguished by its extraordinary beauty, towered high, surmounted by a helmet and sword.

"Whom does it commemorate?"

"A friend. Yes, he was that to me. And let me confess, even more than that. And then came life and separated us. But these earliest impressions remain, at least in a woman's heart. Almost a generation has passed since then, I was still half a child at

gen, ich war noch ein halbes Kind damals, und wär' ich gestorben, wie's mein Wunsch und meine Hoffnung war, so hätt' es
auch auf meinem Grabsteine heißen dürfen: ›Hier ruht das
unschuldige Kind.‹ Aber ich starb nicht und tat, was alle tun,
und vergaß oder schien doch zu vergessen. Ob es gut und ob
ich glücklich war? Ich habe kein Recht zu Konfidenzen. Aber
es wurde mir doch eigen zu Sinn,[20] als ich vor drei Wochen
zum ersten Male diesen Kirchhof betrat und nach so viel
zwischenliegender Zeit und ohne jede Spur von Ahnung,
welches Wiederfinden meiner hier harren würde, diesem Denk-
mal und diesem mir so teuren Namen begegnete.«
»Was trennte Sie? Können Sie's erzählen?«
»Eine Frau in meinen Jahren kann alles erzählen, ihre Fehler
gewiß und ihre Fehltritte beinah. Aber erschrecken Sie nicht,
ich bin allezeit entsetzlich konventionell und immer auf der
graden Straße gewesen, fast mehr, als mir lieb ist. Es heißt zwar,
die Straße sei zu bevorzugen und es mache glücklich, auf einen
glatten Lebensweg zurückblicken zu können. Und ich will es
nicht geradezu bestreiten. Aber interessanter ist der Rückblick
auf ein kupiertes Terrain.«[21]

●

So sprachen sie weiter, und während ihr Gespräch noch an-
dauerte, hatte sich ihnen der alte Mesner genähert, zwei Stock-
laternen in der Rechten und einen großen Kirchenschlüssel an
einem Lederriemen über den Arm gehängt.
»Was gibt es?«
»Ein Begräbnis, gnädige Frau. In a[22] Viertelstund müssens
da sein. A Kind wie a Engel. Aber G'vatter Tod isch a Kenner,
un wenn er kann, nimmt er nichts Schlechts. I werd a paar
Stühl zurecht stelle für die gnädige Frau und den Herrn
Gemoahl.«
»Nicht doch, Mesner, der Herr da ist nicht mein Gemahl. Er
ist schon ein Witwer und hat abgeschlossen.« Und dabei malte
sie mit dem Sonnenschirm in den Sand.
»Hätt i doch g'dacht, Sie wär'n a Paar, un a stattlichs un glück-
lichs dazu, so gut passe Sie zusammen. Und so charmant; besunners die gnädge Frau.«
»Aber Mesner, Sie werden mich noch eitel machen . . . Eine
Frau in meinen Jahren . . . «

the time, and if I had died, as it was my wish and my hope that I should, my tombstone too might have borne the inscription 'Here lies the innocent child.' But I did not die, and I did what everyone does: I forgot, or seemed to forget. Was it good, and was I happy? I have no right to divulge confidences. But I did have a strange feeling when, three weeks ago, I stepped into this cemetery for the first time and, after such a very long time span, without the least suspicion as to what sort of reunion awaited me here, I encountered this monument and this name that is so dear to me."

"What was it that separated you? Can you tell me?"
"A woman in my years can tell anything, certainly her faults, and her lapses almost. But don't be alarmed, I have always been dreadfully conventional, always treading the straight path, almost more so than I wanted to. To be sure, it is said that the broad highway is to be preferred and that it brings you happiness to be able to look back on a smooth journey through life. And I won't actually dispute it. But it is more interesting to look back on broken terrain."

They continued to talk in this vein, and while their conversation was still in progress they were joined by the old sexton, carrying two railway lamps in his right hand and a big church key, which hung from his arm by a leather strap.
"What is happening?"
"A funeral, ma'am. They'll be here in a quarter hour for sure. A child like a angel. But Cousin Death is a expert and when he can, he don't take no shoddy goods. I'll set up a coupla chairs for ma'am and your husban'."

"No, no, sexton, this gentleman is not my husband. He's already a widower and has closed up shop." As she spoke she made patterns in the sand with her parasol.
"I should ha' thought you was a couple, an' a splendid an' happy one at that, you're so well matched. And so charming, madam aspecial."
"But sexton, you're going to make me vain . . . A woman in my years . . ."

»Ach, die Jahre sind nichts, das Herz ist alles. Und so lang es hier noch schlägt, hat keiner abgeschlossen. Abschluß gibt erscht der Tod. Aber da kummen's schon. Und's is Zeit, daß i geh un die Lichter ansteck.«

Indem auch hörte man schon Gesang von der Straße her, und nicht lange mehr, so sahen sie den Zug die Steinstufen heraufkommen, erst die Chorknaben, mit Kerzen und Weihrauchbecken, und dann der Geistliche in seinem Ornat. Dahinter aber der Sarg, der von sechs Trägern, zu deren Seite sechs andere gingen, getragen wurde. Und hinter dem Sarg her kamen die Leidtragenden, und zwischen den Gräbern hin bewegte sich alles auf die Kirchhofskapelle zu.

»Sollen wir uns anschließen?«

»Nein«, antwortete sie. »Ich denke, wir bleiben, wo wir sind; es ist mir, als[23] müßt' es mich dadrinnen erdrücken. Aber mit unserem Ohre wollen wir folgen, die Tür steht auf, und die Luft ist so still. Und ich glaube, wenn wir aufhorchen, so hören wir alles.«

Und dabei flog ein Schmetterling über die Gräber hin, und aus der Kirche her hörte man die Grabresponsorien.

Er nahm ihre Hand und sagte: »Die Tote drinnen vorm Altar predigt uns die Vergänglichkeit aller Dinge, gleichviel, ob wir in der Jugend stehen oder nicht. Uns gehört nur die Stunde. Und eine Stunde, wenn sie glücklich ist, ist viel. Nicht das Maß der *Zeit* entscheidet, wohl aber das Maß des *Glücks*. Und nun frag' ich Sie, sind wir zu alt, um glücklich zu sein?«

»Um abgeschlossen zu haben?«

»Es ist ein sonderbarer Zeitpunkt, den ich wähle«, fuhr er fort, ohne der halb scherzhaften Unterbrechung, in der doch ein gefühlvoller Ton mitklang, weiter zu achten. »Ein sonderbarer Zeitpunkt: ein Friedhof und dies Grab. Aber der Tod begleitet uns auf Schritt und Tritt und läßt uns in den Augenblicken, wo das Leben uns lacht, die Süße des Lebens nur um so tiefer empfinden. Ja, je gewisser das Ende, desto reizvoller die Minute und desto dringender die Mahnung: nutze den Tag.«[24]

●

Als die Zeremonie drinnen vorüber war, folgten beide dem Zuge durch die Stadt, und eine Woche später wechselten sie

"Ah, the years are nothin', the heart's everything. And as long as it keeps tickin', no one has closed up shop. Only death does the closin'. But now they're comin'. An' it's time for me to go an' turn on the lights."

One could already hear the singing from the road and it wasn't long before they saw the procession ascending the stone steps, first the choirboys with candles and incense bowls and then the clergyman in his robes. Behind them came the coffin, carried by six pallbearers, who were flanked by six others. And behind the coffin came the mourners, and the whole procession moved in and out among the graves toward the cemetery chapel.

"Shall we join them?"

"No," she replied. "I think we'll stay where we are; I feel I would stifle in there. But we'll follow them with our ears; the door is open and the air is so still. And I believe if we listen intently, we'll hear everything."

At that moment a butterfly flew over the graves, and from the church one could hear the responses of the funeral service.

He took her hand and said: "The deceased in there before the altar preaches to us the transitoriness of all things, regardless whether our condition is that of youth or not. Only this hour is ours. And an hour of happiness is a lot. It is not the measure of *time* that is decisive but the measure of *happiness*. And now I ask you: Are we too old to be happy?"

"To have closed up shop?"

"It's a strange moment that I choose," he continued, without heeding the half jesting interruption, which carried an undertone of emotion. "A strange moment: a cemetery and this grave. But Death accompanies all our steps and lets us feel the sweetness of life all the deeper in moments when life smiles on us. Yes, the more certain the end, the more alluring the minute, and the more urgent the exhortation: Use the day."

●

When the ceremony inside was over, they both followed the procession through the city, and a week later they exchanged

die Ringe. Verwandte, Freunde waren erschienen. Bei dem kleinen Festmahl aber, das die Verlobung begleitete, trat eine heitere Schwägerin an Braut und Bräutigam heran und sagte: »Man spricht von einem Motto, das Eure Verlobungsringe haben sollen. Oder doch der deine, Marie.«

»Kannst du schweigen?«

»Ich denke.«

»Nun denn, so lies.«

Und sie las: »Eine Frau in meinen Jahren«.

Notes: Fontane, *Eine Frau in meinen Jahren*

1. *gnädige Frau* (literally: gracious lady), madam, dear lady.

2. *Rat*, an honorary title bestowed on men who have distinguished themselves in government, the military, the professions, or business.

3. Wilhelmine Schröder-Devrient (1804–60) was a celebrated dancer and singer, the daughter of the actress Antoinette Sophie Schröder (1781–1868).

4. *cavaliere servente* (Italian), ladies' man, gigolo.

5. *feurige*, Aßmannshausen is a brand of German red champagne.

6. Nüdlingen is a town near Bad Kissingen.

7. The German name is *Eisenkraut* (iron plant).

8. *hoch oben*. The bicycles were the early type with a huge front wheel.

9. *vis-à-vis* (French, literally: face to face), opposite.

10. *um die Wette*, in competition.

11. *aufgehoben, aufheben* means to lift, keep or preserve, hide, cancel, abolish.

12. *eine Frage tun*, more usual: *eine Frage stellen*.

13. *Bildstöckel* = *Marterl*, a cross or plaque commemorating a fatal accident.

14. *nicht doch*, an emphatic negative: no, no.

15. *Generalin*, the wife of General Sir George Brown, a distinguished British soldier.

16. *Offizier*, Captain Robert Halm of Strasburg, West Prussia (now in Poland).

rings. Relatives and friends had appeared. But during the modest meal that celebrated their engagement, a jovial sister-in-law approached the bride and groom and said: "People are talking about a motto that is supposed to be engraved on your engagement rings. Or is it just yours, Mary?"
"Can you keep a secret?"
"I think so."
"Well then, read."
And she read: "A woman in my years."

17. *Großglogau*. No such place is recorded in German atlases. Glogau is a city in Lower Silesia (now belonging to Poland). Perhaps Fontane was referring to Glogau and its suburbs.

18. *Großsattlermeister*. *Groß–* is used in compounds to indicate large, substantial, wholesale; *Großgrundbesitzer*, large landholder; *Großhandel*, wholesale business; *Großindustrie*, heavy industry. In this case it probably indicates that Teschner had a substantial saddlery business.

19. *Traueresche*, formed by analogy with *Trauerweide* (weeping willow).

20. *eigen zu Sinn*, literally: peculiar in my mind.

21. *kupiertes Terrain*, a military term from the French to indicate territory studded with obstacles and traps.

22. Fontane does not reproduce working-class speech precisely but merely suggests its flavor: *a* = *ein, eine, einer*; *müssens* (South German and Austrian) = *müssen sie*; *isch* = *ist*; *Gemoahl* = *Gemahl*, husband, spouse; *i* = *ich*; *besunners* = *besonders*; *erscht* = *erst*; *kummen* = *kommen*.

23. als + subjunctive = *als ob*, with the verb placed after *als*.

24. Horace's *carpe diem* (*Odes* I, 11).

Arthur Schnitzler

1862–1931

Schnitzler was born and lived in Vienna throughout his uneventful life. His father was a prominent throat specialist and for some years the son assisted his father in his practice. But the young Schnitzler became interested in psychiatry and psychic phenomena such as mental telepathy, spiritism, and hypnotism.[1] His first publications were poems that appeared in the literary supplement of the *Neue freie Presse*, Vienna's leading newspaper. His first plays appeared about 1890; their success convinced him that he could live by his pen. In the next forty years he produced the many plays (mostly one-acters), short stories, and novellas that won him the reputation as a leading literary figure in the German-speaking world but brought him into disfavor in government circles and the powerful reactionary, clerical, and anti-Semitic ruling class.

Schnitzler's world is the charming, gracious, vivacious Vienna that we know from popular tradition: the city of coffeehouses, opera, Strauss waltzes, pyschoanalysis, and sex. This world he

[1]At the time hypnotism was regarded as an unscientific interest engaged in by charlatans.

presents to us in a style unmatched for grace, charm, and wit. He treats social problems: religion and politics, the military code of honor, the duel, the relation between parents and children, husband and wife, and above all the many faces of eros, from the Platonic to the most sensual forms of sex. But there is no overwhelming passion in his work, only gay, flirtatious men and women, young and old. There is failure, disillusionment, hostility in his work but no tragedy, only sadness. Schnitzler himself spoke of his "melancholodies." Elemental, atavistic passions express themselves in a subdued voice muted by the veneer of good breeding.

If we probe deeper we find in Schnitzler's work the crisis of modernism full blown. The whole nineteenth-century zeitgeist is there, at least in its negative aspects, culminating in the *fin de siècle* and foreshadowing what was to develop in the twentieth century out of the post-Enlightenment ferment of ideas. For instance:

1. The disintegration of the human personality, postulated by the physicist-philosopher Ernst Mach,[2] who has had a strong influence in science and literature. A "thing," Mach held, is a complex of sensations; and so are the sensations that cluster around a special body that we call an "I"; "thing" and "I" have only a relative constancy. The temporary paralysis of mind and will which Hugo von Hofmannsthal describes in his famous Chandos letter[3] was undoubtedly influenced by the blow that Mach struck at the stability of the physical universe. Writers, and nonwriters too, suddenly discovered that they could not communicate, and romantic loneliness became an almost universal malady;

2. The collapse of traditional ethical values, leading either to nihilism or to the Nietzschean revaluation of values;

3. The growth of democratic sensibility, which has driven the hero out of literature, to be replaced by the antihero, who lacks the will to cope with his environment;[4]

---

[2]Ernst Mach (1838–1916). The definition is from *Analysis of Sensations* (*Analyse der Empfindungen*, 1883).

[3]*Ein Brief* (1902), a letter supposedly written by Philip Lord Chandos to his friend Sir Francis Bacon, excusing himself for his total abandonment of all literary activity.

4. The cult of conspicuous and extravagant pleasure among artists, and the cult of art as a surrogate for religion;

5. The new psychology of the unconscious, which teaches that man is not master in his own house but the slave of his subconscious and unconscious desires, especially the sexual instinct, which led to the breaking of sexual taboos by those who had no inner controls to put in their place.

Which brings us to Freud. Of course Schnitzler was a Freudian. On the writer's sixtieth birthday (in 1922) the creator of psychoanalysis sent him a letter expressing his admiration for Schnitzler's profound psychological insights. Freud writes:

> Whenever I get deeply interested in your beautiful creations I always seem to find behind their poetic glow the same presuppositions, interest, and conclusions as those familiar to me as my own. Your determinism and your skepticism—what people call pessimism—your profound grasp of the truths of the unconscious and of the biological nature of man, the way you take to pieces the social conventions of our society, and the extent to which your thoughts are preoccupied with the polarity of love and death: all this moves me with an uncanny feeling of familiarity. So the impression has been borne in on me that you know through intuition—really from a delicate self-observation—everything that I have discovered in other people by laborious work. Indeed I believe that fundamentally you are an explorer of the depths, as honestly impartial and unperturbed as ever anyone was, and that if you hadn't been so, your artistic gifts, your mastery of language and your creativity would have had free play and made you into something more pleasing to the multitude.[5]

Freud's observation is true about Schnitzler the psychologist; in this area Schnitzler seems to be wholly impartial, as a good analyst should be. But in the sphere of politics, religion, and social problems he comes down unequivocally on the liberal, progressive side. Even in sexual matters, where Schnitzler seems to be wholly objective and nonmoralizing, he is too honest an observer to advocate pagan permissiveness outright. Like Heine

---

[4]See Mario Praz, *The Hero in Eclipse in Victorian Fiction* (1956); Raymond Giraud, *The Unheroic Hero* (1957); Victor Brombert, *The Intellectual Hero* (1960).

[5]Quoted in Ernest Jones, *The Life and Work of Sigmund Freud*, Vol. 3 (1957), 443–444.

before him,[6] he cannot fail to note the harm that dissolute, irresponsible living causes to the individual and to society, the disgust and emptiness that it produces, impairing the ability to differentiate between reality and fantasy.[7]

Schnitzler is a delicate artist, who writes about brutal matters with restraint and decorum, in a style of classical purity. His tones are muted and his colors subdued. His stories are remarkable for their atmosphere of urbanity, irony, and occasionally mystery.

●

The Blind Geronimo and His Brother (*Der blinde Geronimo und sein Bruder*) was written in 1899 and published the following year in the Viennese journal "Die Zeit" (December 1900–January 1901). It deals with a central theme of twentieth-century literature: man's essential loneliness, even with those who are closest to him and for whom he makes the greatest sacrifices. But, surprisingly for Schnitzler, it ends on a positive, optimistic note: understanding and true, selfless love can exist. It proves that Schnitzler was not the professional nihilist that some have made him out to be.

---

[6]See *Neue Gedichte*. Verschiedene 6 and S. S. Prawer, *Heine, the Tragic Satirist* (1961), 22–35.

[7]As in the one act "grotesque" *The Green Cockatoo* (*Der grüne Kakadu*, 1899). Hugo von Hofmannsthal drew similar conclusions about amoral aestheticism as a cult in his verse drama *The Fool and Death* (*Der Tor und der Tod*, 1900).

Title page for Schnitzler's first important play, published in 1893.

Der blinde Geronimo und sein Bruder

Der blinde Geronimo stand von der Bank auf und nahm die
Gitarre zur Hand, die auf dem Tisch neben dem Weinglase
bereit gelegen war.[1] Er hatte das ferne Rollen der ersten Wagen
vernommen. Nun tastete er sich den wohlbekannten Weg bis
zur offenen Türe hin, und dann ging er die schmalen Holzstufen hinab, die frei in den gedeckten Hofraum hinunterliefen.
Sein Bruder folgte ihm, und beide stellten sich gleich neben
der Treppe auf, den Rücken zur Wand gekehrt, um gegen den
naßkalten Wind geschützt zu sein, der über den feuchtschmut-
zigen Boden durch die offenen Tore strich.

Unter dem düsteren Bogen des alten Wirtshauses mußten
alle Wagen passieren, die den Weg über das Stilfser Joch[2]
nahmen. Für die Reisenden, welche von Italien her nach Tirol
wollten, war es die letzte Rast vor der Höhe. Zu langem Au-
fenthalte lud es nicht ein, denn gerade hier lief die Straße
ziemlich eben, ohne Ausblicke, zwischen kahlen Erhebungen
hin. Der blinde Italiener und sein Bruder Carlo waren in den
Sommermonaten hier so gut wie zu Hause.

Die Post fuhr ein, bald darauf kamen andere Wagen. Die
meisten Reisenden blieben sitzen, in Plaids und Mäntel wohl
eingehüllt, andere stiegen aus und spazierten zwischen den
Toren ungeduldig hin und her. Das Wetter wurde immer
schlechter, ein kalter Regen klatschte herab. Nach einer Reihe
schöner Tage schien der Herbst plötzlich und allzu früh herein-
zubrechen.

Der Blinde sang und begleitete sich dazu auf der Gitarre;
er sang mit einer ungleichmäßigen, manchmal plötzlich auf-
kreischenden Stimme, wie immer, wenn er getrunken hatte.
Zuweilen wandte er den Kopf wie mit einem Ausdruck ver-

The Blind Geronimo and His Brother

The blind Geronimo got up from the bench and took his guitar, which had been lying ready on the table near his wine glass, in his hand. He had heard the distant roll of the first carriages. Now he groped his way along the well-known path to the open door, and then he went down the narrow wooden steps that ran down in the open air to the covered courtyard. His brother followed him, and both at once took their position near the staircase, their backs turned to the wall, in order to be protected from the cold, wet wind that was blowing through the open gates over the moist, dirty ground.

All the carriages that took the road over the Stelvio Pass had to pass under the gloomy archway of the old inn. For the travelers who wanted to go from Italy to the Tirol, it was the last resting place before the heights. It did not invite one to stay long, for just at this spot the road was fairly level, without views, between bleak elevations. The blind Italian and his brother Carlo were practically at home here in the summer months.

The stagecoach drove in; soon after that other carriages came. Most of the travelers kept their seats, well wrapped in their plaids and coats; others got out and strolled impatiently back and forth between the gates. The weather became worse and worse; a cold rain splashed down. After a series of beautiful days autumn seemed to set in suddenly and all too early.

The blind man sang and accompanied himself on the guitar; he sang in an uneven voice, which sometimes suddenly turned into a shriek, as always when he had been drinking. At times he turned his head upward as though with an expression of

geblichen Flehens nach oben. Aber die Züge seines Gesichtes mit den schwarzen Bartstoppeln und den bläulichen Lippen blieben vollkommen unbeweglich. Der ältere Bruder stand neben ihm, beinahe regungslos. Wenn ihm jemand eine Münze in den Hut fallen ließ, nickte er Dank und sah dem Spender mit einem raschen, wie irren Blick ins Gesicht. Aber gleich, beinahe ängstlich, wandte er den Blick wieder fort und starrte gleich dem Bruder ins Leere. Es war, als schämten sich seine Augen des Lichts, das ihnen gewährt war, und von dem sie dem blinden Bruder keinen Strahl schenken konnten.

„Bring mir Wein", sagte Geronimo, und Carlo ging, gehorsam wie immer. Während er die Stufen aufwärts schritt, begann Geronimo wieder zu singen. Er hörte längst nicht mehr auf seine eigene Stimme, und so konnte er auf das merken, was in seiner Nähe vorging. Jetzt vernahm er ganz nahe zwei flüsternde Stimmen, die eines jungen Mannes und einer jungen Frau. Er dachte, wie oft diese beiden schon den gleichen Weg hin und her gegangen sein mochten; denn in seiner Blindheit und in seinem Rausch war ihm[3] manchmal, als kämen Tag für Tag dieselben Menschen über das Joch gewandert, bald von Norden gegen Süden, bald von Süden gegen Norden. Und so kannte er auch dieses junge Paar seit langer Zeit.

Carlo kam herab und reichte Geronimo ein Glas Wein. Der Blinde schwenkte es dem jungen Paare zu und sagte: „Ihr Wohl, meine Herrschaften!"

„Danke", sagte der junge Mann; aber die junge Frau zog ihn fort, denn ihr war dieser Blinde unheimlich.

Jetzt fuhr ein Wagen mit einer ziemlich lärmenden Gesellschaft ein: Vater, Mutter, drei Kinder, eine Bonne.

„Deutsche Familie", sagte Geronimo leise zu Carlo.

Der Vater gab jedem der Kinder ein Geldstück, und jedes durfte das seine in den Hut des Bettlers werfen. Geronimo neigte jedesmal den Kopf zum Dank. Der älteste Knabe sah dem Blinden mit ängstlicher Neugier ins Gesicht. Carlo betrachtete den Knaben. Er mußte, wie immer beim Anblick solcher Kinder, daran denken, daß Geronimo gerade so alt gewesen war, als das Unglück geschah, durch das er das Augenlicht verloren hatte. Denn er erinnerte sich jenes Tages auch heute noch, nach beinahe zwanzig Jahren, mit vollkommener

futile pleading. But the features of his face, with its black beard-stubble and its bluish lips, remained completely immobile. His older brother stood beside him, almost motionless. When any-one dropped a coin into his hat he nodded thanks and looked into the face of the giver with a swift, almost wild look. But promptly, almost anxiously, he turned his eyes away again and, like his brother, stared into space. It was as if his eyes felt ashamed of the light that was granted them and of which they could offer no ray to the blind brother.

"Bring me wine," said Geronimo, and Carlo went, obedient as always. While he went up the steps Geronimo began to sing again. He had long stopped listening to his own voice and so he was able to notice what was going on about him. Now he heard two whispering voices quite near him—those of a young man and a young woman. He thought how often these two might have walked back and forth the same way; for in his blindness and in his intoxication it sometimes seemed to him that the same people came over the pass day after day, now from north to south, again from south to north. And so he had known this young couple, too, for a long time.

Carlo came down and handed Geronimo a glass of wine. The blind man raised it to the young couple and said: "To your health, ladies and gentlemen!"

"Thanks," said the young man; but the young woman drew him away, for this blind man made her feel uncomfortable.

Now a carriage with a fairly noisy company drove in: a father, mother, three children, a maid.

"A German family," said Geronimo softly to Carlo.

The father gave each child a coin and each one was allowed to throw his coin into the beggar's hat. Each time Geronimo bowed his head in thanks. The oldest boy looked into the blind man's face with anxious curiosity. Carlo looked at the boy. As always when he saw such children, he had to think that Geronimo had been the same age when the accident through which he had lost his eyesight had happened. For even today, after almost twenty years, he remembered that day with perfect clarity. To this day he could hear in his ear the child's shrill

Deutlichkeit. Noch heute klang ihm der grelle Kinderschrei ins
Ohr, mit dem der kleine Geronimo auf den Rasen hingesunken
war, noch heute sah er die Sonne auf der weißen Gartenmauer
spielen und kringeln und hörte die Sonntagsglocken wieder,
die gerade in jenem Augenblick getönt hatten. Er hatte wie
oftmals mit dem Bolzen nach der Esche an der Mauer geschos-
sen, und als er den Schrei hörte, dachte er gleich, daß er den
kleinen Bruder verletzt haben mußte, der eben vorbeigelaufen
war. Er ließ das Blasrohr aus den Händen gleiten, sprang
durchs Fenster in den Garten und stürzte zu dem kleinen
Bruder hin, der auf dem Grase lag, die Hände vors Gesicht
geschlagen, und jammerte. Über die rechte Wange und den
Hals floß ihm Blut herunter. In derselben Minute kam der
Vater vom Felde heim, durch die kleine Gartentür, und nun
knieten beide ratlos neben dem jammernden Kinde. Nachbarn
eilten herbei; die alte Vanetti war die erste, der es gelang, dem
Kleinen die Hände vom Gesicht zu entfernen. Dann kam auch
der Schmied, bei dem Carlo damals in der Lehre war und der
sich ein bißchen aufs Kurieren verstand; und der sah gleich,
daß das rechte Auge verloren war. Der Arzt, der abends aus
Poschiavo kam, konnte auch nicht mehr helfen. Ja, er deutete
schon die Gefahr an, in der das andere Auge schwebte. Und
er behielt recht. Ein Jahr später war die Welt für Geronimo in
Nacht versunken. Anfangs versuchte man, ihm einzureden,
daß er später geheilt werden könnte, und er schien es zu
glauben. Carlo, der die Wahrheit wußte, irrte damals tage- und
nächtelang auf der Landstraße, zwischen den Weinbergen und
in den Wäldern umher, und war nahe daran, sich umzubringen.
Aber der geistliche Herr, dem er sich anvertraute, klärte ihn
auf, daß es seine Pflicht war, zu leben und sein Leben dem
Bruder zu widmen. Carlo sah es ein. Ein ungeheures Mitleid
ergriff ihn. Nur wenn er bei dem blinden Jungen war, wenn
er ihm die Haare streicheln, seine Stirne küssen durfte, ihm
Geschichten erzählte, ihn auf den Feldern hinter dem Hause
und zwischen den Rebengeländen spazieren führte, milderte
sich seine Pein. Er hatte gleich anfangs die Lehrstunden in der
Schmiede vernachlässigt, weil er sich von dem Bruder gar nicht
trennen mochte, und konnte sich nachher nicht mehr entschließen, sein Handwerk wieder aufzunehmen, trotzdem der

scream with which little Geronimo had sunk on the grass; to this day he saw the sun playing and flickering on the white garden wall and again heard the Sunday bells that had sounded at that very moment. As he had often done, he had been shooting at the ash tree by the wall with his dart; and when he heard the scream he thought at once that he must have hurt his little brother who had just run past. He let the blowpipe slip from his hands, jumped through the window into the garden and rushed over to his little brother, who was lying in the grass, his hands clapped to his face, wailing. The blood was flowing down his right cheek and neck. At the same moment their father came home from the field, through the little garden door, and now both of them kneeled helplessly beside the wailing child. Neighbors hurried over; old woman Vanetti was the first person who succeeded in removing the little boy's hands from his face. Then came the smith, to whom Carlo was apprenticed at that time; he was somewhat adept at medicine, and he saw at once that the right eye was lost. The doctor who came from Poschiavo in the evening couldn't help any more either. In fact he even pointed out the danger for the other eye. And he proved to be right. A year later the world had sunk into night for Geronimo. At first they tried to persuade him that he could be cured later on, and he seemed to believe it. At that time Carlo, who knew the truth, wandered about for days and nights on the highway, between the vineyards, in the forests, and came close to committing suicide. But the ecclesiastic in whom he confided made it clear to him that it was his duty to live and to dedicate his life to this brother. Carlo realized this. He was seized by an immense sympathy. Only when he was with the blind boy, when he could stroke his hair, kiss his forehead, tell him stories, take him for walks in the fields behind the house and between the vineyards, did his anguish decrease. Right from the beginning he had neglected his instruction at the smithy because he did not like to be separated from his brother, and later on he could no longer persuade himself to take up his trade again, even though his father urged him to do so and was concerned about him. One day Carlo noticed that Geronimo had completely stopped talking about his misfortune. He soon knew why: the blind boy had realized that he would never again

Vater mahnte und in Sorge war. Eines Tages fiel es Carlo auf, daß Geronimo vollkommen aufgehört hatte, von seinem Unglück zu reden. Bald wußte er, warum: der Blinde war zur Einsicht gekommen, daß er nie den Himmel, die Hügel, die Straßen, die Menschen, das Licht wieder sehen würde. Nun litt Carlo noch mehr als früher, so sehr er sich auch selbst damit zu beruhigen suchte, daß er ohne jede Absicht das Unglück herbeigeführt hatte. Und manchmal, wenn er am frühen Morgen den Bruder betrachtete, der neben ihm ruhte, ward[4] er von einer solchen Angst erfaßt, ihn erwachen zu sehen, daß er in den Garten hinauslief, nur um nicht dabei sein zu müssen, wie die toten Augen jeden Tag von neuem das Licht zu suchen schienen, das ihnen für immer erloschen war. Zu jener Zeit war es, daß Carlo auf den Einfall kam, Geronimo, der eine angenehme Stimme hatte, in der Musik weiter ausbilden zu lassen. Der Schullehrer von Tola, der manchmal sonntags herüberkam, lehrte ihn die Gitarre spielen. Damals ahnte der Blinde freilich noch nicht, daß die neuerlernte Kunst einmal zu seinem Lebensunterhalt dienen würde.

Mit jenem traurigen Sommertag schien das Unglück für immer in das Haus des alten Lagardi eingezogen zu sein. Die Ernte mißriet ein Jahr nach dem anderen; um eine kleine Geldsumme, die der Alte erspart hatte, wurde er von einem Verwandten betrogen; und als er an einem schwülen Augusttag auf freiem Felde vom Schlag getroffen hinsank und starb, hinterließ er nichts als Schulden. Das kleine Anwesen wurde verkauft, die beiden Brüder waren obdachlos und arm und verließen das Dorf.

Carlo war zwanzig, Geronimo fünfzehn Jahre alt. Damals begann das Bettel- und Wanderleben, das sie bis heute führten. Anfangs hatte Carlo daran gedacht, irgendeinen Verdienst zu finden, der zugleich ihn und den Bruder ernähren könnte; aber es wollte nicht gelingen. Auch hatte Geronimo nirgend Ruhe; er wollte immer auf dem Wege sein.

Zwanzig Jahre war es nun, daß sie auf Straßen und Pässen herumzogen, im nördlichen Italien und im südlichen Tirol, immer dort, wo eben der dichtere[5] Zug der Reisenden vorüberströmte.

see the sky, the hills, the streets, people, the light. Now Carlo suffered even more than before, however much he sought to soothe himself with the thought that he had caused the accident quite unintentionally. And sometimes, when he contemplated his brother in the early morning, as he slept beside him, he was seized by such anxiety at the prospect of seeing him awaken, that the ran out into the garden just so that he would not have to be present when the dead eyes seemed, every day, to seek once more the light that was extinguished for them forever. It was at that time that Carlo hit upon the idea of having Geronimo, who had a pleasant voice, continue his musical education. The schoolmaster from Tola, who sometimes came over on Sundays, taught him to play the guitar. At that time, of course, the blind boy had no idea that the newly learned art would one day serve him as a livelihood.

With that sad summer day, misfortune seemed to have moved permanently into old Lagardi's house. The crops failed one year after another; a relative swindled the old man out of a small sum of money that he had saved; and when he fell down with a stroke and died in the open field on a sultry August day, he left nothing but debts. The little property was sold; the two brothers, without a roof and poor, left the village.

Carlo was twenty years old, Geronimo fifteen. At that time the life of begging and wandering began which they had led till today. At first Carlo had thought of finding some occupation that could support both him and his brother; but he did not succeed. Besides Geronimo could find peace nowhere; he always wanted to be on the road.

For twenty years now they had been moving around on the roads and passes, in northern Italy and southern Tirol, always in the place where the densest throng of tourists streamed past.

Und wenn auch Carlo nach so vielen Jahren nicht mehr die brennende Qual verspürte, mit der ihn früher jedes Leuchten der Sonne, der Anblick jeder freundlichen Landschaft erfüllt hatte, es war doch ein stetes nagendes Mitleid in ihm, beständig und ihm unbewußt, wie der Schlag seines Herzens und sein Atem. Und er war froh, wenn Geronimo sich betrank.

Der Wagen mit der deutschen Familie war davongefahren. Carlo setzte sich, wie er gern tat, auf die untersten Stufen der Treppe, Geronimo aber blieb stehen, ließ die Arme schlaff herabhängen und hielt den Kopf nach oben gewandt.

Maria, die Magd, kam aus der Wirtsstube.

„Habt's[6] viel verdient heut?" rief sie herunter.

Carlo wandte sich gar nicht um. Der Blinde bückte sich nach seinem Glas, hob es vom Boden auf und trank es Maria zu. Sie saß manchmal abends in der Wirtsstube neben ihm; er wußte auch, daß sie schön war.

Carlo beugte sich vor und blickte gegen die Straße hinaus. Der Wind blies, und der Regen prasselte, so daß das Rollen des nahenden Wagens in den heftigen Geräuschen unterging. Carlo stand auf und nahm wieder seinen Platz an des Bruders Seite ein.

Geronimo begann zu singen, schon während der Wagen einfuhr, in dem nur ein Passagier saß. Der Kutscher spannte die Pferde eilig aus, dann eilte er hinauf in die Wirtsstube. Der Reisende blieb eine Weile in seiner Ecke sitzen, ganz eingewickelt in einen grauen Regenmantel; er schien auf den Gesang gar nicht zu hören. Nach einer Weile aber sprang er aus dem Wagen und lief mit großer Hast hin und her, ohne sich weit vom Wagen zu entfernen. Er rieb immerfort die Hände aneinander, um sich zu erwärmen. Jetzt erst schien er die Bettler zu bemerken. Er stellte sich ihnen gegenüber und sah sie lange wie prüfend an. Carlo neigte leicht den Kopf, wie zum Gruße. Der Reisende war ein sehr junger Mensch mit einem hübschen, bartlosen Gesicht und unruhigen Augen. Nachdem er eine ganze Weile vor den Bettlern gestanden, eilte er wieder zu dem Tore, durch das er weiterfahren sollte, und schüttelte bei dem trostlosen Ausblick in Regen und Nebel verdrießlich den Kopf.

„Nun?" fragte Geronimo.

And even though, after so many years, Carlo no longer felt the burning torment with which the shining of the sun, the sight of a pleasant landscape had formerly always filled him, there was still a steady nagging sympathy in him, constant and unknown to him, like the beating of his heart and his breathing. And he was happy when Geronimo got drunk.

The carriage with the German family had driven away. Carlo sat down, as he liked to do, on the lowest steps of the stairway, but Geronimo remained standing, let his arms hang limply and held his head turned upward.

Maria, the maid, came out of the taproom.

"Did you make a lot today?" she called down.

Carlo did not even turn around. The blind man bent down for his glass, picked it up from the ground and drank to Maria. She sometimes sat beside him in the taproom in the evening; he also knew that she was beautiful.

Carlo bent forward and looked out toward the highway. The wind was blowing and the rain pelted down so that the rumbling of the approaching carriage was lost in the loud noise. Carlo stood up and once more took his place at his brother's side.

Geronimo began to sing while the carriage, with only one passenger in it, was still driving up. The coachman hurriedly unhitched the horses, then hurried up to the taproom. For a while the tourist remained sitting in his corner, all wrapped up in a gray raincoat; he did not seem to be listening to the singing at all. But after a while he jumped out of the carriage and walked back and forth in great haste, without going far from the carriage. He kept rubbing his hands against each other to warm himself. Only now did he seem to notice the beggars. He took his position opposite them and looked at them for a long time as if he were testing them. Carlo bowed his head slightly as if in greeting. The tourist was a very young person with a pretty, beardless face and restless eyes. After he had stood before the beggars for quite a while, he hurried again to the gate through which he was to leave; and he shook his head in vexation at the sad prospect in the rain and mist.

"Well?" asked Geronimo.

„Noch nichts", erwiderte Carlo. „Er wird wohl geben, wenn er fortfährt."

Der Reisende kam wieder zurück und lehnte sich an die Deichsel des Wagens. Der Blinde begann zu singen. Nun schien der junge Mann plötzlich mit großem Interesse zuzuhören. Der Knecht erschien und spannte die Pferde wieder ein. Und jetzt erst, als besänne er sich eben, griff der junge Mann in die Tasche und gab Carlo einen Frank.

„O danke, danke", sagte dieser.

Der Reisende setzte sich in den Wagen und wickelte sich wieder in seinen Mantel. Carlo nahm das Glas vom Boden auf und ging die Holzstufen hinauf. Geronimo sang weiter. Der Reisende beugte sich zum Wagen heraus und schüttelte den Kopf mit einem Ausdruck von Überlegenheit und Traurigkeit zugleich. Plötzlich schien ihm ein Einfall zu kommen, und er lächelte. Dann sagte er zu dem Blinden, der kaum zwei Schritte weit von ihm stand: „Wie heißt du?"

„Geronimo."

„Nun, Geronimo, laß dich nur nicht betrügen." In diesem Augenblick erschien der Kutscher auf der obersten Stufe der Treppe.

„Wieso, gnädiger Herr,[7] betrügen?"

„Ich habe deinem Begleiter ein Zwanzigfrankstück gegeben."

„O Herr, Dank, Dank!"

„Ja; also paß auf!"

„Er ist mein Bruder, Herr; er betrügt mich nicht."

Der junge Mann stutzte eine Weile, aber während er noch überlegte, war der Kutscher auf den Bock gestiegen und hatte die Pferde angetrieben. Der junge Mann lehnte sich zurück mit einer Bewegung des Kopfes, als wollte er sagen: Schicksal, nimm deinen Lauf! und der Wagen fuhr davon.

Der Blinde winkte mit beiden Händen lebhafte Gebärden des Dankes nach. Jetzt hörte er Carlo, der eben aus der Wirtsstube kam. Der rief herunter: „Komm, Geronimo, es ist warm heroben, Maria hat Feuer gemacht!"

Geronimo nickte, nahm die Gitarre unter den Arm und tastete sich am Geländer die Stufen hinauf. Auf der Treppe schon rief er: „Laß es mich anfühlen! Wie lang hab' ich schon kein Goldstück angefühlt!"

"Nothing yet," replied Carlo. "He'll probably give when he leaves."

The tourist came back again and leaned against the shaft of the carriage. The blind man began to sing. Now the young man seemed suddenly to listen with great interest. The stable hand appeared and hitched the horses up again. And only now, as though he were just remembering, the young man put his hand in his pocket and gave Carlo a franc.

"O thanks, thanks," Carlo said.

The tourist sat down in the carriage and wrapped himself in his coat again. Carlo picked up the glass from the ground and went up the wooden steps. Geronimo went on singing. The tourist leaned out of the carriage and shook his head with an expression that indicated both superiority and sadness. Suddenly something seemed to occur to him and he smiled. Then he said to the blind man, who was standing scarcely two feet from him: "What is your name?"

"Geronimo."

"Well, Geronimo, just don't let anyone cheat you!" At this moment the coachman appeared on the top step of the staircase.

"How do you mean, sir, cheat me?"

"I gave your companion a twenty-franc piece."

"O thank you, thank you, sir."

"Yes; so look out."

"He is my brother sir, he doesn't cheat me."

The young man hesitated for a while, but while he was still considering, the coachman had mounted his box and whipped up his horses. The young man leaned back with a movement of his head as if he wanted to say "Destiny, take thy course!" and the carriage drove off.

The blind man waved lively gestures of gratitude after him with both hands. Now he heard Carlo who was just coming out of the taproom. He called down: "Come Geronimo, it's warm up here, Maria has made a fire."

Geronimo nodded, took his guitar under his arm, and felt his way up the stairs by the railing. While he was still on the steps he called: "Let me feel it. It's a long time since I've felt a gold piece."

„Was gibt's?" fragte Carlo. „Was redest du da?"

Geronimo war oben und griff mit beiden Händen nach dem
Kopf seines Bruders, ein Zeichen, mit dem er stets Freude oder
Zärtlichkeit auszudrücken pflegte. „Carlo, mein lieber Bruder,
es gibt doch gute Menschen!"

„Gewiß", sagte Carlo. „Bis jetzt sind es zwei Lire und dreißig
Centesimi, und hier ist noch österreichisches Geld, vielleicht
eine halbe Lira."

„Und zwanzig Franken—und zwanzig Franken!" rief Geronimo. „Ich weiß es ja!" Er torkelte in die Stube und setzte sich
schwer auf die Bank.

„Was weißt du?" fragte Carlo.

„So laß doch die Späße! Gib es mir in die Hand! Wie lang
hab' ich schon kein Goldstück in der Hand gehabt!"

„Was willst du denn? Woher soll ich ein Goldstück nehmen?
Es sind zwei Lire oder drei."

Der Blinde schlug auf den Tisch. „Jetzt ist es aber genug,
genug! Willst du es etwa vor mir verstecken?"

Carlo blickte den Bruder besorgt und verwundert an. Er
setzte sich neben ihn, rückte ganz nahe und faßte wie begüti-
gend seinen Arm: „Ich verstecke nichts vor dir. Wie kannst du
das glauben? Niemandem ist es eingefallen, mir ein Goldstück
zu geben."

„Aber er hat mir's doch gesagt!"

„Wer?"

„Nun, der junge Mensch, der hin- und herlief."

„Wie? Ich versteh' dich nicht!"

„So hat er zu mir gesagt: ‚Wie heißt du?' und dann: ‚Gib
acht, gib acht, laß dich nicht betrügen!'"

„Du mußt geträumt haben, Geronimo—das ist ja Unsinn!"

„Unsinn? Ich hab' es doch gehört, und ich höre gut. ‚Laß
dich nicht betrügen; ich habe ihm ein Goldstück . . . '—nein,
so sagte er: ‚Ich habe ihm ein Zwanzigfrankstück gegeben.'"

Der Wirt kam herein. „Nun, was ist's mit euch? Habt ihr das
Geschäft aufgegeben? Ein Vierspänner ist gerade angefahren."

„Komm!" rief Carlo, „komm!"

"What's up?" said Carlo. "What are you talking about?"

Geronimo had reached the top and took his brother's head in both hands, a sign with which he had always expressed joy or tenderness. "Carlo, my dear brother, there really are some good people."

"Certainly," said Carlo. "So far we have two lire and thirty centesimi, and here is some Austrian money too, perhaps half a lira."

"And twenty francs—and twenty francs," cried Geronimo. "I know it's so!" He staggered into the taproom and sat down heavily on the bench.

"What do you know?" asked Carlo.

"Stop your jokes! Give it to me in my hand! What a long time since I've had a gold coin in my hand!"

"What is it you want? Where am I to get a gold coin? There are two or three lire."

The blind man thumped the table. "Now this is enough, enough! Do you perhaps intend to hide it from me?"

Carlo looked at his brother anxiously and in astonishment. He sat down beside him, moved quite close to him and took his arm as though to soothe him: "I'm hiding nothing from you. How can you believe that? It didn't occur to anyone to give me a gold piece."

"But he told me so."

"Who?"

"Well, the young man who was pacing back and forth."

"What? I don't understand you."

"That's what he told me: 'What's your name?' and then: 'Look out, look out, don't let anyone cheat you.'"

"You must have been dreaming, Geronimo—why this is nonsense."

"Nonsense? But I heard it and my hearing is good. 'Don't let anyone cheat you; I gave him a gold piece . . .' no, this is what he said: 'I gave him a twenty-franc piece.'"

The landlord came in. "Well, what's up between you? Have you given up your business? A coach and four has just driven up."

"Come!" cried Carlo. "Come!"

Geronimo blieb sitzen. „Warum denn? Warum soll ich kommen? Was hilft's mir denn? Du stehst ja dabei und—"
Carlo berührte ihn am Arm. „Still, komm jetzt hinunter!"
Geronimo schwieg und gehorchte dem Bruder. Aber auf
den Stufen sagte er: „Wir reden noch, wir reden noch!"
Carlo begriff nicht, was geschehen war. War Geronimo plötzlich verrückt geworden? Denn, wenn er auch leicht in Zorn
geriet, in dieser Weise hatte er noch nie gesprochen.

In dem eben angekommenen Wagen saßen zwei Engländer;
Carlo lüftete den Hut vor ihnen, und der Blinde sang. Der
eine Engländer war ausgestiegen und warf einige Münzen in
Carlos Hut. Carlo sagte: „Danke" und dann, wie vor sich hin:
„Zwanzig Centesimi." Das Gesicht Geronimos blieb unbewegt;
er begann ein neues Lied. Der Wagen mit den zwei Engländern
fuhr davon.

Die Brüder gingen schweigend die Stufen hinauf. Geronimo
setzte sich auf die Bank, Carlo blieb beim Ofen stehen.

„Warum sprichst du nicht?" fragte Geronimo.

„Nun", erwiderte Carlo, „es kann nur so sein, wie ich dir
gesagt habe." Seine Stimme zitterte ein wenig.

„Was hast du gesagt?" fragte Geronimo.

„Es war vielleicht ein Wahnsinniger."

„Ein Wahnsinniger? Das wäre ja vortrefflich! Wenn einer
sagt: ‚Ich habe deinem Bruder zwanzig Franken gegeben,‘ so
ist er wahnsinnig!—Eh,[8] und warum hat er gesagt: ‚Laß dich
nicht betrügen‘—eh?"

„Vielleicht war er auch nicht wahnsinnig . . . aber es gibt Menschen, die mit uns armen Leuten Späße machen . . ."

„Eh!" schrie Geronimo, „Späße?—Ja, das hast du noch sagen
müssen—darauf habe ich gewartet!" Er trank das Glas Wein
aus, das vor ihm stand.

„Aber, Geronimo!" rief Carlo, und er fühlte, daß er vor Be-
stürzung kaum sprechen konnte, „warum sollte ich . . . wie
kannst du glauben . . .?"

„Warum zittert deine Stimme . . . eh . . . warum . . .?"

„Geronimo, ich versichere dir, ich—"

„Eh—und ich glaube dir nicht! Jetzt lachst du . . . ich weiß
ja, daß du jetzt lachst!"

Geronimo sat there. "But why? Why should I come? What use is it to me? When you stand beside me and—"

Carlo touched his arm. "Quiet, come down now!"

Geronimo was silent and obeyed his brother. But on the steps he said: "We'll talk more about this; we'll talk about it."

Carlo did not understand what had happened. Had Geronimo suddenly gone mad? For though he became angry easily, he had never spoken this way before.

Two Englishmen sat in the carriage that had just arrived; Carlo raised his hat to them and the blind man sang. The one Englishman had got out and threw a few coins into Carlo's hat. Carlo said: "Thanks." And then, as though to himself: "Twenty centisimi." Geronimo's face remained impassive; he began a new song. The carriage with the two Englishmen drove off.

The brothers went up the stairs silently. Geronimo sat down on the bench; Carlo remained standing by the stove.

"Why don't you speak?" Geronimo asked.

"Well," Carlo replied, "it can only be as I told you." His voice was trembling slightly.

"What did you say?" Geronimo asked.

"Perhaps the man was insane."

"Insane? That would sure be splendid. If a man says: 'I gave your brother twenty francs,' he's insane—hey, and why did he say: 'Don't let anyone cheat you'—eh?"

"Perhaps he wasn't insane either, but there are people who like to make jokes with us poor folk . . ."

"Hey!" Geronimo shrieked, "jokes?—yes, you had to say that too—I've been waiting for it." He finished the glass of wine that stood before him.

"But Geronimo!" cried Carlo—and he found, in his astonishment, that he was hardly able to talk—"why should I . . . how can you believe . . . ?"

"Why does your voice tremble . . . eh . . . why . . . ?"

"Geronimo, I assure you, I . . ."

"Hey—and I don't believe you. Now you're laughing . . . I know for sure that you're laughing now."

Der Knecht rief von unten: „He, blinder Mann, Leut' sind da!"

Ganz mechanisch standen die Brüder auf und schritten die Stufen hinab. Zwei Wagen waren zugleich gekommen, einer mit drei Herren, ein anderer mit einem alten Ehepaar. Geronimo sang; Carlo stand neben ihm, fassungslos. Was sollte er nur tun? Der Bruder glaubte ihm nicht! Wie war das nur möglich?—Und er betrachtete Geronimo, der mit zerbrochener Stimme seine Lieder sang, angstvoll von der Seite. Es war ihm, als sähe er über diese Stirne Gedanken fliehen, die er früher dort niemals gewahrt hatte.

Die Wagen waren schon fort, aber Geronimo sang weiter. Carlo wagte nicht, ihn zu unterbrechen. Er wußte nicht, was er sagen sollte, er fürchtete, daß seine Stimme wieder zittern würde. Da tönte Lachen von oben, und Maria rief: „Was singst denn noch immer? Von mir kriegst du ja doch nichts!"

Geronimo hielt inne, mitten in einer Melodie; es klang, als wäre seine Stimme und die Saiten zugleich abgerissen. Dann ging er wieder die Stufen hinauf, und Carlo folgte ihm. In der Wirtsstube setzte er sich neben ihn. Was sollte er tun? Es blieb ihm nichts anderes übrig: er mußte noch einmal versuchen, den Bruder aufzuklären.

„Geronimo", sagte er, „ich schwöre dir . . . bedenk' doch, Geronimo, wie kannst du glauben, daß ich—"

Geronimo schwieg, seine toten Augen schienen durch das Fenster in den grauen Nebel hinauszublicken. Carlo redete weiter: „Nun, er braucht ja nicht wahnsinnig gewesen zu sein, er wird sich geirrt haben[9] . . . ja er hat sich geirrt . . ." Aber er fühlte wohl, daß er selbst nicht glaubte, was er sagte.

Geronimo rückte ungeduldig fort. Aber Carlo redete weiter, mit plötzlicher Lebhaftigkeit: „Wozu sollte ich denn—du weißt doch, ich esse und trinke nicht mehr als du, und wenn ich mir einen neuen Rock kaufe, so weißt du's doch . . . wofür brauch' ich denn so viel Geld? Was soll ich denn damit tun?"

Da stieß Geronimo zwischen den Zähnen hervor: „Lüg nicht, ich höre, wie du lügst!"

„Ich lüge nicht, Geronimo, ich lüge nicht!" sagte Carlo erschrocken.

The groom called from below: "Hey, blind man, there are people here."

Quite mechanically the brothers stood up and went down the steps. Two carriages had arrived at the same time, one with three gentlemen, another with an old couple. Geronimo sang: Carlo stood near him, distracted. What could he do? His brother did not believe him! How was this even possible?—And he gave Geronimo, who was singing his songs in a broken voice, an anxious, sidelong look. It seemed to him that he saw thoughts crossing this brow that he had never perceived there before.

The carriages had already left but Geronimo kept on singing. Carlo did not dare to interrupt him. He did not know what to say; he feared that his voice would tremble again. Then there was laughter from above and Maria cried: "Why do you keep on singing? You won't get anything from me."

Geronimo stopped in the middle of a tune; it sounded as if his voice and the strings had snapped at the same time. Then he went up the steps again and Carlo followed him. In the taproom he sat down beside him. What should he do? Nothing else was left for him: he must try once more to enlighten his brother.

"Geronimo," he said, "I swear to you . . . just consider, Geronimo, how can you believe that I . . ."

Geronimo was silent; his dead eyes seemed to look through the window out into the gray mist. Carlo went on: "Well, he needn't have been insane, of course, he may have made a mistake . . . yes, he made a mistake . . ." But he clearly felt that he himself did not believe what he was saying.

Geronimo moved away impatiently. But Carlo kept on talking with sudden animation: "Why should I—you know that I don't eat or drink more than you do, and when I buy a new jacket you know about it . . . what would I need so much money for? What am I to do with it?"

Then Geronimo hissed between his teeth: "Don't lie, I hear how you're lying!"

"I'm not lying, Geronimo, I'm not lying!" said Carlo in fright.

„Eh! hast du ihr's schon gegeben, ja? Oder bekommt sie's erst nachher?" schrie Geronimo.

„Maria?"

„Wer denn, als Maria? Eh, du Lügner, du Dieb!" Und als wollte er nicht mehr neben ihm am Tische sitzen, stieß er mit dem Ellbogen den Bruder in die Seite.

Carlo stand auf. Zuerst starrte er den Bruder an, dann verließ er das Zimmer und ging über die Stiege in den Hof. Er schaute mit weit offenen Augen auf die Straße hinaus, die vor ihm in bräunlichen Nebel versank. Der Regen hatte nachgelassen. Carlo steckte die Hände in die Hosentaschen und ging ins Freie. Es war ihm, als hätte ihn sein Bruder davongejagt. Was war denn nur geschehen? . . . Er konnte es noch immer nicht fassen. Was für ein Mensch mochte das gewesen sein? Einen Franken schenkt er her und sagt, es waren zwanzig! Er mußte doch irgendeinen Grund dazu gehabt haben . . . Und Carlo suchte in seiner Erinnerung, ob er sich nicht irgendwo jemanden zum Feind gemacht, der nun einen anderen hergeschickt hatte, um sich zu rächen . . . Aber soweit er zurückdenken mochte, nie hatte er jemanden beleidigt, nie irgendeinen ernsten Streit mit jemandem vorgehabt. Er hatte ja seit zwanzig Jahren nichts anderes getan, als daß er in Höfen oder an Straßenrändern gestanden war[10] mit dem Hut in der Hand . . . War ihm vielleicht einer wegen eines Frauenzimmers[11] böse? . . . Aber wie lange hatte er schon mit keiner was zu tun gehabt . . . die Kellnerin in La Rosa war die letzte gewesen, im vorigen Frühjahr . . . aber um die war ihm gewiß niemand neidisch . . . Es war nicht zu begreifen! . . . Was mochte es da draußen in der Welt, die er nicht kannte, für Menschen geben? . . . Von überall her kamen sie . . . was wußte er von ihnen? . . . Für diesen Fremden hatte es wohl irgendeinen Sinn gehabt, daß er zu Geronimo sagte: Ich habe deinem Bruder zwanzig Franken gegeben . . . Nun ja . . . Aber was war nun zu tun? . . . Mit einemmal war es offenbar geworden, daß Geronimo ihm mißtraute! . . . Das konnte er nicht ertragen! Irgend etwas mußte er dagegen unternehmen . . . Und er eilte zurück.

Als er wieder in die Wirtsstube trat, lag Geronimo auf der Bank ausgestreckt und schien das Eintreten Carlos nicht zu bemerken. Maria brachte den beiden Essen und Trinken. Sie

"Hey! have you given it to her already, yes? Or will she get it only later?" Geronimo shrieked.

"Maria?"

"Who else but Maria? Hey, you liar, you thief!" And, as though he didn't want to sit beside him at the table any longer, he thrust his elbow into his brother's side.

Carlo stood up. At first he stared at his brother, then he left the room and went into the courtyard by way of the staircase. With wide open eyes he looked at the highway, which faded before him in brownish mist. The rain had abated. Carlo put his hands into his trouser pockets and went out into the open. He felt as though his brother had driven him away. What had really happened? . . . He couldn't grasp it even now. What kind of person could that have been? He offers a franc and says it was twenty. He must surely have had some reason for it . . . And Carlo searched his memory: had he somewhere made an enemy of someone who had now sent another man here to take revenge . . . But as far back as he could think, he had never insulted anyone, had never had a serious quarrel with anyone. For he had done nothing in the last twenty years except to stand around in courtyards and at curbs with his hat in his hand . . . Could it be that someone was angry with him because of a woman? . . . But how long it was since he had had anything to do with one . . . the waitress in La Rosa had been the last one, the previous spring . . . but certainly no one envied him because of her . . . It was incomprehensible! . . . What sort of people could there be out there in that world which he did not know? . . . They came from everywhere . . . what did he know about them? . . . There must have been some reason why this stranger said to Geronimo: "I gave your brother twenty francs . . ." Well, yes . . . But what was to be done now? . . . Suddenly it had become obvious that Geronimo distrusted him! . . . This he could not bear! He must do something against it . . . And he hurried back.

When he entered the taproom again Geronimo lay stretched out on the bench and seemed not to notice Carlo's entrance. Maria brought both of them food and drink. They did not say

sprachen während der Mahlzeit kein Wort. Als Maria die Teller abräumte, lachte Geronimo plötzlich auf und sagte zu ihr: „Was wirst du dir denn dafür kaufen?"

„Wofür denn?"

„Nun, was? Einen neuen Rock oder Ohrringe?"

„Was will er denn von mir?" wandte sie sich an Carlo.

Indes dröhnte unten der Hof von lastenbeladenen Fuhrwerken, laute Stimmen tönten herauf, und Maria eilte hinunter. Nach ein paar Minuten kamen drei Fuhrleute und nahmen an einem Tische Platz; der Wirt trat zu ihnen und begrüßte sie. Sie schimpften über das schlechte Wetter.

„Heute nacht werdet ihr Schnee haben", sagte der eine.

Der zweite erzählte, wie er vor zehn Jahren Mitte August auf dem Joch eingeschneit und beinahe erfroren war. Maria setzte sich zu ihnen. Auch der Knecht kam herbei und erkundigte sich nach seinen Eltern, die unten in Bormio wohnten.

Jetzt kam wieder ein Wagen mit Reisenden. Geronimo und Carlo gingen hinunter, Geronimo sang, Carlo hielt den Hut hin, und die Reisenden gaben ihr Almosen. Geronimo schien jetzt ganz ruhig. Er fragte manchmal: „Wieviel?" und nickte zu den Antworten Carlos leicht mit dem Kopfe. Indes versuchte Carlo selbst seine Gedanken zu fassen. Aber er hatte immer nur das dumpfe Gefühl, daß etwas Schreckliches geschehen und daß er ganz wehrlos war.

Als die Brüder wieder die Stufen hinaufschritten, hörten sie die Fuhrleute oben wirr durcheinanderreden und lachen. Der jüngste rief dem Geronimo entgegen: „Sing uns doch auch was vor, wir zahlen schon!—Nicht wahr?" wandte er sich an die anderen.

Maria, die eben mit einer Flasche rotem Wein kam, sagte: „Fangt heut nichts mit ihm an, er ist schlechter Laune."[12]

Statt jeder Antwort stellte sich Geronimo mitten ins Zimmer hin und fing an zu singen. Als er geendet, klatschten die Fuhrleute in die Hände.

„Komm her, Carlo!" rief einer, „wir wollen dir unser Geld auch in den Hut werfen wie die Leute unten!" Und er nahm eine kleine Münze und hielt die Hand hoch, als wollte er sie in den Hut fallen lassen, den ihm Carlo entgegenstreckte. Da

a word during the meal. When Maria cleared off the dishes, Geronimo suddenly gave a laugh and said to her: "What are you going to buy for it?"

"For what?"

"Well, what? A new skirt or earrings?"

"What does he want from me?" she said turning to Carlo.

Meanwhile the courtyard below echoed with heavily loaded vehicles, loud voices reached upstairs, and Maria hurried down. After a few minutes three drivers came and took their places at a table; the landlord went up to them and greeted them. They cursed the bad weather.

"Tonight you'll get snow," one of them said.

The second one told how, ten years ago in the middle of August, he had been snowed in on the pass and had almost been frozen. Maria sat down beside them. The servant came up too and inquired about his parents, who lived down below in Bormio.

Now another carriage with passengers came. Geronimo and Carlo went down, Geronimo sang, Carlo held out his hat, and the tourists gave their alms. Geronimo now seemed quite calm. He sometimes asked: "How much?" and nodded lightly with his head to Carlo's answers. Meanwhile Carlo himself tried to gather his thoughts together. But he always had the obscure feeling that something terrible had happened and that he was quite helpless.

When the brothers went up the steps again, they heard the drivers upstairs talking at the same time and laughing. The youngest one called out to Geronimo: "Sing something for us too, we'll pay you!—Won't we?" said he, turning to the others.

Maria, who was just coming with a bottle of red wine, said: "Don't start anything with him today, he's in a bad mood."

Instead of giving an answer Geronimo took his position in the middle of the room and began to sing. When he had finished the drivers applauded.

"Come here, Carlo!" one of them cried, "We'll throw our money into your hat too, like the people down below." And he took a small coin and held up his hand as though he would drop it into the hat that Carlo stretched out to him. At that

griff der Blinde nach dem Arm des Fuhrmannes und sagte: „Lieber mir, lieber mir! Es könnte daneben[13] fallen—daneben!"
„Wieso daneben?"
„Eh, nun! zwischen die Beine Marias!"
Alle lachten, der Wirt und Maria auch, nur Carlo stand regungslos da. Nie hatte Geronimo solche Späße gemacht! . . .

„Setz' dich zu uns!" riefen die Fuhrleute. „Du bist ein lustiger Kerl!" Und sie rückten zusammen, um Geronimo Platz zu machen. Immer lauter und wirrer war das Durcheinanderreden; Geronimo redete mit, lauter und lustiger als sonst, und hörte nicht auf zu trinken. Als Maria eben wieder hereinkam, wollte er sie an sich ziehen; da sagte der eine von den Fuhrleuten lachend: „Meinst du vielleicht, sie ist schön? Sie ist ja ein altes häßliches Weib!"

Aber der Blinde zog Maria auf seinen Schoß. „Ihr seid alle Dummköpfe", sagte er. „Glaubt ihr, ich brauche meine Augen, um zu sehen? Ich weiß auch, wo Carlo jetzt ist—eh!—dort am Ofen steht er, hat die Hände in den Hosentaschen und lacht."

Alle schauten auf Carlo, der mit offenem Munde am Ofen lehnte und nun wirklich das Gesicht zu einem Grinsen verzog, als dürfte er seinen Bruder nicht Lügen strafen.[15]

Der Knecht kam herein; wenn die Fuhrleute noch vor Dunkelheit in Bormio sein wollten, mußten sie sich beeilen. Sie standen auf und verabschiedeten sich lärmend. Die beiden Brüder waren wieder allein in der Wirtsstube. Es war die Stunde, um die sie sonst manchmal zu schlafen pflegten. Das ganze Wirtshaus versank in Ruhe wie immer um diese Zeit der ersten Nachmittagsstunden. Geronimo, den Kopf auf dem Tisch, schien zu schlafen. Carlo ging anfangs hin und her, dann setzte er sich auf die Bank. Er war sehr müde. Es schien ihm, als wäre er in einem schweren Traum befangen. Er mußte an allerlei denken, an gestern, vorgestern und alle Tage, die früher waren, und besonders an warme Sommertage und an weiße Landstraßen, über die er mit seinem Bruder zu wandern pflegte, und alles war so weit und unbegreiflich, als wenn es nie wieder so sein könnte.

Am späten Nachmittage kam die Post aus Tirol und bald darauf in kleinen Zwischenpausen Wagen, die den gleichen

point the blind man seized the driver's arm and said: "Better give it to me, better to me. It might fall outside."

"How do you mean outside."

"Well, between Maria's legs."

They all laughed, the landlord and Maria too, only Carlo stood there motionless. Geronimo had never made such jokes before . . .

"Sit down with us," the drivers cried. "You're a merry fellow." And they moved closer together, to make room for Geronimo. The general talk grew louder and louder and more and more confused. Geronimo joined in, louder and merrier than usual, and did not stop drinking. When Maria came in again, he wanted to draw her to him; one of the drivers said laughing: "Can you possibly think she's beautiful? Why she's an old, ugly woman."

But the blind man drew Maria down on his lap. "You're all stupid," he said. "Do you think I need my eyes to see? I even know where Carlo is now. Hey, he's standing there by the stove, has his hands in his pants pockets, and is laughing."

They all looked at Carlo, who was leaning against the stove with his mouth open, and now really twisted his face into a grin, as if he mustn't make a liar out of his brother.

The servant came in; if the drivers wanted to reach Bormio before dark, they had to hurry. They stood up and took a noisy leave. The two brothers were alone again in the taproom. It was the hour when they sometimes took a nap. The whole inn fell into a calm, as always at this time during the first afternoon hours. Geronimo, with his head on the table, seemed to be sleeping. At first Carlo walked back and forth, then he sat down on the bench. He was very tired. It seemed to him that he was experiencing a heavy dream. He had to think of all sorts of things—of yesterday, the day before yesterday, and all the days that came before, and especially of warm summer days and white highways over which he was accustomed to walk with his brother—and it was all so far away and unintelligible, as if it could never be the same again.

In the late afternoon the stagecoach from Tirol came and soon afterward, at brief intervals, carriages that were taking

Weg nach dem Süden nahmen. Noch viermal mußten die
Brüder in den Hof hinab. Als sie das letztemal heraufgingen,
war die Dämmerung hereingebrochen, und das Öllämpchen,
das von der Holzdecke herunterhing, fauchte. Arbeiter kamen,
die in einem nahen Steinbruche beschäftigt waren und ein paar
hundert Schritte unterhalb des Wirtshauses ihre Holzhütten
aufgeschlagen hatten. Geronimo setzte sich zu ihnen; Carlo
blieb allein an seinem Tische. Es war ihm, als dauerte seine
Einsamkeit schon sehr lange. Er hörte, wie Geronimo drüben
laut, beinahe schreiend, von seiner Kindheit erzählte: daß er
sich noch ganz gut an allerlei erinnerte, was er mit seinen
Augen gesehen, Personen und Dinge: an den Vater, wie er auf
dem Felde arbeitete, an den kleinen Garten mit der Esche an
der Mauer, an das niedrige Häuschen, das ihnen gehörte, an
die zwei kleinen Töchter des Schusters, an den Weinberg hinter
der Kirche, ja an sein eigenes Kindergesicht, wie es ihm aus
dem Spiegel entgegengeblickt hatte. Wie oft hatte Carlo das
alles gehört. Heute ertrug er es nicht. Es klang anders als sonst:
jedes Wort, das Geronimo sprach, bekam einen neuen Sinn
und schien sich gegen ihn zu richten. Er schlich hinaus und
ging wieder auf die Landstraße, die nun ganz im Dunkel lag.
Der Regen hatte aufgehört, die Luft war sehr kalt, und der
Gedanke erschien Carlo beinahe verlockend, weiterzugehen,
immer weiter, tief in die Finsternis hinein, sich am Ende irgend-
wohin in den Straßengraben zu legen, einzuschlafen, nicht
mehr zu erwachen.—Plötzlich hörte er das Rollen eines Wagens
und erblickte den Lichtschimmer von zwei Laternen, die immer
näher kamen. In dem Wagen, der vorüberfuhr, saßen zwei
Herren. Einer von ihnen mit einem schmalen, bartlosen Ge-
sichte fuhr erschrocken zusammen, als Carlos Gestalt im Lichte
der Laternen aus dem Dunkel hervortauchte. Carlo, der stehengeblieben war, lüftete den Hut. Der Wagen und die Lichter
verschwanden. Carlo stand wieder in tiefer Finsternis. Plötzlich schrak er zusammen. Das erstemal in seinem Leben machte
ihm das Dunkel Angst. Es war ihm, als könnte er es keine
Minute länger ertragen. In einer sonderbaren Art vermengten
sich in seinem dumpfen Sinnen die Schauer, die er für sich
selbst empfand, mit einem quälenden Mitleid für den blinden
Bruder und jagten ihn nach Hause.

the same road to the south. The brothers had to go down into the courtyard four more times. When they went up for the last time twilight had fallen and the little oil lamp that hung down from the wooden ceiling was sputtering. In came some laborers who worked in a nearby stone quarry and had put up their wooden huts a few hundred feet below the inn. Geronimo sat down beside them; Carlo remained at his table alone. He felt as if his loneliness had already lasted a long time. He heard Geronimo over there telling about his childhood, talking loudly, almost shouting: that he still remembered everything quite well; persons and things that he had seen with his eyes: his father working in the field, the little garden with the ash tree beside the wall, the low little house that belonged to them, the shoemaker's two little daughters, the vineyard behind the church, in fact, even his own child's face looking back at him from the mirror. How often Carlo had heard all this. Today he could not bear it. It sounded different than usual: every word that Geronimo spoke acquired a new sense and seemed to turn against him. He stole out and returned to the highway, which was now quite dark. The rain had stopped, the air was very cold, and the idea of going on appeared almost enticing to Carlo—to go on and on, deep into the darkness, and in the end to lie down somewhere in a ditch, fall asleep, not to awake again. Suddenly he heard the rumbling of a carriage and caught sight of the gleam of light from two lamps that came nearer and nearer. In the carriage that rode by were two gentlemen. One of them, with a narrow, beardless face, started back in fright as Carlo's face emerged out of the darkness in the light of the lamps. Carlo, who had stopped, raised his hat. The carriage and lights vanished. Carlo stood in deep darkness again. Suddenly he started. For the first time in his life he was afraid of the dark. He felt as if he couldn't bear it one minute longer. In his dull brooding the horror he felt with himself mingled strangely with a tormented sympathy for his blind brother and drove him home.

Als er in die Wirtsstube trat, sah er die beiden Reisenden, die vorher an ihm vorbeigefahren waren, bei einer Flasche Rotwein an einem Tische sitzen und sehr angelegentlich miteinander reden. Sie blickten kaum auf, als er eintrat.

An dem anderen Tische saß Geronimo wie früher unter den Arbeitern.

„Wo steckst du denn, Carlo?" sagte ihm der Wirt schon an der Tür. „Warum läßt du deinen Bruder allein?"

„Was gibt's denn?" fragte Carlo erschrocken.

„Geronimo traktiert die Leute. Mir kann's ja egal sein, aber ihr solltet doch denken, daß bald wieder schlechtere Zeiten kommen."

Carlo trat rasch zu dem Bruder und faßte ihn am Arme. „Komm!" sagte er.

„Was willst du?" schrie Geronimo.

„Komm zu Bett", sagte Carlo.

„Laß mich, laß mich! Ich verdiene das Geld, ich kann mit meinem Gelde tun, was ich will—eh!—alles kannst du ja doch nicht einstecken! Ihr meint wohl, er gibt mir alles! O nein! Ich bin ja ein blinder Mann! Aber es gibt Leute—es gibt gute Leute, die sagen mir: ‚Ich habe deinem Bruder zwanzig Franken gegeben!'"

Die Arbeiter lachten auf.

„Es ist genug", sagte Carlo, „komm!" Und er zog den Bruder mit sich, schleppte ihn beinahe die Treppe hinauf bis in den kahlen Bodenraum, wo sie ihr Lager hatten. Auf dem ganzen Wege schrie Geronimo: „Ja, nun ist es an den Tag gekommen, ja, nun weiß ich's! Ah, wartet nur! Wo ist sie? Wo ist Maria? Oder legst du's ihr in die Sparkassa?[16]—Eh, ich singe für dich, ich spiele Gitarre, von mir lebst du—und du bist ein Dieb!" Er fiel auf den Strohsack hin.

Vom Gang her schimmerte ein schwaches Licht herein; drüben stand die Tür zu dem einzigen Fremdenzimmer des Wirtshauses offen, und Maria richtete die Betten für die Nachtruhe her. Carlo stand vor seinem Bruder und sah ihn daliegen mit dem gedunsenen Gesicht, mit den bläulichen Lippen, das feuchte Haar an der Stirne klebend, um viele Jahre älter aussehend, als er war. Und langsam begann er zu verste-

When he entered the taproom he saw the two tourists who had driven past him before, sitting at a table over a bottle of red wine and talking with each other very earnestly. They scarcely looked up when he entered.

At the other table Geronimo sat among the workers as before.

"Where have you been, Carlo?" the landlord said to him when he was still at the door. "Why do you leave your brother alone?"

"Why, what's wrong?" asked Carlo in fright.

"Geronimo is treating people. It makes no difference to me, of course, but you should consider that bad times will soon be coming again."

Carlo quickly stepped up to his brother and grasped his arm. "Come," he said.

"What do you want?" Geronimo shrieked.

"Come to bed," said Carlo.

"Leave me, leave me! *I* earn the money, I can do what I want with my money—hey—you certainly can't pocket it all. I suppose you think he gives it all to me. Oh no. I'm only a blind man. But there are people—there are good people who tell me: 'I gave your brother twenty francs.'"

The laborers laughed loudly.

"It's enough," said Carlo, "come." And he drew his brother to him, almost dragged him up the steps to the bleak attic room where they had their bed. All the way up Geronimo shrieked: "Yes, now it's come to light, yes, now I know it! Oh, just wait. Where is she? Where's Maria? Or are you putting it in her bank account?—Hey, I sing for you, I play the guitar, you live on me—and you're a thief!" He fell down on his straw sack.

From the hall a weak light shone in; over there the door to the only guest room in the inn stood open, and Maria was preparing the beds for the night. Carlo stood before his brother and saw him lying there with his bloated face, his bluish lips, his damp hair clinging to his forehead, looking many years older than he was. And he slowly began to understand. The blind man's distrust could not date from today; it must have

hen. Nicht von heute konnte das Mißtrauen des Blinden sein,
längst mußte es in ihm geschlummert haben, und nur der
Anlaß, vielleicht der Mut hatte ihm gefehlt, es auszusprechen.
Und alles, was Carlo für ihn getan, war vergeblich gewesen;
vergeblich die Reue, vergeblich das Opfer seines ganzen Lebens. Was sollte er nun tun?—Sollte er noch weiterhin Tag für
Tag, wer weiß wie lange noch, ihn durch die ewige Nacht
führen, ihn betreuen, für ihn betteln und keinen anderen Lohn
dafür haben als Mißtrauen und Schimpf? Wenn ihn der Bruder
für einen Dieb hielt, so konnte ihm ja jeder Fremde dasselbe
oder Besseres leisten als er. Wahrhaftig, ihn allein lassen, sich
für immer von ihm trennen, das wäre das klügste. Dann mußte
Geronimo wohl sein Unrecht einsehen, denn dann erst würde
er erfahren, was es heißt, betrogen und bestohlen werden, einsam und elend sein. Und er selbst, was sollte er beginnen? Nun,
er war ja noch nicht alt; wenn er für sich allein war, konnte er
noch mancherlei anfangen. Als Knecht zum mindesten fand
er überall sein Unterkommen. Aber während diese Gedanken
durch seinen Kopf zogen, blieben seine Augen immer auf den
Bruder geheftet. Und er sah ihn plötzlich vor sich, allein am
Rande einer sonnbeglänzten Straße auf einem Stein sitzen, mit
den weit offenen, weißen Augen zum Himmel starrend, der
ihn nicht blenden konnte, und mit den Händen in die Nacht
greifend, die immer um ihn war. Und er fühlte, so wie der
Blinde niemand anderen auf der Welt hatte als ihn, so hatte
auch er niemand anderen als diesen Bruder. Er verstand, daß
die Liebe zu diesem Bruder der ganze Inhalt seines Lebens
war, und wußte zum ersten Male mit völliger Deutlichkeit: nur
der Glaube, daß der Blinde diese Liebe erwiderte und ihm
verziehen, hatte ihn alles Elend so geduldig tragen lassen. Er
konnte auf diese Hoffnung nicht mit einem Male verzichten.
Er fühlte, daß er den Bruder gerade so notwendig brauchte
als der Bruder ihn. Er konnte nicht, er wollte ihn nicht verlassen. Er mußte entweder das Mißtrauen erdulden oder ein
Mittel finden, um den Blinden von der Grundlosigkeit seines
Verdachtes zu überzeugen ... Ja, wenn er sich irgendwie das
Goldstück verschaffen könnte! Wenn er dem Blinden morgen
früh sagen könnte: „Ich habe es nur aufbewahrt, damit du's

slumbered in him for a long time, and he had only lacked the occasion, perhaps the courage, to express it. And everything that Carlo had done for him had been in vain; in vain the remorse, in vain the sacrifice of his whole life. What was he to do now? Should he continue to lead him through the eternal night, on and on, day after day, who knows for how long, caring for him, begging for him, and having no other reward for it except distrust and abuse? If his brother took him for a thief, then any stranger could serve him as well or even better. Truly, to leave him alone, to separate from him forever—that would be the wisest thing. Then Geronimo would indeed have to realize his injustice, for he would learn only then what it means to be cheated and robbed, to be lonely and wretched. And he himself—what should he do? Well, he really wasn't old yet; if he was by himself, he could still do many sorts of things. As a hired hand, at least, he would get his keep anywhere. But while these thoughts went through his head, his eyes were fixed steadily on his brother. And suddenly he saw him before him sitting alone on a stone at the side of a road bathed in sunlight, staring with his wide open, white eyes at the sky that could not blind him, stretching his hands out into the night that was always about him. And he felt that, just as the blind man had no one else in the world except him, so he too had no one else except this brother. He understood that the love for this brother was the whole content of his life and he knew for the first time with complete clarity: only the belief that the blind man returned this love and had forgiven him had permitted him to bear all the misery so patiently. He could not renounce this hope all at once. He felt that he needed his brother just as much as his brother him. He could not, he did not want to abandon him. He either had to endure his distrust or find a means of convincing the blind man of the baseless nature of his suspicion . . . Yes, if he could somewhere procure the gold coin! If he could tell the blind man tomorrow morning: "I only kept it so that you wouldn't spend it on drink with the laborers—so that people wouldn't steal it from you" . . . or anything else at all . . .

nicht mit den Arbeitern vertrinkst, damit es dir die Leute nicht
stehlen" . . . oder sonst irgend etwas . . .

Schritte näherten sich auf der Holztreppe: die Reisenden gingen zur Ruhe. Plötzlich durchzuckte seinen Kopf der Einfall,
drüben anzuklopfen, den Fremden wahrheitsgetreu den heutigen Vorfall zu erzählen und sie um die zwanzig Franken zu
bitten. Aber er wußte auch gleich: das war vollkommen aus-
sichtslos! Sie würden ihm die ganze Geschichte nicht einmal
glauben. Und er erinnerte sich jetzt, wie erschrocken der eine
blasse zusammengefahren war, als er, Carlo, plötzlich im Dunkel vor dem Wagen aufgetaucht war.

Er streckte sich auf den Strohsack hin. Es war ganz finster
im Zimmer. Jetzt hörte er, wie die Arbeiter laut redend und
mit schweren Schritten über die Holzstufen hinabgingen. Bald
darauf wurden beide Tore geschlossen. Der Knecht ging noch
einmal die Treppe auf und ab, dann war es ganz still. Carlo
hörte nur mehr das Schnarchen Geronimos. Bald verwirrten
sich seine Gedanken in beginnenden Träumen. Als er erwachte, war noch tiefe Dunkelheit um ihn. Er sah nach der
Stelle, wo das Fenster war; wenn er die Augen anstrengte,
gewahrte er dort mitten in dem undurchdringlichen Schwarz
ein tiefgraues Viereck. Geronimo schlief noch immer den
schweren Schlaf des Betrunkenen. Und Carlo dachte an den
Tag, der morgen war; und ihn schauderte. Er dachte an die
Nacht nach diesem Tage, an den Tag nach dieser Nacht, an
die Zukunft, die vor ihm lag, und Grauen erfüllte ihn vor der
Einsamkeit, die ihm bevorstand. Warum war er abends nicht
mutiger gewesen? Warum war er nicht zu den Fremden gegangen und hatte sie um die zwanzig Franken gebeten? Vielleicht hätten sie doch Erbarmen mit ihm gehabt. Und doch—
vielleicht war es gut, daß er sie nicht gebeten hatte. Ja, warum
war es gut? . . . Er setzte sich jäh auf und fühlte sein Herz
klopfen. Er wußte, warum es gut war: Wenn sie ihn abgewiesen
hätten, so wäre er ihnen jedenfalls verdächtig geblieben—so
aber . . . Er starrte auf den grauen Fleck, der matt zu leuchten
begann . . . Das, was ihm gegen seinen eigenen Willen durch
den Kopf gefahren, war ja unmöglich, vollkommen unmöglich!
. . . Die Tür drüben war versperrt—und überdies: sie konnten

Steps were approaching on the wooden staircase; the tourists were going to bed. Suddenly the idea flashed through his mind: to knock at their door, tell the strangers the true story of today's occurrences, and ask them for the twenty francs. But he knew at once: that was completely hopeless! They wouldn't even believe the whole story. And he now remembered how the pale man had shrunk away in fright when he, Carlo, had suddenly appeared in the darkness in front of the carriage.

He stretched out on the straw sack. It was quite dark in the room. Now he heard the laborers going down the wooden steps with heavy tread, talking loudly. Soon after that both gates were locked. The servant went up and down the stairs once more, then all was quite still. Carlo now heard only Geronimo's snoring. Soon his thoughts became confused in incipient dreams. When he awoke, there was still deep darkness about him. He looked at the spot where the window was; when he strained his eyes, he perceived there, in the center of the impenetrable black, a deep gray rectangle. Geronimo was still sleeping the heavy sleep of the intoxicated. And Carlo thought of the day that was tomorrow; and he shuddered. He thought of the night after this day, of the day after this night, of the future that lay before him, and horror filled him at the loneliness that faced him. Why had he not been more courageous in the evening? Why had he not gone to the strangers and asked them for the twenty francs? Perhaps they might have had pity on him after all. And yet—perhaps it was good that he had not asked them. Yes, why was it good? . . . He sat up suddenly and he felt his heart beating. He knew why it was good: if they refused him, he would have remained an object of suspicion to them all the same—but now . . . He stared at the gray spot, which began to shine faintly . . . What had gone through his head against his own will, was impossible of course, completely impossible! . . . The door over there was locked— and besides: they could wake up . . . Yes, there—the gray, shining, spot in the middle of the darkness was the new day———

aufwachen . . . Ja, dort—der graue leuchtende Fleck mitten im
Dunkel war der neue Tag— — —

Carlo stand auf, als zöge es ihn dorthin, und berührte mit
der Stirn die kalte Scheibe. Warum war er denn aufgestanden?
Um zu überlegen? . . . Um es zu versuchen? . . . Was denn? . . .
Es war ja unmöglich—und überdies war es ein Verbrechen.
Ein Verbrechen? Was bedeuten zwanzig Franken für solche
Leute, die zum Vergnügen tausend Meilen weit reisen? Sie
würden ja gar nicht merken, daß sie ihnen fehlten . . . Er ging
zur Türe und öffnete sie leise. Gegenüber war die andere, mit
zwei Schritten zu erreichen, geschlossen. An einem Nagel im
Pfosten hingen Kleidungsstücke. Carlo fuhr mit der Hand über
sie . . . Ja, wenn die Leute ihre Börsen in der Tasche ließen,
dann wäre das Leben sehr einfach, dann brauchte bald niemand mehr betteln zu gehen . . . Aber die Taschen waren leer.
Nun, was blieb übrig? Wieder zurück ins Zimmer, auf den
Strohsack. Es gab vielleicht doch eine bessere Art, sich zwanzig
Franken zu verschaffen—eine weniger gefährliche und recht-
lichere. Wenn er wirklich jedesmal einige Centesimi von den
Almosen zurückbehielte, bis er zwanzig Franken zusammen-
gespart, und dann das Goldstück kaufte . . . Aber wie lang
konnte das dauern—Monate, vielleicht ein Jahr. Ah, wenn er
nur Mut hätte! Noch immer stand er auf dem Gang. Er blickte
zur Tür hinüber . . . Was war das für ein Streif, der senkrecht
von oben auf den Fußboden fiel? War es möglich? Die Tür war
nur angelehnt, nicht versperrt? . . . Warum staunte er denn
darüber? Seit Monaten schon schloß die Tür nicht. Wozu auch?
Er erinnerte sich: nur dreimal hatten hier in diesem Sommer
Leute geschlafen, zweimal Handwerksburschen und einmal
ein Tourist, der sich den Fuß verletzt hatte. Die Tür schließt
nicht—er braucht jetzt nur Mut—ja, und Glück! Mut? Das
Schlimmste, was ihm geschehen kann, ist, daß die beiden aufwachen, und da kann er noch immer eine Ausrede finden. Er
lugt durch den Spalt ins Zimmer. Es ist noch so dunkel, daß
er eben nur die Umrisse von zwei auf den Betten lagernden
Gestalten gewahren kann. Er horcht auf: sie atmen ruhig und
gleichmäßig. Carlo öffnet die Tür leicht und tritt mit seinen
nackten Füßen völlig geräuschlos ins Zimmer. Die beiden Betten stehen der Länge nach an der gleichen Wand dem Fenster

Carlo stood up, as if he were drawn to that place, and touched the cold window pane with his forehead. Why had he really got up? To think it over? . . . To try it? . . . Try what? . . . It was impossible, of course—and besides it was a crime. A crime? What do twenty francs mean to such people who travel a thousand miles for their pleasure? They wouldn't even notice that it was missing . . . He went to the door and opened it softly. Facing him was the other door, to be reached by taking two steps, locked. On a nail in the jamb, articles of clothing were hanging. Carlo passed his hand over them . . . Yes, if people left their wallets in their pockets, life would be very simple; then, soon, no one would have to go begging any more . . . But the pockets were empty. Well, what was there left to do? Back to his room again, on the straw sack. Perhaps there really was a better way of procuring twenty francs—less dangerous and more honest. If he really held back a few centesimi from the alms every time, until he had saved up twenty francs, and then bought the gold coin . . . But how long would that take—months, perhaps a year. Oh, if only he had courage! He was still standing in the hall. He looked over toward the door . . . What sort of line was that which fell vertically to the floor from above? Was it possible? The door was ajar, not locked? . . . but why was he astonished at that? The door had not been locked for months. And why should it? He remembered: this summer people had slept here only three times—artisans twice, and once a tourist who had hurt his foot. The door doesn't lock now he only needs courage—yes, and luck. Courage? The worst that can happen to him is that the two men will wake up, and then he can always find an excuse. He peers through the crack into the room. It is still so dark that he can just perceive the mere outlines of two figures lying on the beds. He listens: they are breathing calmly and evenly. Carlo opens the door lightly and, without a sound, walks into the room in his bare feet. The two beds stand lengthwise against the same wall opposite the window. In the center of the room is a table; Carlo steals up to it. He runs his hand over its surface and feels a bunch of keys, a pen knife, a little book—nothing more . . . Well, of course! . . . That he could even imagine they would lay their

gegenüber. In der Mitte des Zimmers ist ein Tisch; Carlo
schleicht bis hin. Er fährt mit der Hand über die Fläche und
fühlt einen Schlüsselbund, ein Federmesser, ein kleines Buch—
weiter nichts ... Nun natürlich! ... Daß er nur daran denken
konnte, sie würden ihr Geld auf den Tisch legen! Ah, nun
kann er gleich wieder fort! ... Und doch, vielleicht braucht es
nur einen guten Griff, und es ist geglückt ... Und er nähert
sich dem Bett neben der Tür; hier auf dem Sessel liegt etwas—er
fühlt danach—es ist ein Revolver ... Carlo zuckt zusammen
... Ob er ihn nicht lieber gleich behalten sollte? Denn warum
hat dieser Mensch den Revolver bereitliegen? Wenn er erwacht
und ihn bemerkt ... Doch nein, er würde ja sagen: Es ist drei
Uhr, gnädiger Herr, aufstehn! ... Und er läßt den Revolver
liegen.

Und er schleicht tiefer ins Zimmer. Hier auf dem anderen
Sessel unter den Wäschestücken ... Himmel! das ist sie ... das
ist eine Börse—er hält sie in der Hand! ... In diesem Moment
hört er ein leises Krachen. Mit einer raschen Bewegung streckt
er sich der Länge nach zu Füßen des Bettes hin ... Noch einmal dieses Krachen—ein schweres Aufatmen—ein Räuspern—
dann wieder Stille, tiefe Stille. Carlo bleibt auf dem Boden
liegen, die Börse in der Hand, und wartet. Es rührt sich nichts
mehr. Schon fällt der Dämmer blaß ins Zimmer herein. Carlo
wagt nicht aufzustehen, sondern kriecht auf dem Boden vorwärts bis zur Tür, die weit genug offen steht, um ihn durch-
zulassen, kriecht weiter bis auf den Gang hinaus, und hier erst
erhebt er sich langsam, mit einem tiefen Atemzug. Er öffnet die
Börse; sie ist dreifach geteilt: links und rechts nur kleine Sil-
berstücke. Nun öffnet Carlo den mittleren Teil, der durch einen
Schieber nochmals verschlossen ist, und fühlt drei Zwanzig-
frankenstücke. Einen Augenblick denkt er daran, zwei davon
zu nehmen, aber rasch weist er diese Versuchung von sich,
nimmt nur ein Goldstück heraus und schließt die Börse zu.
Dann kniet er nieder, blickt durch die Spalte in die Kammer,
in der es wieder völlig still ist, und dann gibt er der Börse einen
Stoß, so daß sie bis unter das zweite Bett gleitet. Wenn der
Fremde aufwacht, wird er glauben müssen, daß sie vom Sessel
heruntergefallen ist. Carlo erhebt sich langsam. Da knarrt der
Boden leise, und im gleichen Augenblick hört er eine Stimme

money on the table! Ah, now he can get out at once! . . . And
yet, perhaps all that is needed is one good snatch and it's done
. . . And he approaches the bed near the door; here on the easy
chair something is lying—he feels for it—it's a revolver . . .
Carlo starts . . . Wouldn't it be better to take possession of it
right now? Why does this man have a revolver lying in readiness? If he wakes up and notices him . . . But no, he would just
say: It's three o'clock, sir, time to get up . . . And he lets the
revolver lie there.

And he steals deeper into the room. Here on the other easy
chair, among the linen . . . Heavens! that's it . . . that's a wallet—
he holds it in his hand . . . At this moment he hears a slight creaking. With a swift movement he stretches out full length at the
foot of the bed . . . Again this creaking—heavy breathing—
clearing of the throat—then silence again, deep silence. Carlo
remains lying on the floor, the wallet in his hand, waiting.
Nothing stirs any more. The dawn is already casting its pale
light into the room. Carlo does not dare to stand up but crawls
forward on the floor to the door, which is open far enough to
let him through; he crawls on, out into the hall, and only here
does he slowly get to his feet, taking a deep breath. He opens
the wallet; it is divided into three compartments: at the left and
right there are only small silver coins. Now Carlo opens the
middle part, which is also closed by a clasp, and feels three
twenty-franc pieces. For a moment he thinks of taking two of
them, but he quickly rejects this temptation, takes out only one
gold piece and closes the wallet. Then he kneels down, looks
through the crack into the room in which there is complete
silence again, and then he shoves the wallet forward so that it
glides under the second bed. When the stranger awakes he will
have to believe that it fell down from the chair. Carlo rises
slowly. Then the floor creaks slightly and at the same moment
he hears a voice from inside: "What is it? What's up?" Carlo
takes two swift steps backward, holding his breath, and slips

von drinnen: „Was ist's? Was gibt's denn?" Carlo macht rasch zwei Schritte rückwärts, mit verhaltenem Atem, und gleitet in seine eigene Kammer. Er ist in Sicherheit und lauscht . . . Noch einmal kracht drüben das Bett, und dann ist alles still. Zwischen seinen Fingern hält er das Goldstück. Es ist gelungen— gelungen! Er hat die zwanzig Franken, und er kann seinem Bruder sagen: ‚Siehst du nun, daß ich kein Dieb bin!' Und sie werden sich noch heute auf die Wanderschaft machen—gegen den Süden zu, nach Bormio, dann weiter durchs Veltlin . . . dann nach Tirano . . . nach Edole . . . nach Breno . . . an den See von Iseo wie voriges Jahr . . . Das wird durchaus nicht verdächtig sein, denn schon vorgestern hat er selbst zum Wirt gesagt: „In ein paar Tagen gehen wir hinunter."

Immer lichter wird es, das ganze Zimmer liegt in grauem Dämmer da. Ah, wenn Geronimo nur bald aufwachte! Es wandert sich[17] so gut in der Frühe! Noch vor Sonnenaufgang werden sie fortgehen. Einen guten Morgen dem Wirt, dem Knecht und Maria auch, und dann fort, fort . . . Und erst wenn sie zwei Stunden weit sind, schon nahe dem Tale, wird er es Geronimo sagen.

Geronimo reckt und dehnt sich. Carlo ruft ihn an: „Geronimo!"

„Nun, was gibt's?" Und er stützt sich mit beiden Händen und setzt sich auf.

„Geronimo, wir wollen aufstehen."

„Warum?" Und er richtet die toten Augen auf den Bruder. Carlo weiß, daß Geronimo sich jetzt des gestrigen Vorfalles besinnt, aber er weiß auch, daß der[18] keine Silbe darüber reden wird, ehe er wieder betrunken ist.

„Es ist kalt, Geronimo, wir wollen fort. Es wird heuer[19] nicht mehr besser; ich denke, wir gehen. Zu Mittag können wir in Boladore sein."

Geronimo erhob sich. Die Geräusche des erwachenden Hauses wurden vernehmbar. Unten im Hof sprach der Wirt mit dem Knecht. Carlo stand auf und begab sich hinunter. Er war immer früh wach und ging oft schon in der Dämmerung auf die Straße hinaus. Er trat zum Wirt hin und sagte: „Wir wollen Abschied nehmen."

„Ah, geht ihr schon heut?" fragte der Wirt.

into his own room. He is safe and listens . . . Once more the
bed over there creaks and then all is silent. Between his fingers
he holds the gold piece. He has succeeded—succeeded. He has
the twenty francs and he can say to his brother: "Do you see
now that I'm not a thief!" And they will set out on the road
this very day—toward the south, to Bormio, then through the
Valtellina . . . then to Tirano . . . . to Edolo . . . to Breno . . . to
Lake Iseo like last year . . . This will be in no way suspicious,
for the day before yesterday he himself had told the landlord:
"In a few days we're going down."

It gets brighter all the time; the whole room lies before him
in a gray twilight. Ah, if only Geronimo would wake up soon.
It's so nice to hike in the early morning. They will set out even
before sunrise. A "good morning" to the landlord, to the servant
and Maria too, and then off, off . . . And only when they are
two hours' distant, near the valley, will he tell Geronimo.

Geronimo stirs and stretches. Carlo calls to him: "Geronimo."

"Well, what's up?" And he supports himself with both his
hands and sits up.
"Geronimo, we'll get up."
"Why?" And he fixes his dead eyes on his brother. Carlo
knows that Geronimo now remembers the event of yesterday,
but he also knows that he will not utter a syllable about it until
he is drunk again.
"It's cold, Geronimo, let's leave. It won't improve this year
any more; I think we'll go. By noon we can be in Boladore."

Geronimo got up. The sounds of the waking house became
audible. Down in the courtyard the landlord was talking to the
servant. Carlo got up and went down. He was always up early
and often went out on the highway when it was still twilight.
He went over to the landlord and said: "We want to take leave."

"Ah, are you leaving today?" asked the landlord.

„Ja. Es friert schon zu arg, wenn man jetzt im Hof steht, und der Wind zieht durch."

„Nun, grüß' mir den Baldetti, wenn du nach Bormio hinunterkommst, und er soll nicht vergessen, mir das Öl zu schicken."

„Ja, ich will ihn grüßen. Im übrigen—das Nachtlager von heut." Er griff in den Sack.

„Laß sein, Carlo", sagte der Wirt. „Die zwanzig Centesimi schenk' ich deinem Bruder; ich hab' ihm ja auch zugehört. Guten Morgen."

„Dank", sagte Carlo. „Im übrigen, so eilig haben wir's nicht. Wir sehen dich noch, wenn du von den Hütten zurückkommst; Bormio bleibt am selben Fleck stehen, nicht wahr?" Er lachte und ging die Holzstufen hinauf.

Geronimo stand mitten im Zimmer und sagte: „Nun, ich bin bereit zu gehen."

„Gleich", sagte Carlo.

Aus einer alten Kommode, die in einem Winkel des Raumes stand, nahm er ihre wenigen Habseligkeiten und packte sie in ein Bündel. Dann sagte er: „Ein schöner Tag, aber sehr kalt."

„Ich weiß", sagte Geronimo. Beide verließen die Kammer.

„Geh leise", sagte Carlo, „hier schlafen die zwei, die gestern abend gekommen sind." Behutsam schritten sie hinunter. „Der Wirt läßt dich grüßen", sagte Carlo; „er hat uns die zwanzig Centesimi für heut nacht geschenkt. Nun ist er bei den Hütten draußen und kommt erst in zwei Stunden wieder. Wir werden ihn ja im nächsten Jahre wiedersehen."

Geronimo antwortete nicht. Sie traten auf die Landstraße, die im Dämmerschein vor ihnen lag. Carlo ergriff den linken Arm seines Bruders, und beide schritten schweigend talabwärts. Schon nach kurzer Wanderung waren sie an der Stelle, wo die Straße in langgezogenen Kehren weiterzulaufen beginnt. Nebel stiegen nach aufwärts, ihnen entgegen, und über ihnen die Höhen schienen von den Wolken wie eingeschlungen. Und Carlo dachte: Nun will ich's ihm sagen.

Carlo sprach aber kein Wort, sondern nahm das Goldstück aus der Tasche und reichte es dem Bruder; dieser nahm es zwischen die Finger der rechten Hand, dann führte er es an die Wange und an die Stirn, endlich nickte er. „Ich hab's ja gewußt", sagte er.

"Yes. The cold is getting too bad now, when you stand in the yard and the wind blows through it."

"Well, my regards to Baldetti when you get down to Bormio, and tell him not to forget to send me the oil."

"Yes, I'll give him your regards. And—for last night's bed." He put his hand into his bag.

"Never mind, Carlo," said the landlord. "I'll present the twenty centesimi to your brother; after all, I've listened to him too. Good morning."

"Thanks," said Carlo. "For that matter, we're not in that much of a hurry. We'll see you again when you come back from the huts; Bormio will still be in the same place, won't it?" He laughed and went up the wooden steps.

Geronimo stood in the middle of the room and said: "Well, I'm ready to go."

"Right away," said Carlo.

Out of an old chest that stood in a corner of the room he took their few belongings and packed them into a bundle. Then he said: "A beautiful day, but very cold."

"I know," said Geronimo. They both left the bedroom.

"Go softly," said Carlo, "the two men who came last night are sleeping here." They went down cautiously. "The landlord sends you his regards," said Carlo; "he didn't charge us the twenty centesimi for tonight. Now he's out by the huts and won't be back for two hours. But we'll see him again next year."

Geronimo did not reply. They went out on the highway that lay in the twilight before them. Carlo took his brother's left arm and they both went down toward the valley silently. After a short stroll they were already at the spot where the road begins to run on in sweeping turns. Mists rose up toward them, and the heights above them seemed as though swallowed up by the clouds. And Carlo thought: now I'll tell him.

But Carlo did not say a word; he took the gold coin out of his pocket and handed it to his brother; the latter took it between his fingers of his right hand, then he touched it to his cheek and forehead, finally he nodded. "I knew it," he said.

„Nun ja",[20] erwiderte Carlo und sah Geronimo befremdet an.

„Auch wenn der Fremde mir nichts gesagt hätte, ich hätte
es doch gewußt."

„Nun ja", sagte Carlo ratlos. „Aber du verstehst doch, warum
ich da oben vor den anderen—habe gefürchtet, daß du das
Ganze auf einmal—Und sieh, Geronimo, es wäre doch an der
Zeit, hab' ich mir gedacht, daß du dir einen neuen Rock kaufst
und ein Hemd und Schuhe auch, glaube ich; darum habe
ich . . ."

Der Blinde schüttelte heftig den Kopf. „Wozu?" Und er strich
mit der einen Hand über seinen Rock. „Gut genug, warm
genug; jetzt kommen wir nach dem Süden."

Carlo begriff nicht, daß Geronimo sich gar̄nicht zu freuen
schien, daß er sich nicht entschuldigte. Und er redete weiter:
„Geronimo, war es denn nicht recht von mir? Warum freust
du dich denn nicht? Nun haben wir es doch, nicht wahr? Nun
haben wir es ganz. Wenn ich dir's oben gesagt hätte, wer weiß
. . . Oh, es ist gut, daß ich dir's nicht gesagt habe—gewiß!"

Da schrie Geronimo: „Hör' auf zu lügen, Carlo, ich habe
genug davon!"

Carlo blieb stehen und ließ den Arm des Bruders los. „Ich
lüge nicht."

„Ich weiß doch, daß du lügst! . . . Immer lügst du! . . . Schon
hundertmal hast du gelogen! . . . Auch das hast du für dich
behalten wollen, aber Angst hast du bekommen, das ist es!"

Carlo senkte den Kopf und antwortete nichts. Er faßte wieder
den Arm des Blinden und ging mit ihm weiter. Es tat ihm weh,
daß Geronimo so sprach; aber er war eigentlich erstaunt, daß
er nicht trauriger war.

Die Nebel zerteilten sich. Nach langem Schweigen sprach
Geronimo: „Es wird warm." Er sagte es gleichgültig, selbst-
verständlich, wie er es schon hundertmal gesagt, und Carlo
fühlte in diesem Augenblick: für Geronimo hatte sich nichts
geändert. Für Geronimo war er immer ein Dieb gewesen.

„Hast du schon Hunger?" fragte er.

Geronimo nickte, zugleich nahm er ein Stück Käse und Brot
aus der Rocktasche und aß davon. Und sie gingen weiter.

"Is that so?" Carlo replied, and looked at Geronimo in surprise.

"Even if the stranger had told me nothing, I would have known it anyhow."

"Is that so?" said Carlo helplessly. "But you do understand why up there—before the others—I was afraid that you would spend all of it at once. And see, Geronimo, it is really time, I thought to myself, that you should buy yourself a new coat and a shirt and shoes too, I think; that's why I—"

The blind man shook his head vehemently. "What for?" And he ran his one hand over his coat. "Good enough, warm enough; now we'll get to the south."

Carlo did not understand why Geronimo did not seem to be glad at all, why he did not apologize. And he went on: "Geronimo, didn't I do right? Why aren't you glad? Now we have it, don't we? Now we have the whole of it. If I'd told you about it up there who knows . . . Oh, it's good that I didn't tell you—for sure!"

Then Geronimo shrieked: "Stop lying, Carlo, I have enough of that."

Carlo stopped and released his brother's arm. "I'm not lying."

"I know quite well that you're lying! . . . You're always lying! . . . You've lied a hundred times already! . . . You wanted to keep this one for yourself too, but you got scared, that's what it is."

Carlo lowered his head and did not reply. He took the blind man's arm again and went on with him. It hurt him that Geronimo talked this way; but he was really astonished at not being sadder.

The mists parted. After a long silence Geronimo spoke: "It's getting warm." He said it indifferently, casually, as he had said it a hundred times before, and Carlo felt at this moment: nothing had changed for Geronimo. For Geronimo, he had always been a thief.

"Are you hungry yet?" he asked.

Geronimo nodded; at the same time he took a piece of cheese and bread out of his jacket pocket and ate it. And they went on.

Die Post von Bormio begegnete ihnen; der Kutscher rief sie
an: „Schon hinunter?" Dann kamen noch andere Wagen, die
alle aufwärts fuhren.

„Luft aus dem Tal", sagte Geronimo, und im gleichen Augenblick, nach einer raschen Wendung, lag das Veltlin zu ihren
Füßen.

‚Wahrhaftig—nichts hat sich geändert,' dachte Carlo . . .
‚Nun hab' ich gar für ihn gestohlen—und auch das ist umsonst
gewesen.'

Die Nebel unter ihnen wurden immer dünner, der Glanz
der Sonne riß Löcher hinein. Und Carlo dachte: ‚Vielleicht war
es doch nicht klug, so rasch das Wirtshaus zu verlassen . . . Die
Börse liegt unter dem Bett, das ist jedenfalls verdächtig.' . . .
Aber wie gleichgültig war das alles! Was konnte ihm noch
Schlimmes geschehen? Sein Bruder, dem er das Licht der
Augen zerstört, glaubte sich von ihm bestohlen und glaubte es
schon jahrelang und wird es immer glauben—was konnte ihm
noch Schlimmes geschehen?

Da unter ihnen lag das große weiße Hotel wie in Morgenglanz
gebadet, und tiefer unten, wo das Tal sich zu weiten beginnt,
lang hingestreckt, das Dorf. Schweigend gingen die beiden weiter, und immer lag Carlos Hand auf dem Arm des Blinden.
Sie gingen an dem Park des Hotels vorüber, und Carlo sah auf
der Terrasse Gäste in lichten Sommergewändern sitzen und
frühstücken. „Wo willst du rasten?" fragte Carlo.

„Nun, im ‚Adler', wie immer."

Als sie bei dem kleinen Wirtshause am Ende des Dorfes ange-
langt waren, kehrten sie ein. Sie setzten sich in die Schenke
und ließen sich Wein geben.

„Was macht ihr so früh bei uns?" fragte der Wirt.

Carlo erschrak ein wenig bei dieser Frage. „Ist's denn so
früh? Der zehnte oder elfte September—nicht?"

„Im vergangenen Jahr war es gewiß viel später, als ihr herun-
terkamt."

„Es ist so kalt oben", sagte Carlo. „Heut nacht haben wir
gefroren. Ja richtig, ich soll dir bestellen, du möchtest nicht
vergessen, das Öl hinaufzuschicken."

Die Luft in der Schenke war dumpf und schwül. Eine sonder-
bare Unruhe befiel Carlo; er wollte gern wieder im Freien sein,

The stagecoach from Bormio met them; the coachman called to them: "Going down already?" Then other carriages came too, all going up.

"Air from the valley," said Geronimo, and at the same moment, after a sudden turn, the Valtellina lay at their feet.

"Truly—nothing has changed," Carlo thought . . . "Now I've even stolen for him—and this too has been for nothing."

The mists below them became thinner all the time; the light of the sun tore holes in them. And Carlo thought: "Perhaps it wasn't really wise to leave the inn so quickly . . . The wallet is lying under the bed . . . that is certainly suspicious." But how little all that mattered! What other evil could befall him? His brother, the light of whose eyes he had destroyed, thought himself robbed by him and had thought so for years and will always think so what other evil could befall him?

There below them the great white hotel lay as though bathed in morning splendor, and deeper below them, where the valley begins to broaden, the village stretched out in a long line. The two went on silently and all the time Carlo's hand lay on the blind man's arm. They went past the park of the hotel, and Carlo saw guests in light summer clothes sitting on the terrace and eating breakfast. "Where do you want to rest?" Carlo asked.

"Well, in the *Eagle,* as always."

When they reached the little inn at the end of the village, they went in. They sat down in the taproom and ordered wine.

"What are you doing here so early?" asked the landlord.

Carlo was a little frightened at this question. "But is it so early? The tenth or eleventh of September, isn't it?"

"Last year it was certainly much later when you came down."

"It's so cold up there," said Carlo. "Last night we froze. Oh yes, I'm to tell you you mustn't forget to send the oil up."

The air in the taproom was heavy and sultry. A strange uneasiness befell Carlo; he very much wanted to be in the open

auf der großen Straße, die nach Tirano, nach Edole, nach dem
See von Iseo, überallhin, in die Ferne führt! Plötzlich stand
er auf.

„Gehen wir schon?" fragte Geronimo.

„Wir wollen doch heut mittag in Boladore sein, im ‚Hirschen'
halten die Wagen Mittagsrast; es ist ein guter Ort."

Und sie gingen. Der Friseur Benozzi stand rauchend vor seinem Laden. „Guten Morgen", rief er. „Nun, wie sieht's da oben
aus? Heut nacht hat es wohl geschneit?"

„Ja, ja", sagte Carlo und beschleunigte seine Schritte.

Das Dorf lag hinter ihnen, weiß dehnte sich die Straße zwischen Wiesen und Weinbergen, den rauschenden Fluß entlang.
Der Himmel war blau und still. ‚Warum hab' ich's getan?' dachte
Carlo. Er blickte den Blinden von der Seite an. ‚Sieht sein
Gesicht denn anders aus als sonst? Immer hat er es geglaubt—
immer bin ich allein gewesen—und immer hat er mich gehaßt.'
Und ihm war, als schritte er unter einer schweren Last weiter,
die er doch niemals von den Schultern werfen dürfte, und als
könnte er die Nacht sehen, durch die Geronimo an seiner Seite
schritt, während die Sonne leuchtend auf allen Wegen lag.

Und sie gingen weiter, gingen, gingen stundenlang. Von Zeit
zu Zeit setzte sich Geronimo auf einen Meilenstein, oder sie
lehnten beide an einem Brückengeländer, um zu rasten. Wieder
kamen sie durch ein Dorf. Vor dem Wirtshause standen Wagen,
Reisende waren ausgestiegen und gingen hin und her; aber
die beiden Bettler blieben nicht. Wieder hinaus auf die offene
Straße. Die Sonne stieg immer höher; Mittag mußte nahe sein.
Es war ein Tag wie tausend andere.

„Der Turm von Boladore", sagte Geronimo. Carlo blickte
auf. Er wunderte sich, wie genau Geronimo die Entfernungen
berechnen konnte: wirklich war der Turm von Boladore am
Horizont erschienen. Noch von ziemlich weither kam ihnen
jemand entgegen. Es schien Carlo, als sei[21] er am Wege gesessen
und plötzlich aufgestanden. Die Gestalt kam näher. Jetzt sah
Carlo, daß es ein Gendarm war, wie er ihnen so oft auf der
Landstraße begegnete. Trotzdem schrak Carlo leicht zusammen. Aber als der Mann näher kam, erkannte er ihn und war
beruhigt. Es war Pietro Tenelli; erst im Mai waren die beiden
Bettler im Wirtshaus des Raggazzi in Morignone mit ihm zusam-

air again, on the great highway that leads to Tirano, to Edolo, to Lake Iseo, everywhere, far away. Suddenly he stood up.

"Are we going already?" asked Geronimo.

"Don't we want to be in Boladore at noon today? The carriages stop at the *Stag* for their midday rest; it's a good place."

And they went. The barber Benozzi stood in front of his shop smoking. "Good morning," he cried. "Well, how does it look up there? I suppose it snowed last night?"

"Yes, yes," said Carlo, hastening his steps.

The village lay behind them, the road stretched white between meadows and vineyards, along the murmuring river. The sky was blue and still. "Why did I do it?" Carlo thought. He gave the blind man a sidelong glance. "Does his face look any different than usual? He always thought so—I've always been alone—and he has always hated me." And he felt as if he were walking on under a heavy burden that he would never be permitted to throw off his shoulders and as if he could see the night through which Geronimo walked at his side, while the sun lay shining on all the roads.

And they went on, walked, walked for hours. From time to time Geronimo sat down on a milestone, or they both leaned against the railing of a bridge to rest. Again they walked through a village. In front of the inn stood carriages; tourists had gotten out and were walking back and forth; but the two beggars did not stay. Again they went out onto the open highway. The sun rose higher and higher; midday must be near. It was a day like a thousand others.

"The tower of Boladore," said Geronimo. Carlo looked up. He was astonished how exactly Geronimo could calculate distances: the tower of Boladore had really appeared on the horizon. Someone was coming toward them from a fairly long distance away. It seemed to Carlo that the man had been sitting by the road and had suddenly stood up. The figure came closer. Now Carlo saw that it was a gendarme, the kind he met so often on the highway. Still, Carlo felt a slight tremor. But when the man came closer he recognized him and was calmed. It was Pietro Tenelli; only last May the two beggars had sat beside him in Ragazzi's inn in Morignone, and he had told them a

men gesessen, und er hatte ihnen eine schauerliche Geschichte erzählt, wie er von einem Strolch einmal beinahe erdolcht worden war.

„Es ist einer[22] stehengeblieben", sagte Geronimo.

„Tenelli, der Gendarm", sagte Carlo.

Nun waren sie an ihn herangekommen.

„Guten Morgen, Herr Tenelli", sagte Carlo und blieb vor ihm stehen.

„Es ist nun einmal so",[23] sagte der Gendarm, „ich muß euch vorläufig beide auf den Posten nach Boladore führen."

„Eh!" rief der Blinde.

Carlo wurde blaß. ‚Wie ist das nur möglich?' dachte er. ‚Aber es kann sich nicht darauf beziehen. Man kann es ja hier unten noch nicht wissen.'

„Es scheint ja euer Weg zu sein", sagte der Gendarm lachend, „es macht euch wohl nichts, wenn ihr mitgeht."

„Warum redest du nichts, Carlo?" fragte Geronimo.

„O ja, ich rede . . . Ich bitte, Herr Gendarm, wie ist es denn möglich . . . was sollen wir denn . . . oder vielmehr, was soll ich . . . wahrhaftig, ich weiß nicht . . ."

„Es ist nun einmal so. Vielleicht bist du auch unschuldig. Was weiß ich. Jedenfalls haben wir die telegraphische Anzeige ans Kommando bekommen, daß wir euch aufhalten sollen, weil ihr verdächtig seid, dringend verdächtig, da oben den Leuten Geld gestohlen zu haben. Nun, es ist auch möglich, daß ihr unschuldig seid. Also vorwärts!"

„Warum sprichst du nichts, Carlo?" fragte Geronimo.

„Ich rede—o ja, ich rede . . ."

„Nun geht endlich! Was hat es für einen Sinn, auf der Straße stehenzubleiben! Die Sonne brennt. In einer Stunde sind wir an Ort und Stelle. Vorwärts!"

Carlo berührte den Arm Geronimos wie immer, und so gingen sie langsam weiter, der Gendarm hinter ihnen.

„Carlo, warum redest du nicht?" fragte Geronimo wieder.

„Aber was willst du, Geronimo, was soll ich sagen? Es wird sich alles herausstellen; ich weiß selber nicht . . ."

Und es ging ihm durch den Kopf: ‚Soll ich's ihm erklären, ehe wir vor Gericht stehen? . . . Es geht wohl nicht. Der Gendarm hört uns zu . . . Nun, was tut's?[24] Vor Gericht werd' ich

gruesome story of how he had once almost been stabbed by a tramp.

"Someone has stopped," said Geronimo.
"Tenelli, the gendarme," said Carlo.
Now they had come up to him.
"Good morning, Mr. Tenelli," said Carlo and stopped before him.
"That's the way it is," said the gendarme. "For the present I must take you both to the station at Boladore."
"Hey!" cried the blind man.
Carlo turned pale. "But how is this possible?" he thought. "But it can't have anything to do with this. They can't know about it down here yet."
"It seems to be on your way, doesn't it?" the gendarme laughed. "It doesn't really matter to you if you come along with me."
"Why don't you say anything, Carlo?" Geronimo asked.
"Oh yes, I'm talking . . . Please, gendarme, how is it possible . . . what are we supposed to . . . or rather, what am I supposed to . . . really, I don't know . . ."
"That's the way it is. Perhaps you're really innocent. What do I know? Anyway we got a telegraphic report at the station to stop you because you are suspected, strongly suspected, of having stolen money from the people up there. Well, it's possible, of course, that you're innocent. So come on."

"Why don't you say anything, Carlo?" asked Geronimo.
"I'm talking—oh yes, I'm talking . . ."
"Well, come on! What sense is there in stopping on the road? The sun is burning. In an hour we'll be on the spot. On with you."
Carlo touched Geronimo's arm as always, and so they went on slowly, the gendarme behind them.
"Carlo, why don't you talk?" Geronimo asked again.
"But what do you want, Geronimo, what am I to say? Everything will come to light; I don't know myself . . ."
And it went through his head: "Shall I explain it to him before we stand before the court? . . . It won't do, I fear. The gendarme is listening to us . . . Well, what does it matter? Before the court

ja doch die Wahrheit sagen. ‚Herr Richter‘, werd ich sagen, ‚es
ist doch kein Diebstahl wie ein anderer. Es war nämlich so: . . .‘
Und nun mühte er sich, die Worte zu finden, um vor Gericht
die Sache klar und verständlich darzustellen. ‚Da fuhr gestern ein Herr über den Paß . . . es mag ein Irrsinniger gewesen
sein—oder am End' hat er sich nur geirrt . . . und dieser
Mann . . .‘

Aber was für ein Unsinn! Wer wird es glauben? . . . Man
wird ihn gar nicht so lange reden lassen.—Niemand kann diese
dumme Geschichte glauben . . . nicht einmal Geronimo glaubt
sie . . . —Und er sah ihn von der Seite an. Der Kopf des Blinden
bewegte sich nach alter Gewohnheit während des Gehens wie
im Takte auf und ab, aber das Gesicht war regungslos, und die
leeren Augen stierten in die Luft.—Und Carlo wußte plötzlich,
was für Gedanken hinter dieser Stirne liefen . . . . ‚So also stehen
die Dinge‘, mußte Geronimo wohl denken.—‚Carlo bestiehlt
nicht nur mich, auch die anderen Leute bestiehlt er . . . Nun,
er hat es gut, er hat Augen, die sehen, und er nützt sie aus . . .
‘—Ja, das denkt Geronimo, ganz gewiß . . . Und auch, daß man
kein Geld bei mir finden wird, kann mir nicht helfen,—nicht
vor Gericht, nicht vor Geronimo. Sie werden mich einsperren
und ihn . . . Ja, ihn geradeso wie mich, denn er hat ja das
Geldstück.—Und er konnte nicht mehr weiter denken, er fühlte
sich so sehr verwirrt. Es schien ihm, als verstünde er überhaupt
nichts mehr von der ganzen Sache, und er wußte nur eines:
daß er sich gern auf ein Jahr in den Arrest setzen ließe . . .
oder auf zehn, wenn nur Geronimo wüßte, daß er für ihn allein
zum Dieb geworden war.

Und plötzlich blieb Geronimo stehen, so daß auch Carlo inne-
halten mußte.

„Nun, was ist denn?" sagte der Gendarm ärgerlich. „Vorwärts, vorwärts!" Aber da sah er mit Verwunderung, daß der
Blinde die Gitarre auf den Boden fallen ließ, seine Arme erhob
und mit beiden Händen nach den Wangen des Bruders tastete.
Dann näherte er seine Lippen dem Munde Carlos, der zuerst
nicht wußte, wie[25] ihm geschah, und küßte ihn.

„Seid ihr verrückt?" fragte der Gendarm. „Vorwärts! vorwärts! Ich habe keine Lust zu braten."

I'll tell the truth, of course. 'Your Honor,' I'll say: 'This is no theft like any other. It was this way, you must know . . .' And now he struggled to find the words with which he could present the matter to the court clearly and intelligibly. "Yesterday a gentleman was riding over the pass . . . he may have been a madman—or he was only mistaken after all . . . and this man . . ."

But what nonsense! Who will believe it? They won't even let him talk that long.—No one can believe this stupid story . . . not even Geronimo believes it . . .—And he gave him a sidelong glance. As usual, the blind man's head was moving rhythmically up and down as he walked, but his face was motionless and his empty eyes stared into the air. And Carlo suddenly knew what sort of thoughts were racing behind this brow . . . "That's the way things are, Geronimo must probably be thinking, 'Carlo steals not only from me, he steals from other people too' . . . Well, he's lucky, he has eyes that see and he's making use of them . . .—Yes, that's what Geronimo is thinking, I'm quite certain . . . And also the fact that they will find no money on me can't help me—not before the court, not before Geronimo. They'll lock me up and him, too . . . Yes, him just as much as me, for he has the coin, of course." And he could not think any more, he felt so very confused. It seemed to him that he understood nothing more of the whole matter, and he knew only one thing: that he would be glad to be put under arrest for a year . . . or for ten, if only Geronimo knew that he had become a thief for him alone.

And suddenly Geronimo stopped, so that Carlo too had to stop.

"Well, what's wrong?" the gendarme said peevishly. "Go on, go on." But then he saw in astonishment that the blind man dropped his guitar on the ground, raised his two arms, and groped for his brother's cheeks with both hands. Then he brought his lips close to Carlo's mouth, who at first didn't know what was happening, and kissed him.

"Are you two crazy?" the gendarme asked. "Keep going, keep going. I have no wish to roast."

Geronimo hob die Gitarre vom Boden auf, ohne ein Wort zu sprechen. Carlo atmete tief auf und legte die Hand wieder auf den Arm des Blinden. War es denn möglich? Der Bruder zürnte ihm nicht mehr? Er begriff am Ende—? Und zweifelnd sah er ihn von der Seite an.

„Vorwärts!" schrie der Gendarm. „Wollt ihr endlich—!" Und er gab Carlo eins[26] zwischen die Rippen.

Und Carlo, mit festem Druck den Arm des Blinden leitend, ging wieder vorwärts. Er schlug einen viel rascheren Schritt ein als früher. Denn er sah Geronimo lächeln in einer milden, glückseligen Art, wie er es seit den Kinderjahren nicht mehr an ihm gesehen hatte. Und Carlo lächelte auch. Ihm war, als könnte ihm jetzt nichts Schlimmes mehr geschehen,—weder vor Gericht, noch sonst irgendwo auf der Welt.—Er hatte seinen Bruder wieder . . . Nein, er hatte ihn zum erstenmal . . .

Notes: Schnitzler, *Der blinde Geronimo und sein Bruder*

1. *war*, South German for *hatte*.
2. *Stilfser Joch*, Stelvio Pass.
3. *war ihm als*, it seemed to him as if.
4. *ward* = *wurde*.
5. *dichtere*, unusually dense (absolute comparative).
6. *habt's* = *habt ihr* (colloquial Austrian).
7. *gnädiger Herr*, sir.
8. *eh!* an Austrian exclamation equivalent to *sowieso* = anyhow or anyway; here perhaps equivalent to the meaningless American "you know" or "O.K." or "hey."
9. *wird* . . . , the future perfect, used to express high probability in the past = must have.
10. *war*, South German for *hatte*.
11. *Frauenzimmer*, the older word for *woman*; now used in a comical or derogatory sense.
12. *schlechter Laune* (genitive), in a bad mood.
13. *daneben*, i.e., outside the hat.

Geronimo picked up his guitar from the ground, without saying a word. Carlo drew a deep breath and again laid his hand on his blind brother's arm. Was it really possible? His brother was no longer angry with him? He finally realized—? And he gave him a dubious, sidelong glance.

"Go on!" the gendarme roared. "Will you . . . !" And he gave Carlo a punch between the ribs.

And Carlo, guiding the blind man's arm with firm pressure, went forward again. He took a much faster pace than before. For he saw Geronimo smile in that gentle, happy way that he had not seen in him since his childhood. And Carlo smiled too. He felt as if nothing bad could happen to him now—neither before the court nor anywhere else in the world.—He had his brother again . . . No, he had him for the first time . . .

15. *Lügen strafen*, make a liar of
16. *Sparkassa*, Austrian for *Sparkasse*.
17. *wandert sich*, equivalent to the gerund *wandering*.
18. *der*, he (emphatic).
19. *heuer*, this year (Austrian).
20. *nun ja*, is that so? irrelevant words spoken in perplexity.
21. *sei*, South German for *habe*.
22. *einer*, someone.
23. *es* . . . , that's just the way it is.
24. *was tut's*, what does it matter.
25. *wie*, what.
26. *eins*, i.e., a punch.

Thomas Mann '

1875–1955

The brothers Mann, Heinrich[1] and Thomas, placed considerable value on their mixed blood. Their father was a patrician,
a senator of the free Hanseatic city of Lübeck on the north
German coast; their mother, a beautiful, artistically gifted South
American, was part Creole. The fortunes of the family are
chronicled in Thomas Mann's first novel, *The Buddenbrooks* (*Buddenbrooks*, 1901),[2] which tells how a race of vigorous, aggressive
merchants rises to wealth and prominence in the grain ship-
ping business but declines as its members develop an interest
in culture and the arts, the growth in civilization being accompanied by a diminution in vigor and adaptability. At the
death of the senator in 1891 the family business was dissolved
and the Mann children became writers, actors, musicians, and
scholars.

[1]Heinrich Mann (1871–1950) wrote fiction, drama, and essays. He was a
distinguished man of letters who spent the last fifteen years of his life in
California.
[2]*The Buddenbrooks* is the correct English title. The family name is Budden-
brook.

After an unhappy schooling young Thomas joined his widowed mother in Munich, working as an unsalaried clerk in an insurance office. But he had already tasted the sweet waters of literary recognition; so after a year he gave up business as a career and joined his brother Heinrich in Italy, where he labored for three years on *Buddenbrooks* and wrote short stories, which were published in various German magazines. When he returned to Munich he worked for two years as a junior editor of the literary journal *Simplicissimus*. The publication of *Buddenbrooks*, after a brief lull, established his reputation as an author of the first rank; he entered on the precarious existence of a free-lance writer. His outward life was uneventful: marriage to the beautiful daughter of a distinguished scholar, a brood of gifted children, a series of literary successes, culminating in the award of the Nobel prize for literature in 1929.

There were family sorrows, recurring periods of depression, and in the earlier years financial concerns. The First World War produced a private crisis. The Mann home in Lübeck had been "apolitical," that is to say, traditionally conservative. This atmosphere the Mann brothers absorbed and took with them when they left home. Heinrich outgrew it quickly and moved toward the views of a liberal democrat, while Thomas remained untouched by the political and social agitation that had been stirring in European society since the French Revolution. He remained a German patriot and had even been planning a novel that would glorify the policies of Frederick the Great. Yet he firmly believed that he was apolitical. At the outbreak of the war he published two highly chauvinistic articles and an essay "Frederick and the Grand Coalition" ("Friedrich und die große Koalition," 1915), in which he justified Frederick's Machiavellian policies on pragmatic grounds (because they were successful and therefore right) and by the jesuitical argument that the end justifies the means. That same year Heinrich published an essay on Emile Zola[3] in which he attacked the German ideology and censured his brother (though not by name) for his chauvinism. A bitter enmity arose between the brothers,

---

[3]Emile Zola (1840–1902), French writer of the naturalist school, of which he is regarded as the founder.

lasting until the war's end. Thomas replied with a massive volume *Reflections of an Apolitical Person* (*Betrachtungen eines Unpolitischen*, 1918), a polemic against his brother, whom he labeled a "Zivilisationsliterat."[4] After the German defeat and the establishment of the Weimar Republic, Thomas abandoned his Prussian ideology and became a staunch supporter of the democratic new Germany. He foresaw the dangers of National Socialism for Germany and of fascism for the world and warned of this danger by pen and word of mouth. When the Nazis came to power in 1933, he was lecturing abroad. His children advised him not to return. After a temporary sojourn in France and Switzerland, the Mann family emigrated to the United States in 1938; they were received with the warmth and dignity that was their due. They became American citizens and lived in Los Angeles until 1952. The wave of intolerance that came to be known as McCarthyism was so distressing to Thomas Mann that he and his wife returned to Switzerland, where they lived to the end of their days.

Mann's literary oeuvre consists almost entirely of prose; it comprises a series of novels, of which the most memorable are *Buddenbrooks* (in two volumes), *The Magic Mountain* (*Der Zauberberg*, 1924, in two volumes), *Joseph and His Brothers* (*Joseph und seine Brüder*, 1933–42, in four volumes), and *Doktor Faustus* (1947); many stories, two of which are classics: *Tonio Kröger* (1903) and *Death in Venice* (*Der Tod in Venedig*, 1911); an impressive body of political essays and literary criticism; and hundreds of occasional pieces that reveal him as a generous colleague toward young and struggling artists in whose behalf he was always ready to intercede.

Thomas Mann was an avid, though not omnivorous reader. He had a strong philosophical bent and showed an astonishing erudition, acquired ad hoc in the fields of medicine (for *The*

---

[4]*Zivilisationsliterat*, a difficult word to translate. *Zivilisation* is often used in German to designate technical progress, as opposed to *Kultur*, which denotes civilization as it concerns mental, moral, social, and aesthetic development. *Literat* is similarly used as a derogatory term for a second-rate, superficial writer, the way we sometimes use the term *journalist* pejoratively for an inferior writer. A *Zivilisationsliterat* is therefore a second-rate writer who is concerned with politics and superficial problems rather than with deep culture.

Magic Mountain), in archaeology and biblical and midrashic literature (for the *Joseph* tetralogy), and modern musical theory (for *Dr. Faustus*). The strongest influences on his early intellectual development were Schiller and Heine in his schooldays, and thereafter Wagner, Nietzsche and Schopenhauer, the German romantics, Russian and Scandinavian writers, the nineteenth-century French and British novelists, Theodor Fontane, and in later life Goethe.

Mann was a highly subjective writer; his works, like Goethe's, are fragments of a great confession but in a much more literal sense. In an early notebook Mann wrote: "The use of personal experience has been everything to me; inventing out of thin air is not my thing; I have always considered the world to be more gifted than I am." Or as he puts it in another context: "I was always a dreamer and doubter, who was always concerned with saving and justifying my own life, and I never flattered myself that I could teach people to improve themselves and to be converted."[5] How much of his family, and his friends (and enemies?) has gone into his work has been demonstrated by scholarship and may be gathered from reading his numerous letters and notebooks. Like Goethe, Mann underwent a radical change in outlook from youth to maturity; the change was in fact, the same: from a romantic to a classical view of life.

There is a central theme running through Mann's work: it is the conflict between *Natur* and *Geist* (nature and spirit), that is, between the physical world of the senses—practical, instinctive life on the one hand—and intellect in its broadest sense of the immaterial—mind, spirit, psyche (as understood by modern psychology) on the other. Is there a topic in human thought more fundamental? In early modern times this dichotomy between nature (or life) and spirit was strikingly brought to the world's attention by Rousseau[6] in his "First Discourse" (1750)

---

[5]The last clause is a montage from Faust's opening monologue: Bilde mir nicht ein, ich könnte was lehren / Die Menschen zu bessern und zu bekehren.

[6]Jean-Jacques Rousseau (1712–78) was one of the most influential writers of modern times: novelist, musicologist, author of works on politics, sociology, education, and one of the world's great autobiographies, *Les Confessions*. He was a seminal thinker who prepared the way for the romantic movement in Europe.

as a paradox that was welcomed by the people of the Age of Reason,[7] who had grown tired of living by reason. Rousseau's thesis was that as long as man lived by his instincts, like the animal and the savage, he was morally good and happy; when he began to reason, to reflect on life, he became corrupt and miserable. Of course Rousseau's myth (for that is what it is) was anything but original. It was known to the writer of Genesis 2, who told "of man's first disobedience and the fruit / of that forbidden tree, whose mortal taste / brought death into the world and all our woe." The Greeks knew of it;[8] it was treated by the great Western and Eastern writers, if not explicitly, then by implication. But in the modern mind the myth is associated with Rousseau, and it became the fountainhead of romanticism in the catch phrase "the return to nature," that is, to instinct. In his early work Thomas Mann adopts the Rousseau myth by depicting the conflict between the *Bürger*[9] and the artist-intellectual. But by the end of the nineteenth century, when Mann began to write, Rousseauistic irrationalism had been reinforced by Darwin's theory of evolution, which was interpreted by some social thinkers as justifying the laissez-faire economic and social doctrines that dominated that age in the name of Darwin's "survival of the fittest." Darwin's biological theory was borrowed to legitimize the predatory instincts of capitalists toward labor, of imperialist nations against their colonial victims, and of the bourgeoisie as the new ruling class in the industrial West.

What is Thomas Mann's conception of the *Bürger* in his early writings? He is the middle-class businessman or professional man, soldier, civil servant; a self-confident, extraverted, industrious, nonintellectual type. His values are the conventional

[7]*The Age of Reason*, the title given to the Enlightenment because it advocated reason as the guide to living.

[8]See Arthur Lovejoy and George Boas, *Primitivism and Related Ideas in Classical Antiquity* (1935).

[9]*Bürger* is a difficult word to render in English. It means citizen, burgher (i.e., townsman), member of the middle class, bourgeois. But the word has by extension come to mean a conventional man, a square. The adjective *bürgerlich* has become a synonym for respectable, conventional. *Die Einrichtung war bürgerlich* = The furnishings were conventional.

mores of the tribe. He is conservative in politics, insofar as he has any interest in politics. He is a realist and a pragmatist (what works is right). The world given us by the senses is the real world to him. He may have an interest in the arts; if he does, it is no more than a perfunctory one. He is the philistine the romantics ridiculed, whom Flaubert and Baudelaire hated, against whom the neoromantics of 1900 and the hippies of the 1960s rebelled. But the earth and the fullness thereof was, and still is, his.[10]

The antithesis of the *Bürger*, the artist-intellectual, is wholly dedicated to the life of the spirit, the realm of ideas, ideals, and beauty. The world of the intellect is for him true reality, while the real world of the *Bürger* is alien to him.[11] He is a person with a frail physical constitution, delicate nerves, and a fragile sensibility, irritated by noise and disgusted by vulgarity. But he is capable of intense mental concentration in the execution of an intellectual or artistic undertaking. Romantic writers have noted the affinity between spirit, disease, and death. Thomas Mann quotes with approval Platen's poem "Tristan":

> Wer die Schönheit angeschaut mit Augen
> Ist dem Tode schon anheimgegeben.[12]

> [Whoever has beheld beauty with his eyes
> Is already dedicated to death.]

[10]A similar portrait of the *Bürger* will be found in John Galsworthy's *The Forsyte Saga*, Sinclair Lewis's *Main Street* and *Babbitt*, and Somerset Maugham's superb story *The Alien Corn*.

[11]Cf. Schiller's poem "The Division of the Earth" ("Die Teilung der Erde"), which tells how Zeus at the Creation summoned humans of all trades and vocations and told them to divide the world among themselves in a brotherly way. They went and grabbed what they could in a most unbrotherly way. Last of all came the poet, but too late; the whole earth had already been parceled out. "Where were you when the earth was divided?" the god demanded. "With you," the poet reminded Zeus; "my eyes were fixed on your countenance, my ears attuned to Heaven's harmonies." The solution? Zeus suggests: "If you are willing to dwell with me in my Heaven, you shall always be welcome."

[12]*August von Platen* (1796–1835) was a skillful poet who wrote in the classical mode during the romantic period. This poem was characterized by Thomas Mann as "the fundamental and primordial formula of all romanticism. It represents a world in which the imperative to live, the laws of life, reason, and morality mean nothing."

Beauty is of course part of the realm of spirit. The schoolboy Mann, who was a passionate admirer of Heine, no doubt read in the *Journey from Munich to Genoa* (*Reise von München nach Genua*) the following two passages: "The Tyroleans are handsome, cheerful, honest, decent, and unfathomably dull-minded. They are a healthy human species, perhaps because they are too stupid to be capable of being sick." And later on in the same travelogue Heine contrasts the barbarous British tourists in Italy with the refined native Italians.

> Albion's son, although he wears white linen and pays for everything in cash is still a civilized barbarian compared to the Italian, who manifests a state of civilization in transition to barbarism. The Englishman reveals a restrained coarseness, the Italian a wanton refinement. And, moreover, the pale, Italian faces, the suffering white in their eyes, the sickly delicacy of their lips, how mysteriously aristocratic they are, compared to the stiff British faces with their plebeian, ruddy health! The whole Italian people is inwardly sick, and sick people are always really more aristocratic than the healthy; for only a sick person is a human being, his limbs have a history of suffering, they are spiritualized. I even believe that suffering could turn animals into humans; I once saw a dog in the agony of death who looked almost human to me. [13]

Now Heine was not a Rousseauist, for his sympathy is not with the healthy British bourgeois but with the sick, spiritualized Italians. But the young Goethe, author of *Werther* and the early *Faust* version, *was* a Rousseauist. For these two characters feel Rousseau's disgust with knowledge and reason and want to escape into the real world of the senses, which is the world of the *Bürger*. This romantic will to escape into primitivism or adventure (bohemianism) persists through the nineteenth century and enjoys a renascence in *fin de siècle* neoromanticism and in the various anti-intellectual, back-to-nature movements that have erupted in the twentieth century.

As for the German romantics, they felt no philosophical qualms about supporting both sides in the fray. They rebelled against rationalism in the name of emotion and intuition; that

---

[13]*Heine: Werke*, ed. Elster, III, 235, 270.

is, they supported nature against spirit; but they also championed the artist-intellectual against the *Bürger*, whom they
called a "philistine." The truth is that the nature-spirit
dichotomy, as it has been presented so far, is untenable; it is
an oversimplification of a highly complex situation.

The association of spirit with disease is of course rooted in
the popular mind. The brawny but brainless football player
and the puny, bespectacled professor are stereotypes of the
cartoonist's art. From disease to death is a straight and direct
path; hence the lure that death holds for the artist-intellectual—
a ubiquitous theme in Mann's work. In this context death has
two meanings: a literal one, for many artists and intellectuals
burn themselves out at an early age, and a metaphorical one,
for they become dead to life and live only in their work.

The artist-intellectual is critical of the status quo; he is a
reformer, a Utopian, dreaming of possible worlds—at least on
paper, in the laboratory, or in the classroom. Because he ex-
pends all his energies on his creative or scientific work, he has
none left for "living," for the social amenities that play so large
a role in good society. Or perhaps the source of his social inep-
titude is the need for freedom from all restraint after the discipline exacted from him by his cerebral labors. It may well be
that this social disease is related to the physical disease and the
lure of death. In any case, the artist-intellectual tolerates in
himself the slovenly demeanor that we associate with bohemians
and hippies. He becomes socially inept, is clumsy on the dance
floor, and feels "out of it" at a social gathering. This is the
picture of the artist that Baudelaire paints in his poem "L'Alba-
tros," in which the poet is compared to an albatross, "the
king of the azure sky," who loses his grace and his strength
when he is placed in a group of common sailors. Baudelaire
concludes:

> The poet is like this prince of the clouds
> who is a friend of the storm and mocks the archer:
> but, exiled on the ground amidst the jeers [of the crowd],
> he is prevented by his giant wings from walking.

This is part of the romantic view of the poet as *vates* or seer,
prophet and teacher, and purveyor of aesthetic delight, the

poet as "the unacknowledged legislator of mankind" (Shelley). The view of the artist as a nonparticipant in life has historic roots in German aesthetics. Kant, followed by Schopenhauer, introduced a new aspect into the artistic enterprise. They saw the creative artist as a passive observer of life, a scientific student, so to speak, who monitors the behavior of people objectively, dispassionately, and records what he observes. In the third book of *The World as Will and Representation* (*Die Welt als Wille und Vorstellung*, 1819) Schopenhauer gave eloquent expression to this view of the artist's (and the scientist's) work. Far from intending to slight the artist by this designation of his function, Schopenhauer meant to exalt him; for the artist has "seen through" the folly of the common man, who is a slave to his will (or instincts) as he plods through his miserable existence. The artist, as a will-less, objective observer of life, stands on a higher plane. Kant and Schiller would have agreed with this value judgment.

But a social Darwinist or a Freudian might well cry sour grapes. He would counter that the artist stands aside from life because he is unfit to live it successfully. In Thomas Mann's early work there is plenty of support for this Darwinian thesis. In fact this denigration of the artist forms the tail end of a long literary tradition that goes back to Plato, who banished poets from his ideal republic because they make up lies and try to pass them off as true. Writers have had to defend their craft against a phalanx of detractors. In the Renaissance Sir Philip Sidney composed his defense of "poor poetry which, from almost highest admiration, is fallen to be the laughing stock of children." Shelley felt the need to write another defense of poetry. In the early years of our century Bernard Shaw rode into the lists once more, proclaiming *The Sanity of Art* against the attacks of Tolstoy and Max Nordau.[14] For various reasons the nineteenth century spawned a growing number of attacks on the lofty position that the artist had occupied through the

---

[14]*Max Nordau* (1849–1923), Zionist leader and social critic, whose book *Degeneration* (1893) enjoyed a *succès de scandale* because of its wholesale condemnation of all modernism in Western culture of the day. Shaw wrote *The Sanity of Art* (1907) to refute Nordau's views.

centuries. Kierkegaard's attack on the amoral, aesthetic view
of life, the general decline of the hero in nineteenth-century
fiction, the tendency of realism to present man in depravity
rather than in his glory, and the Darwinian dogma already
mentioned—all these and other factors contributed to a reversal
of position: the passivity, the dispassionate objectivity of the
artist could be seen as a weakness rather than a strength.

But meanwhile the most devastating onslaught ever made
against the artist came from Friedrich Nietzsche as a result of
his experience with the work of Richard Wagner.[15] Nietzsche's
position may be summed up in the following propositions: (1)
one cannot be an artist without being sick; (2) the artist denies,
or at least falsifies, reality; (3) art is a compensation for failure
in life (an anticipation of Freud); (4) the writer is an actor who
pretends passion where he feels none; (5) the artist is a vampire
who shamelessly makes literature out of his own feelings.

Shaw himself, while defending art and the artist with one
hand, dealt out doughty blows with the other through his plays
Candida and *The Doctor's Dilemma*.[16] And in *The Revolutionist's
Handbook*[17] Shaw wrote: "He who can, does; he who cannot
teaches," and he might have added "or writes."

In the light of all this historical material, some of which the
Mann brothers must have known at first hand, it is not surprising that these two scions of a conservative family and a provincial
environment entered the literary arena with a jaundiced view
of their profession. True, they were themselves infected with
the virus of spirit;[18] but they had enough of the *Bürger* in them
to feel divided against themselves. Heinrich outgrew this
dichotomy very soon; Thomas's development was slower. In
his early stories there is a regular pattern: an outsider (artist

[15]Nietzsche began as an admirer of Wagner's art but later became a bitter
opponent of Wagner's music, personality, and view of life. His principal
polemics against Wagner are *The Wagner Case* (*Der Fall Wagner*) and *Nietzsche
against Wagner* (*Nietzsche contra Wagner* (both 1888).

[16]In *Candida* (1897) the poet Marchbanks is depicted as a dependent weakling;
in *The Doctor's Dilemma* (1906) the painter Dubedat is a selfish scoundrel.

[17]A collection of aphorisms attached to the play *Man and Superman*.

[18]This is one of the paradoxes of romanticism: Rousseau wrote a book advocating that there should be no books.

or intellectual, sometimes even a cultured businessman) en-
counters "life" in some form and is defeated in the encounter.
He cannot stand up against crude but robust life. These early
stories embody a coarse form of social Darwinism. The author
gives us no hint as to where his sympathies lie until we come
to the artist stories (*The Buffoon*) [*Der Bajazzo*], *Tristan*, *Tonio
Kröger*), where it becomes clear that the artist deserves the defeat
he suffers. In *Tonio Kröger* we are given one of the two sharpest
denunications of the artist's character in all literature. It occurs
in the fourth chapter in the celebrated conversation between
Tonio and the Russian painter Lisaveta Ivanovna.

As Mann's thinking on the topos of *Natur* and *Geist* deepened,
he saw that social Darwinism was too simplistic. It failed to take
cognizance of the ambivalence about life and art that Thomas
Mann felt in his own mind. So in *Tonio Kröger* he showed his
own inner division and his devotion to art at war with his strong
bourgeois instincts, which made him long for "the bliss of the
commonplace" like his conventional, unintellectual school-
friend Hans Hansen, who read only horse stories, who cared
nothing about the intensely moving scene in Schiller's *Don Carlos*
in which the king of Spain wept. But Hans Hansen got to dance
with the blonde Inge Holm, who did not fall on the dance floor
like Tonio's intellectual partner, Magdalene Vermehren. Chapters 3 and 4 of *Tonio Kröger* give a superb analysis of the *Natur-
Geist* conflict as Thomas Mann saw it at this time, describing
the life of the spirit in unusually harsh terms. *Erkenntnisekel*,
disgust brought about by knowledge, by "seeing through" life
and people's motives, induces in the man of spirit a surfeit of
intellect and makes him yearn for the bliss of nature; yet he
goes back to his painful literary existence. This state of being
torn by two opposing forces is unbearable. So, as the despairing
Faust curses all life, the despairing Tonio gives vent to his
pent-up unhappiness in the harshest condemnation of life in
the spirit.

But in spite of these misgivings, despite all the nasty things
that Tonio says about men of letters in his conversation with
the Russian painter, he concludes his letter to her (written from
abroad) with the question whether this dichotomy in his psyche,
this pull toward the bliss of the commonplace, does not make

him a deeper artist than the mere *littérateur* who has no such rift in his soul. It is a sort of minor Copernican revolution[19] that Thomas Mann has achieved with the formulation of his problem. It became a turning point in his weltanschauung and led to an intense speculation bent on rehabilitating spirit from the stigma that had been attached to it in anti-intellectual periods.

Perhaps, Mann began to argue, intellect and true art were not incompatible, as the enemies of spirit claimed. Perhaps art could be put in the service of life rather than serving sickness and death. Or perhaps it must pass through the valley of the shadow of death, only to emerge from it to renewed, regenerated life. It was a long path that led to the ultimate cure for the romantic malady. But there were milestones on the way. One was the profound analysis that Schiller had contributed to the problem in his great essay *On Naive and Sentimental Literature* (*Über naive und sentimentalische Dichtung*, 1795), for which Thomas Mann felt a boundless admiration.

Schiller had distinguished two types of art and artist: naive and sentimental (today we would say realist and idealist). He began with the assertion that naive, nonintellectual, intuitive art, produced semiconsciously, by inspiration, without effort, like Goethe's, was superior to reflective art. We adults admire the child's naiveté and wish we could trade in our intellectual sophistication for it. But after a hundred pages of subtle, complex, highly erudite argumentation Schiller decided that sentimental (that is, idealist) art has nothing to be ashamed of. He even hinted that for the modern sophisticated world it has more relevance than the naive art of the Greeks—or of his friend

---

[19]*Copernican revolution,* a term used to describe the revolutionary point of view introduced into philosophy by Immanuel Kant (1724–1804). The British empiricists had viewed the human mind as a blank slate on which experience impresses sensations, which are turned into concepts. The difficulties raised by this view led Kant to postulate the theory that the mind is not a passive receptacle but an active, constitutive agent that supplies certain ways of organizing experience. The innovation was called Copernican because Copernicus suggested the same kind of turnabout in astronomy: the sun does not revolve about the earth but the earth about the sun. Mann's refusal to judge his divided consciousness as a weakness but as a strength is a similar *volte face.*

and rival Goethe. But perhaps the solution lay in a synthesis of the two types.

Thomas Mann recognized that Schiller's (perhaps unconscious) motive in writing the essay was to assert his own sense of worth in the face of the crushing effect that the towering genius of Goethe exerted on him. Goethe apparently wrote with ease, he was a naive artist, whereas Schiller wrenched every line out of his conscious intellect. Did this mean that Goethe was an artist and Schiller was not? Not so. Both were men of spirit, only they worked in different ways: Goethe through realism, Schiller through an idealist vision. It was wrong to deny Schiller the title of creative artist because he created only by overcoming, by formidable effort, instead of warbling his native woodnotes wild.

The resolution of this inner crisis in Schiller's psyche is the theme of A Difficult Hour (Schwere Stunde, 1905). From the point of view of Thomas Mann's development this story (for it is a piece of fiction) marks a station in Mann's progress toward the justification of spirit, a bridging of the abyss he had set up between art and life.

But there were relapses. One such is chronicled in the superb novella Death in Venice (Der Tod in Venedig, 1912), which recounts how an eminent middle-aged writer of the Schiller type, a Leistungsethiker,[20] craves the luxury of savoring life before it is too late. He wants to experience beauty, not the beauty of artistic creation but beauty in the flesh, like Faust in his pact with the devil. He goes to Venice, where he comes under the spell of an angelic-looking boy, whom he worships from a distance. When cholera breaks out, he lacks the will power to tear himself away from his idol but stays on in the stricken city until death claims him. Such is the fate of Geist when it loses control and sets out to experience life.

The second relapse arose out of Mann's bitter quarrel with his older brother and the polemical book it engendered, Betrachtungen eines Unpolitischen. Once more Mann called into service the Natur-Geist antithesis, loading spirit with a plethora of

---

[20]Leistungsethiker, a moralist through achievement or effort, entailing self-control.

undesirable effects, identifying German culture (= *Natur*) with
soul, depth, humanity, and identifying French spirit (*Geist*) with
mass democracry, intellect, legalism, superficiality, hypocrisy.
It defends a position that Mann had long ago abandoned and
leads him into a morass of contradictions and absurditics.

The first important statement of the new Thomas Mann, the
liberal democrat, was the magisterial essay *Goethe und Tolstoy*
(1922) in which he pairs off two "naive" writers, Goethe and
Tolstoy, against two "sentimental" or reflective artists, Schiller
and Dostoevski. His judgment is that both sides are partially
right, the aesthetic truth lies in a synthesis between them:
"Effortless nature is crude. Effortless spirit is without root or
substance. A noble encounter of nature and spirit, as they
mutually yearn for each other, that is humanity." Two years
later, in *Der Zauberberg*, he has Hans Castorp, the novel's hero,
vow that he will not permit himself to be lured into seductive
death but will go through death into the service of life.[21]

Thomas Mann had made a discovery about Schiller's basic
thesis that the sentimental man yearns to become naive again.
Mann realized that the reaction was reversible: the naive man
also wants to be spirit. The history of human culture bears this
out. For since we are born naive, how does spirit develop at
all? The human organism must, so to speak, be programmed
to become dissatisfied with itself and to be transformed into its
antithesis: spirit. If the two antitheses meet halfway and stop,
a satisfactory synthesis, a harmonious mean, is formed. This
agrees with Schiller's conception of beauty as a harmonious
fusion between nature and spirit, as depicted in the essay *On
the Aesthetic Education of Mankind* (*Über die ästhetische Erziehung
des Menschen*, 1794). What Thomas Mann wrote after the seminal essay *Goethe und Tolstoy* develops this new insight and illus-
trates it through widely divergent examples of social interaction
in the great novels of his last decades and in the essays on great
men of thought and letters: Nietzsche, Freud, Schopenhauer,
Chekhov, and finally Schiller again.

●

When stated so abstractly these generalizations about artists,
intellectuals, and bourgeois characters may sound farfetched.

[21]In the crucial section of chapter 6 titled *Schnee*.

But in fact there is a substantial literature on the subject written by artists and scholars of reputation, even of fame. The impulse to classify into two or three or four categories is widespread. And, what is more important, when such theories are sugar-coated by a work of fiction, they are much easier to swallow. To understand how it was possible for a young man of Mann's intelligence and experience to work with such a set of assumptions, it is important to note what is clear from his letters: that he suffered from deep feelings of inadequacy, self-doubt, and inner contradiction. These letters show him searching for an identity and deeply troubled by doubts about the place of art in the social structure. It is difficult for twentieth-century North Americans, with our idolization of show biz personalities, to imagine a successful writer doubting the validity of his creative endeavor and the applause it brought him, but the evidence of Mann's correspondence is convincing and this helps us to understand the tenor of his work.

At least we should be grateful to Thomas Mann for rejecting out of hand the adulation that artists have awarded themselves for centuries—"the unacknowledged legislators of mankind," "a second maker, a just Prometheus under God"—and the stones that the public and the critics have hurled at them through the centuries by associating genius with insanity, linking intellect with physical debility, and so on.

A writer's reputation does not rest on his grasp of metaphysics or political science but on his ability to capture and communicate the quality of life through the interaction of people with the environment and with one another. Through *Buddenbrooks*, *Tonio Kröger*, *Der Tod in Venedig*, the great novels of the twenties and thirties, *Dr. Faustus* and *Felix Krull*, Thomas Mann has earned for himself a place among the foremost men of letters of the twentieth century and among the classical writers of world literature.

●

Schwere Stunde, which Thomas Mann called "a subjective sketch," was written upon request, in the spring of 1905, for the Schiller centennial number of the magazine *Simplicissimus*, of which Mann was at that time a junior editor. It appeared in the issue of May 9, the anniversary of Schiller's death. In pre-

paration for the work Mann read Schiller's correspondence
with Goethe and Körner as well as biographical and critical
works. Although neither Schiller's name nor any of his works
is mentioned in the text, it is clear that the setting is the winter
of 1796–97, when Schiller was struggling to complete his most
ambitious work, the *Wallenstein* trilogy.

The conception of Schiller as a *Leistungsethiker*, with affinities
to Tonio Kröger, Gustav von Aschenbach, and other Mann
characters, is grounded in the author's own psyche. In a letter
of January 17, 1906 to his older brother Heinrich, Mann speaks
of his aim in writing *Fiorenza* and *Schwere Stunde* and in the
novel he was then planning on the life of Frederick the Great.
All these works, he writes, are studies in greatness and heroism,
designed to make the reader *feel* what true greatness is by giving
him an intimate and living presentation of it, by capturing its
tone. In his correspondence and his autobiographical and literary essays Mann has often referred to his own labored method
of creation, which sometimes filled him with despair but at
other times gave him great satisfaction because of the results
it produced. In August of 1904, when he was working on the
drama *Fiorenza*, he wrote to his fiancée Katja Pringsheim almost
verbatim the passage printed on p. 372. When he read about
Schiller's difficulties with literary creation, he realized that the
great poet was, like himself, a man of will, who overcame by
heroic effort the difficulties and the pain that literary creation
entailed.

Half a century later Thomas Mann wrote and read another
commemorative essay on Schiller, *Versuch über Schiller*, on the
occasion of the one hundred and fiftieth anniversary of the
poet's death. In it he referred to the earlier tribute and
suggested that it is fresher, deeper, happier, and more enduring
than the more elaborate essay of his old age.

Schwere Stunde is composed in *erlebte Rede*, a narrative technique that records the thoughts of a character without using
direct or even indirect quotation, as if the narrator were himself
empathically experiencing the speaker's words. It is related to
the stream of consciousness technique that we know from
Schnitzler, Dorothy Richardson, Proust, Joyce, and Faulkner.
But *erlebte Rede* is a much older literary device; it was known

to the Romans, used by medieval writers, and became popular in the nineteenth century through writers like Jane Austen, Flaubert, and Fontane.

Jacket design for Thomas Mann's *The Buddenbrooks* by Wilhelm Schulz (1903)

Schwere Stunde

Er[1] stand vom Schreibtisch auf, von seiner kleinen, gebrech-
lichen Schreibkommode, stand auf wie ein Verzweifelter und
ging mit hängendem Kopfe in den entegengesetzten Winkel
des Zimmers zum Ofen, der lang und schlank war wie eine
Säule. Er legte die Hände an die Kacheln, aber sie waren fast
ganz erkaltet, denn Mitternacht war lange vorbei, und so lehnte
er, ohne die kleine Wohltat empfangen zu haben, die er suchte,
den Rücken daran, zog hustend die Schöße seines Schlafrockes
zusammen, aus dessen Brustaufschlägen das verwaschene Spit-
zenjabot heraushing, und schnob mühsam durch die Nase, um
sich ein wenig Luft zu verschaffen; denn er hatte den Schnupfen wie gewöhnlich.

Das war ein besonderer und unheimlicher Schnupfen, der
ihn fast nie völlig verließ. Seine Augenlider waren entflammt
und die Ränder seiner Nasenlöcher ganz wund davon, und in
Kopf und Gliedern lag dieser Schnupfen ihm wie eine schwere,
schmerzliche Trunkenheit. Oder war an all der Schlaffheit und
Schwere das leidige Zimmergewahrsam schuld, das der Arzt
nun schon wieder seit Wochen über ihn verhängt hielt? Gott
wußte, ob er wohl daran tat. Der ewige Katarrh und die
Krämpfe in Brust und Unterleib mochten es nötig machen,
und schlechtes Wetter war über Jena,[2] seit Wochen, seit
Wochen, das war richtig, ein miserables und hassenswertes Wetter, das man in allen Nerven spürte, wüst, finster und kalt, und
der Dezemberwind heulte im Ofenrohr, verwahrlost und gott-
verlassen, daß es klang nach nächtiger Heide im Sturm und
Irrsal und heillosem Gram der Seele. Aber gut war sie nicht,
diese enge Gefangenschaft, nicht gut für die Gedanken und
den Rhythmus des Blutes, aus dem die Gedanken kamen. . .

A Difficult Hour

He got up from his desk, from his small, fragile secretary, got up like a desperate man and went, with drooping head, to the opposite corner of the room, to the stove, which was tall and slender like a pillar. He placed his hands on the tiles but they were now almost cold, for midnight was long past, and so he leaned with his back against them without receiving the small comfort that he sought, coughed and gathered the folds of his dressing gown about him, between the lapels of which the faded lace jabot hung out, and blew his nose strenuously, to get a little air; for he had a catarrh, as usual.

It was a special and uncanny catarrh, which almost never left him completely. His eyelids were inflamed and the edges of his nostrils were quite sore from it, and this catarrh lay in his head and limbs like a heavy, painful intoxication. Or was this nasty confinement to his room, which the doctor had once again held over his head for weeks now, responsible for all the weakness and heaviness? Heaven knew whether he was doing the right thing. The eternal catarrh and the cramps in his chest and abdomen might have made it necessary. And there had been bad weather over Jena for weeks, for weeks, that was true, a miserable and hateful weather that one felt in every nerve, desolate, dark, and cold. And the December wind howled in the stovepipe, wild and God-forsaken, so that it sounded like a heath in a storm by night—and like straying, hopeless mental grief. But it was not good, this narrow prison, not good for the thoughts and the rhythm of the blood out of which the thoughts came. . .

[365]

Das sechseckige Zimmer, kahl, nüchtern und unbequem, mit
seiner geweißten Decke, unter der Tabaksrauch schwebte,
seiner schräg karierten Tapete, auf der oval gerahmte Silhouet-
ten hingen, und seinen vier, fünf dünnbeinigen Möbeln, lag
im Lichte der beiden Kerzen, die zu Häupten des Manuskripts
auf der Schreibkommode brannten. Rote Vorhänge hingen
über den oberen Rahmen der Fenster, Fähnchen nur, symme-
trisch geraffte Kattune; aber sie waren rot, von einem warmen,
sonoren Rot, und er liebte sie und wollte sie niemals missen,
weil sie etwas von Üppigkeit und Wollust in die unsinnlich
enthaltsame Dürftigkeit seines Zimmers brachten. . . .

Er stand am Ofen und blickte mit einem raschen und
schmerzlich angestrengten Blinzeln hinüber zu dem Werk, von
dem er geflohen war, dieser Last, diesem Druck, dieser Gewis-
sensqual, diesem Meer, das auszutrinken,[3] dieser furchtbaren
Aufgabe, die sein Stolz und sein Elend, sein Himmel und seine
Verdammnis war. Es schleppte sich, es stockte, es stand—schon
wieder, schon wieder! Das Wetter war schuld und sein Katarrh
und seine Müdigkeit. Oder das Werk? Die Arbeit selbst? Die
eine unglückselige und der Verzweiflung geweihte Empfängnis
war?

Er war aufgestanden, um sich ein wenig Distanz davon zu
verschaffen, denn oft bewirkte die räumliche Entfernung vom
Manuskript, daß man Übersicht gewann, einen weiteren Blick
über den Stoff, und Verfügungen zu treffen vermochte. Ja, es
gab Fälle, wo das Erleichterungsgefühl, wenn man sich abwen-
dete von der Stätte des Ringens, begeisternd wirkte. Und das
war eine unschuldigere Begeisterung, als wenn man Likör
nahm oder schwarzen, starken Kaffee.—Die kleine Tasse stand
auf dem Tischchen. Wenn sie ihm über das Hemmnis hülfe?
Nein, nein, nicht mehr! Nicht der Arzt nur, auch ein zweiter
noch, ein Ansehnlicherer, hatte ihm dergleichen behutsam
widerraten, der Andere, der dort, in Weimar, den er mit einer
sehnsüchtigen Feindschaft liebte. Der war weise. Der wußte zu
leben, zu schaffen; mißhandelte sich nicht; war voller Rücksicht
gegen sich selbst. . . .

Stille herrschte im Hause. Nur der Wind war hörbar, der die
Schloßgasse hinuntersauste, und der Regen, wenn er prickelnd
gegen die Fenster getrieben ward. Alles[4] schlief, der Hauswirt

The hexagonal room, bare, plain, and uncomfortable, with its white-washed ceiling, under which the tobacco smoke floated, its wall paper with oblique squares, on which hung silhouettes in oval frames, and its four or five spindly-legged pieces of furniture, lay in the light of the two candles, which burned at the head of the manuscript on the secretary. Red drapes hung over the upper window frames, mere tatters, pieces of calico gathered symmetrically; but they were red, of a warm, sonorous red; and he loved them and never wanted to be without them, because they brought something of luxury and voluptuousness into the nonsensuous, abstemious meagerness of his room. . .

He stood by the stove and peered, with a swift and painfully strained blinking of his eyes, at the work from which he had fled, this burden, this pressure, this torment of conscience, this sea that he had to drink up, this terrible task that was his pride and his misery, his heaven and his damnation. It dragged, it got stuck, it stood still—once again, once again! It was the fault of the weather and his catarrh and his weariness. Or was it the work? The work itself? Which was an unhappy conception and doomed to despair?

He had stood up to get some distance, for often a removal in space from the manuscript gave one perspective, a longer view of the material, and enabled one to make decisions. Yes, there were cases where the feeling of relief gained from turning away from the place of struggle produced inspiration. And that was a more innocent inspiration than when one took liquor or black, strong coffee.—The little cup stood on the small table. Suppose it should help him over the obstacle? No, no, no more! Not only the doctor, another person too, a more prominent one, had advised him prudently against such things, that other one, that man there in Weimar, whom he loved with a yearning enmity. He was wise. He knew how to live, how to create; did not abuse himself; was full of consideration toward himself. . .

Silence reigned in the house. Only the wind could be heard, roaring down the Schlossgasse, and the rain when it was driven and pattered against the windows. Everyone was asleep, the landlord and his family, Lotte and the children. And he stood

und die Seinen, Lotte und die Kinder. Und er stand einsam
wach am erkalteten Ofen und blinzelte gequält zu dem Werk
hinüber, an das seine kranke Ungenügsamkeit ihn nicht glauben ließ,—Sein weißer Hals ragte lang aus der Binde hervor,
und zwischen den Schößen des Schlafrocks sah man seine nach
innen gekrümmten Beine. Sein rotes Haar war aus der hohen
und zarten Stirn zurückgestrichen, ließ blaß geäderte Buchten
über den Schläfen frei[6] und bedeckte die Ohren in dünnen
Locken. An der Wurzel der großen, gebogenen Nase, die un-
vermittelt in eine weißliche Spitze endete, traten die starken
Brauen, dunkler als das Haupthaar, nahe zusammen, was
dem Blick der tiefliegenden, wunden Augen etwas tragisch
Schauendes gab. Gezwungen, durch den Mund zu atmen,
öffnete er die dünnen Lippen, und seine Wangen, sommer-
sprossig und von Stubenluft fahl, erschlafften und fielen ein. . .
    Nein, es mißlang, und alles war vergebens! Die Armee! Die
Armee hätte gezeigt werden müssen! Die Armee war die Basis
von allem! Da sie nicht vors Auge gebracht werden konnte—
war die ungeheure Kunst denkbar, sie der Einbildung aufzu-
zwingen? Und der Held war kein Held; er war unedel und
kalt! Die Anlage war falsch und die Sprache war falsch, und
es war ein trockenes und schwungloses[6] Kolleg in Historie,
breit, nüchtern und für die Schaubühne verloren!
    Gut, es war also aus. Eine Niederlage. Ein verfehltes Unter-
nehmen. Bankerott. Er wollte es Körnern[7] schreiben, dem
guten Körner, der an ihn glaubte, der in kindischem Vertrauen
seinem Genius anhing. Er würde höhnen, flehen, poltern—der
Freund; würde ihn an den Carlos[8] gemahnen, der auch aus
Zweifeln und Mühen und Wandlungen hervorgegangen und
sich am Ende, nach aller Qual, als ein weithin Vortreffliches,
eine ruhmvolle Tat erwiesen hat. Doch das war anders gewesen.
Damals war er der Mann noch, eine Sache mit glücklicher Hand
zu packen und sich den Sieg daraus zu gestalten. Skrupel und
Kämpfe? O ja. Und krank war er gewesen, wohl kränker als
jetzt, ein Darbender, Flüchtiger, mit der Welt Zerfallener,
gedrückt und im Menschlichen bettelarm. Aber jung, ganz jung
noch! Jedesmal, wie tief auch gebeugt, war sein Geist geschmei-
dig emporgeschnellt, und nach den Stunden des Harms waren
die anderen des Glaubens und des inneren Triumphes gekom-

in solitude and awake at the cold stove and blinked in torment
at the work in which his pathological insatiability did not permit
him to believe. His white neck stood far out of the neckband
and between the skirts of his dressing gown one could see his
knock-kneed legs. His red hair, brushed back from his high,
delicate brow, exposed pale-veined bays above his temples and
covered his ears in thin curls. At the base of the large, curved
nose, which ended abruptly in a whitish point, the well-marked
eyebrows came close together; they were of a darker color than
the hair of his head and gave the deep-set, smarting eyes a
somewhat tragic appearance. Compelled to breathe through
his mouth, he opened his thin lips; and his cheeks, covered
with freckles and pale from the air inside the room, grew slack
and hollow. . .

No, it was a failure, and it was all in vain! The army! The
army should have been shown. The army was the basis of
everything! But since it could not be brought before the eyes,
was the tremendous art conceivable that would force it on the
imagination? And the hero was no hero; he was common and
cold. The setting was wrong and the diction was wrong and it
was a dry and prosaic lecture in history, elaborate, colorless,
and a total loss for the stage.

Good, so it was over. A defeat. An undertaking that had
failed. Bankruptcy. He wanted to write Körner about it, the
good Körner who believed in him, who clung to his genius with
childish confidence. He would mock, implore, bluster—that
friend; would remind him of *Carlos*, which had also emerged
from doubts and efforts and changes and in the end, after all
the torment, had revealed itself as something really excellent,
a meritorious achievement. But that had been different. At that
time he had still been the man to take hold of a thing with a
lucky hand and to shape it into victory. Scruples and struggles?
Oh yes. And he had been ill, probably more so than now, a
starving man, a refugee, at odds with the world, oppressed and
a beggar in his human sympathy. But young, still quite young.
Each time his spirit had bobbed up nimbly, however deeply it
had been bent; and after the hours of grief, those others of
faith and inner triumph had come. These no longer came,

men. Die kamen nicht mehr, kamen kaum noch. Eine Nacht
der flammenden Stimmung, da man auf einmal in einem genia-
lisch leidenschaftlichen Lichte sah, was werden könnte, wenn
man immer solcher Gnade genießen dürfte, mußte bezahlt werden mit einer Woche der Finsternis und der Lähmung. Müde
war er, siebenunddreißig erst alt und schon am Ende. Der
Glaube lebte nicht mehr, der an die Zukunft, der im Elend sein
Stern gewesen. Und so war es, dies war die verzweifelte
Wahrheit: Die Jahre der Not und der Nichtigkeit, die er für
Leidens- und Prüfungsjahre gehalten, sie eigentlich waren
reiche und fruchtbare Jahre gewesen; und nun, da ein wenig
Glück sich herniedergelassen, da er aus dem Freibeutertum
des Geistes in einige Rechtlichkeit und bürgerliche Verbindung
eingetreten war, Amt und Ehren trug, Weib und Kinder besaß,
nun war er erschöpft und fertig. Versagen und verzagen—das
war's, was übrigblieb.

Er stöhnte, preßte die Hände vor die Augen und ging wie
gehetzt durch das Zimmer. Was er da eben gedacht, war so
furchtbar, daß er nicht an der Stelle zu bleiben vermochte, wo
ihm der Gedanke gekommen war. Er stezte sich auf einen Stuhl
an der Wand, ließ die gefalteten Hände zwischen den Knien
hangen und starrte trüb auf die Diele nieder.

Das Gewissen . . . Wie laut sein Gewissen schrie! Er hatte
gesündigt, sich versündigt gegen sich selbst in all den Jahren,
gegen das zarte Instrument seines Körpers. Die Ausschweifun-
gen seines Jugendmutes, die durchwachten Nächte, die Tage
in tabakrauchiger Stubenluft, übergeistig und des Leibes un-
eingedenk, die Rauschmittel, mit denen er sich zur Arbeit gesta-
chelt—das rächte, rächte sich jetzt!

Und rächte es sich, so wollte er den Göttern trotzen, die
Schuld schickten und dann Strafe verhängten. Er hatte gelebt,
wie er leben mußte, er hatte nicht Zeit gehabt, weise, nicht Zeit,
bedächtig zu sein. Hier, an dieser Stelle der Brust, wenn
er atmete, hustete, gähnte, immer am selben Punkt dieser
Schmerz, diese kleine, teuflische, stechende, bohrende Mahnung, die nicht schwieg, seitdem vor fünf Jahren in Erfurt das
Katarrhfieber, jene hitzige Brustkrankheit, ihn angefallen;—
was wollte sie sagen? In Wahrheit, er wußte es nur zu gut, was

scarcely ever came. One night of flaming mood when, in a passionate light of genius, one suddenly saw what could be created, if one were still permitted to enjoy such grace, had to be paid for with a week of darkness and paralysis. He was tired, only thirty-seven years old and already at the end. His faith was no longer alive, his faith in the future, which had been his star in his wretchedness. And so it was; this was the desperate truth: the years of distress and nothingness which he had considered his years of suffering and testing—these had really been rich and fruitful years; and now that a little good fortune had descended on him, when he had moved from a condition of intellectual piracy into a certain integrity and bourgeois bondage, had an office and honors, possessed a wife and children, now he was exhausted and finished. To fail and despair—that's what was left for him.

He groaned, pressed his hands to his eyes and walked through the room as if possessed. What he had just thought was so terrible that he could not remain in the spot where the thought had come to him. He sat down on a chair near the wall, let his folded hands hang between his knees, and stared down dully at the floor.

His conscience . . . How loudly his conscience was crying! He had sinned, sinned against himself all these years, against the delicate instrument of his body. The excesses of his youthful spirits, the nights spent awake, the days in a room whose confined air was saturated with tobacco smoke, the excessive intellectuality and heedlessness of his body, the intoxicating stimulants with which he had goaded himself to work—this was now avenging itself.

And if it was taking vengeance, he would defy the gods who sent guilt and then imposed a penalty. He had lived as he had to live, he had not had time to be wise, no time to be cautious. Here, at this spot in his chest, when he breathed, coughed, yawned, always at the same point: this pain, this small, devilish, piercing, boring exhortation, which was never silent since that time in Erfurt five years ago when catarrhal fever, that inflammation of his chest, had seized him;—what did it mean? In truth he knew only too well what it meant—no matter what his

sie meinte,—mochte der Arzt sich stellen[9] wie er konnte und
wollte. Er hatte nicht Zeit, sich mit kluger Schonung zu begegnen,[10] mit milder Sittlichkeit hauszuhalten. Was er tun wollte,
mußte er bald tun, heute noch, schnell.—Sittlichkeit? Aber wie
kam es zuletzt, daß die Sünde gerade, die Hingabe an das
Schädliche und Verzehrende ihn moralischer dünkte als alle
Weisheit und kühle Zucht? Nicht sie, nicht die verächtliche
Kunst des guten Gewissens waren das Sittliche, sondern der
Kampf und die Not, die Leidenschaft und der Schmerz!

Der Schmerz . . . Wie das Wort ihm die Brust weitete! Er
reckte sich auf, verschränkte die Arme; und sein Blick, unter
den rötlichen zusammenstehenden Brauen, beseelte sich mit
schöner Klage. Man war noch nicht elend, ganz elend noch
nicht, solange es möglich war, seinem Elend eine stolze und
edle Benennung zu schenken. Eins war not: Der gute Mut,
seinem Leben große und schöne Namen zu geben! Das Leid
nicht auf Stubenluft und Konstipation zurückzuführen! Gesund
genug sein, um pathetisch sein—um über das Körperliche hin-
wegsehen, hinwegfühlen zu können! Nur hierin naiv sein, wenn
auch sonst wissend in allem! Glauben, an den Schmerz glauben
können . . . Aber er glaubte ja an den Schmerz, so tief, so innig,
daß etwas, was unter Schmerzen geschah, diesem Glauben
zufolge weder nutzlos noch schlecht sein konnte. Sein Blick
schwang sich zum Manuskript hinüber, und seine Arme ver-
schränkten sich fester über der Brust. . . . Das Talent selbst—
war es nicht Schmerz? Und wenn *das* dort, das unselige Werk,
ihn leiden machte, war es nicht in der Ordnung so und fast
schon ein gutes Zeichen? Es hatte noch niemals gesprudelt,
und sein Mißtrauen würde erst eigentlich beginnen, wenn es
das täte. Nur bei Stümpern und Dilettanten sprudelte es, bei
den Schnellzufriedenen und Unwissenden, die nicht unter dem
Druck und der Zucht des Talentes lebten. Denn das Talent,
meine Damen und Herren dort unten, weithin im Parterre,[11]
das Talent ist nichts Leichtes, nichts Tändelndes, es ist nicht
ohne weiteres[12] ein Können. In der Wurzel ist es *Bedürfnis,* ein
Kritisches Wissen um das Ideal, eine Ungenügsamkeit, die sich
ihr Können nicht ohne Qual erst schafft und steigert. Und den
Größten, den Ungenügsamsten ist ihr Talent die schärfste
Geißel. . . . Nicht klagen! Nicht prahlen! Bescheiden, geduldig

doctor could or might say. He did not have time to act with prudent care toward himself, to be thrifty with a gentle virtue. What he wanted to do he had to do soon, this very day, quickly.—Virtue? But how did it happen, after all, that it was precisely sin, surrender to what was harmful and consuming, which seemed to him more moral than all wisdom and cool discipline? Not this, not the contemptible art of good conscience was virtue, but struggle and distress, passion and pain.

Pain . . . How the word caused his chest to swell. He stood upright, folded his arms; and his eyes, under the reddish, joined eyebrows, were animated with beautiful lament. One was not wretched yet, not quite wretched yet, as long as it was possible to give one's misery a proud and noble name. One thing was needed: the good courage to give one's life great and beautiful names! Not to attribute one's suffering to the stuffy air in the room and constipation. To be healthy enough to be able to have lofty feelings, to be able to disregard the physical, to cease feeling it. To be naïve in this alone, though sophisticated in everything else. To believe, to be able to believe in pain . . . But he did believe in pain, so deeply, so fervently, that anything that happened amid pain could not, according to this faith, be either useless or bad. His eye turned to the manuscript, and his arms folded more tightly over his chest. . . . Talent itself—was it not pain? And if that thing over there, the unhappy work, caused him suffering, wasn't it proper and almost a good sign in itself? It had never gushed yet, and his distrust would really begin if it should do so. It gushed only for bunglers and dilettantes, for those who were easily satisfied and ignorant, who did not live under the pressure and discipline of talent. For talent, ladies and gentlemen down there far away in the orchestra, talent is not a facile thing, not a bauble; it is not a mere ability. At its root it is a *need*, a critical knowing of the ideal, a dissatisfaction that only creates and increases its skill; and not without torment. And for the greatest, the most exacting, their talent is the sharpest scourge.—Not to complain! Not to boast! To think modestly, patiently of what one endured!

denken von dem, was man trug! Und wenn nicht ein Tag in
der Woche, nicht eine Stunde von Leiden frei war—was weiter?
Die Lasten und Leistungen, die Anforderungen, Beschwerden,
Strapazen gering achten, *klein* sehen,—das war's, was groß
machte!

Er stand auf, zog die Dose und schnupfte gierig, warf dann
die Hände auf den Rücken und schritt so heftig durch das
Zimmer, daß die Flammen der Kerzen im Luftzuge flatterten. . . . Größe! Außerordentlichkeit! Welteroberung und Un-
sterblichkeit des Namens! Was galt alles Glück der ewig Unbekannten gegen dies Ziel? Gekannt sein,—gekannt und geliebt
von den Völkern der Erde! Schwatzet von Ichsucht, die ihr
nichts wißt von der Süßigkeit dieses Traumes und Dranges!
Ichsüchtig ist alles Außerordentliche, sofern es leidet. Mögt ihr
selbst zusehen, spricht es, ihr Sendungslosen, die ihr's auf Erden
so viel leichter habt! Und der Ehrgeiz spricht: Soll das Leiden
umsonst gewesen sein? Groß muß es mich machen! . . .

Die Flügel seiner großen Nase waren gespannt, sein Blick
drohte und schweifte. Seine Rechte war heftig und tief in den
Aufschlag seines Schlafrockes geschoben, während die Linke
geballt herniederhing. Eine fliegende Röte war in seine hageren
Wangen getreten, eine Lohe, emporgeschlagen aus der Glut
seines Künstleregoismus, jener Leidenschaft für sein Ich, die
unauslöschlich in seiner Tiefe brannte. Er kannte ihn wohl,
den heimlichen Rausch dieser Liebe. Zuweilen brauchte er nur
seine Hand zu betrachten, um von einer begeisterten Zärtlichkeit für sich selbst erfüllt zu werden, in deren Dienst er
alles, was ihm an Waffen des Talentes und der Kunst gegeben
war, zu stellen beschloß. Er durfte es, nichts war unedel daran.
Denn tiefer noch, als diese Ichsucht, lebte das Bewußtsein, sich
dennoch bei alldem im Dienste von irgend etwas Hohem, ohne
Verdienst freilich, sondern unter einer Notwendigkeit, unei-
gennützig zu verzehren und aufzuopfern. Und dies war seine
Eifersucht: daß niemand größer werde als er, der nicht auch
tiefer als er um dieses Hohe gelitten.

Niemand! . . . Er blieb stehen, die Hand über den Augen, den
Oberkörper halb seitwärts gewandt, ausweichend, fliehend.
Aber er fühlte schon den Stachel dieses unvermeidlichen

And if there was not a day in the week, not an hour that was free from suffering—what of it? To make light of one's burdens and achievements, of demands, difficulties, hardships, to see them as *petty*—it was that which made one great.

He stood up, took out his snuffbox and sniffed eagerly, then swiftly put his hands behind his back and strode so vehemently through the room that the candle flames fluttered in the draft. . . . Greatness! Extraordinariness! World conquest and an immortal name! What value was there in the happiness of the perpetually unknown compared with this goal? To be know—known and loved by the peoples of the earth! Prattle about egotism, you who know nothing of the sweetness of this dream and urge! Everything extraordinary is egotistical, insofar as it suffers. May you observe it yourselves, it speaks, you without a mission, for whom things on earth are so much easier! And ambition speaks: shall the suffering have been in vain? It must make me great! . . .

The nostrils of his large nose were taut, his eyes looked threatening and wild. His right hand was thrust vehemently and deeply into the opening of his dressing gown while his left hand hung down clenched. A fleeting red had spread over his haggard cheeks, a fire thrown up from the glow of his artist's egoism, that passion for his ego which burned inextinguishably in his depth. He knew it well, the secret intoxication of this love. At times he needed only to look at his hand to be filled with an enthusiastic tenderness for himself, in whose service he resolved to place everything that was given to him as weapons of his talent and art. He was permitted to do so; there was nothing ignoble about it. For even deeper than this egotism lay the consciousness that he was nevertheless, in spite of it all, unselfishly consuming and sacrificing himself in the service of something lofty; without any merit on his part, it is true, merely out of a feeling of necessity. And this was his jealousy: that no one should become greater than he, who had not also suffered more deeply than he for the sake of this lofty thing.

No one! . . . He stopped, his hand over his eyes, his torso turned half sideways, avoiding, fleeing. But he already felt the goad of this unavoidable thought in his heart, the thought of

Gedankens in seinem Herzen, des Gedankens an ihn, den
anderen, den Hellen, Tatseligen, Sinnlichen, Göttlich-Unbe-
wußten, an *den* dort, in Weimar, den er mit einer sehnsüchtigen
Feindschaft liebte. . . . Und wieder, wie stets, in tiefer Unruhe,
mit Hast und Eifer, fühlte er die Arbeit in sich beginnen, die
diesem Gedanken folgte: das eigene Wesen und Künstlertum
gegen das des anderen zu behaupten und abzugrenzen. . . .
War er denn größer? Worin? Warum? War es ein blutendes
Trotzdem, wenn er siegte? Würde je sein Erliegen ein tra-
gisches Schauspiel sein? Ein Gott, vielleicht,—ein Held war er
nicht. Aber es war leichter, ein Gott zu sein, als ein Held!—
Leichter . . . Der andere hatte es leichter! Mit weiser und glücklicher Hand Erkennen und Schaffen zu scheiden, das mochte
heiter und quallos und quellend fruchtbar machen. Aber war
Schaffen göttlich, so war Erkenntnis Heldentum, und beides
war der, ein Gott und ein Held, welcher erkennend schuf!

Der Wille zum Schweren . . . Ahnte man, wieviel Zucht und
Selbstüberwindung ein Satz, ein strenger Gedanke ihn kostete?
Denn zuletzt war er unwissend und wenig geschult, ein dumpfer
und schwärmender Träumer. Es war schwerer, einen Brief des
Julius[13] zu schreiben, als die beste Szene zu machen,—und war
es nicht darum auch fast schon das Höhere?—Vom ersten
rhythmischen Drange innerer Kunst nach Stoff, Materie, Möglichkeit des Ergusses—bis zum Gedanken, zum Bilde, zum
Worte, zur Zeile: welch Ringen! welch Leidensweg! Wunder
der Sehnsucht waren seine Werke, der Sehnsucht nach Form,
Gestalt, Begrenzung, Körperlichkeit, der Sehnsucht hinüber in
die klare Welt des anderen, der unmittelbar und mit göttlichem
Mund die besonnten Dinge bei Namen nannte.[14]

Dennoch, und jenem zum Trotz: Wer war ein Künstler, ein
Dichter gleich ihm, ihm selbst? Wer schuf, wie er, aus dem
Nichts, aus der eigenen Brust? War nicht als Musik,[15] als reines
Urbild des Seins ein Gedicht in seiner Seele geboren, lange
bevor es sich Gleichnis und Kleid aus der Welt der Erscheinungen lieh? Geschichte, Weltweisheit, Leidenschaft: Mittel
und Vorwände, nicht mehr, für etwas, was wenig mit ihnen zu
schaffen, was seine Heimat in orphischen[16] Tiefen hatte. Worte,
Begriffe: Tasten nur, die sein Künstlertum schlug, um ein
verborgenes Saitenspiel klingen zu machen. . . Wußte man das?

him, the other one, the bright one, happy in doing, sensuous, divinely unconscious—of *that man* there, in Weimar, whom he loved with a yearning enmity. . . . And once again, as always, in deep disquiet, with haste and zeal, he felt stirring within him the labor that followed this thought: to assert and delimit his own essence and artistry against that of the other. . . Was he really greater? In what? Why? When he triumphed, was it a bloody "despite"? Would his defeat ever be a tragic spectacle? A god, perhaps—he was no hero. But it was easier to be a god than a hero. Easier . . . The other had an easier time of it. To differentiate knowing and creating with a wise and lucky hand—that could make one serene and free from torment and gushingly fertile. But if creation was divine, knowledge was heroism and he was both, a god and a hero, who created knowingly.

The will to achieve the difficult . . . Did anyone suspect how much discipline and self-control a sentence, a rigorous thought cost him? For in the final analysis he was ignorant and had little schooling, a muddled, enthusiastic dreamer. It was harder to write a letter of Julius than to produce the best scene—and was it not, for that reason alone, almost the higher achievement?— From the first rhythmic impulse of inner art toward matter, material, a potential eruption—to the thought, image, word, line: what a struggle, what a way of suffering! His works were miracles of yearning, yearning for form, shape, limitation, corporeality; yearning for the clear world of the other one, who, directly and with divine lips, named the sunlit things by their names.

And yet, and despite the other: who else was an artist, a poet like himself? Who created, as he did, out of nothing, out of his own breast? Was not a poem born in his soul as music, as a pure archetype of being, long before it borrowed a symbol and dress from the world of phenomena? History, world wisdom, passion: means and pretexts, no more, for something that had little to do with them, that had its habitat in Orphic depths. Words, concepts: mere keys that his artistry struck to draw music out of a hidden instrument. . . . Was this known? They praised him highly, the good people, for the power of emotion

Sie priesen ihn sehr, die guten Leute, für die Kraft der Gesinnung, mit welcher er die oder jene Taste schlug. Und sein Lieblingswort, sein letztes Pathos, die große Glocke, mit der er zu den höchsten Festen der Seele rief, sie lockte viele herbei... Freiheit[17]... Mehr und weniger, wahrhaftig, begriff er darunter, als sie, wenn sie jubelten. Freiheit—was hieß das? Ein wenig Bürgerwürde doch nicht vor Fürstenthronen?[18] Laßt ihr euch träumen, was alles ein Geist mit dem Worte zu meinen wagt? Freiheit wovon? Wovon zuletzt noch? Vielleicht sogar noch vom Glücke, vom Menschenglück, dieser seidenen Fessel, dieser weichen und holden Verpflichtung...

Vom Glück... Seine Lippen zuckten; es war, als kehrte sein Blick sich nach innen, und langsam ließ er das Gesicht in die Hände sinken... Er war im Nebenzimmer. Bläuliches Licht floß von der Ampel, und der geblümte Vorhang verhüllte in stillen Falten das Fenster. Er stand am Bette, beugte sich über das süße Haupt auf dem Kissen ... Eine schwarze Locke ringelte sich über die Wange, die von der Blässe der Perle schien, und die kindlichen Lippen waren im Schlummer geöffnet ... Mein Weib! Geliebte! Folgtest du meiner Sehnsucht und tratest du zu mir, mein Glück zu sein? Du bist es, sei still! Und schlafe! Schlag jetzt nicht diese süßen, langschattenden Wimpern auf, um mich anzuschauen, so groß und dunkel, wie manchmal, als fragtest und suchtest du mich! Bei Gott, bei Gott, ich liebe dich sehr! Ich kann mein Gefühl nur zuweilen nicht finden, weil ich oft sehr müde vom Leiden bin und vom Ringen mit jener Aufgabe, welche mein Selbst mir stellt. Und ich darf nicht allzusehr dein, nie ganz in dir glücklich sein, um dessentwillen, was meine Sendung ist...

Er küßte sie, trennte sich von der lieblichen Wärme ihres Schlummers, sah um sich, kehrte zurück. Die Glocke mahnte ihn, wieweit schon die Nacht vorgeschritten, aber es war auch zugleich, als zeigte sie gütig das Ende einer schweren Stunde an. Er atmete auf, seine Lippen schlossen sich fest; er ging und ergriff die Feder... Nicht grübeln! Er war zu tief, um grübeln zu dürfen! Nicht ins Chaos hinabsteigen, sich wenigstens nicht dort aufhalten! Sondern aus dem Chaos, welches die Fülle ist, ans Licht emporheben, was fähig und reif ist, Form zu gewinnen. Nicht grübeln! Arbeiten! Begrenzen, ausschalten, gestalten, fertig werden!...

with which he struck this or that key. And his favorite word, his final transport, the great bell with which he summoned people to the highest banquets of the soul—it enticed many. . . Freedom . . . Truly, he understood more and less by it than they when they exulted. Freedom—what did it mean? Surely not a little civic dignity before the thrones of princes? Do you venture to dream of all that a spirit dares to mean by the word? Freedom from what? And from what after that? Perhaps even from happiness, from human happiness, that silken bond, that soft and sweet obligation. . .

From happiness . . . His lips twitched; it was as if his eye were turning inward and slowly he let his face sink into his hands. . . He was in the next room. A bluish light flowed from the lamp, and the flowered curtain concealed the window in silent folds. He stood by the bed, bent over the sweet head on the pillow . . . A black lock curled over her cheek, which seemed to have the pallor of a pearl, and the childlike lips were open in slumber . . . My wife! Beloved! Did you obey my yearning and did you come to me to be my happiness? You are that, be still! And sleep. Don't open those sweet, long shadowy lashes now to look at me with those big and dark eyes, as you sometimes do, as if you were questioning and seeking me. By Heaven, by Heaven, I love you very much. Only at times I can't find my feeling because I'm often very tired from suffering and from struggling with that task which my self imposes on me. And I must not be too much yours, never wholly happy in you, for the sake of that which is my mission. . .

He kissed her, separated himself from the pleasant warmth of her slumber, looked around and went back. The chiming clock reminded him how far the night had already progressed; but at the same time it was as if it kindly announced the end of a difficult hour. He drew a deep breath, his lips closed firmly; he went and took his pen. . . No brooding! He was too far down to be permitted to brood. No descent into chaos; at least no tarrying there. But raise out of the chaos that is fullness, into the light, what is capable and ripe for winning form. No brooding! Work! Limit, exclude, shape, complete! . . .

Und es wurde fertig, das Leidenswerk. Es wurde vielleicht nicht gut, aber es wurde fertig. Und als es fertig war, siehe, da war es auch gut. Und aus seiner Seele, aus Musik und Idee, rangen sich neue Werke hervor, klingende und schimmernde Gebilde, die in heiliger Form die unendliche Heimat wunderbar ahnen ließen, wie in der Muschel das Meer saust, dem sie entfischt ist.

Notes: Mann, *Schwere Stunde*

1. Friedrich Schiller (1759–1805) was ten years younger than Goethe. He was a dramatist, poet, historian, and philosopher and a liberal champion of free thought, in contrast to Goethe, who after a youthful fling at rebellion, was a political and social conservative. From 1799 until his death Schiller lived in Weimar, in close association with Goethe, with whom he had already corresponded in a series of notable letters. Schiller's health was always delicate; in his later years he produced his literary and philosophical writings in the shadow of death. These circumstances play a role in Thomas Mann's story.

2. Schiller was at this time professor of History at the University of Jena in Thuringia.

3. *auszutrinken.* Supply *war* (the last word in the sentence), had to be drunk up.

4. *alles,* everyone.

5. *ließ frei,* exposed.

6. *schwunglos* without verve, fire, inspiration, i.e. dull.

7. Christian Gottfried Körner was a wealthy man, an admirer and patron of Schiller. There is an extensive published correspondence between the two men.

8. Schiller's early drama *Don Carlos* (1787).

9. *sich stellen,* take a position.

10. *sich begegnen,* i.e., treat himself.

11. Schiller, a rhetorician by instinct, imagines he is delivering a speech.

12. *ohne weiteres,* simply (literally: without further ado).

13. The original title of Schiller's *Philosophische Briefe* was *Briefe Julius' an Raphael.*

And it was completed—that labor of suffering. Perhaps it did not turn out well, but it was completed. And when it was completed, behold, it was good too. And out of his soul, out of music and idea, new works struggled forth, ringing and gleaming structures, which in a sacred form offered a wonderful intuition of the infinite source of their being—as the sea roars in the shell that was fished from it.

14. This is a paraphrase of the opening thesis of Schiller's essay *Über naive und sentimentalische Dichtung*.

15. In a letter to Goethe (March 18, 1796) Schiller wrote that his creative works originated in a certain musical mental mood without a clear object.

16. Orphic; allusion to the Greek mysteries associated with the name of Orpheus.

17. The ideal of freedom pervades all of Schiller's work.

18. An allusion to the line *Männerstolz vor Königsthronen* (manly pride before the thrones of kings) in Schiller's ode *An die Freude* (*To Joy*).

Franz Kafka

1883–1924

Franz Kafka was born in Prague, the capital of Bohemia (now Czechoslovakia), at that time part of the Austro-Hungarian empire. The official culture in that historic city was German, but the majority of the population was Czech; life in the Jewish community exposed the young Kafka to a rich Jewish heritage and isolated him, to a degree, from the Gentile world. Kafka attended the German *Gymnasium* in Prague, then took a law degree at the German university. After a year of private practice he entered the service of the government-sponsored Workers' Insurance Institute, where he worked for ten years, after which he was retired on a pension because he had contracted severe tuberculosis. During the First World War he helped to manage an asbestos factory owned by his brother-in-law, who was away on military service. He formed a lasting friendship with the novelist Max Brod,[1] who became his literary mentor and ultimately his literary executor. It was Brod who disregarded

---

[1]Max Brod (1884–1968) author of novels, short stories, lyric poetry, and works on philosophy, religion, biography, and history.

Kafka's wish that his unpublished works be destroyed at his death. Three times Kafka was engaged to be married, twice to the same woman, Felice Bauer; he broke all three engagements. He had relationships with other women, notably a brief love affair with the brilliant journalist Milena Jesenskà. He spent the last years of his life in various sanatoria. In Dora Dymant he found a devoted companion who nursed him while he lived in dire poverty in Berlin. He died of tuberculosis of the throat in a sanatorium near Vienna.

Apart from the admiration of a small circle of friends, the only literary recognition Kafka achieved was the award of the Fontane prize for his story *The Stoker* (*Der Heizer,* 1913), which later became the opening chapter of his novel *Amerika* (1917).

Kafka's writings comprise three unfinished novels, nine superb stories, a miscellany of parables, sketches, and aphorisms, a remarkable diary extending over the period 1910—1923, and several volumes of letters.

Quantitatively, it is not an imposing literary output. Yet Kafka has had a more powerful impact on literate society than any other writer of the twentieth century. His fiction, depicting a world seen through a distorting mirror, has convinced readers that this is the way our life is; such is our existence in industrial and postindustrial society. More vividly, more profoundly than any other contemporary writer, Kafka has captured the anxiety, suffering, turmoil, the frustrated hope and longing that constitute the human condition. Our age, Max Brod wrote, will one day be called the age of Kafka.

Kafka's world is one in which irrationality, injustice, cruelty, and despair abound. The life he presents resembles a nightmare; it is a world in which all the laws of human thinking, feeling, and acting are suspended, in which cause and effect are reversed. *Because* a man is accused of a crime, the nature of which he does not even suspect, he begins to feel guilty—of what? He is never told by the officers of the court who process his trial, although he spends a whole year trying to find out. The narrator of *The Trial* (*Der Prozess,* 1925) makes it clear through his opening sentence that Joseph K., the hero, is innocent. "Someone must have slandered Joseph K., for without

having committed any crime he was arrested one morning." At
the end of the year the bewildered victim admits his guilt (for
form's sake? as a result of brainwashing? we are not told) and
half leads, is half led by, his executioners to an open place,
where he is executed "like a dog," and dies, not really convinced
of his guilt.

This is but one example of what has come to be known as
kafkaesque, a topsy-turvy world pervaded by anxiety and frustration: individual, social, and cosmic.

Writing at age thirty to his prospective father-in-law, Kafka
characterized himself as follows:

> My whole essence is focused on literature . . . If I ever abandon it,
> I shall no longer be alive. All that I am and am not results from
> this fixation. I am taciturn, unsocial, peevish, hypochondriacal, and
> literally sickly . . . I live in the midst of my family—the best, most
> loving people—more estranged than a stranger. In the past few
> years I have spoken on the average less than twenty words per day
> with my mother; with my father I have hardly ever exchanged
> more than a greeting. With my married sisters and brothers-in-law
> I am not on speaking terms, though I feel no anger toward them.
> I lack all sense of synchronous living with my family . . .

This statement was designed to explain why it was unwise for
Felice Bauer to embark on a joint life with him, but apparently
it failed to frighten her into withdrawing. It was Kafka who
broke the engagement, twice. We know from various sources
that Kafka's self-characterization is not exaggerated. He might
have added to it that he was indecisive, lacked self-confidence
to a pathological degree, and felt ashamed of his body, though
he was well built, with an attractive face and steel-blue eyes.
He was over solicitous of others' needs and rights, with an
uncertain ego structure, given to isolation and depression,
highly sensitive to noise, hyperexcitable, yielding occasionally
to rages. His sexual drive was either repressed or inadequate.
It has been suggested that he was a homosexual who was afraid
to admit it and that all his work is a defense of homosexuality.
He needed the companionship of women but feared physical

contact with them, for he tended to regard sex as dirty. He was a vegetarian and had a distaste for food altogether.

This is how Kafka conceived his mission in life:

> To tread the path of renunciation by refusing to use one's native predatory claws, never to hurt anyone as far as this is humanly possible . . . to transform one's own being into a burning and yet serene heart full of love and of love alone, to open oneself to a spirituality that is infinite and to know that in freedom one becomes further and further removed from material inhibitions, though one never loses sight of the material and spiritual need of mankind and seeks to render assistance in that need . . .

Max Brod, who knew Kafka better than anyone else, believed that Kafka lived this ideal in his daily life, that he was a living example to modern man. Milena Jesenskà confirmed Brod's view: "He was a man and artist of such scrupulous conscience that he remained wary even where others, the deaf, felt themselves to be secure." In a less rhapsodic mood Brod described his friend as "a mixture of hopelessness and constructive will." But he added, "In him these two opposites did not cancel each other out but elevated each other into infinitely complicated structures."

Kafka suffered from an anxiety neurosis. His father was a gigantic, self-made businessman of domineering, even brutal temperament, toward whom Franz developed a severe feeling of fear, to which he gave eloquent expression in his famous *Letter to My Father* (*Brief an den Vater*, 1917). Nor did his mother give him enough love to counteract the destructive influence of the tyrannical father. But he suffered from another kind of anxiety too. "My essential being is *Angst*," he wrote to Milena; the word keeps recurring in his letters to her. Kafka relates it to the "dirt" that is in him. He makes it clear that by dirt he means his falling away from the ideal of perfection and purity (*Ganzheit, Reinheit*) which he talks about in his diaries and aphorisms; the relapse into a state in which nature, the instincts, rebel against spirit. But the "constructive will" of which Brod speaks must not be forgotten. Many have testified to his outward serenity, his orderly life-style, his courtesy, friendliness, good companionship, and fine sense of humor. They marveled at

his purity of heart and mind, his honesty and integrity, his intense intellectual curiosity. He was in this world but not of it. It will not do to ask: Which is the real Kafka? the *poète maudit*[2] or the good companion? the morbid pessimist or the visionary idealist? Both are real. Kafka wrote in his diary: "I can derive temporary satisfaction from works like *A Country Doctor*,[3] assuming that they are successful (very improbably). But happiness comes to me only when I can elevate the world into the realm of the pure, true and immutable." One of his aphorisms reads: "Man cannot live without a lasting trust in something indestructible within him, although the indestructible element may be permanently concealed from him." By pointing to the idealistic, constructive, loving tone of the aphorisms and other reflective writings, Brod was able to explain away the tone of despair that pervades Kafka's fiction by claiming that it shows erring man in all his terror and abandon, who has lost the indestructible element, who has become uncertain in his belief, to whom the pristine faith has become almost unattainable, almost incomprehensible, although it still echoes within him with a faint ring. Brod is not alone; Martin Buber, too, sees Kafka as a positive religious thinker. And there are others: Wilhelm Emrich argues that behind the negative picture of life presented in the fiction, behind the puzzles, obscurities, and contradictions, there is a hidden truth, integrity, and beauty. Kafka himself wrote (surely with reference to himself): "Some deny the misery by pointing to the sun, others deny the sun by pointing to the misery." It is clear from what Kafka himself has written that he regarded himself as belonging to the latter class. Brod admits at one point of his apology that Kafka's work "is a mixture of nine elements of despair and one of hope." We may concede him that one part of hope; but it is hard to escape the conclusion that his protagonists—the searchers for salvation, grace, acceptance, and guidance—are not helped but actually thwarted and misled by those in power

---

[2] *poète maudit,* cursed poet: the conception of the poet as an outcast in modern society, despised by the philistines because he sees how empty their lives are. The phrase was coined by the French poet Paul Verlaine.

[3] *Ein Landarzt* (1920), one of Kafka's enigmatic parabolic stories.

and authority in this world, those whose official duty is to help and guide the honest quester. Erich Heller's phrase "negative transcendence," that is, diabolism elevated to a metaphysical principle, though it sounds harsh, comes closer to the message that most readers carry away from Kafka's fiction. Stefan Andres and Heinz Politzer support the negative interpretation. Politzer writes: "What we see in his novels, stories, and parables is absurdity and nihilism. Kafka is the parabolical writer of helplessness, who poses desperate questions to which we are given no answers."

But Kafka was not a philosopher, he was a creative writer who had a Flaubertian[4] conscience vis-à-vis the written word. How did he express his vision of life? What sort of art did he create?

He was an *Erlebnisdichter;* what he wrote was grounded in his own experience, in his personal life, his immediate surroundings (family, friends, the physical environment in which he lived) and chance observation, contemporary history, the zeitgeist, and his wide reading. He assigns to his characters names that point to himself: K, Josef K., Samsa and Bendemann (the sequence of letters in Samsa and Bende parallels that of the name Kafka). The description of the doorkeeper in *Before the Law* (*Vor dem Gesetz*) is based on doormen who stood outside the palaces of Prague. But to conclude from this that Kafka's work is essentially autobiographical or sociological is to read him superficially. Any sensitive reader feels the profound concern for man's condition and man's fate that emanates from these mystery-laden writings. Above all, they must not be interpreted psychologically. Kafka himself has warned us against such a misreading. He is not interested in revealing the motives from which individuals or groups act. Like the other expressionist[5] writers, he broke with the dominant tradition of fiction and drama since the Renaissance, which concerned itself prin-

---

[4]Gustave Flaubert (1821–80), one of the masters of French realism, a great stylist, was fanatically precise about choosing the right word (*le mot juste*).

[5]*Expressionism* was a European movement in the arts (c. 1910–c. 1930) which sought to penetrate beneath the surface of reality (the concern of naturalism and impressionism) to the true essence of things and to express this essence as an inner vision in ecstasy, often distorting everyday reality.

cipally with the study of individual psychology. Kafka does not write about men and women but about mankind and the human condition. As we read the little parable *A Commentary* (*Ein Kommentar*) we feel instantly, instinctively that the unnamed man in an unnamed place who sets out for the railroad station, the policeman whom he consults, the street, the clock tower "stand for" something deeper, something universal, cosmic.

But it is one of Kafka's many paradoxes that these cosmic tales are told in the most matter-of-fact, unadorned style, full of the accurate but irrelevant detail that was so dear to the naturalists. "It is a naturalistic representation of a fantastic world, which becomes credible through the minute precision of his images," André Gide wrote of Kafka. His style is one of classical clarity, honesty, strength, and integrity. It has an affinity with the style of Johann Peter Hebel, whose *Schatzkästlein* Kafka cherished. The contrast between content and form in Kafka's work is striking; it challenges the cast-iron rule in aesthetics that content and form must merge into each other. They don't in Kafka; perhaps the contrast underscores the unreality of the content.

Most parables in world literature permit only one clear, unequivocal interpretation; if they did not, they would confuse the reader or listener and miss their didactic purpose. Kafka's parables are an exception. The early interpreters of his work agreed that its character was "theological" in the broad sense of ontological, asking the basic questions about life and man. But after World War II, when Kafka became a powerful influence on the thinking world, the approaches to his work multiplied: the psychoanalysts, the sociologists, Jewish apologists, the existentialists, the Marxians, and latterly the structuralists and deconstructionists all lined up at the grindstone, whetting their axes. An examination of the recently published *Kafka Handbuch* (edited by Hartmut Binder) shows that Kafka exegesis has become an industry. The contemporary humorist Wolfgang Hildesheimer was moved to write an essay titled *Ich schreibe kein Buch über Kafka* (I am not writing a book about Kafka).

Some of Kafka's parables are transparent enough; others are difficult to fathom, some bewilderingly so. Friedrich Beissner has written that the best introduction to Kafka's work is through

the short fiction. In this spirit the following selection has been made. Nothing that is said about Kafka can be definitive, perhaps because Kafka was not a problem-solver but a problem-poser. In his fiction he set up various models, imagined situations that suggested different ways of reading the riddle of life. His models are described in such general terms that they admit of the most diverse, antithetical interpretations. This ambiguity is, of course, a mark of great literature.

What Camus said of *Der Prozess* applies to all of Kafka's work: "It is the fate and perhaps the greatness of his work that it offers every possibility but confirms none."

●

Since Kafka's parables lend themselves to such diverse interpretations, each of them has been furnished with a commentary, which follows the text of the parable.

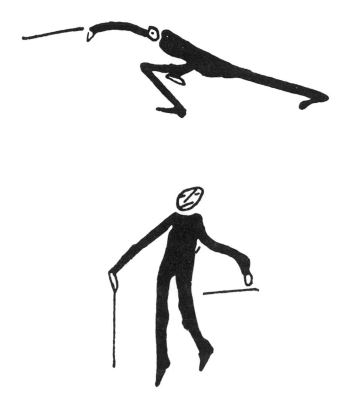

Drawings by Franz Kafka

Vor dem Gesetz

Vor dem Gesetz steht ein Türhüter. Zu diesem Türhüter kommt ein Mann vom Lande und bittet um Eintritt in das Gesetz. Aber der Türhüter sagt, daß er ihm jetzt den Eintritt nicht gewähren könne. Der Mann überlegt und fragt dann, ob er also später werde eintreten dürfen. »Es ist möglich«, sagt der Türhüter, »jetzt aber nicht.« Da das Tor zum Gesetz offensteht wie immer und der Türhüter beiseite tritt, bückt sich der Mann, um durch das Tor in das Innere zu sehn. Als der Türhüter das merkt, lacht er und sagt: »Wenn es dich so lockt, versuche es doch, trotz meines Verbotes hineinzugehn. Merke aber: Ich bin mächtig. Und ich bin nur der unterste Türhüter. Von Saal zu Saal stehn aber Türhüter, einer mächtiger als der andere. Schon den Anblick des dritten kann nicht einmal ich mehr ertragen.« Solche Schwierigkeiten hat der Mann vom Lande nicht erwartet; das Gesetz soll doch jedem und immer zugänglich sein, denkt er, aber als er jetzt den Türhüter in seinem Pelzmantel genauer ansieht, seine große Spitznase, den langen, dünnen, schwarzen tatarischen Bart, entschließt er sich, doch lieber zu warten, bis er die Erlaubnis zum Eintritt bekommt. Der Türhüter gibt ihm einen Schemel und läßt ihn seitwärts von der Tür sich niedersetzen. Dort sitzt er Tage und Jahre. Er macht viele Versuche, eingelassen zu werden, und ermüdet den Türhüter durch seine Bitten. Der Türhüter stellt öfters kleine Verhöre mit ihm an, fragt ihn über seine Heimat aus und nach vielem andern, es sind aber teilnahmslose Fragen, wie sie große Herren stellen, und zum Schlusse sagt er ihm immer wieder, daß er ihn noch nicht einlassen könne. Der Mann, der sich für seine Reise mit vielem ausgerüstet hat, verwendet alles, und sei es noch so wertvoll, um den Türhüter zu

Before the Law

Before the Law stands a doorkeeper. To this doorkeeper there comes an ordinary man and requests entry into the Law. But the doorkeeper says that he cannot grant him entry now. The man reflects on this and then asks whether he will be permitted to enter later on. "It's possible," says the doorkeeper, "but not now." Since the door to the Law stands open, as always, and the doorkeeper steps to one side, the man bends down to look through the door into the interior. When the doorkeeper notices this he laughs and says: "If the urge is so great, try to enter in spite of my prohibition. But mark you, I am powerful. And I am only the lowest doorkeeper. From hall to hall, however, there stand doorkeepers, one more powerful than the other. Even I cannot endure the mere sight of the third one." Such difficulties the man from the country did not expect; after all, he thinks, the Law is supposed to be accessible to everyone and at all times; but as he now looks more closely at the doorkeeper, in his fur coat, with his large sharp nose, with his long, sparse, black Tartar beard, he decides that he would rather wait until he receives permission to enter. The doorkeeper gives him a footstool and lets him sit down beside the door. There he sits for days and years. He makes many attempts to be admitted and wearies the doorkeeper with his requests. The doorkeeper often institutes brief interrogations with him, questions him about his native town and about many other matters, but they are indifferent questions, the kind that are put by men of high authority, and in the end he tells the man every time that he cannot admit him yet. The man, who has equipped himself amply for his journey, spends everything, however valuable it is, in his attempt to bribe the doorkeeper. The latter,

bestechen. Dieser nimmt zwar alles an, aber sagt dabei: »Ich nehme es nur an, damit du nicht glaubst, etwas versäumt zu haben.« Während der vielen Jahre beobachtet der Mann den Türhüter fast ununterbrochen. Er vergißt die andern Türhüter und dieser erste scheint ihm das einzige Hindernis für den Eintritt in das Gesetz. Er verflucht den unglücklichen Zufall, in den ersten Jahren rücksichtslos und laut, später, als er alt wird, brummt er nur noch vor sich hin. Er wird kindisch, und, da er in dem jahrelangen Studium des Türhüters auch die Flöhe in seinem Pelzkragen erkannt hat, bittet er auch die Flöhe, ihm zu helfen und den Türhüter umzustimmen. Schließlich wird sein Augenlicht schwach, und er weiß nicht, ob es um ihn wirklich dunkler wird, oder ob ihn nur seine Augen täuschen. Wohl aber erkennt er jetzt im Dunkel einen Glanz, der unverlöschlich aus der Türe des Gesetzes bricht. Nun lebt er nicht mehr lange. Vor seinem Tode sammeln sich in seinem Kopfe alle Erfahrungen der ganzen Zeit zu einer Frage, die er bisher an den Türhüter noch nicht gestellt hat. Er winkt ihm zu, da er seinen erstarrenden Körper nicht mehr aufrichten kann. Der Türhüter muß sich tief zu ihm hinunterneigen, denn der Größenunterschied hat sich sehr zu ungunsten des Mannes verändert. »Was willst du denn jetzt noch wissen?« fragt der Türhüter, »du bist unersättlich.« »Alle streben doch nach dem Gesetz«, sagt der Mann, »wieso kommt es, daß in den vielen Jahren niemand außer mir Einlaß verlangt hat?« Der Türhüter erkennt, daß der Mann schon an seinem Ende ist, und, um sein vergehendes Gehör noch zu erreichen, brüllt er ihn an: »Hier konnte niemand sonst Einlaß erhalten, denn dieser Eingang war nur für dich bestimmt. Ich gehe jetzt und schließe ihn.«

●

Commentary to *Vor dem Gesetz*

This parable is the core of the novel *The Trial* (Der Prozeß), of which it forms the penultimate chapter. Kafka called it a legend, but it is as much a parable as any of his shorter pieces. It was written in December 1914, when Kafka was working on *The Trial*, and published separately in an obscure magazine. The novel did not appear until 1925, a year after Kafka's death.

it is true, accepts it all, but says: "I only accept it so that you may not think you've neglected anything." During these many years the man observes the doorkeeper almost without interruption. He forgets the other doorkeepers, and this first one seems to him to be the only hindrance to his entry into the Law. He curses his bad luck, in his first years harshly and loudly; later, when he grows old, he merely mutters to himself. He becomes childish, and since, in his years of studying the doorkeeper, he has come to know even the fleas in his fur coat, he begs even the fleas to help him convert the doorkeeper. Finally the light in his eyes grows dim and he does not know whether the space about him is really growing darker or whether his eyes are only deceiving him. But now he does in fact recognize in the darkness an inextinguishable gleam of light that breaks through the door of the Law. Now he has not much longer to live. Before his death all the experiences of the whole time coalesce in his mind into one question, which he has not yet put to the doorkeeper. He beckons to him, since he can no longer command his stiffening body to sit up. The doorkeeper must bend low to him, for they have grown very much apart in size, to the man's disadvantage. "What do you want to know now?" the doorkeeper asks, "you are insatiable." "After all, everybody strives for the Law," says the man, "how does it happen that in these many years no one but me has sought admittance to it?" The doorkeeper realizes that the man is already near his end, so in order that his words may still reach his fading hearing, he bellows at him: "No one could be granted admittance here but you, for this entrance was destined for you alone. And now I'm going to lock it."

●

Commentary (continued)

The introductory note on Kafka gives some details about this great novel. As one follows the series of interrogations and investigations that constitute the action of the work, and the steps taken by Josef K to discover the charge on which he has been taken into custody, it becomes clear that this is no ordinary trial we are dealing with. This trial (or procedure, process—the

German word means all three) is a pilgrim's progress through
life in search of salvation, the word being taken in a broader
than the biblical sense. In the discussion that follows the recita-
tion of the parable, Josef K refers to the parable as a "message
or gospel of salvation" (die erlösende Mitteilung). The phrase
applies to the whole novel, which is not about a civil or criminal
offense, but about existential guilt, the sense of inadequacy or
despair felt by men of good will who strive to understand God's
ways with man but find no satisfying answer to their quest.

1. "Der Mann vom Lande" sounds as awkward in German
as its equivalent in English. It is a literal translation of the
Hebrew phrase *am ha-aretz*, which in Hebrew and Yiddish
denotes an uneducated man, usually with the pejorative over-
tone of "ignoramus." In this parable Kafka does not use it in
an insulting sense but rather neutrally for the average man,
the *homme moyen sensuel*, Mr. Everyman, who is untrained in the
Law but yearns to enjoy the benefits that accrue to those who
are admitted to the Law.

2. When Kafka speaks of the Law he is translating the Hebrew word *Torah*, which is often rendered as "the Law," although it literally means "the teaching" [of Moses, the prophets,
and the rabbis]. When Jesus says: "Think not that I am come
to destroy the law or the prophets" (Matthew 5:17), he is referring to the whole body of prescriptions and prohibitions that
constitute the Mosaic religion, which covers the total sphere of
human activity: man's relationship to God and to his fellow
man, as embodied in his conception of justice, good living,
personal hygiene, theology, and ritual. For Kafka, who was not
an orthodox Jew, the Law meant the code of ethics that regulates
human relations, belief in the existence of a world order that
is rational and humane, one that enables us to believe that the
universe is being directed by an intelligent and benevolent deity.
Hermann Hesse goes too far perhaps when he equates Kafka's
Law with God, but it does suggest a rational and humane world
order, one in which there is no place for the sort of parables
that Kafka felt compelled to write. It is relevant to note here
that in the Jewish religion the concept of law in the narrow
sense plays a significant role. A large portion of the Pentateuch
and the Talmud is devoted to *halakha*, which means law. On

the Holy Days (Rosh Hashana and Yom Kippur) the whole of mankind faces a trial in the celestial court, where God sits in judgment, takes testimony from the good angels and from Satan about the conduct of every living soul, and inscribes us all in the "book of life" or of death. There can be no doubt that these traditional Jewish conceptions left their imprint on Kafka's mind, at least as literary metaphors. To "enter the Torah" is a phrase used in the Jewish liturgy. It may well be the source of Kafka's basic image of entering the Law, which means the hope of being admitted to the company of those who accept the world and life in it as a just and humane enterprise.

3. To help man attain this blessed condition there are special guides, teachers, and mentors whose business it is to enlighten the seeker and make it easier for him to gain admittance to the Law but also to keep out those who are unworthy of entering. The doorkeeper may be thought of as a priest but he may also be a parent, a teacher, a philosopher, or a great artist. Kafka, echoing Tolstoy, once noted that writing is a form of prayer. For great books have been guides to many seekers for the way to enter the Law. One thinks of the Book of Job, Sophocles' *Oedipus,* Dante's *Divine Comedy,* Bunyan's *Pilgrim's Progress,* and Kafka's *Castle.* Great books, paintings, sculptures, cathedrals, musical compositions have changed people's lives. Rilke, contemplating the torso of an archaic statue of Apollo, read from it the admonition: You must change your life (Du mußt dein Leben ändern). Many artists have been seekers themselves; some have felt that they had been admitted to the Law; others were uncertain but kept hoping and dreaming; still others, like Thomas Hardy, felt that there was nothing behind the door, not even the gleam of light that shines for Kafka's Everyman at the end of his life.

4. In the debate that follows the narration of the parable the priest points to a contradiction between the doorkeeper's early statement that the gate to the Law always remains open and his closing remark: "Now I'm going to lock it." The priest dismisses this contradiction as a fallacy but does not explain why it is fallacious. The explanation is simple: In the text of the parable the entrance to the Law is denoted at first by the word *Tor* (lines 6 and 8) which means gate, gateway, portal [of

a castle]; later (in lines 21 and 44) by the word *Tür*. It seems that Kafka pictured the edifice of the Law as a building approached by a portal or gate, after which one enters a mansion consisting of a series of chambers one behind the other, each supplied with a door that is guarded by a doorkeeper. The parable tells us that the gateway to the Law is always open but that a doorkeeper stands before the door of each inner chamber. Apparently the man from the country had no difficulty in getting inside the gate; but in the house itself he sits in total darkness. When the doorkeeper tells him at the end of his life: "This entrance [*Eingang* in the third last line of the parable] was reserved for you alone," he means this door, not the outside gate.

5. The priest also maintains that Josef K is mistaken in his belief that the Court is hostile to him. The priest's arguments are mostly specious and pedantic. For instance: When Josef K asks the priest why the doorkeeper did not tell the man from the country until shortly before his death that this door had been especially reserved for him ("his message of salvation") the priest replies: because he wasn't asked till then. This is technically correct; it is true that it did not occur to the simple quester before then to ask why no one else had appeared before the door to seek admittance to the Law. But this circumstance does not alter the fact that the fervent seeker did everything in his power to enter the Law. If the doorkeeper and those he represents had been interested in encouraging the man from the country in his quest, they should have informed him that this door had been especially reserved for him. Instead the doorkeeper discouraged him by telling him about the phalanx of doorkeepers who were all dedicated to the mission of keeping him out of the Law.

6. Hartmut Binder adds an additional charge of his own against our poor rustic. Binder sees the focal point of the parable in the circumstance that the man from the country makes no attempt to test the doorkeeper's claims by simply walking through the door, since, as he tells the doorkeeper, the Law is open to everyone. But is such an expectation reasonable? Here we have an unsophisticated, unlettered man of deep faith in the world order who, on the strength of the doorkeeper's state-

ment that some day later he may be admitted, is willing to spend his whole life waiting and planning and scheming to get in. He believes in the Law and its representatives, the door-keepers, each more powerful than the one below him. Can such a man be expected to defy the priestly or secular hierarchy and walk through the forbidden door, especially when the door-keeper keeps telling him "Yes, but not yet"? Are we not in a parallel situation to that in the parable *Ein Kommentar*, printed below? Surely in a well-ordered world it would be the duty of the doorkeepers to instruct Mr. Everyman how to get through the door into the Law, just as the policeman in *Ein Kommentar* should tell the traveler how to get to the railway station. But, like the policeman there, the doorkeepers obstruct the way to the Law and confuse the simple believer. To tell the earnest and truly dedicated seeker at the end of his lifelong wait that this door was reserved especially for him is a malicious mockery. The wise Oedipus defied the oracle and ended in disaster. Our man from the country obeys the oracle and ends in disaster. No wonder he feels that the world is built on a lie.

7. There is not room here to pursue the priest's flimsy de-fense of his colleague, the doorkeeper. But the cleric's final statement is significant. He tells Josef K that the doorkeeper is above human judgment by virtue of the fact that he is in the service of the Law. This claim Josef K rejects because it implies infallibility in the servants of the Law and the priest has admitted that not all the doorkeeper's views are true. To this the priest counters that they may not be true but they are necessary. "A melancholy opinion" replies Josef K; "it bases the world order on a lie."

What is meant by the formula "not true but necessary"? The priest argues for the Macchiavellian principle of *raison d'Etat*: what is good for the State, for society, for an organized religious order is true even if it runs counter to individual morality and the dictates of reason, justice, common sense and even facts. Captain Dreyfus was guilty of treason even after the evidence showed that he had been framed, because to admit that the judicial condemnation was wrong would do grievous harm to the authority of the State and the army. It was necessary that he should remain guilty, therefore he *was* guilty. Similarly it

was necessary to assume that Galileo's contention that the earth revolves about the sun was subversive of the Church's teaching; therefore it was false. Similarly Darwin's theory of evolution runs counter to the teaching of Genesis; therefore evolution must yield to the necessity of upholding the structure of faith. The priest's position is like that of the Grand Inquisitor in Dostoevski's parable in *The Brothers Karamazov*. It is to this that Josef K replies: "A melancholy opinion; it bases the world on a lie."

These comments do not offer a solution to the enigma *Vor dem Gesetz* but suggest approaches to an interpretation of this and the following texts. As we noted in the biographical introduction, Kafka, who was himself a seeker, did not offer solutions but set up models that occurred to him as possible data that *might* lead to a theodicy that *could possibly* justify the ways of God to man. Perhaps he did not even go this far but took the position that Thomas Hardy did.

Drawings by Franz Kafka

Der Schlag ans Hoftor

Es war im Sommer, ein heißer Tag. Ich kam auf dem Nach-
hauseweg mit meiner Schwester an einem Hoftor vorüber. Ich
weiß nicht, schlug sie[1] aus Mutwillen ans Tor oder aus
Zerstreutheit oder drohte sie nur mit der Faust und schlug gar
nicht. Hundert Schritte weiter an der nach links sich wenden-
den Landstraße begann das Dorf. Wir kannten es nicht, aber
gleich nach dem ersten Haus kamen Leute hervor und winkten
uns, freundschaftlich oder warnend, selbst erschrocken, ge-
bückt vor Schrecken. Sie zeigten nach dem Hof, an dem wir
vorübergekommen waren, und erinnerten uns an den Schlag
ans Tor. Die Hofbesitzer werden uns verklagen, gleich werde
die Untersuchung beginnen. Ich war sehr ruhig und beruhigte
auch meine Schwester. Sie hatte den Schlag wahrscheinlich gar
nicht getan, und hätte sie ihn getan, so wird deswegen nirgends
auf der Welt ein Beweis geführt.[2] Ich suchte das auch den
Leuten um uns begreiflich zu machen, sie hörten mich an,
enthielten sich aber eines Urteils. Später sagten sie, nicht nur
meine Schwester, auch ich als Bruder werde angeklagt werden.
Ich nickte lächelnd. Alle blickten wir zum Hofe zurück, wie
man eine ferne Rauchwolke beobachtet und auf die Flamme
wartet. Und wirklich, bald sahen wir Reiter ins weit offene
Hoftor einreiten. Staub erhob sich, verhüllte alles, nur die
Spitzen der hohen Lanzen blinkten. Und kaum war die Truppe
im Hof verschwunden, schien sie gleich die Pferde gewendet
zu haben und war auf dem Wege zu uns. Ich drängte meine
Schwester fort, ich werde alles allein ins Reine bringen. Sie
weigerte sich, mich allein zu lassen. Ich sagte, sie solle sich aber
wenigstens umkleiden, um in einem besseren Kleid vor die
Herren[3] zu treten. Endlich folgte sie und machte sich auf den

The Knock at the Manor Gate

It was summer, a hot day. On the way home with my sister I
passed by the gate of an estate. I don't know whether she
knocked at the gate out of mischief or absentmindedly or
whether she didn't knock at all but only made a threatening
fist at it. A hundred feet farther on the country road, where it
turned left, the village began. We didn't know it, but right after
the first house people came out and waved to us, in friendship
or in warning, terrified themselves, bent low with terror. They
pointed to the manor house that we had passed and reminded
us of the knock on the gate. The owners of the manor house
would charge us, the inquiry would begin at once. I was very
calm and calmed my sister too. She had probably not knocked
at all, and if she had, nowhere in the world were such matters
a cause for investigation. I tried to make this clear to the people
around us, they listened to me but withheld judgment. Later
they said that not only my sister but I too, as her brother, would
be charged. I nodded with a smile. We all looked back at the
manor house, the way one observes a distant smoke cloud,
waiting for the flame. And sure enough, we soon saw horsemen
riding through the wide open manor gate. Dust rose, covering
everything, only the tips of the tall lances glittered. And scarcely
had the troop vanished in the courtyard when they seemed to
have turned the horses around and were on the way toward
us. I pushed my sister out of the way, I would clear everything
up myself. She refused to leave me alone. I told her she should
at least change her clothes, so that she could appear before the
authorities in a better dress. Finally she obeyed and set off on
the long way home. The horsemen were already beside us; still
sitting on their horses, they asked after my sister. She's not

langen Weg nach Hause. Schon waren die Reiter bei uns, noch
von den Pferden herab fragten sie nach meiner Schwester. Sie
ist augenblicklich nicht hier, wurde ängstlich geantwortet,
werde aber später kommen. Die Antwort wurde fast gleichgültig aufgenommen; wichtig schien vor allem, daß sie mich gefunden hatten. Es waren hauptsächlich zwei Herren, der Richter,
ein junger, lebhafter Mann, und sein stiller Gehilfe, der Aß-
mann genannt wurde. Ich wurde aufgefordert in die
Bauernstube einzutreten. Langsam, den Kopf wiegend, an den
Hosenträgern rückend, setzte ich mich unter den scharfen
Blicken der Herren in Gang. Noch glaubte ich fast, ein Wort
werde genügen, um mich, den Städter, sogar noch unter Ehren,
aus diesem Bauernvolk zu befreien. Aber als ich die Schwelle
der Stube überschritten hatte, sagte der Richter, der vorge-
sprungen war und mich schon erwartete: »Dieser Mann tut mir
leid.« Es war aber über allem Zweifel, daß er damit nicht meinen
gegenwärtigen Zustand meinte, sondern das, was mit mir
geschehen würde. Die Stube sah einer Gefängniszelle ähnlicher
als einer Bauernstube. Große Steinfliesen, dunkel, ganz kahle
Wand, irgendwo eingemauert ein eiserner Ring, in der Mitte
etwas, das halb Pritsche, halb Operationstisch war.

Könnte ich noch andere Luft schmecken[4] als die des Gefängnisses? Das ist die große Frage oder vielmehr, sie wäre es, wenn
ich noch Aussicht auf Entlassung hätte.

●

Commentary to *Der Schlag ans Hoftor*

"The Knock on the Manor Gate (Der Schlag ans Hoftor)"
was written early in 1917 and first published in the collection
At the Building of the Chinese Wall (*Beim Bau der chinesischen Mauer*,
1931). This is one of Kafka's dream stories. Its outstanding
feature is the rapid movement in time and space so characteristic
of the dream experience. The manor house changes into a
peasant's living room, then into a courtroom, then a jail cell,
finally into an operating table (for torturing the prisoner?).
Although the village begins after a turn of the road, so that
the peasants can't see the manor house, they are already aware
of the misdemeanor committed by the two protagonists and

here at the moment, came the anxious answer, but would come later. The answer was received almost with indifference; what seemed important above all was that they had found me. There were chiefly two gentlemen, the judge, a young, lively man, and his quiet assistant, whose name was Assmann. I was ordered to go into the farmhouse living room. Slowly, tossing my head and tugging at my suspenders, I began moving under the sharp eyes of the gentlemen. I still almost believed that a word would suffice to liberate me, the city man, even with honor, from this group of peasants. But when I had crossed the threshold of the living room, the judge, who had hastened ahead and was already waiting for me, said: "I feel sorry for this man." But it was beyond all doubt that he meant by that not my present state but what was going to happen to me. The room looked more like a prison cell than a farmhouse living room. Large stone flags, dark, a very bare wall, at some point in it an iron ring was cemented in, at the center something that was half bunk, half operating table.

Could I smell any other air than prison air? That is the great question, or rather it would be, if I still had any prospect of being released.

•

Commentary (continued)

quake with fear of the consequences it may produce. The troop of horsemen change from warriors in the service of the manor house into a judge and his assistant, whose name is Assmann (the irrelevant detail is characteristic of the dream) and who is very different in temperament from his superior. The judge has already made up his mind that the man is guilty, and the punishment is already being carried out.

The irony of the situation is that it was not the man who knocked on the gate but his sister, and it is doubtful whether she knocked at all or only made a fist. Even if she did knock, what is her crime? Is it *lèse majesté* or rebellious defiance or

youthful contempt for authority? The narrator, who is her accused brother, states that nowhere in the world is such an act a cause for criminal prosecution; yet almost instantly he, not the sister, is condemned and is sitting in the prison cell wondering if he will ever get out and, if he does, whether he will be able to endure the air of freedom.

Psychiatry recognizes a category of dream called the "anxiety dream." In this account of such a dream the protagonist's state of mind changes from supreme confidence to despair. It is one of the many instances in Kafka's work in which unmotivated (or inadequately motivated) guilt is presented as a frightening, crippling human experience.

Notes: Kafka, *Der Schlag ans Hoftor*

1. *schlug sie* = ob sie schlug.
2. *einen Beweis führen*, to take evidence or proof.
3. *Herren*, here lords, men in authority, gentlemen (in its older connotation).
4. *schmecken*, to taste is used colloquially for *smell*.

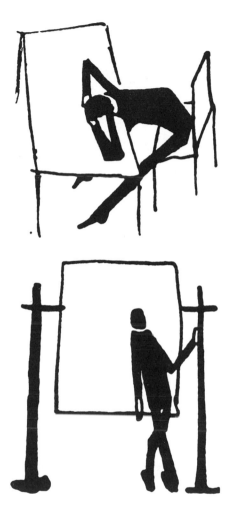
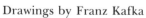

Drawings by Franz Kafka

Ein alltäglicher Heroismus

Ein alltäglicher Vorfall: sein Ertragen[1] eine alltägliche Verwirrung. A hat mit B aus H ein wichtiges Geschäft abzuschließen.
Er geht zur Vorbesprechung nach H, legt den Hin- und Her-
weg in je zehn Minuten zurück und rühmt sich zu Hause dieser
besonderen Schnelligkeit. Am nächsten Tag geht er wieder
nach H, diesmal zum endgültigen Geschäftsabschluß. Da dieser
voraussichtlich mehrere Stunden erfordern wird, geht A sehr
früh morgens fort. Obwohl aber alle Nebenumstände, wenigstens nach A's Meinung, völlig die gleichen sind wie am Vor-
tag, braucht er diesmal zum Weg nach H zehn Stunden. Als
er dort ermüdet abends ankommt, sagt man ihm, daß B, ärgerlich wegen A's Ausbleiben, vor einer halben Stunde zu A in
sein Dorf gegangen sei und sie sich eigentlich unterwegs hätten
treffen müssen. Man rät A zu warten. A aber, in Angst wegen
des Geschäftes, macht sich sofort auf und eilt nach Hause.

Diesmal legt er den Weg, ohne besonders darauf zu achten,
geradezu in einem Augenblick zurück. Zu Hause erfährt er, B
sei doch schon gleich früh gekommen—gleich nach dem Weg-
gang A's;[2] ja, er habe A im Haustor getroffen, ihn an das
Geschäft erinnert, aber A habe gesagt, er hätte jetzt keine Zeit,
er müsse jetzt eilig fort.

Trotz diesem unverständlichen Verhalten A's sei aber B doch
hier geblieben, um auf A zu warten. Er habe zwar schon oft
gefragt, ob A nicht schon wieder zurück sei, befinde sich aber
noch oben in A's Zimmer. Glücklich darüber, B jetzt noch zu
sprechen und ihm alles erklären zu können, läuft A die Treppe
hinauf. Schon ist er fast oben, da stolpert er, erleidet eine
Sehnenzerrung und fast ohnmächtig vor Schmerz, unfähig

An Everyday Heroism

An everyday occurrence; enduring it is an everyday heroism. A has an important business deal to conclude with B of H. He goes to H for a preliminary conference, covers the round trip in ten minutes each way and boasts of his speed when he gets home. Next day he goes to H again, this time to close the deal. Since this will presumably take several hours, A leaves very early next morning. But although the attendant circumstances are identical to those of yesterday—at least so it seems to A—it now takes him ten hours to reach H. When he gets there in the evening, exhausted, he is told that B, annoyed by A's failure to appear, had set out half an hour ago for A's village and that they really must have met on the way. A is advised to wait. But worried about the business deal, A sets out at once for home. This time he actually completes the journey, without giving the matter a thought, in one moment. At home he learns that B had arrived there very early in the morning, right after A's departure; in fact he had met A at the front door, had reminded him of their business deal, but A had said he had no time now, he had to hurry away. In spite of this incomprehensible behavior by A, B had remained here waiting for A. He had kept asking whether A was back yet but was now upstairs in A's room. Happy that he will still be able to talk to B and explain everything to him, A runs up the stairway. He is almost at the top when he stumbles, suffers a torn ligament, and, almost fainting from pain, unable even to cry out, only whimpering, he hears in the darkness how B—it is not clear whether from a great distance or close by him—stomps down the stairs in a fury and vanishes for good.

sogar zu schreien, nur winselnd im Dunkel hört er, wie B—undeutlich ob in großer Ferne oder knapp neben ihm—wütend
die Treppe hinunterstampft und endgültig verschwindet.

●

Commentary to *Ein alltäglicher Heroismus*

Written on October 21, 1917, An Everyday Heroism (*Ein alltäglicher Heroismus*) is a philosophical reflection in the form of a
textbook problem in mathematics. It has been printed under
the title *An Everyday Confusion* (*Eine alltägliche Verwirrung*), which
was supplied by Max Brod as a result of a misreading of the
opening sentence in the manuscript. Brod's title is misleading
as to the interpretation of the text and as to Kafka's judgment
of the event he portrays.

Here are six possible interpretations of this reflection:

1. In the light of the opening sentence one may say that
Kafka presents A's behavior as an everyday (that is, unheroic,
unsung) heroism. He anticipates what Albert Camus demonstrated later in his essay *The Myth of Sysiphus:* that Sysiphus'
perpetual rolling of the stone uphill, in spite of the repeated
frustration of his labor by Fate, is a noble or heroic act. According to Camus, the Greek myth celebrates man's nobility, which
consists in this: that Sysiphus continues to strive *because* (not
although) he knows that his existence, and therefore his effort,
is absurd, indeed meaningless. His knowledge of his condition
makes him superior to his fate. As he walks down the hill to
begin pushing the stone uphill once more, he reflects on his
wretched condition; this lucidity of mind constitutes his victory.
It is the same recognition that Oedipus achieves at the end of
Sophocles' tragedy. Camus writes: "The absurd man Sysiphus
says yes, and his effort will henceforth be unceasing . . .
Sysiphus teaches the higher fidelity that negates the gods and
raises rocks." Sysiphus lives under no illusion that in pushing
the rock uphill after repeated defeats he is doing God's will.
His own decision not to accept defeat, and the very effort itself
involved in the repeated act, give him dignity and fill his heart
with joy. Applying this interpretation to our text, we may be
certain that as soon as A is able to walk again, he will make a

new effort to close the deal with B or, failing that, will set out to make new deals. It is possible to argue that despite his many defeats and in spite of his fate, Sysiphus lives in the hope that the stone will one day stay put. Kafka's A, too, has the will to survive and to succeed; hope cannot be eradicated from his soul.

Is it necessary to add that the "business deal" about which Kafka writes is not a slap in the face of capitalism or the bourgeoisie? Kafka knew that there are many ways of serving God, or, in his language, of gaining admittance to the Law. Some wait all their lives before the gate; others go about their daily business. The fate that befalls A could strike him no matter what his business or profession, as will become evident from the third interpretation (below).

2. In §51 of *The World as Will and Representation* (*Die Welt als Wille und Vorstellung*) Schopenhauer writes that the most poignant type of tragedy is that in which the catastrophe is brought about by the mere confrontation of the characters, without involving a fateful error on the part of the hero (Aristotle's *hamartia*[3]) or an unheard of accident or the machinations of an evil antagonist. But in this most terrible type of tragedy, characters who are ethically normal people, under conditions that occur frequently, prepare the greatest misfortune for one another, knowingly and with open eyes, and neither side is wholly in the wrong. This type of tragedy demonstrates that we live in an irrational world governed by blind forces, which is the essence of Schopenhauer's philosophy.

3. There is a minor but important theme in world literature, which Germans have named *die Tücke des Objekts* (the malice of [inanimate] objects). The Italian Renaissance poet Tasso was convinced that a *faletto* or haunting spirit took pleasure in disarranging his papers, running off with his money, and playing a thousand other mischievous tricks on him. You bring someone to your house and find that you have left the house key inside; your spectacles are never there when you need them; after searching for them frantically, you are told that you have parked them on your head; a speck of dirt that flies into your eye as you step into the street prevents you from keeping an important business engagement; when you drop a slice of buttered bread it "always" falls buttered side down; you walk in the market

place along with scores of other people, but *you* are the one
who stumbles over the bushel of apples and you end up on the
ground with the apples rolling in all directions (the opening
scene of *The Golden Pot* (*Der goldene Topf*), a novella by E. T. A.
Hoffmann); you sit in a hushed concert hall, listening with rapt
attention to a divine performer, when you are suddenly overcome by an uncontrollable urge to sneeze. In Ludwig Tieck's
novella *The Witches' Sabbath* (*Der Hexensabbath*) the painter
Labitte can never finish a canvas, because at the moment of
highest inspiration he always begins to sneeze. He regards this
frustration as the work of the devil. An English writer, John
Beresford, has collected 1,243 types of such petty frustrations
in two volumes, *Miseries of Human Life* (1806–07). And Friedrich
Theodor Vischer has written a work of fiction, *Another One*
(*Auch Einer*, 1879), in which *die Tücke des Objekts* is developed
into a philosophical system containing a cosmology, a natural
philosophy, a theology, an aesthetic and ethic. Superficial
thinkers may talk of absent-mindedness and chance, but we
select few who have lived with this plague know better. There
are *foletti* out there, an army of them: sprites, gremlins, imps,
kobolds, who make their living by torturing sensitive people,
earnest souls who plan a business deal with all the care that
Kafka's anti-hero A puts into his preparations only to discover
that the *foletti* have been there again. Of course these clever
devils permit you minor successes along the way to encourage
you so that they may enjoy your ultimate discomfiture all the
more. In a world like Kafka's, governed by Murphy's law—anything that can go wrong will go wrong—it was inevitable that
the *Tücke des Objekts* theme should find a place in his writings.
And Kafka is in very good company: Lawrence Sterne (*Tristram
Shandy*), Jean Paul Richter (in several of his novels, but especially
in *The Comet* [*Der Komet*], E. T. A. Hoffmann (in *The Golden Pot*
[*Der goldene Topf*]), Lewis Carroll (*Alice in Wonderland*), and Isaac
Bashevis Singer. Comic writers are naturally drawn to this
theme, because those who are not themselves afflicted by the
syndrome tend to view it from the comic side. Wilhelm Busch,
Robert Benchley, James Thurber, and Ogden Nash (in a delightful "poem," "Two goes into two once, if you can get it
there") have exploited this fertile theme. A film actor, the late

Edgar Kennedy, made it his specialty: his famous "slow burn" was a crescendo of annoyance, rising to exasperation and fury as he finally acknowledged defeat by the *foletti*. There is a marvelous short film in which Robert Benchley decides to spend a pleasant, relaxed evening at home. He appears in the living room in a dressing gown with a magazine in his hand and makes for the easy chair in front of the television set. Then everything goes wrong; Murphy's law is working overtime; and he ends the evening in a state of near insanity.

Ein alltäglicher Heroismus is a classic example of *die Tücke des Objekts* at work.

4. The *Tücke* syndrome may be funny to those who are immune to it, but it borders on tragedy for its victims, as Vischer's *Another One* demonstrates. Its tragic aspect is frustration as a chronic phenomenon, an attitude to life which has been a staple of literature but which has become a central theme in modern times, that is, since the Renaissance. "As flies to wanton boys are we to the gods; / They kill us for their sport", says Gloucester in *King Lear*. These are the bitter words of a noble, despairing man. They have been echoed by many since they were first uttered on the Elizabethan stage. The notion that God is an Aristophanes who enjoys the human comedy that is being enacted on earth, to the discomfiture of its inhabitants, has been expressed often by modern writers, brilliantly by Heine and Anatole France. Thomas Hardy ends his tragic novel *Tess of the d'Urbervilles* with this reflection: "Justice was done and the President of the Immortals, in Aeschylean phrase, had ended his sport with Tess." A related notion is the suggestion that God is not in control of the universe, which is being managed (or mismanaged) by a demiurge or the devil. A far cry from the Lord's optimistic prediction at the beginning of *Faust*: "Ein guter Mensch, in seinem dunklen Drange / Ist sich des rechten Weges wohl bewußt" (A good man, in his dark urge, is well aware of the right way), or from Hugo von Hofmannsthal's acceptance of a world order as it is, in *The Great Salzburg World Theater (Das Salzburger große Welttheater)*.

5. The parallel with the *Oedipus* of Sophocles should be explored. Kafka's anti-hero is a good man, a businessman trying to make a living and working at it with energy. He goes out of

his way to succeed. Some Kafka interpreters, seeking a flaw in
his character in order to justify his utter failure, have pounced
upon his "excessive zeal." An aphorism from Kafka's *Er* is
quoted: "The original sin for which man was driven out of
paradise was impatience." Nineteenth-century scholars used to
justify Oedipus' ghastly fate on the same grounds of impatience
and excessive zeal. Oedipus got what he deserved for being an
eager beaver. More haste, less speed, and so on. Excessive zeal
for what? one asks.To escape the two most horrendous crimes,
parricide and incest? Can any zeal be called excessive in such
a cause? It is Oedipus' goodness, his nobility that brings disaster
on him. *Because* he is a noble man he cannot sit by and allow
the oracle to fulfill itself but must try to outwit it. That is the
motive force of his zeal. Can this be seriously advanced as an
Aristotelian *hamartia*? Similarly in Kafka: A, intent on assuring
a successful issue to his enterprise, aided by Fate during the
rehearsal stage, eager to make assurance doubly şure at the
consummation of the deal by setting out earlier than necessary,
is rewarded by crushing disaster. Recent commentators on
Oedipus interpret the play as an absurdist questioning of the
world order by the deeply religious Sophocles. It seems logical
to interpret Kafka's text in the same way.

6. A Marxian interpreter, Helmut Richter, sees this parable
of Kafka's as a purely artificial construct. "The accidental failure
of the two men to communicate with each other is systematized
so monstrously that nothing is left but absolute nonsense . . .
What we get here is not a reality that is disfigured by contradictions but a reality disfigured by the attitude of an observer who
has been decisively influenced by these contradictions." I think
he means that the contradictions and absurdities represented
in this paradigm are not inherent in the dialectical world order
as part of the world process, to be resolved in the Hegelian
synthesis, but are the subjective reaction of someone who is
going through life with the "wrong" (that is, non-Marxian) at-
titudes. Richter's position is representative of that taken by
Marxian criticism, which condemns Kafka for believing that
"man is sick and powerless and the world around him horrible
and unalterable;"[4] whereas Marxians know that only capitalist-
imperialist society is horrible and unalterable and that a Marx-

ian world order can alter all that, liquidating the social factors that cause the symptoms Kafka writes about.

So Kafka was not a Marxist, Richter tells us; agreed. As to the "artificial construct," that is what parables are: fictional illustrations of a moral lesson to be learned. They neglect to give names to the characters, fail to specify the location or time of the events they relate, and thereby universalize the point made by the parable: it can happen to anyone, everyone, all the time, everywhere. Richter's comment is patronizing: if only Kafka had been schooled in Marxist thinking, he would have been saved from writing such defeatist, subversive, counterrevolutionary heresy. For Marxists know better: all human problems can be solved by social engineering and by a correct interpretation of the historical process.

Notes: Kafka, *Ein alltäglicher Heroismus*

¹*Ertragen* means both *endurance* and *result.*

²This contradicts the statement of B's relatives that B had left H only half an hour before A's arrival there, which was in the evening.

³*Hamartia* is the tragic error committed by the hero of Greek tragedy, the cause of the misfortune that befalls him. See Aristotle's *Poetics* 13.

⁴The words of Soviet "Kafkologist" Dmitri Zatonsky, as reported by Stanley Corngold in the "German Quarterly," vol. 55 (May 1983), p. 522.

Kleine Fabel

"Ach", sagte die Maus, "die Welt wird enger mit jedem Tag.
Zuerst war sie so breit, daß ich Angst hatte, ich lief weiter und
war glücklich, daß ich endlich rechts und links in der Ferne
Mauern sah, aber diese langen Mauern eilen so schnell aufeinander zu, daß ich schon im letzten Zimmer bin, und dort
im Winkel steht die Falle, in die ich laufe." — "Du mußt nur
die Laufrichtung ändern", sagte die Katze und fraß sie.

●

Commentary to *Kleine Fabel*

Written toward the end of 1920, *A Little Fable (Kleine Fabel)* is
perhaps Kafka's most pessimistic parable. Life, human destiny,
is a cat-and-mouse game. Like the man from the country in
Vor dem Gesetz the mouse sets out on a quest for a way of life.
For the young person the world is too large, too formless; this
produces the anxiety of agoraphobia. So you limit your scope,
concentrate your ambition on a narrower goal. But this does
not bring satisfaction either, it merely yields a different form
of anxiety: claustrophobia. Now the world has walls, but these
seem to close in on you and threaten to crush you. Only too

A Little Fable

"Ah," said the mouse, "the world is getting tighter every day. At first it was so broad that I felt anxiety, I kept running and was happy to see finally walls to the right and left of me in the distance, but these long walls are speeding toward each other so fast that I'm already in the last room and there in the corner stands the trap into which I'm running." — "You need only change the direction in which you're running," said the cat and gobbled it up.

●

Commentary (continued)

soon you meet your nemesis: it is a trap that will stop your quest altogether. But just in time a counselor appears: the cat. Unlike the policeman in *Ein Kommentar* or the doorkeeper in *Vor dem Gesetz*, the cat seems really interested in the pilgrim's plight. His advice is simple: merely change your direction, go back to the formless world of your youth; that anxiety is better for you than this trap. But before the mouse has a chance to try this new direction, the cat solves the problem by cutting the Gordian knot.

Ein Kommentar

Es war sehr früh am Morgen, die Straßen rein und leer, ich ging zum Bahnhof. Als ich eine Turmuhr mit meiner Uhr verglich, sah ich, daß es schon viel später war, als ich geglaubt hatte, ich mußte mich sehr beeilen, der Schrecken über diese Entdeckung ließ mich im Weg unsicher werden, ich kannte mich in dieser Stadt noch nicht sehr gut aus, glücklicherweise war ein Schutzmann in der Nähe, ich lief zu ihm und fragte ihn atemlos nach dem Weg. Er lächelte und sagte: »Von mir willst du den Weg erfahren?« »Ja«, sagte ich, »da ich ihn selbst nicht finden kann.« »Gibs auf, gibs auf«, sagte er und wandte sich mit einem großen Schwunge ab, so wie Leute, die mit ihrem Lachen allein sein wollen.

●

Commentary to *Ein Kommentar*

This parable is known under the title *Give It Up* (*Gibs auf*), but Kafka's manuscript bears the title given here. It was written in December 1922 and first published in a Prague Jewish almanac. The title provokes the question: a commentary on what? A possible answer: on life. After subjecting the text to a laborious, casuistic, kafkaesque analysis, Heinz Politzer[1] concludes that this is not a realistic story but a parable. Even a cursory reading makes this clear. The affinity with *Vor dem Gesetz* is obvious. Mr. Everyman sets out on a quest for "the way." His preparations leave nothing to be desired: he sets out early, there are no hindrances or frustrating circumstances on the way to his goal: the railway station (= the castle, which is the goal in the novel by that title; the doorway to the Law). But the man cannot

A Commentary

It was very early in the morning, the streets clean and empty, I was going to the railway station. When I compared a tower clock with my pocket watch I saw that it was already much later than I had thought, I really had to hurry, the fright caused by this discovery made me uncertain of the way, I was still unfamiliar with this city, fortunately there was a policeman nearby, I ran to him and asked him breathlessly for the way. He smiled and said: "You want to know the way from *me?*" "Yes," I said, "since I can't find it myself." "Give it up, give it up," he said and turned aside with a sweeping gesture like people who want to be alone with their laughter.

●

Commentary (continued)

reach his destination because he is a stranger in the town (= the world). He meets an agent of the Law, a *Schutzmann* (= a protecting man), a security guard, who should be eager to help him. But this guardian of law and order sneers at the confused quester: "You expect to learn the way from *me?*" and turns his back on the simpleton, unwilling to embarrass him with his ridicule.

This parable reinforces the conclusion reached by the man from the country in *Vor dem Gesetz:* that the world is built on a lie.

Note: Kafka, *Ein Kommentar*

1. Heinz Politzer, *Franz Kafka, Parable and Paradox* (1962), p. 1 ff.

Heinrich Böll

1917–

A born storyteller by the grace of God, like Homer, Balzac, Dickens, Tolstoy, and in our own day Isaac Singer, Heinrich Böll writes fiction and essays that appeal to a broad spectrum of readers. In his lectures on aesthetics, delivered at the University of Frankfort in 1964, he refused to draw a sharp line between "true literature" and entertainment and propounded an "aesthetic of the human," that is, an art based on the ordinary concerns of life: the five senses (especially the sense of smell, which pervades his work as it does Heine's), the business of eating, sleeping, sex, clothing, working, the less pleasant functions of mankind, and the everyday social contact between people. Böll's novels have made the best-seller lists and have received the acclaim of the highbrows too. He has won a dozen or so literary prizes, including the most coveted one, the Nobel prize for literature, in 1972.

There are descriptive passages and episodes in his works that bear comparison with the best in Balzac, Flaubert, and Henry James. Two examples suffice. The fourth chapter of the novel *Unguarded House* (*Haus ohne Hüter*, 1954) opens with a factual

account of a visit to the dentist by Frau Brielach, a comely
widow who is driven by postwar conditions to live by her physical
attractiveness to men. The dentist tells her that she will lose all
her teeth unless she undergoes periodontal treatment. The cost
of this treatment is wholly beyond her financial reach. The
conversation between them is low-key, matter-of-fact, wholly
unemotional. But I know of no passage in literature more poignant than this in conveying the mental anguish of a human
creature faced with a hopeless situation.

Or take the opening of the novel *Group Portrait with Lady*
(*Gruppenbild mit Dame,* 1971). We are given a whole chapter of
vital statistics about Leni Gruyten, the forty-eight-year-old
"heroine": her height, weight, the color of her hair and eyes,
the way she wears her hair, her vocational history, her financial
situation, recorded with the bureaucratic pedantry of a police
report. This goes on for a whole chapter; yet one reads on.
And I know of no critic who has complained that this is the
way a seven-year-old girl would start a novel. For the fact is
that Böll carries it off because he is a superb storyteller, just as
Homer carries off his famous catalog of ships.

Heinrich Böll was born in 1917, when it was clear that the
First World War was finally being lost by Germany and her
allies. His early years were spent in his native Cologne, where
he experienced, along with many millions of Germans, hunger,
political turmoil, inflation, *the inflation,* the failure of the German
experiment in democracy, the beginning and growth of German
fascism, and the crash of 1929, which led to the Great Depression of the thirties. He was born into a lower middle class family
of devout Catholics. Both parents were vehemently opposed to
the Nazi movement, as they had been outraged by the mili-
tarism of the Wilhelmine regime. Heinrich attended a Roman
Catholic school that did not embrace the Nazi ideology, so that
a few of its pupils could refuse to join the Hitler Youth Movement without suffering drastic consequences. After finishing
the *Gymnasium*[1] he was apprenticed to a second-hand bookseller
in Bonn. He began to write about this time (1937) and produced
half a dozen novels, none of which has been published. After

[1]*Gymnasium.* See note 1 on pp. 53.

three months of study at the university he was drafted into the
national labor force and, when war broke out in 1939, into the
army. For six years he was shunted over Nazi Europe: through
Poland, France, Russia, Rumania, and Hungary. He was seriously wounded several times and contracted typhoid fever. During a sick leave in 1942 he married; two years later he was so
fed up with army life that he deserted and returned to his wife
and child but rejoined his regiment before his defection was
discovered. Shortly before the war ended Böll was taken prisoner by the Americans, who moved him to France and Belgium,
where he was released and sent home to Cologne. He worked
in the family cabinet shop, resumed his academic studies and
began writing again. A few of his short stories appeared in
reputable newspapers and periodicals. For a year (1950) he
worked in the municipal statistical office, but boredom drove
him from this job to risk the precarious existence of a free-lance
writer. His faith in his own talent, however, was rewarded, for
in that same year he won the prize of the "Group of 47"[2] for
a satirical story *The Black Sheep* (*Die schwarzen Schafe*). From then
on Böll's life settled into the intellectual excitement produced
by his writings and the political controversies in which he found
himself more and more involved. He has written steadily:
novels, short stories, essays on current events and manners,
book reviews, radio and television scripts. He has given many
interviews and made many speeches. With his wife he has translated from contemporary English, American, and French literature. From 1971 to 1974 he served as president of the International PEN Club.[3] He lived for a while in Ireland and has
traveled widely in Europe, including Soviet bloc countries. He
has toured and lectured in the United States and visited Israel.
But his permanent home is still his native Cologne, which forms
the setting for much of his writing.

[2]*Gruppe 47*. A loose association of young writers of liberal, democratic, or
socialist persuasion who met annually from 1947 to 1977 to discuss matters of
common interest and to criticize one another's work. An annual prize was
awarded for the best work read at the conference.

[3]*PEN*. A club of writers formed in England, which spread over the literate
world. It stood for freedom of speech, international understanding, and the
abolition of political and racial hatred.

Theodor W. Adorno[4] writes of Böll that he could have made
life easy for himself by becoming Germany's official, representative writer, for he combines in his person the contradictory
qualities of a highly successful man of letters, an indisputably
progressive liberal, and a practicing Catholic. It required,
Adorno believes, extraordinary intellectual and moral strength
to resist this temptation, and Henrich Böll possesses that
strength. "The grapes did not hang too high for him to reach
them," Adorno concludes, "he spat them out." This moral courage to tell the truth as he sees it has got him into many scrapes
with both right and left; but he has never hesitated to enter
the lists on behalf of some wrong to be righted, some villainy
to be exposed, some warning to be issued to the nation or
humanity at large. Not that Böll is a belligerent personality or
that he likes the limelight; for those who know him well testify
to his innate modesty, unpretentiousness, his genuine dislike
of pomp, cant, snobbery, hypocrisy, and phoniness, all of which
are inseparable from public life. So he has steadfastly refused
to think of himself as a public person or celebrity. "A writer
publishes," he said in an interview, "but he is not a public
person." "Perhaps the most modest and least vain of contemporary German writers," Iring Fetscher said of him. Böll warns
us repeatedly against making images and icons out of artists,
who are given much more influence than they deserve. Böll
does not believe in hero worship or monuments or leaders or
gurus, and he wants no followers or disciples. The essential
trait of his character is nonconformism; he is a nonjoiner, an
outsider. Some have called him an anarchist, in the sense that
he does not believe in salvation through organization, except
when a crisis produces a spontaneous joint action to ward off
an evil situation.[5] We are not talking of ideology but of personal
character, of habitual, perhaps instinctive behavior. It is therefore not surprising that Böll's protagonists are antiestablish-
ment types, not professional rebels but natural, congenital antis.

Since Böll is an "anarchist" he should have no concern for

---

[4]Theodor W. Adorno (1903–69). An eminent sociologist, musicologist and
essayist.
[5]As happens at the end of the novel *Gruppenbild mit Dame*.

the political and social problems that beset his country or the world. Yet his commitment is so strong and deep that it has earned him the reputation as a moralist and the conscience of Germany. He protests against this and insists that his stories and novels are about love and that his principal concern is to play with literary forms, persons, and situations. But the printed record shows that his fertile and sharp intellect has explored the human condition as it manifests itself through German history in the twentieth century. And the discerning reader will discover that his regional fiction is a reflection of what ails the Western world at large.

At times he lets the cat out of the bag, as when he characterizes art as a good hiding place for intellectual dynamite and social time bombs. Or again when he writes: "There is nothing that doesn't concern us, that is: everything concerns us to some extent." And still again he mediates between the two antithetical positions: (1) the function of literature is to guard and defend human dignity through the word, but (2) the writer must not be a public conscience, a decrier of social and political wrongs, because that makes him a didactic preacher.[6]

"Anarchy and Tenderness" is the title that Bernt Balzer gave to his introductory essay to Böll's collected works. These are the two poles of Heinrich Böll's psyche. They represent a dialectical state of mind, for the anarchist is essentially a me-firster, while tenderness is an altruistic, self-sacrificing quality. Böll's expression of tenderness is preeminently exemplified through the role that women play in his writings. He points to the centrality of feminine influence in the life of Christ: Mary, Martha, the Magadelen, Veronica—women's hands ministering to Jesus.

Böll once told an interviewer that there are only two topics worth writing about: religion and love.[7] Love at any level, from the coarsest carnality to eros as the generating principle of the universe, to the love of God that passes all understanding or Spinoza's intellectual love of God, involves the most intimate

[6]Possibly an echo of Heine's admonition in his well-known political poem "Die Tendenz": Aber halte deine Dichtung / Nur so allgemein als möglich (But keep your writing as general as possible).

[7]George Orwell, and Heinrich Heine a century before him, expressed themselves in similar terms.

relationship between a human being and something outside oneself, and it demands respect, generosity, self-sacrifice, self-transcendence.[8] We can agree that love is a fit subject for high literature. But religion? What attraction can it have for left-wing intellectuals like Heine, Orwell, or Böll? for Böll the rebel, who has pronounced so many harsh judgments against the Roman Catholic church and its hierarchy? The fact is that committed liberal writers have recognized that secular humanism alone will not satisfy the needs of the human soul unless it is supplemented by a deeper experience that is akin to religion.[9] This experience goes beyond ethical behavior; it is a very different sphere of activity from that which goes on in parliaments or in the market place. Böll has adhered to Roman Catholicism even to the extent of paying his tithes to the church, strange though this may sound for an "anarchist" who distrusts all organization. He rebels when the church becomes untrue to its founding fathers and defends big business and exploitive capitalism and makes concordats with repressive political regimes. It would not surprise him, he writes in one place, if the churches would ally themselves with an atheistic society to destroy a person or a group that, out of mere trust in God, cast its lot not with society but with humanity at large. What irks Böll especially, as it irked Bernard Shaw, is the church's identification of morality with sexual morality and its failure to recognize marriage as a sacrament between two people bound together by love, whether it has been formalized and legalized by church or state.

If we ask what Böll is commited to, the answer is that he champions the old "eternal truths", the common decencies of civilized behavior; justice, honesty, integrity, love (instead of hate), peace instead of war, a fair distribution of the common wealth instead of its lopsided accumulation by the grasping few. Just as important is what he is against: crass materialism, nationalism, racism, amoral technology, ruthless efficiency, bureaucratic bungling and insensitivity, pedantry, and snob-

[8] Goethe's "stirb und werde" (die to become a higher being) in the poem "Blissful Yearning" ("Selige Sehnsucht").

[9] This contradicts the thesis of Freud's *Future of an Illusion* (1928). But we think differently about such matters today.

bery. He is a socialist of sorts, but not the sort that has established itself in the Soviet bloc and the third world.

There is a strong Utopian streak in Böll. So when he saw German society, after its almost total destruction in 1945, rebuild itself after the model of capitalist private enterprise, drawing former Nazis into the highest administrative posts of the Federal Republic, he spoke out sharply, sometimes savagely, against this new-old social order. Böll is a formidable dialectician and polemicist. He delivered both lusty and deft blows at what he regarded as the betrayal of basic principles of civilization. Theoretically, he was wholly justified in his feelings of indignation; but he forgot that neither the democratic society of the West nor the socialist bloc of the East was any closer to the ideal world he dreamed of.

Böll's early writings were naturally saturated with the experiences of the war and the Nazi nightmare that caused it. He wrote about them tragically; but his exquisite sense of humor soon asserted itself and he began to express himself in satire. Story after story in the fifties satirizes some aspect of German life or some general human foible. His satire has a delicate but telling thrust, which is, however, free from bitterness. He deplores the malicious humor of Wilhelm Busch.

Ideologically, there is in Böll's work a development from sheer negativism, a sort of Luddite syndrome,[10] through resignation, to a belief in the possibility of escaping into the Voltairian private garden,[11] although Böll himself will never cease to speak his mind where he sees or smells evil. In his middle years he felt the inadequacy of satire as a literary weapon. His clown Hans Schnier says so: "They laugh but learn little." Böll had similar doubts about the efficacy of irony. The distance, detachment, and critical balance that the ironic mode provides is a narcotic for the privileged few, says old Fähmel in *Billiards at Nine Thirty* (*Billard um halb zehn*). We see and proclaim the truth, so we need do nothing about it. To understand all is to

[10]The Luddites were English artisans who rioted in 1811 and destroyed the power looms that were taking away their bread.

[11]An allusion to the admonition at the end of *Candide* to cultivate one's own garden, i.e., to live one's own private life and ignore society.

forgive all, as the French proverb has it. Irony can become an excuse for inaction. So for a time Böll seemed to abandon irony and satire.

The "aesthetic of the human" mentioned above points to realistic literary theory. This is what the realists of the nineteenth century had in mind, as we saw in the introduction to Stifter. So does Böll's rejection of inwardness (*Innerlichkeit*). There is no doubt about it: Böll is a realist. His love of detailed description, his predilection for ordinary life, his courage in depicting sordid aspects of existence as something quite natural—all this belongs to the canon of realism. But like the realists too, Böll has affinities with romanticism: he tends to idealize characters, he demands absolute freedom for the artist to express himself, to go to extremes, "beyond limits," so that he may learn through trial and error where the limits are. He quotes Chesterton: "Exaggeration is the definition of art."

Böll has been criticized for creating black-and-white characters. The criticism is justified up to a point. From *Billard um halb zehn* Böll began to distribute virtue and vice more evenly on both sides of the conflict. The clown Hans Schnier is more complex and more contradictory than any of the earlier protagonists. And in *Gruppenbild mit Dame* and *Protective Custody* (*Fürsorgliche Belagerung*, 1979) we meet the whole spectrum of human conduct with a mixture of both good and bad in most of the characters.

To the charge that he was an old-fashioned writer, clinging to the narrative traditions of the nineteenth century, Böll countered that fashion belongs to the sphere of tailoring and hairdressing but has no place in art. He writes pithy, graceful, rhythmical prose, spiced with striking metaphors ("dark halls in which a melancholy humility had turned sour"), occasional aphorisms, and much delightful wit. But in truth Böll's style is not old-fashioned at all. He has experimented widely with different narrative forms and points of view, with the manipulation of narrative time, the technique of montage, flashbacks, and other current literary gimmicks. The ordinary reader doesn't notice them because he is so absorbed by the story; the scholar will find them if he looks.

The finest tribute to Böll's genius was penned by Ludwig Marcuse. Böll's essay "Mutter Ey," Marcuse wrote, is "a little idyll composed by God."[12] Agreed; but it should be pointed out that there are many other literary gems among his writings for which the same Author might well claim to be the source of inspiration; above all the incomparable little parable on freedom "They did *not* fly away" ("Weggeflogen sind sie nicht").

The Railway Station of Zimpren (*Der Bahnhof von Zimpren*) first appeared in the weekly periodical *Die Zeit* in 1958. It has been interpreted as a satire on the advertising industry. But its scope is surely wider. What Böll satirizes is the whole sphere of capitalist enterprise, illustrated by the specific example of an oil boom that is quickly followed by a bust. The vicissitudes of fortune narrated here could apply equally to the automobile industry, a furniture business, or an educational conglomerate. The tone of the satire is not harsh but gentle, so that our amusement is not malicious but indulgent. The events themselves are not humorous, they could have been treated tragically, as the history of many American ghost towns shows. But Böll chose to make us laugh this folly out of existence: *castigare ridendo mores*.[13]

In choosing a representative story from Heinrich Böll's work, one is confronted with an embarrassment of wealth. There are various categories: tragic war stories, sketches of contemporary life, many and varied character studies, and much satire. For Böll's short stories belong to his earlier period, when the satirical strain was strong in him. It therefore seemed right to reprint one of his satirical pieces which shows his delightful sense of humor alive at a time when he felt deeply distressed by the state of his country and the world.

[12]Ludwig Marcuse, "Neben den Erzählungen," in the collection of essays *In Sachen Böll*, edited by Marcel Reich-Ranicki. Ludwig Marcuse, essayist, critic, and literary scholar who taught at the University of Southern California, is not to be confused with the philosopher Herbert Marcuse.

[13]To chastise manners (or behavior) by ridiculing them.

Der Bahnhof von Zimpren

Für die Bahnbeamten des Verwaltungsbezirks Wöhnisch ist der Bahnhof von Zimpren längst[1] zum Inbegriff des Schreckens geworden. Ist jemand nachlässig im Dienst oder macht sich auf andere Weise bei seinen Vorgesetzten unbeliebt, so flüstert man sich zu: »Der, wenn der so weitermacht, wird noch nach Zimpren versetzt.« Und doch ist vor zwei Jahren noch eine Versetzung nach Zimpren der Traum aller Bahnbeamten des Verwaltungsberzirks Wöhnisch gewesen.

Als man nahe bei Zimpren erfolgreiche Erdölbohrungen vornahm, das flüssige Gold in meterdicken Strahlen aus der Erde quoll, stiegen die Grundstückspreise zunächst aufs Zehnfache. Doch warteten die klugen Bauern, bis der Preis, da auch nach vier Monaten noch das flüssige Gold in meterdicken Strahlen der Erde entströmte, aufs Hundertfache gestiegen war. Danach zog der Preis nicht mehr an, denn die Strahlen wurden dünner, achtzig, dreiundsechzig, schließlich vierzig Zentimeter dick; bei dieser Dicke blieb es ein halbes Jahr lang, und die Grundstückspreise, die erst aufs Fünfzigfache des Originalpreises gefallen waren, stiegen wieder aufs Neunundsechzigfache. Die Aktien der SUB TERRA SPES wurden nach vielen Schwankungen endlich stabil.

Nur eine einzige Person in Zimpren hatte diesem unverhofften Segen widerstanden: die sechzigjährige Witwe Klipp, die mit ihrem schwachsinnigen Knecht Goswin weiterhin ihr Land bebaute, während um ihre Felder herum Kolonien von Wellblechbaracken, Verkaufsbuden, Kinos enstanden, Arbeiterkinder in öligen Pfützen »Prospektor« spielten. Bald erschienen in soziologischen Fachzeitschriften die ersten Studien über das

The Railway Station of Zimpren

For the railway officials of the administrative district of Wöhnisch the railway station of Zimpren became a long time ago the very embodiment of terror.

If someone is negligent in the service or makes himself unpopular in some other way among his superiors, they whisper to each other: "That fellow, if he continues to perform like this, will be transferred to Zimpren yet." And yet, only two years ago, to be transferred to Zimpren was still the dream of every railway official in the district of Wöhnisch.

When successful oil drilling was begun near Zimpren and the liquid gold gushed out of the earth in meter-thick streams, real-estate prices immediately increased tenfold. But when four months later the liquid gold was still gushing out of the earth in meter-thick streams, smart farmers waited for the price to increase a hundredfold. After that, prices no longer went up because the streams became thinner: eighty, sixty-three, finally forty centimeters thick; this thickness lasted half a year, and real-estate prices, which had at first fallen fiftyfold from the original price, increased again to sixty-ninefold. After many such fluctuations the shares of Sub Terra Spes finally stabilized.

Only one single person in Zimpren had resisted this unexpected blessing: the sixty-year-old widow Klipp, who continued to cultivate her land with her feeble-minded hired man Goswin while around her fields colonies of corrugated shacks, commercial stands, and movie houses sprang up and the workers' children played "prospector" in oily puddles. Soon the first studies on the phenomenon of Zimpren appeared in sociological journals, shrewd essays, clever analyses, which aroused

Phänomen Zimpren, gescheite Arbeiten, geschickte Analysen, die in den entsprechenden Kreisen entsprechendes Aufsehen erregten. Es wurde auch ein Reportage-Roman »Himmel und Hölle von Zimpren« geschrieben, ein Film gedreht, und eine junge Adlige veröffentlichte in einer illustrierten Zeitung ihre höchst dezenten Memoiren »Als Straßenmädchen in Zimpren«. Die Bevölkerungszahl von Zimpren stieg innerhalb von zwei Jahren von dreihundertsiebenundachtzig auf sechsundfünfzigtausendachthundertneunzehn.

Die Bahnverwaltung hatte sich rasch auf den neuen Segen eingestellt: ein großes, modernes Bahnhofsgebäude mit großem Wartesaal, Benzinbad, Aktualitätenkino, Buchhandlung, Speisesaal und Güterabfertigung wurde mit einer Geschwindigkeit errichtet, die der fälschlicherweise für sprichwörtlich gehaltenen Langsamkeit der Bahnverwaltung offensichtlich widersprach. Der Chef des Verwaltungsbezirks Wöhnisch gab eine Parole heraus, die noch lange in aller Munde blieb: »Die Zukunft unseres Bezirks liegt in Zimpren.« Verdiente Beamte, deren Beförderung bisher am Planstellenmangel gescheitert war, wurden nun rasch befördert, nach Zimpren versetzt, und auf diese Weise sammelten sich in Zimpren die besten Kräfte[2] des Bezirks. Zimpren wurde in einer rasch einberufenen außerordentlichen Sitzung der Fahrplankommission zur D-Zug-Station[3] erhoben. Die Entwicklung gab zunächst diesem Eifer recht: immer noch strömten zahlreiche Arbeitsuchende nach Zimpren und standen begierig vor den Personalbüros Schlange.[4]

In den Kneipen, die sich in Zimpren auftaten, wurden die gute Witwe Klipp und ihr Knecht Goswin zu beliebten Gestalten; als folkloristischer Überrest, Repräsentanten der Urbevölkerung, gaben beide überraschende Beweise ihrer Trinkfestigkeit und einer Neigung zu Sprüchen, die den Zugewanderten bald schon eine stete Quelle der Heiterkeit wurden. Gern spendeten sie Flora Klipp einige Glas Starkbier, um sie sagen zu hören: »Trauet der Erde nimmer, nimmer traut ihr, denn einhundertacht Zentimeter tief«; und Goswin wiederholte nach zwei, drei Schnäpsen, sooft es verlangt wurde, den Spruch, den die meisten seiner Zuhörer schon aus den Bekenntnissen der jungen Adligen kannten, die sich—zu Unrecht übrigens—auch

appropriate attention in appropriate circles. In addition a documentary novel was written with the title *The Heaven and Hell of Zimpren*, a film was made, and a young aristocratic lady published her highly chaste memoirs, "A Street Woman in Zimpren," in an illustrated magazine. Within two years the population of Zimpren rose from 387 to 56,819 inhabitants.

The railway administration had quickly adjusted itself to the new blessing: a large modern railway station was erected, with a large waiting room, a dry-cleaning establishment, a documentary cinema, a bookstore, a dining room, and a baggage depot—with a speed that patently gave the lie to the falsely proverbial slowness of the railway bureaucracy. The head of the administrative district of Wöhnisch published a slogan that was repeated by everyone for a long time: "The future of our district lies in Zimpren." Deserving bureaucrats whose promotion had until now been frustrated by a lack of permanent established positions were now rapidly promoted, transferred to Zimpren; and thus the best minds of the district were assembled in Zimpren An extraordinary session of the schedule commission was swiftly convened to elevate Zimpren to the rank of an express train station. This zealous move was at first justified by further developments: numerous people in search of work kept streaming to Zimpren, lining up eagerly at the personnel offices.

In the taverns that opened up in Zimpren the good widow Klipp and her hired man Goswin became popular figures; as folkloristic remnants, representatives of the original population, they both offered astonishing proof of their drinking prowess and a penchant for proverbs that soon became a steady source of merriment for the newcomers. These gladly treated Flora Klipp to several glasses of strong beer to hear her say: "Never trust the earth, never trust it beyond a depth of one hundred and eight centimeters"; and Goswin, after two or three whiskeys, repeated to anyone who requested it the saying that most of his audience already knew from the confessions of the young aristocratic lady, who—unjustly, by the way—had

intimer Beziehungen zu Goswin gerühmt hatte; wer Goswin
ansprach, bekam zu hören: »Ihr werdet's ja sehen, sehen werdet ihr's.«

Inzwischen gedieh Zimpren unaufhaltsam; was ein ungeord-
netes Gemeinwesten aus Baracken, Wellblechbuden, fragwür-
digen Kneipen gewesen war, wurde eine wohlgeordnete kleine
Stadt, die sogar einmal einen Kongreß von Städtebauern beher-
bergte. Die SUB TERRA SPES hatte es längst aufgegeben, der
Witwe Klipp ihre Felder abzuschwatzen, die recht günstig in
der Nähe des Bahnhofs gelegen waren und auf eine schlimme
Weise zunächst die Entwicklung zu hindern schienen, später
aber von klugen Architekten als »äußerst rares Dekorum«
städtebaulich eingeplant und gepriesen wurden; so wuchsen
Kohlköpfe, Kartoffeln und Rüben genau an der Stelle, wo die
SUB TERRA SPES so gerne ihr Hauptverwaltungsgebäude und
ein Schwimmbad für Ingenieure der gehobenen Laufbahn
errichtet hätte.

Flora Klipp blieb unerbittlich, und Goswin wiederholte unerbittlich, wie die Respons einer Litanei, seinen Spruch: »Ihr
werdet's ja sehen, sehen werdet ihr's.« Mit dem ihm eigenen
Fleiß und mit Zärtlichkeit dünnte er weiterhin Rüben aus,
flantze Kartoffeln in schnurgerader[5] Reihe und beklagte in
unartikulierten Lauten den öligen Ruß, der das Blattgrün
verunzierte.

Es klang wie ein Gerücht, wurde auch wie ein solches geflü-
stert: daß die Erdölstrahlen dünner geworden seien; nicht
vierzig Zentimeter seien sie mehr dick, sondern—so raunte man
sich zu—sechsunddreißig; tatsächlich waren sie nur noch
achtundzwanzig Zentimeter dick, und als man offiziell noch
ihre Dicke mit vierunddreißig Zentimetern angab, betrug sie
nur noch neunzehn. Die halbamtliche Lüge wurde so weit
getrieben, daß man schließlich, als nichts, gar nichts mehr der
geduldigen Erde entströmte, noch verkünden ließ, der Strahl
sei noch fünfzehn Zentimeter dick. So ließ man das Öl, als es
schon vierzehn Tage lang überhaupt nicht mehr strömte,
offiziell weiterströmen; in nächtlicher Heimlichkeit wurde aus
entfernt gelegenen Bohrzentren der SUB TERRA SPES in Tankwa-
gen Öl herangebracht, das man der ahnungslosen Bahnverwaltung als Zimprensches Öl zur Verladung übergab. Doch setzte

boasted of having intimate relations with Goswin; anyone who addressed Goswin received the reply: "You shall see it indeed; see it you shall."

Meanwhile Zimpren flourished irresistibly; what had been a haphazard community of shacks, corrugated tin huts, and quesionable taverns became a well-ordered small town that once even played host to a convention of city designers. The firm Sub Terra Spes had long ago given up hope of wheedling the widow Klipp out of her fields, which were advantageously situated near the railway station and at first seemed to affect the development program adversely but were later incorporated by clever architects into the city plan and lauded as "extremely rare decorum"; and so cabbage heads, potatoes, and turnips grew on the very spot where Sub Terra Spes would have wished to erect its main administration building and a swimming pool for the engineers of the elevated train.

Flora Klipp remained inexorable, and Goswin repeated inexorably, like the response in a litany, his maxim: "You'll see it, you may be sure, see it you shall." With his characteristic zeal and with tenderness he continued to thin out turnips, plant potatoes in perfectly straight rows, and in inarticulate sounds to bemoan the oily soot that was disfiguring the green of the leaves.

It sounded like a rumor and was whispered about like one: that the streams of oil had grown thinner; they were no longer forty centimeters thick but—so they whispered to one another—thirty-six; in fact they were now only twenty-eight centimeters thick, and when the thickness was officially given out as thirty-four centimeters, it only amounted to nineteen. The semiofficial lie was carried so far that finally, when nothing, absolutely nothing, any longer flowed from the patient earth, it was still announced that the stream was still fifteen centimeters thick. And so, fourteen days after the oil had stopped flowing it was officially allowed to flow on; under the secrecy of night oil was hauled in tanker trucks from Sub Terra Spes drilling centers situated far away, and this was turned over to the unsuspecting railway administration to be loaded as oil from Zimpren. In the official production reports, however, the thickness of the

man in den offiziellen Produktionsberichten die Dicke des Strahls langsam herab: von fünfzehn auf zwölf, von zwölf auf sieben—und dann mit einem kühnen Sprung auf Null, wobei man das Versiegen als vorläufig bezeichnete, obwohl alle Eingeweihten wußten, daß es endgültig war.

Für den Bahnhof von Zimpren wurde gerade diese Zeit zu einer Blütezeit; wenn auch weniger Tankzüge mit Öl den Bahnhof verließen, so strömten die Arbeitsuchenden gerade jetzt mit einer Heftigkeit nach, die man der Geschicklichkeit des Pressechefs der SUB TERRA SPES zuschreiben muß; gleichzeitig aber strebten schon die Entlassenen von Zimpren weg, und selbst jene, die beim Abbau der Anlagen noch ganz gut für ein Jahr hätten ihr Brot verdienen können, kündigten, von den Gerüchten beunruhigt, und so erlebten die Billettschalter und die Gepäckaufbewahrung einen solchen Andrang, daß der verzweifelte Bahnhofsvorsteher, der seine besten Beamten kurz vor dem Zusammenbruch sah, Verstärkung anforderte. Es wurde eine außerordentliche Sitzung des Verwaltungsrates anberaumt und rasch eine neue—die fünfzehnte—Planstelle für Zimpren bewilligt. Es soll—wenn man dem Geflüster der Leute glauben darf—auf dieser außerordentlichen Sitzung heiß hergegangen sein; viele Mitglieder des Verwaltungsrates waren gegen die Bewilligung einer neuen Planstelle, doch der Chef des Verwaltungsbezirks Wöhnisch soll gesagt haben: »Es ist unsere Pflicht, dem unberechtigten pessimistischen Gemurmel der Masse eine optimistische Geste entgegenzusetzen.«

Auch der Büfettier der Bahnhofsgaststätte in Zimpren erlebte einen Andrang, der dem am Fahrkartenschalter entsprach: die Entlassenen mußten ihre Verzweiflung, die Zuströmenden ihre Hoffnung begießen, bis schließlich, da sich beim Bier die Zungen rasch lösten, allabendlich eine beide Gruppen verbindende verzweifelte Sauferei stattfand. Bei diesen Saufereien stellte sich heraus, daß der schwachsinnige Goswin durchaus imstande war, seine Respons aus dem Futur ins Präsens zu transponieren, denn er sagte jetzt: »Nun seht ihr's, seht ihr's nun?«

Verzweifelt versuchte das gesamte höhere technische Personal der SUB TERRA SPES, das Öl wieder zum Strömen zu bringen. Ein wettergebräunter, verwegen aussehender Mensch

stream was slowly reduced: from fifteen to twelve, from twelve to seven, and then with a bold leap to zero; at the same time the exhaustion was designated as temporary, although all the insiders knew that it was permanent.

For the railway station at Zimpren this period actually became a golden age; though fewer oil tankers left the station, men looking for work now streamed in with a density that must be credited to the skill of the head of the press bureau of Sub Terra Spes. At the same time those people of Zimpren who had lost their jobs were trying to get away from there, and even those who could quite easily have earned their bread for another year by helping to dismantle the equipment gave notice because they were disturbed by the rumors; and so the ticket office and the baggage depot experienced such a crush that the desperate stationmaster, who saw his best men facing a nervous breakdown demanded reinforcements. An extraordinary session of the administrative council was called and a new permanent position for Zimpren, the fifteenth, was sanctioned. If we can believe what people whispered, this extraordinary session was supposedly a turbulent one; many members of the administrative council were opposed to the sanctioning of a new permanent position; but the head of the administrative district of Wöhnisch is supposed to have said: "It is our duty to oppose the unjustified pessimistic grumbling of the masses with a gesture of optimism."

The manager of the buffet in the station restaurant of Zimpren also experienced a rush, corresponding to that felt at the ticket window; those who had been dismissed from their jobs had to wet their despair and those who were streaming into the place their hope, until finally, since the beer quickly loosened tongues, every evening a desperate boozing took place which brought the two groups together. At these booze fests it became evident that the feeble-minded Goswin was perfectly able to transpose his response from the future to the present, for he now said "Now you see it. Do you see it now?"

Desperately the total senior technical personnel of Sub Terra Spes tried to get the oil to flow again. A weather-beaten, daring-looking fellow dressed in a cowboylike outfit was flown in from

in cowboyartigem Gewand wurde aus fernen Gefilden per Flugzeug herangeholt; tagelang erschütterten gewaltige Sprengungen Erde und Menschen, doch auch dem Wettergebräunten gelang es nicht, auch nur einen einzigen Strahl von einem Millimeter Dicke aus der dunklen Erde zu locken. Von einem ihrer Äcker her, wo sie gerade Mohrrüben auszog, beobachtete Flora Klipp stundenlang einen sehr jungen Ingenieur, der verzweifelt einen Pumpenschwengel drehte; schließlich stieg sie über den Zaun, packte den jungen Mann an der Schulter, und da sie ihn weinen sah, nahm sie ihn an die Brust und sagte beschwichtigend: »Mein Gott, Junge, 'ne Kuh, die keine Milch mehr gibt, gibt nun mal keine Milch mehr.«

Da das Versiegen der Quellen so offensichtlich den Prognosen widersprach, wurde den immer düsterer klingenden Gerüchten als Würze eine Vokabel beigestreut, die die Gehirne ablenken sollte: Sabotage. Man scheute nicht davor zurück, Goswin zu verhaften, zu verhören, und obwohl man ihn mangels Beweises freisprechen mußte, so wurde doch eine Einzelheit aus seinem Vorleben bekanntgegeben, die manches Kopfschütteln verursachte: Er hatte in seiner Jugend zwei Jahre in einem Häuserblock gewohnt, in dem auch ein kommunistischer Straßenbahner gewohnt hatte. Nicht einmal die gute Flora Klipp wurde von Mißtrauen verschont; es fand eine Haussuchung bei ihr statt, doch wurde nichts Belastendes gefunden außer einem roten Strumpfband, für dessen Existenz Flora Klipp einen Grund angab, der die Kommission nicht ganz überzeugte: sie sagte, sie habe in ihrer Jugend eben gern rote Strumpfbänder getragen.

Die Aktien der SUB TERRA SPES wurden so wohlfeil wie fallende Blätter im Herbst, und man gab als Grund für die Aufgabe des Unternehmens Zimpren bekannt: politische Ursachen, die bekanntzugeben dem Staatswohl widerspreche, zwängen sie, das Feld zu räumen.

Zimpren verödete rasch; Bohrtürme wurden abmontiert, Baracken versteigert, der Grundstückspreis fiel auf die Hälfte seines ursprünglichen Wertes, doch hatte nicht ein einziger Bauer Mut, sich auf dieser schmutzigen, zertrampelten Erde zu versuchen. Die Wohnblocks wurden auf Abbruch verkauft, Kanalisationsröhren aus der Erde gerissen. Ein ganzes Jahr

distant fields; for days the earth and the people on it were shaken by powerful explosions, but even the weather-beaten fellow did not succeed in luring even a single one-millimeter-thick stream out of the dark earth. From one of her fields, on which she was just then pulling carrots, Flora Klipp observed a very young engineer desperately turning a pump handle for hours; finally she climbed over the fence, grasped the young man by the shoulder, and when she saw that he was in tears, she pressed him to her bosom and said to him soothingly: "Good Lord, lad, a cow that don't give no more milk just don't give no more milk."

Since the exhaustion of the source was such a flagrant contradiction of the prognoses that had been made, a new word was added to the rumors, which sounded more and more gloomy, as a spice to distract people's minds: the word *sabotage*. They did not shrink from arresting Goswin and interrogating him; and although he had to be released for lack of evidence, one detail from his former life was nevertheless made public, causing much head-shaking: in his youth he had lived for two years in a tenement house in which a communistic railway worker had lived too. Not even the good Flora Klipp was spared the ordeal of distrust; her house was searched but nothing incriminating was found except a red garter, for the existence of which Flora Klipp gave a reason that did not quite convince the commission: she said that in her youth she had just fancied red garters.

The shares of Sub Terra Spes became as cheap as falling leaves in autumn, and the reason for abandoning the enterprise was made public: political causes which, if they were made known, would endanger the welfare of the state, compelled them to clear out.

Zimpren rapidly became desolate; drilling rigs were dismantled, shacks were auctioned off, the price of real estate fell to half its original value: yet there wasn't a single farmer with enough courage to take a risk on this dirty, ravaged earth. The dwelling units were sold for scrap, the sewer pipes were torn out of the ground. For a whole year Zimpren was the El Dorado

lang war Zimpren das Dorado der Schrott- und Altwarenhänd-
ler, die nicht einmal die Güterabfertigung der Bahn frequen-
tierten, da sie ihre Beute auf alten Lastwagen abtransportierten:
Spinde und Spitaleinrichtungen, Biergläser, Schreibtische und
Straßenbahnschienen wurden auf diese Weise aus Zimpren
wieder weggeschleppt.

Lange Zeit hindurch bekam der Chef des Verwaltungsbezirks
Wöhnisch täglich eine anonyme Postkarte mit dem Text: »Die
Zukunft unseres Bezirks liegt in Zimpren.« Alle Versuche, den
Absender ausfindig zu machen, blieben erfolglos. Noch ein
halbes Jahr lang blieb Zimpren, da es in den internationalen
Fahrplänen als solche verzeichnet war, D-Zug-Station. So hiel-
ten hitzig daherbrausende Fernzüge auf diesem nagelneuen
Bahnhof mittlerer Größe, wo niemand ein- noch ausstieg; und
gar mancher Reisende, der sich gähnend aus dem Fenster
lehnte, fragte sich, was sich so mancher Reisende auf mancher
Station fragt: »Wozu halten wir denn hier?« Und sah er richtig:
standen Tränen in den Augen dieses intelligent aussehenden
Bahnbeamten, der mit schmerzlich zuckender Hand den Wink-
löffel hochhielt, um den Zug zu verabschieden?

Der Reisende sah richtig: Bahnhofsvorsteher Weinert weinte
wirklich; er, der sich seinerzeit von Hulkihn, einer Eilzugstation
ohne Zukunft, nach Zimpren hatte versetzen lassen, er sah hier
seine Intelligenz, sah seine Erfahrung, seine administrative
Begabung verschwendet. Und noch eine Person machte dem
gähnenden Reisenden diese Station unvergeßlich: jener zer-
lumpte Kerl, der sich auf seine Rübenhacke stützte und dem
Zug, der hinter der Schranke langsam anzog, nachbrüllte: »Nun
seht ihr's ja, seht ihr's nun?«

Im Laufe zweier trübseliger Jahre bildete sich in Zimpren
zwar wieder eine Gemeinde, eine kleine nur, denn die kluge
Flora Klipp hatte, als der Grundstückspreis endlich auf ein
Zehntel seines ursprünglichen Wertes gefallen war, fast ganz
Zimpren aufgekauft, nachdem der Boden von Altwaren- und
Schrotthändlern gründlich gesäubert worden war; doch auch
Frau Klipps Spekulation erwies sich als voreilig, da es ihr nicht
gelang, ausreichend Personal zur Bewirtschaftung des Bodens
nach Zimpren zu locken.

for secondhand and scrap metal dealers, who didn't even come near the freight shed, carting off their booty on old trucks; cabinets and hospital fixtures, beer glasses, desks, and street-car tracks were hauled away from Zimpren in this way.

For a long time the head of the administrative district of Wöhnisch received an anonymous postcard every day with the text "The future of our district is in Zimpren." All attempts to discover the identity of the sender failed. For half a year longer Zimpren remained an express train station, since it was designated as such in the international railway schedules. So steaming long-distance trains that raced by with a roar made a stop at this brand-new medium-sized station at which no one got out of or into the train; and many a traveler who leaned out of the window asked himself with a yawn the question that so many travelers ask at many railway stations: "Why are we stopping here anyway?" And was he seeing right? Were there tears in the eyes of this intelligent-looking railway official who, with a hand that trembled with pain, held up the sign that signaled the departure of the train?

The traveler had been right: Stationmaster Weinert was really weeping; he who in his day had had himself transfered from Hulkihn, an express train station without a future, saw his intelligence, his experience, his administrative gifts squandered in this place. And another person made this station unforgettable to the yawning traveler; that ragged fellow who supported himself on a turnip spade and roared after the train as it slowly pulled out of the station: "Now you see it, don't you? Do you see it now?"

It is true that in the course of two gloomy years a community once more developed in Zimpren, a small one, for the smart Flora Klipp had bought up almost the whole of Zimpren after the price of real estate hade fallen to a tenth of its original value and when the ground had been thoroughly cleansed of its secondhand and scrap metal dealers; but her speculations, too, turned out to be premature, since she did not succeed in luring enough personnel to Zimpren to farm the land.

Das einzige, das unverändert in Zimpren blieb, war der neue
Bahnhof; für einen Ort mit hunderttausend Einwohnern be-
rechnet, diente er nun siebenundachtzig. Groß ist der Bahnhof,
modern, mit allem Komfort ausgestattet. Die Bezirksverwal-
tung hatte seinerzeit nicht gezögert, den üblichen Prozentsatz
der Bausumme zur künstlerischen Verschönerung auszuwer-
fen; so ziert ein riesiges Fresko des genialen Hans Otto Winkler
die fensterlose Nordfront des Gebäudes; das Fresko, zu dem
die Bahnverwaltung das Motto »Der Mensch und das Rad« gestellt hat, ist in köstlichen graugrünen, schwarzen und orange-
farbenen Tönen ausgeführt, es stellt eine Kulturgeschichte des
Rades dar, doch der einzige Betrachter blieb, da die Bahnbeamten die Nordseite mieden, lange Zeit der schwachsinnige Goswin, der angesichts des Freskos sein Mittagbrot verzehrte, als
er das Gelände, das ursprünglich die Laderampe der SUB TERRA
SPES bedeckte, für die Kartoffelaussaat vorbereitete.

Als der neue Fahrplan herauskam, in dem Zimpren endgültig
als D-Zug-Station gestrichen wurde, brach der künstliche Op-
timismus der Bahnbeamten, den sie einige Monate lang zur
Schau trugen, zusammen. Hatten[6] sie sich mit dem Wort Krise
zu trösten versucht, so war nun nicht mehr zu übersehen, daß die
Permanenz des erreichten Zustandes das optimistische Wort
Krise nicht mehr rechtfertigte. Immerhin bevölkerten fünfzehn
Beamte—davon sechs mit Familie—den Bahnhof, an dem nun
die D-Züge verächtlich durchbrausten; den täglich drei Güter-
züge schweigend passierten, auf dem aber nur noch zwei Züge
wirklich hielten: ein Personenzug, der von Senstetten kommt
und nach Höhnkimme weiterfährt; ein anderer, der von Höhnkimme kommt und nach Senstetten fährt; tatsächlich bot[7]
Zimpren nur noch zwei Planstellen, während fünfzehn dort
besetzt waren.

Der Chef des Verwaltungsbezirks schlug—kühn wie immer—
vor, die Planstellen einfach abzuschaffen, die verdienten Beamten in aufstrebende Bahnhöfe zu versetzen, doch erhob der
»Interessenverband der Bahnbeamten« gegen diesen Beschluß
Einspruch und verwies—mit Recht—auf jenes Gesetz, das die
Abschaffung einer Planstelle so unmöglich macht wie die Abset-
zung des Bundeskanzlers. Auch brachte der Interessenverband
das Gutachten eines Erdölprospektors bei, der behauptete, man

The only thing in Zimpren that remained unchanged was the new railway station; planned for a city with a hundred thousand inhabitants, it now served eighty-seven. The station is large, modern, provided with every comfort. The district administration had in its day not hesitated to allot the usual percentage of the building costs for artistic beautification; thus the windowless northern elevation of the building is decorated with a huge fresco by the brilliant painter Hans Otto Winkler. The fresco, for which the railway administration supplied the motto "Man and the Wheel," was executed in exquisite tones of gray-green, black, and orange; it depicts the cultural history of the wheel; but since the railway officials avoided the north side, the only person who looked at it was, for a long time, the feeble-minded Goswin, who ate his lunch before the fresco when he was preparing the soil that had been originally covered by the loading ramp of the Sub Terra Spes for the potato crop.

When the new railway schedule was published, in which Zimpren was definitely removed from the list of express train stations, the artificial optimism that the railway officials had exhibited for some months finally collapsed. While they had tried to comfort themselves with the word *crisis,* it could no longer be ignored that the permanent state that had now been reached no longer justified the optimistic word *crisis.* Nevertheless fifteen officials—six of them with their families—populated the station, through which the express trains now roared contemptuously; which three freight trains passed in silence every day; but at which only two trains now really stopped: a local, which comes from Senstetten and goes on to Höhnkimme, another that comes from Höhnkimme and goes to Senstetten. In point of fact Zimpren now offered only two permanent positions, while fifteen were actually occupied.

The head of the administrative district—bold as ever— proposed that the permanent position should simply be abolished and the deserving bureaucrats transferred to stations that were showing growth; but the "Union of Railway Officials" objected to this decision and pointed—justly—to the law that makes the abolition of a permanent position as impossible as it is to dismiss the chancellor of the German federal government. The union also produced the testimony of an oil prospector, who stated

habe in Zimpren nicht tief genug gebohrt, habe vorzeitig die
Flinte ins Korn geworfen.[8] Es bestehe immer noch Hoffnung auf
Erdöl in Zimpren, doch sei ja bekannt, daß die Prospektoren der
SUB TERRA SPES nicht an Gott glaubten.[9]

Der Streit zwischen Bahnverwaltung und Interessenverband
schleppte sich von Instanz zu Instanz, gelangte vors Präze-
denzgericht, das sich gegen die Bahnverwaltung entschied—
und so bleiben die Planstellen in Zimpren bestehen und müssen
besetzt gehalten werden.

Besonders heftig beklagte sich der junge Bahnsekretär Suchtok, dem einst in der Schule eine große Zukunft prophezeit
worden war, der aber jetzt in Zimpren seit zwei Jahren einer
Abteilung vorsteht, die nicht einen einzigen Kunden gehabt
hat: der Gepäckaufbewahrung. Dem Vorsteher der Fahrkar-
tenabteilung geht es ein klein wenig besser, aber eben nur ein
ganz klein wenig. Den Leuten in der Signalabteilung bleibt
immerhin der Trost, daß sie die Drähte—wenn auch nicht für
Zimpren—summen hören, was beweist, daß irgendwo—wenn
auch nich in Zimpren—etwas geschieht.[10]

Die Frauen der älteren Beamten haben einen Bridge-Klub
gegründet, die der jüngeren ein Federball-Team aufgestellt,
aber sowohl den bridgespielenden wie den federballspielenden
Damen wurde die Lust verdorben durch Flora Klipp, die sich,
da es ihr an Arbeitskräften mangelt, auf den Feldern um den
Bahnhof herum abrackerte, nur hin und wieder ihre Arbeit
unterbrach, um ins Bahnhofsgebäude hinüberzurufen: »Beam-
tengesindel, erzfaules.«[11] Auch härtere Ausdrücke fielen, ordi-
näre, die jedoch nicht literaturfähig[12] sind. Goswin fühlte sich
durch die hübschen jungen Frauen, die auf dem Bahnhofsge-
lände Federball spielten, ebenfalls provoziert und bewies, daß
er sein Vokabularium vergrößert hatte, denn er schrie: »Huren,
nichts als Huren!«—ein Ausspruch, den jüngere, unverheira-
tete Bahnbeamte auf seine Bekanntschaft mit der jungen Adligen zurückführten.

Schließlich kamen die jüngeren wie die älteren Damen überein, diesen sich wiederholenden Tadel nicht auf sich sitzen
zu lassen; Klagen wurden eingereicht, Termine anberaumt,
Rechtsanwälte reisten herbei, und Bahnsekretär Suchtok, der
seit zwei Jahren vergeblich auf Kundschaft gewartet hatte, rieb

that they hadn't drilled deep enough in Zimpren, that they had thrown in the towel too soon. There was still hope for oil in Zimpren, but it was well known that the prospectors of the Sub Terra Spes did not believe in God.

The dispute between the railway officials and the union dragged on from court to court, came before the Court of Precedence, which decided against the railway administration; and so the permanent positions in Zimpren remain and must be filled.

An especially vehement complaint was registered by the young railway secretary Suchtok, for whom a great future had been foretold in his school years but who has now been in Zimpren for two years as head of a division that has not had one customer, not a single one: namely, the baggage-checking department. The head of the ticket department is a tiny bit better off, but only a tiny bit. The people in the signal division can at least find comfort in the fact that they hear the wires hum, though not for Zimpren, which proves that somewhere, though not in Zimpren, something is happening.

The wives of the older bureaucrats have formed a bridge club, those of the younger officials have put together a badminton team; both the bridge players and the badminton ladies have had their fun spoiled for them by Flora Klipp who, suffering from a dearth of field help, worked herself to the bone around the railway station; only now and then did she interrupt her work to shout into the railway station, "Bureaucratic riffraff, lazybones!" Harsher expressions fell too, vulgar ones that can't be repeated in a respectable publication. Goswin too felt provoked by the attractive young women playing badminton on the railway station property and demonstrated that he had enlarged his vocabulary by shouting "Whores, nothing but whores!" an expression the younger, unmarried railway bureaucrats traced back to his acquaintance with the young noblewoman.

Finally both the younger and older women agreed not to put up with this repeated censure. Complaints were registered, trial dates were set, attorneys arrived, and railway secretary Suchtok, who had been waiting in vain for two years for some customers, rubbed his hands in glee: on one single day two briefcases and

sich die Hände: an einem einzigen Tag wurden zwei Aktentaschen und drei Schirme abgegeben. Doch als er selber diese
Gegenstände entgegennehmen wollte, wurde er von seinem
Untergebenen, dem Bahnschaffner Uhlscheid, belehrt, daß er,
der Sekretär, zwar die Oberaufsicht führe, daß Entgegennahme
der Gegenstände aber seine, Uhlscheids, Aufgabe sei. Tatsächlich hatte Uhlscheid recht, und Suchtok[13] bleib nur der
Triumph, daß er abends, als die Gepäckstücke wieder abgeholt
wurden, die Gebühren kassieren durfte: fünfmal dreißig Pfen-
nige; das erstemal in zwei Jahren klingelte die nagelneue
Registrierkasse.

Der kluge Bahnhofsvorsteher hat inzwischen mit Flora Klipp
einen Kompromiß geschlossen: sie hat sich bereit erklärt, ihre—
wie sie eingesehen hat—unberechtigten Beschimpfungen ein-
zustellen; außerdem hat sie die Garantie dafür übernommen,
daß auch Goswin sich keinerlei Injurien mehr erlauben wird.
Als Gegenleistung, jedoch sozusagen privat, da dies offiziell
nicht möglich ist, hat er Witwe Klipp die Herrentoilette zur
Aufbewahrung ihres Ackergerätes und die Damentoilette zu
dem vom Architekten bestimmten Zweck zur Verfügung gestellt. Witwe Klipp darf sogar—doch muß dies streng geheim
bleiben, da es weit über die Natur einer Gefälligkeit hinausgeht—ihren Traktor im Güterschuppen unterstellen und ihr
Mittagbrot in den weichen Polstern des riesigen Speisesaals
einnehmen. Aus reiner Herzensgüte, da ihr der junge Suchtok
leid tut, gibt Witwe Klipp hin und wieder ihren Proviantbeutel
oder ihren Regenschirm bei der Gepäckaufbewahrung ab.

Nur wenigen Beamten ist es bisher gelungen, von Zimpren
versetzt zu werden; doch immer müssen die vakant werdenden
Stellen neu besetzt werden, und es ist im Verwaltungsbezirk
Wöhnisch längst ein offenes Geheimnis, daß Zimpren ein
Strafbahnhof ist: so häufen sich dort Rauf- und Trunkenbolde,
aufsässige Elemente, zum Schrecken jener anständigen Elemente, denen es noch nicht gelungen ist, ihre Versetzung
durchzudrücken.

Betrübt gab der Bahnhofsvorsteher vor wenigen Tagen seine
Unterschrift unter den jährlichen Kassenbericht, der Einnah-
men in Höhe von dreizehn Mark achtzig auswies; zwei Rückfahrkarten nach Senstetten wurden verkauft: das war der

three umbrellas were checked in. But when he wanted to receive these articles himself, he was informed by his subordinate, the railway guard Uhlscheid, that while he, the secretary, was indeed the supervisor, it was his, Uhlscheid's, duty to receive the objects. Uhlscheid was in fact right, and Suchtok was only able to enjoy the triumph of taking in the fees when the articles were claimed in the evening: five times thirty pfennigs; the brand-new cash register rang for the first time in two years.

The smart stationmaster has meanwhile made a compromise with Flora Klipp: she has declared herself ready to stop her—as she realizes—unjustified insults; she has, moreover, assumed the guarantee that Goswin too would not permit himself any more insults of any kind. In return for this favor, but privately so to speak, since this is not officially possible, he has placed the men's rest room at her disposal for storing her agricultural implements and the ladies' room for the purpose assigned to it by the architect. The widow Klipp is even permitted—but this must be kept a strict secret, since it goes far beyond the nature of a favor—to park her tractor in the freight shed and to eat her lunch on the soft cushions of the huge dining room. Out of sheer goodness of heart, since she feels sorry for young Suchtok, the widow Klipp now and then checks her lunch box or her umbrella at the baggage checking counter.

Few bureaucrats have thus far succeeded in being transferred out of Zimpren; still, the positions that become vacant must be replaced every time, and it has been an open secret in the administrative district of Wöhnisch for a very long time that Zimpren is a penal railway station; and so ruffians and drunkards, rebellious elements, gather there, to the terror of those decent folk who have not yet succeeded in pushing their transfer through.

Sadly the stationmaster put his signature a few days ago to the treasurer's annual report, which showed receipts of fifteen marks and eighty pfennigs, from two round trips to Senstetten; they were for the sacristan of Zimpren and his sole acolyte,

Küster von Zimpren mit seinem einzigen Meßdiener, die zum alljährlich fälligen gemeinsamen Ausflug bis Senstetten fuhren, um dort die herrliche Lourdes-Grotte[14] zu besichtigen; zwei Rückfahrkarten nach Höhnkimme, der Station vor Zimpren, das war der alte Bandicki, der mit seinem Sohn zum Ohrenarzt fuhr; eine einfache Fahrkarte nach Höhnkimme: das war die uralte Mutter Glusch, die dort ihre verwitwete Schwiegertochter besuchte, um ihr beim Einkochen von Pflaumen zur Hand zu gehen; sie wurde zurück von Goswin auf dem Gepäckständer des Fahrrades mitgenommen; achtmal Gepäck— die beiden Aktentaschen und die drei Regenschirme der Rechtsanwälte, zweimal der Proviantbeutel, einmal der Regenschirm von Flora Klipp. Und zwei Bahnsteigkarten: das war der Pfarrer, der Küster und Meßdiener an den Zug begleitete und wieder vom Zug abholte.

Das ist eine trübselige Bilanz für den begabten Bahnhofsvorsteher, der sich seinerzeit von Hulkihn weggemeldet hatte, weil er an die Zukunft glaubte. Er glaubt längst nicht mehr an die Zukunft. Er ist es, der immer noch heimlich anonyme Postkarten an seinen Chef schickt, der sogar hin und wieder mit verstellter Stimme anruft, um seinem Chef mündlich zu wiederholen, was auch auf den Postkarten steht: »Die Zukunft unseres Bezirks liegt in Zimpren.«

Neuerdings ist zwar Zimpren zum Pilgerziel eines jungen Kunststudenten geworden, der sich vorgenommen hat, über das Werk des inzwischen verstorbenen Hans Otto Winkler zu promovieren; stundenlang weilt dieser junge Mensch in dem leeren, komfortablen Bahnhofsgebäude, um auf gutes Fotowetter zu warten und dort seine Notizen zu vervollständigen; auch verzehrt er dort sein belegtes Brot, den Mangel eines Ausschanks beklagend. Das lauwarme Leitungswasser ist seiner Kehle widerwärtig; befremdet hat er festgestellt, daß in der Herrentoilette »bahnfremde Gegenstände« aufbewahrt werden. Der junge Mann kommt ziemlich häufig, da er das riesige Fresko nur partiell fotografieren kann; doch leider wirkt er sich nicht positiv auf die Bahnhofskasse aus, denn er ist mit einer Rückfahrkarte ausgestattet und benutzt auch die Gepäckaufbewahrung nicht. Der einzige, der einen gewissen Nutzen aus der Reiselust des Kunststudenten zieht, ist der junge Brehm,

who took the annual trip together to Senstetten to inspect the splendid Lourdes grotto there; two round trips to Höhnkimme, the station before Zimpren, bought by old Bandicki, who went to the ear doctor with his son; one single fare to Höhnkimme bought by ancient Mother Glusch, who visited her widowed daughter-in-law there, to give her a hand in cooking her plums for jam; she came back to Zimpren riding on the parcel rack of Goswin's bicycle; eight items of baggage: the two lawyers' briefcases and their three umbrellas; Flora Klipp's lunch box twice and her umbrella once. And two platform tickets: that was for the priest, who accompanied the sexton and his acolyte to the train and met them at the train on their return.

That is a sad balance sheet for the gifted stationmaster, who had in his day asked to be transferred from Hulkihn because he had faith in the future. He has long ago lost his faith in the future. He is the man who keeps sending the secret anonymous postcards to his boss; who even calls him up now and then and repeats to him, in a disguised voice, the message on the postcards: "The future of our district lies in Zimpren."

To be sure recently Zimpren has become the goal of a pilgrimage made by a young art student, who has undertaken a doctoral dissertation on the work of Hans Otto Winkler, who has meanwhile died. For hours this young person sits in the empty, comfortable station building, waiting for good photographing weather and completing his notes; he also eats his sandwich there, lamenting the absence of a bar. The lukewarm tap water hurts his throat; he has noted with surprise that articles foreign to the railway system are stored in the men's room. The young man comes to the station fairly frequently, since he can take only partial photographs of the gigantic fresco; but unfortunately his visits do not produce a positive effect on the station's cash register, for he is provided with a return ticket and doesn't make use of the baggage checkroom. The only person who derives a certain benefit from the art student's love of travel is young Brehm, a railway guard who was transferred to Zimpren

ein Bahnschaffner, der wegen Trunkenheit im Dienst nach
Zimpren strafversetzt wurde; ihm ist es vergönnt, die Rückfahrkarte des Studenten zu lochen; eine Bevorzugung durch
das Schicksal, die den Neid seiner Kollegen erweckt. Er war es
auch, der die Beschwerde über den Zustand der Herrentoilette
entgegennahm und den Skandal heraufbeschwor, der für
einige Zeit Zimpren noch einmal interessant machte. Wohl
jeder entsinnt sich noch des Prozesses, der die »bahnfremde
Verwendung bahneigener Gebäude«[15] zum Gegenstand hatte.
Doch ist auch das längst vergessen. Der Bahnhofsvorsteher
erhoffte sich von diesem Skandal eine Strafversetzung von
Zimpren weg, doch war seine Hoffnung vergeblich, denn
man kann nur *nach* Zimpren strafversetzt werden, nicht *von*
Zimpren weg.

Notes: Böll, *Bahnhof von Zimpren*

1. *längst*, the superlative to indicate very high degree.
2. *Kräfte*, energies, human resources.
3. *D-Zug-Station*, D stands for *Durchgangs*, i.e. a train with corridors which make it possible to walk from coach to coach.
4. *Schlange stehen*, stand in line, form a queu.
5. *schnurgerade*, with a string, to plant the vegetables in a straight line.
6. *hatten . . .* , an if-clause, here with concessive force.
7. *bot*, i.e. justified.
8. *die Flinte ins Korn werfen*, to throw the rifle into the wheat field, i.e., to throw in the sponge.
9. This is of course sheer slander. The idea that anyone who doubts the noble purposes of the big oil company must be an atheist, a communist, or a subversive.
10. The title of one of Böll's satirical stories is *Es wird etwas geschehen*.
11. *erzfaul*, literally: arch (i.e. immensely) lazy.
12. *literaturfähig*, formed by Böll by analogy with *salonfähig*, fit for admission to polite society.
13. *Suchtok* is a dative of interest; the subject of the sentence is *Triumph*.

for being drunk on duty; he is privileged to punch the student's return ticket, a favor bestowed on him by Fate, which arouses his colleagues' envy. It was he, moreover, who received the complaint about the condition of the men's room and precipitated the scandal that made Zimpren interesting again for some time. Everybody probably still remembers the trial that had as its theme "the railway-alien utilization of railway owned buildings." But that too has long been forgotten. The stationmaster hoped to get a punitive transfer away from Zimpren out of this scandal, but he hoped in vain, for one can only get a punitive transfer *to* Zimpren, not *away from* it.

14. *Lourdes-Grotte*, a shrine in the form of a grotto in imitation of the one in Lourdes, France, erected to commemorate the appearance of the Virgin Mary to the peasant girl Bernadette Soubirous (1858), who was later canonized as St. Bernadette.

15. This is bureaucratese for "the misuse of railway buildings for purposes that have nothing to do with railway matters." The wooden English of the translation tries to capture the spirit of the German.

Designer: UC Press Staff
Compositor: Prestige Typography
Printer: Vail-Ballou
Binder: Vail-Ballou
Text: 10 pt. Baskerville
Display: Baskerville